Dedication

Dedicated to my grandchildren: Kristi, Joel, Lisa, Mark, John, Elisabeth, Matthew, William, Joshua and Rachel. I love you. Thanks for inspiring me to share memories.

And to my daughters: Karen, Martha, Mary and Joy, along with their husbands, Lee, Paul, Herb and Ken.

And especially to my wife: Alberdena.

Also to my parents: Dad and Mom.

Let me add one more, that would be to the memory of Little Beth.

Acknowledgements

Special appreciation must go to my wife, Alberdena, who helped in so many ways with writing these memories.

My grandchildren for wanting me to tell them stories. They gave me the challenge to write.

Thanks goes to those who shared information with me, some were family members, while others were some of our old neighbors.

I'm thankful to God, my Heavenly Father, for gifting me with memory. The Holy Spirit did His leading. I want to exalt my Lord and Savior, Jesus Christ. Now to God alone be the glory!

A BOY IN HOOSIERLAND

WM. M. HOFFMAN

HOFF MANSE

PUBLISHING

Rev William M Hoffman
903 Berg Blvd SE
Stewartville MN 55976-1483

Library of Congress
Catalog Card Number 95-95275

ISBN 1-57579-006-8

Front Cover: The State of Indiana is outlined and the dot marks the spot where De Motte is located. In that general area is the setting for *A Boy in Hoosierland.*

Printed in United States of America

 PINE HILL PRESS, INC.
Freeman, S. Dak. 57029

Making Memories

All of us have memories. Some are fond memories. Not all bring us joy. Yet it is a wonderful experience to share some of yesterday. When we do, then we draw upon those memories. Really there are more of them than we realize.

While I was growing up, I never knew anything about computers. Yet I have been living with one, according to Dr. Earl Radmacher. That man said, as I recall, "The human mind is a fabulous computer. As a matter of fact, no one has been able to design a computer as intricate and efficient as the human mind."

They are now claiming that the brain is capable of recording 800 memories per second! More than that, this can be done for 75 years without ever getting tired.

I recently saw an advertisement about a book published by Reader's Digest which told a most interesting fact. The fact is this: the human memory stores up to 500 times more information than a set of encyclopedia.

Beyond that, Dr. Radmacher added something else, "You never really forget anything. Everything is on permanent file in your brain."

So it is all there—on file. Plus one does not forget. However, being human some of us still have a problem, which is, we have trouble with recall!

One seminary professor used to joke about forgetting. He claimed his "forgettory" worked better than his memory!

As I have been asked about events and experiences of my childhood and youth, I thought I could recall a few. Some were easy to remember.

But I soon made a wonderful discovery, as I began to write my life's story. I had many more precious memories on file than I ever dreamed. Once I began searching back into the treasury of my memory, there I had made many, many deposits. Now investments over the years are rewarding me with the riches of memories. It is a divinely endowed gift to be able to remember. Now I get excited as I pick out gems from my memory bank. I'm so glad my children and grandchildren challenged me to share out of my treasury.

I have accepted the challenge. So I write about my days in Indiana. So I had an enjoyable visit to Hoosierland in my memory. Even fun. A few not so enjoyable, sometimes it has been painful.

Times I laughed as I wrote. Tears also flowed. As I read the stories again, I have laughed so hard I could hardly continue to read. Other times I have had my emotions so stirred that I couldn't go on reading. I've choked up. My heart was so touched I could only see the pages through tears.

But, believe me, I had a good childhood in Indiana. (No, I didn't always think so as a kid.) However, from where I am now, gratitude grabs my heart. I am thankful for my Dad and Mom, brothers and sisters, grandparents, and many friends. I was truly blessed by the Providence of God, my Heavenly Father. I learned about Jesus loving me, even as a little boy. The old First Reformed Church, Dutch Corners, was my spiritual parent in the family of God. For it all, I thank God for my childhood and youth in De Motte.

I was by no means perfect. Nor am I perfect now, far from it. Neither was my family perfect. But there is a place of forgiveness by the grace of God. That is something we must remember—always!

Let me add, my gratitude goes to God, our Father in Heaven. Jesus made a great sacrifice for this sinner, so that I know I'm saved by grace. Grace alone! The Holy Spirit has touched my life, so that I have been able to respond to His love and grace.

I owe so much to my Father in Heaven. But I also owe so much to my family and friends.

Now I want to share with you out of the treasure of the riches of this life, given to me by the grace of God. Together we'll share, may we all enjoy our trip down memory lane.

Take your time, pause now and then. As you stroll among the treasure of my memories, may you then recall many more of your own. Realize how blessed you have been. God is so good!

My Father in Heaven has been good to me. I trust that you'll personally know about His goodness touching those experiences and events of your own life, which you may not have recalled for some time. Let me take you to Hoosierland!

Born in Hoosierland

I was born in the Hoosier State, Indiana. As a native, I do think of myself as a Hoosier. What does the word Hoosier mean? One old Indiana poet wrote a poem about "The Hoosiers' Nest." That goes back to probably 1830. That newspaper man was asked about the meaning, then would refer to the poem. It tells of a stranger riding up on his horse to a cabin, but before dismounting would call out a greeting. Strangers all through Indiana did that in early days. Then from within came a question, "Who's there?" From that answer came the word Hoosier.

Who's this boy born in Hoosierland?

I was named William Hoffman, after my grandfather. The date of my birth is March 18, 1925. My record of birth is in Rensselaer, Indiana. I was born on the farm, so the certificate

Sena Hoffman with her new baby, William, standing by our Baby Overland.

1

recorded my birth in Jasper County Indiana. That is south of the Kankakee River. The Hoosiers' Nest is just north of the river in Porter County.

The information for my birth is found in Book No. H6, Page No. 96, with the recording date: 3-18-25. I was born the first child of Martin and Sena (Walstra) Hoffman.

That record of birth does not list a middle name. However, the De Motte Bank put "M" on the front of my savings passbook. I asked Dad what that meant, since we had a Martin J. in the family. Dad gave me permission to make my own choice. I chose the name "Melvin" when I was about 13 years old.

The day I was born in March the men were hauling manure from the cow yard into the fields before spring plowing. Mom, a young mother-to-be, was raking leaves in the yard in the morning. In the afternoon she informed Dad that he should get the doctor. So Dad told the hired man to keep an eye on things while he went to De Motte, 5 miles away. The doctor came to our home for the delivery. "Doc" had been drinking before he came, as they put it, he was "under the weather."

The weather had problems, too. It was a lovely day on the farm. However, other places had a big problem. Few people know about that day or remember what happened. History tells that the most devastating tornado hit the Midwest the day I was born. It took in Missouri, Illinois and Indiana. Figures vary, but some claim 823 died, with some 2,990 injured. (I found other figures, which claimed the death toll at 689 and the injured at 1,980.) It was a bad one, no matter what figures you choose. This tornado had surges upward to 100 to 200 mph. It was only 300 yards wide, yet winds on the edge of it reached up to speeds of 500 mph. It was strong enough to fling cars over rooftops. It even derailed trains. Yet is was a calm day on the farm when I was born in Hoosierland.

My folks lived in the old farm house on the hill. At that time it was a square four-room home. Attached to the house was an old summer kitchen. Under that unfinished room was our cellar, which you entered by a trap-door in the floor. A wood burning heater stove was in the living room. In the kitchen was our black cook stove. A two-burner laundry stove was in the summer kitchen. An old bathtub was later put in a corner, which meant we had to run across the room to get warm by the little laundry stove. That's the stove that branded me! I backed into the hot stove while bending over to dry myself one Saturday. My bottom was burned! I guess I was branded on the old farm. (I believe it was a Hoosier brand.)

Throughout the years various additions were made to this old house on the hill. Dad said he had to do that as the family grew. Grow it did. Later two brothers and four sisters joined us in our home.

When I was born Dad was 31; Mom was 19.

My brothers and sisters were born as follows:

Paul born October 27, 1926
Lois June born June 4, 1929
Martin J. born March 27, 1932
Wilma Jean born September 19, 1935
Carolyn Ruth born July 31, 1938
Rita Jo born August 7, 1940

As I mentioned earlier, I was named after my Grandpa, William Hoffman. My father called Grandpa "Daddy." His mother he called "Ma." We knew her as "Little Grandma." And she was little. When I was born Grandpa was 64, while Little Grandma was 59. She was a Borgman.

When my Dad was born May 10, 1893, they were 33 and 27 years old. Dad was the fifth child born to William and Melena Hoffman.

I have never forgotten what my Little Grandma told me as a small boy. She and I were visiting in her little kitchen. It was such a day for a heart-to-heart talk with a grandson. Dad was busy taking care of other things for them. I was sitting on a chair by the window. Grandma turned her chair from the table, then faced me. She started to talk about my Dad. What I heard from Little Grandma shocked me!

3

She had four babies the first five years of marriage. More than she wanted in a row. Then she discovered she was expecting another baby—my father.

She almost wanted him to go away!

Frankly she told me, "I never wanted your father." I could hardly believe it. How could she feel that way?

I understand she admitted getting on the kitchen table, then jumped off! She even drank vinegar, hoping the sour stuff would cause her to lose the baby.

All her efforts failed. May 10, 1893, my father was born!

Quickly adding to her story, Grandma said, "Now that I am old, your father is one who never forgets me. He always remembers." As a small boy, about that time, I needed to hear her say that. She assured me she was glad she had my Dad! I have never forgotten her story. I still feel God in His Providence gave my father over 90 years because he did honor his father and mother. Of that I am absolutely convinced.

Since Dad was born in Chicago and in the year 1893, there was something special about that. That was the year of a World's Fair in Chicago, which my grandparents attended. In fact, Dad was a babe in arms when they went there.

Grandma told how she crawled over a rope-fence, but Grandma and her baby did not belong there! It was where they kept the elephants. She soon discovered one elephant made gestures of irritation—in one big hurry Grandma Hoffman and little Martin cleared the fence! It was safer on the other side.

40 years later there was another World's Fair in Chicago. Dad took Grandma there in 1933. She was 67 years old then. Both were back at the fair for the second time together.

That was a big day. Little Grandma got really tired, but she was not the only one. Late in the afternoon she sat on a bench to rest. I can't say she could relax very much.

Right next to her was an ice cream vendor. Constantly the vendor cried, "Ice cream! Ice cream! Ice cream!" Following that she would rattle off the kinds of ice cream she had. Rapidly she repeated, "Chocolate! Vanilla! and Pecan-toffee!" Never-ending was her cry.

Finally in utter exasperation Grandma spoke up, "Girl (Meisje), Hoede de bek!" (Girl, hold your mouth!")

It didn't happen. The vendor continued to cry. She was not about to hold her mouth. Besides she probably didn't have the slightest idea what Grandma said to her, "Girl, Hoede de bek!"

After a little rest, we walked away, with the vendor still trying to sell more ice cream. She kept it ringing in our ears, "Ice cream! Ice cream..." But as we walked slowly, it was fading away. Yet I still remember the one special flavor—pecan-toffee.

Another picture of Little Grandma is in church. Her head, with her black hat, was just above the back of the pew.

Dad took her to the morning service, which was still in Dutch when I was a boy.

Sometimes I went along with them to church. Dad took his mother many, many times on Sunday. That little baby once in her womb, one she wanted to reject, now was a big man taking his little mother to God's House to worship.

God's ways can be so mysterious!

Left, Grandpa William Hoffman, and right, Little Grandma Hoffman. Unknown relatives, man in the middle, and the cousin holding Grandma's hand.

My Dad's parents on their front porch in Indiana.

Grandpa and Grandma Hoffman's little farm was three and a half miles south of our place. There were two driveways. South of the chicken houses and driveway were their fruit trees. A few trees were north of the north driveway. As kids we spent time playing in the orchard. With our cousins we had fun running around, sometimes getting in a tree.

I can still picture them picking apples.

Grandpa Hoffman liked to sit in a swivel chair in his kitchen, by the table. He was always leaning back in his chair. Tipped back— his feet were off the floor. Grandpa would be holding an open newspaper in his hands. It seemed he was always reading the paper when we got there.

Sometimes he'd smoke while he read.

As we opened the door, Grandpa would look around the edge of his paper, then say, "Hello, Boyke." Other times I was called "Lieve." That was the name my Dad used, too. It was an endearing expression of love and affection. (Some variations are: lieveling—darling, pet; lief—dear, beloved; liefde—love; liefje—o love, sweetheart.)

When I got called "Lieve" I would get a pat, or my hand was held, softly rubbing it. I knew they loved me.

WALSTRA FAMILY: Back row, Minnie, Garret, Henry, John, Cornelius, Samuel. Middle row, Gertrude, Jake, Grandpa Peter (Hijt), Grandma Forsena (Mem), Andrew, Louis. Front row, Danny (Grandpa's lap), Jennie, Sena (Mom, on Grandma's lap). Dorothy, not pictured.

7

I also remember Grandpa and Grandma Walstra. We called them "Hijt" and "Mem." Grandpa Walstra was 67 when I was born, while Grandma was 64.

They lived in a big house on what was called "Range Line" road. It was between De Motte and Thayer, Indiana. Their house was on the west side of the road. The driveway brought us to a big mulberry tree. Generally we drove around the mulberry tree whenever we visited there.

On one visit the mulberries were ripe. And I ate too many! I'll never forget that visit. I was one sick boy, who didn't want to eat another mulberry!

They had an orchard south of the big mulberry tree.

Their house was big, with a porch on the front and back. A swing was on the front porch, so we played on it many times.

When we came into the big kitchen we headed for the bench behind the table. Grandpa Walstra sat in his chair, near the pantry. Grandma had a curtain in the pantry doorway.

Their house had a smell that was always the same. It was a smell between Grandpa's smoking and Grandma's spice cake. Most visits we'd get tea and a small piece of her brown spice cake. A few times when I sat behind the table we got a very little glass of wine. (They had a name for it, slokje, which described it.) It wasn't much, just only a couple swallows. They didn't offer that to us very often, but we did have it a few times.

If other people came after church, then we could expect to hear a theological discussion. Many times the men would get started by something the minister had in his sermon. The talk would be in both Dutch and English; sometimes, as a boy, I did not understand what they were talking about. Some of my uncles could get excited, and loud!

As kids we would generally leave the older ones, with our escape through the door into the big hallway. Most of the time it was chilly in the hall. If nobody was watching, then we'd open doors to peek into the other rooms. They were cold, and had that smell in them, too. If we got a chance, we would go upstairs, where there were a lot more rooms to see. Nobody hardly ever got into them. All the furniture was old fashioned, but very clean and neat. Nothing was out of place. For us there were so many interesting things to see—pictures and furniture we generally never saw in other homes. We found it fun to go from one room to the next. We were very quiet, hoping nobody would want to know where we were. Finally somebody would call, again it was time to go.

Grandpa Walstra was in his 70s when I remember going to their place. He was bald, with only a little hair around his neck. As kids we'd ask about his hair, really, the lack of hair. We questioned when his hair was going to grow. Everytime we got the same answer, "Grandpa's hair will grow in the spring, when the grass is green." Each year spring would come and go, many springs! But Grandpa's hair never did grow on his bald head!

That bald head fascinated us kids. He had fun with us, with his bald head being a nice spot to put his cup and saucer. After finishing his tea or coffee, then he picked that time to put it right in the middle of his bald head. We almost expected that during every visit.

Sometimes it stayed put. Too often he'd have to make a quick grab for it as it began to slide off his slippery bald head. Most of the time he would catch them in time.

Not always. Every now and then he missed. It was a crash when it hit the floor. Naturally, at those times, there were pieces of the cup and saucer all over Grandma's kitchen floor.

Nobody knows how often this happened. My Mom said she would not know how often they had to clean up the broken pieces off the floor. Many times. But as kids we really enjoyed Grandpa's little show. No matter how many times he repeated it, we always thought it was a lot of fun— for us.

When it came time for chores we either went to the chicken coop with Grandma or to the barn with Grandpa.

The chicken coop was close to the mulberry tree. I'd go there to help feed the chickens and gather the eggs.

To me it seemed like the barn was a long way from the house. They had a very sandy yard. Grandpa would go there to milk his cows. When he was older he didn't have very many. But when they lived on a ranch they had over one hundred cows to milk. They would bring a whole hay rack full of milk cans to the train. That was the way they shipped milk in the early days. From what I remember they could put 33 cans of milk on one hay rack.

However, when I was a small boy "Hijt" had only a few cows. Several times I'd watch him clean the barn. There was a big manure pile back of his barn.

As I knew them, Hijt and Mem, they were older than my Dad's parents. There was more Dutch spoken in their home. That left us kids in the dark, so we'd ask what they were talking about. Generally these questions came when we got in the car. Sometimes we found out, then again, other times we never found out. My parents did the same thing, talked in Dutch, if they didn't want us to know something. But my Dad didn't always understand what Hijt and Mem were saying, especially if they talked too fast. Then Dad would ask them to talk slower.

Our grandparents came from different parts of the Netherlands. Mom's parents came from Friesland; Dad's came from Gronigen. The Walstras were Fries, with the Frisian background. The Hoffmans had the Gronigen background.

Mom's family came to America when she was only six months old. They settled in Grand Rapids, Michigan, when they first arrived. Within a year or so they moved to Indiana. Dad's family lived in the Chicago area.

Grandpa Hoffman was a truck farmer at the time. I heard once that the general area was across from where the Midway Airport is now located. At one time they were fairly well off. A story is told of having a beautiful team in front of a surrey which was used when going to church on Sunday. Later the family moved to Indiana.

Of course in coming to America, some changes took place for both families. Pieter K. Walstra became Peter K. Walstra. Grandma's name was Forsina, nee Nicolai, Walstra, with a later spelling of her name as Forsine.

Grandpa Hoffman was Wiebe Hofma. (Dad told about Grandpa being close to his mailbox once, where his name "Wiebe" was painted. A man, not knowing him personally, yet

10

HOFFMAN FAMILY: Back row, Ralph, Jake, Martin (Dad). Middle, Grace, Ricca, Grandma Melena Hoffman, George, Grandpa William Hoffman, Fred. Front, Little William, Ben.

11

wanting to be friendly, greeted him, "Hello, Wipe!") Several changes took place with his name when he made it William Hoffman. "Hofma" became "Hoffman" by teachers in Chicago adding an extra "f" and the "n" at the end. Dad said they told the teachers their name was Hofma, but it was of no use. Finally Grandpa told the children to forget it, so their name became Hoffman through the school system. In the '50s I asked Dad about the spelling and got that story. He also mentioned Grandma's maiden name was "Borgman." This was after both of my grandparents had died, so there was no other change. It remained Melena, nee Borgman, Hoffman.

As I looked at their family picture, taken when Dad's little brother William was still living, it was taken approximately in 1907. It was taken at Suchy, corner of Ashland & 50th St., in Chicago. In that family picture Grandpa Hoffman did not have his injured eye. It had to be after this that a team ran-away with him. Ducking just in time, it prevented his death. Otherwise he would have been crushed against a large corner post. However, with the lines around his body, Grandpa was drug by the runaway team. That's when he had injuries to his cheek and eye. After that accident, his eye always teared, which had to be wiped constantly with a handkerchief. It caused him trouble the rest of his life.

The Citizens Bank   IN ACCOUNT WITH

Martin Hoffman

1926

June 3	5314	CHECKS LISTED & RETURNED
May 22	3473	E. 6 Pearco 1541
March 29	3028	
Dec 30	7780	BALANCE 6180
1932	21595	21595
Jan ✓ BALANCE	6180	CHECKS LISTED & RETURNED
		Checks 3002
July 16	2000	
July 31	5000	
		BALANCE 10178
	13180	13180

Dad's bank book in Hebron during 1926 and 1932

13

Depression Days

I was born during what was know as "The Roaring Twenties." World War I was over. History tells the story of the dollar being strong.

A study shows that the economy was strong for about eight years. A new Ford sold for $550. Gas cost 20¢ a gallon. And you paid 9¢ for a loaf of bread.

By the way, Babe Ruth who hit 54 home runs in one season, 60 in another, got only $20,000 as his salary. (In the '90s some make $35,000 per inning!)

Those Roaring Twenties ended with a whimper. That was Black Friday, October 29, 1929, which was the beginning of The Great Depression.

It did not all fail at once, for the worst year to come was after that financial catastrophe, which later had a worldwide effect. That worst year came in 1932. About three and a half years after the stock market crash 25% of the people were out of work.

Franklin D. Roosevelt was elected President.

On March 4, 1933, the banking system of the United States collapsed. Our President ordered the banks closed. That's when he declared a nationwide holiday.

I was seven when Dad talked with Mom about having all their money in one bank, which he felt was not good at all. After breakfast that morning he headed for the bank. His plan was to take half his money out of the De Motte State Bank and deposit it in the Citizens Bank in Hebron.

Dad only got half of his plan accomplished.

I still see Dad coming home with money in his hand. It was the $200 taken out of the bank in De Motte. He had driven about ten miles to Hebron to make his deposit. As he walked to the front door of the bank it was being locked. The banker pulled down the shade on the door, then motioned to Dad to go away. But Dad continued to bang on the door, finally he opened it, only to tell Dad to leave. Dad tried to tell him he wanted to put money in the bank. That was when the banker said he could not let Dad in the bank for it was closed by order of the President. That same thing happened across America that same day.

President Roosevelt gave one of his famous fireside chats on the radio, this one was on March 12, 1933. After that chat, the banks started opening again. The bank holiday was lifted gradually.

Once Dad showed me that he had less than $10.00 in the bank on which to run the whole farm.

A hired man got on an average $216 a year. It was no easy life on the farm in those years. For in the middle of all those hard times we had some very dry years. Out West it was known as the "Dust Bowl Days."

But then it was hard in the whole world. The throes of such change was happening in many places, especially in Europe, where Spain was under the totalitarian rule of Generalissimo Francisco Franco, but even worse was the Fascism in Italy under "Il Duce" Benito Mussolini. Yet far worse in Germany, Nazism, which was under "Der Fuhrer" Adolf Hitler. As a boy I hated to hear their names mentioned in the news on the radio. It struck fear in my heart.

But we had plenty of problems of our own in America with the Great Depression. President Roosevelt came out with a new program, as he called it, The New Deal.

As a kid I began to catch on to the alphabet in a new way. Posters, symbols and stickers were everywhere. The radio and papers used them too. Here are the ones I remember: NRA, CCC, PWA, and WPA. I'll mention some of these later, as they did change our lives.

Many things were happening in the times and world in which I grew up as a boy in Hoosierland. I'm still thankful I got to live my early years in Indiana.

A few other changes happened in those times, which I now know touched our family, too.

15

Early in our century parents were called Papa and Mama. However, when I was a boy, a change took place—and we made the change as a family. It became popular to call your father "Dad" and mother "Mom." That is one change which stuck in our family.

My Early Discoveries

I discovered my father was old!

I made this discovery when I was only 7 years old!

Maybe I was only 7, but I knew for certain that my Dad was really old. It stopped me in my tracks. I stood still. I could only stare at him.

Dad was 39!

There was the evidence, right at my feet. His teeth were falling out. One was lying silently still on the kitchen floor. What more evidence was needed?

I was in total shock. Everything came to a stand-still in that moment.

It stopped our parade!

Mom had told us that it was time for bed. Naturally as kids, we wanted to postpone that business—as long as possible.

Our chorus of request: "Can't we have an apple?" After all, a snack is needed before going to bed. We'd get an apple. Mom agreed to our request, but then to bed!

After each kid got an apple, I led the parade. Around and around the kitchen table I led the evening parade. Each kid chomping away on an apple during the march.

Dad was watching. He was sitting by the chimney, a warm spot to sit. Dad, too, had his apple. He took one big bite out of his apple—that's when it all happened.

Just as he made his bite, one of his incisors broke off. It came out of his mouth. It fell on the floor, danced a couple of times on the linoleum. Then it laid deathly still. Everyone was captured by a strange quietness.

Dad broke the silence. (But he used a word we were not suppose to use!) Dad said that word, then as an old man added, ."..! 39 and the teeth are falling out of my head!"

That's when it happened. In a single moment of time, it all changed—everything!

My father went from a young man to an old man!

And do you know what this old man did? Dad grinned. There it was, a gapping space, only a stump remained in that spot. Once again I looked at the evidence at my feet.

Besides Dad admitted it. He was 39! And his teeth were falling out of his mouth.

As I said, our parade came to a standstill. We couldn't move. After such shocking news, how could a parade go on?

To this day I have no idea how long I stood there. I know it took awhile for me even to realize I had witnessed a big transformation. I was there! I saw it with my own eyes.

One moment Dad was young. The next he was old!

Afterwards Dad told me that he had pyorrhea alveolaris. It was loosening his teeth in their sockets. (It sounds like peridontitis, as it is called today.) If this periodontal disease is not treated, then eventually, the bony sockets can become so eroded that the teeth become loose and must be extracted. Dad did end up getting all his teeth pulled.

Living in my memory is that evening I made this revealing discovery.

At the age of 7 I discovered my father was very old at 39!

Even at an earlier age I made another great discovery. I discovered one of my very best friends. That friend was my old thumb. I found such comfort when I sucked my thumb.

My Dad when he was a young man.

But if I was to enjoy the greatest satisfaction I had to suck my thumb while holding my "oodle." My "oodle" was a small blanket with a fringe on it. Naturally I liked to touch the soft fringe. Oh, to rub it on my cheek, across my face, under my nose, even under my chin, ever so gently rub it against my skin—pure enjoyment. That sensation was the best

Left, George and Martin in their Sunday best, even with boxing gloves.

for a little Hoosier boy. Such friendships meant everything.

Since little boys drag their security blankets almost everywhere, especially when tired, mine got dirty. How does one get the dirty thing into the washing machine? Separation is next to impossible.

A mother has to know when to make such a move. Mom got it washed, then hurried to the clothesline.

A boy can only suffer separation so long. After play, a boy gets tired. That's when I went on a search for my "oodle" friend. My best friend and I would make this clean discovery on the clothesline. There was my "oodle" hanging! A clean smell. Right then and there, we'd have such a good time— Billy, his thumb and the "oodle." We hung out together, with the clothesline supporting a tired little boy who could hardly stand on his feet anymore.

I can't tell you what happened to my "oodle." We parted early in my life. But my best friend, my thumb, stuck together.

I got a reminder later how much I sucked my thumb. While in grade school I got a big blister on it. Strange looking, very white, requiring a doctor's attention. Dr. E. E. Leesen took a look at it. He cut off this white skin. In asking questions Dr. Leesen wanted to know if I sucked my thumb earlier in my life. I did! I had to admit it. He felt I had injured it, so I was suffering a delayed reaction. At times a few little scars can be seen. They are the only reminder of our special friendship between a little boy and his thumb.

I have only a faint memory, still I can picture the shadowy experience. Mom's reminder has helped me recall this one. This has to do with playing under the big corn crib. I picked the southern side, perhaps with more light. A few chickens got under there, too. I'd crawl between the cement blocks to get under the crib. Naturally, I was out of sight, so Mom could not spot me. It was a secret place to hide. No matter how much she called, I refused to answer her. Also I crawled under far enough so she could not reach me. I sat at a safe distance, out of her reach.

Mom could be on her hands and knees pleading, but the little boy would only grin. There I would continue to play in the dust and dirt, with leaves, corn husks, and chicken feathers, and more. Once she found me with that "ockie" stuff in my mouth! It was a relief to find me, which took away some fears. Still she had a job of begging me to come out from under the big crib.

Later Paul was old enough to join me. That's when it got extremely dangerous. First our play took us to the cars of the hired men. Many times they parked their cars by the crib. It was fun to play in their cars. As boys we also discovered they kept matches in their cars. While we knew it was wrong to play with matches, still we were tempted to do it anyway. Wanting to escape being caught, we crawled under the crib to play with the matches. We could strike them on the rough timber. One at a time—strike—watch the flame.

Then wave it out. Sometimes quickly throw it down. Right in the middle of all those dry leaves, feathers, corn husks, and other junk. It was extremely dangerous! If a fire ever got started, I have no idea if we would have made it out of there. It certainly could have been a deadly threat.

The folks got after us for that kind of play. Dad told his hired men to lock their cars. Sometimes they did, but not always. Finally Dad got ropes to wrap around the cars, to keep us out of them. Dad knotted those ropes tightly, hoping to keep little hands from untying them.

After recalling this, I can only conclude this showed God was kind enough to watch over naughty little boys in Hoosierland!

I made another early discovery—about the love of money. It cost this "little man's best friend"—my black puppy.

There is a family picture, where Paul and I are together, while I'm holding this little puppy.

Down the road, south of our farm buildings, some men were cutting brush along the ditch. This was one of the work projects during the early depression years. As boys we walked down there to see what they were doing. These men were working near the old turtle hole and on the banks of the Cook Ditch.

How much is that puppy? I'm holding the puppy I sold for a quarter. My brother Paul is standing next to me.

While watching them, they began to talk with us. It wasn't long before they asked questions about my dog. Teasing, they wanted to know if I'd sell my puppy. At the time I could not tell them whether I did or didn't.

I do remember I was offered 25¢. That got my attention. Libby De Vries offered me the quarter. At the time it seemed like a lot of money. (Understand this, a few men were working for 50¢ a day, others got a

21

buck, a dollar.) To a little boy 25¢ sounded like a whole lot of money.

I agreed to the sale. My puppy didn't agree, for he kept trying to follow me home. They wanted me to tie him up. At home I found a short piece of binder twine, which I took back with me. With twine around his neck I tied the puppy to the bumper of a car parked along the road. Turning I headed for home, while my puppy was yipping and jumping by the car bumper. I walked home without him, but 25¢ richer!

In my hand was my new proud possession: a whole quarter!

The rest of the day I felt pretty good, until sunset. As the sun sank in the west my heart sank inside. I was lonesome. I felt empty without my puppy. With a heavy heart I went into the house, Mom was found in the kitchen. To her I made my plea, I wanted my puppy back. Something Mom could not do anything about. My little black puppy was gone!

I stood in the middle of our kitchen—a poor boy! Oh, the riches of a quarter was in his clenched hand. It felt worthless. No longer did I feel I had riches. In disgust I fired the quarter across the room. I had nothing—my puppy was gone. Hurting, I cried. I was so lonesome. I was brokenhearted. Never again could I pet my puppy. Nor hug him. Run with him. Nor feel him lick my face. I could only cry out my heart. It turned out to be one of the saddest evenings in my life. A little boy had sold his best friend for 25¢!

What I did that day taught me a few hard lessons. I discovered the love of money was the root of some real heartaches. Also I discovered money could not buy happiness. Overall one expensive lesson for me, but still I learned about the worth of life's values.

In life we can pay big prices for our lessons. Even play can be costly. I discovered that truth in my Grandma Hoffman's chickenhouse. Our family was there; so was Aunt Bess with her girls. My cousin Jean and I went into the chickenhouse. I have no idea why we did, but two adventurous kids did.

Jean reached into a nest of eggs. She took out one egg. A split-second later she fired it at the front of the coop. One smashed egg! She laughed. One more try. Jean made another direct hit!

Jean was a few months older than I. In this play, I have no idea when I joined her. But I did. Once we got going, we went from one nest to the next to get our "fire power" in this game. It became like a war zone. Smashed egg yokes were running down the whole front wall of Grandma's chicken coop. It was a sickly yellow, dripping mess. What a sight!

That strange sight greeted Little Grandma when she came to gather her eggs for the day. But the nests were empty. She couldn't even scramble all the eggs we broke. Besides we were caught "yellow-handed" in the act. Grandma had her two guilty egg-breakers. Grabbing both of us by an arm, she promptly marched us to the house. The only pause took place at the gate, where she had to push us through it after opening it. We knew we were in trouble. Big trouble! Little Grandma made it clear—it was big trouble!

Naturally our crimes were reported to our parents. Plus an inspection had to be made of the devastated war zone. The parents could see for themselves. Every egg had been smashed. Not one was spared. A yellow, dripping mess covered the whole front of the hen house. Boards and windows were covered. It was ugly. (In my mind's eye I can still see it, to this very day.)

Little Grandma was asked how many eggs she got each day. Then Aunt Bess and Dad took out their pocketbooks to pay for the damage. They paid.

Afterwards came our turn. Jean got it first. She paid dearly, Aunt Bess was very angry over breaking all those eggs. It was a rough spanking! Jean really yelled! It got to me—I dreaded what I might get.

Aunt Bess gave Jean her punishment immediately after paying Little Grandma for half the eggs. Dad was not so quick to deal with me. While Jean was still crying—loudly, not keeping the pain to herself, Dad turned to me. Oh, boy... He simply, yet firmly, told me never to do that again. With my heart beating fast, I shook my head, letting him know I heard him! And that was it for me.

However, it was not over for my cousin. Jean, nor her mother, were getting over it that quickly. While Jean was still licking her wounds, Aunt Bess gave her another licking. That frightened me, every time she got spanked. Before it was over, Jean got it several more times.

Believe me I was very quiet in the back seat of the car on the way home. My parents talked about what happened. I do recall my Dad and Mom felt my aunt was out of control for punishing my cousin repeatedly.

But our "fun" with all those smashed egg yokes was no joke!

I lost a summer. Most of it anyway. I almost missed the whole summer of 1932. Earlier I celebrated my 7th birthday. Shortly after that birthday, my youngest brother was born. Martin J. was born on March 27, 1932.

I wasn't there when he was born. Overnight I stayed at Uncle Dick and Aunt Ricca's place. The Tysens lived on the curve going out of De Motte, to the south. It was not the best night for me, for I did plenty of crying. I had such a toothache most of the night.

At first they thought I was homesick. Maybe I was, a little, but my biggest problem was a rotten tooth which really ached.

Anyway, while I was away, I had a little brother born on that Easter Sunday.

Mom nursed him.

Nursing brought very little satisfaction as far as Marty was concerned. He cried. Often! Most of the time! It seemed like he cried all the time!

So when he cried in the crib, even after shortly eating, Mom asked his "big" brother to go to him. I had to take care of him. I'd roll the crib. I'd shake it. Anything, all to get this little guy to stop his crying.

Mom took as much time as she could. Other work had to get done, so I was expected to help.

He was crying that spring when I got out of school for the summer. Of course, with school out, I had even more opportunity to help Mom.

Again and again, she would make her requests: "Bill, go see about Marty."

"Bill, see what the baby wants."

"Bill, try to rock him a little, see if he'll stop crying."

"Bill, can you take care of him while I do..."

I'd go see. There he was crying in his crib. With the shades down in the living room, I'd go to him in the crib. I rolled it. Shook it. Pushed it back and forth.

Those old casters finally had dents in the rug. Even more, eventually it was threadbare in spots. Casters soon were caught. Before the summer was over holes were in the carpet.

Those summer days were long for me. His cries were long.

I could take it so long in that darkened room, then I had to pull the shade aside. I had to look, just a peek outside. What was I looking for? Out there, that's where the other kids were. Playing!

As a seven year old I wanted to be out there too. They were having fun. I was stuck in the house—taking care of my kid brother—and summer was passing me by. Would I ever get to play again?

Several times Mom caught me in my frustration. She'd look in, just to check on us. There I was, spinning the crib in a circle. Around and around I spun that old crib.

Marty didn't realize it, I'm sure, but he was on a merry-go-round a number of times that summer. No, he was not riding a little wooden horse either. He was riding flat on his back in his crib, not on a carrousel.

One thing is certain, he travelled a long way that summer, but never left the living room.

As I said, I almost lost that summer. I didn't miss it all. Little Grandma Hoffman saved part of it for me.

One Sunday afternoon we stopped after church. Grandma gave us some tea, along with some goodies.

While we were having our lunch, Mom had Marty on her lap, but he was crying anyway. Little Grandma asked to take "that boy", which she did. At first she tried to calm his crying. It wasn't working.

So she got up, heading for her pantry. The door was in the corner of her kitchen. That time I followed her, just to see what she was going to do. I stood in the doorway to watch Grandma.

She reached for a package of Holland Rusk on a shelf. One piece was taken out. After putting it in a saucer, sugar was sprinkled over it. Stepping around me, she took the teakettle from the stove. Grandma poured a little warm water on the rusk. With a spoon she mushed it up.

After going to the table, she sat down with Marty in her arms. She started feeding him.

He liked it!

Marty ate it all!

Without waiting, Little Grandma went for a second helping. He ate that too. Marty really liked it!

He liked it so much...well, he fell sound asleep...

Grandma told Mom that her baby was hungry. Mom just did not have enough nurse.

Grandma went to her pantry for her package of rusk. Standing in the pantry door, she commented to me that Grandpa had to have some for breakfast. She took out one piece. Then she broke another one in half, so she had enough for next morning's breakfast.

Little Grandma gave Mom the rest of the package that Sunday afternoon. Suggesting to Mom more could be bought later in the week.

Marty liked his Holland Rusk. He seemed very eager to eat the stuff. Great, it stopped all that crying! Well, not all of it, but until he wanted more rusk!

I hurried outside to play. I was in a big hurry, for summer was almost gone. I almost missed it.

Thanks to Little Grandma's discovery, I did get to play a little the summer of 1932.

I discovered another thing early in life. As a kid, I could pout.

If things did not go my way, I would pout. If I didn't like what was going on, I'd pout. A little thing could happen to me, that's all it took, I was peeved. That was my nature. Around home I became pouter #1.

I don't know how many family members realized it, maybe all of them did. Then again, maybe not. Dad didn't miss it. Dad could spot my pouting right away. My body language always gave me away. And he was not about to let me continue my pouting. Dad would speak up, challenging me. Generally he said the same thing to me. It had enough humor so that it worked every time. My pouting streak would be broken, even when I was determined to resist his efforts.

Dad would simply say, "Willie, you better pick up your bottom lip, or you'll step on it!"

Every time he did the same thing, oh, I wanted to be angry at what he said. If I could stay mad, then I felt I could keep on pouting. Inside, I was almost ready to laugh. But I didn't dare look at him. Yet when our eyes met, it was all over. Dad's humor was enough to tip the scale, with a grin I had to give up—again.

I had to make the change, after we smiled at each other.

The change? I would pick up my bottom lip—before I stepped on it!

During the Depression days there were people who were known as tramps. Every now and then one would be walking along a road or highway. Generally he carried a few belongings, wrapped in a bundle. That bundle hung at the end of a stick, hanging over his shoulder.

Nor was it unusual to see people riding the rails. They would be on a train going through De Motte or on the old Monon Railroad. One would see a hobo standing in an open door of a boxcar. If they hopped off, then they would go to a home to ask for food. As kids we heard many stories about these people.

One day I decided to run away. I made my decision: I was going to be a tramp. Mom got the news first. Maybe a few others heard my announcement. However, before this prodigal left home he had to gather it all together. While I can't remember exactly all I did take with me, I do remember I took food!

27

A number of sandwiches were fixed. I had jelly on a few of them. Maybe I took an apple. There must have been more than that, but I can't recall what it was. I do remember putting it all in a big red handkerchief. I knotted the four corners together. A stick, I needed a stick. My belongings were hung from it. This young prodigal left his family, with only a slight glance over his shoulder.

I hit the road away from home. My wayward path led me through the woods north of the big barn. Sometimes I kept to the trail through the woods, with some steps being off the trail into the thick of the trees. Finally I made my way out to the Old Grade. I left the farm near the four corners, on the northwest edge of our property.

I made this a deliberate choice, I did not care to get too far into the far country. Actually I was safe within sight of the home place, .2 of a mile from home. But our fenceline was closer yet, likely no more than fifty feet away.

On that corner there was a large sycamore tree. I walked over to that tree, after looking all directions at the four corners. I sat next to the tree, on the northside.

Once I travelled that far, I made another discovery, this little tramp was hungry. Time to eat. I ate all my food in one sitting. No leftovers!

While eating my lonely meal, I had time to reflect, I even questioned such a life. I began to wonder about this life of a tramp I had chosen. I faced another decision, where would I get my next meal? Where would I go from here?

It was time to go back to my father and home.

Well, not directly. My longing for home was not that great. I would roam around in the woods near home, for an hour or so.

Finally I was home again. Oh, I came home without any fanfare. Simply put, the prodigal son had returned. That's all there was to this tramp life. I discovered the whole family accepted me back as if I had never left home. My stay in the far country was never mentioned by anyone.

It was so good to be home again. One little tramp's roaming day was over. I was back home—to stay!

Our Horse and Buggy Days

For most people those days were left behind. About the time I was born, a man from the Midwest commented on the changes happening: "I can tell you what's happening in just four letters—A-U-T-O." Roads had to change, too. The feeling was those "horse highways" had to change for their cars.

Even so, we did not miss out on those good old horse and buggy days. And we didn't. Hitch up old Benny and get in the buggy for a ride. As kids we had more fun with an old-fashioned buggy ride.

Dad picked up an old buggy on a farm sale. It was still in very good condition when we got it. It was not unusual for Dad to come home with a pair of shafts on the roof of our car. He had several pairs around. We needed extras, for we started breaking them with our rides through the woods. We did not always miss the stumps!

Another thing we had was the spring wagon, with a high seat in front and space in the back of the wagon to carry things. I guess one could think of it as an old-fashioned farm pickup. The horsepower came from horses.

We liked the old buggy Dad bought. With it we travelled all over the countryside. Benny, boys, and a buggy was a common sight. As kids we knew the areas around the marsh as well as anybody. We explored it all.

Our trips took us over old roads or trails through the many wooded areas. Some were no more than short-cuts early settlers used. A few were back-roads of old logging trails. If we spotted one, likely we would soon be checking it out. The main roads in the marsh were just plain old dirt roads. Gentle old Benny was in no hurry, neither were we. So a slow ride by boys in their buggy was a lot of fun.

A buggy ride and boy-talk was enjoyed, almost any day.

One day we took a ride in the rain. In those days we said it was "raining cats and dogs." Since the buggy had a canvas top we kept dry. Almost dry. Except when the wind was blowing rain into our laps. We took care of that. We got Dad's canvas, which we hung over the top of the buggy, draping it over the dashboard, and around the sides. That was one way to keep out the rain. It was so neat to be inside our little room. Of course we couldn't see where we were going. That didn't bother us—Benny knew the way home. Just sit back and have a good time. Benny plodded along. We never peeked as he took us towards home from the Hodge Ditch bridge.

Out of the hard rain came a voice shouting and yelling at us!

Immediately we jerked back the canvas. Who was yelling at us?

A farmer. The first sight I had was his horses both rearing up into the air, while still hitched to his wagon. When they came down, the horses attempted to drag his wagon into the ditch. Naturally the farmer thought he was going in for sure. Evidently his horses were spooked by our strange covered-buggy. The farmer bawled us out while trying to control his horses and still stay out of the ditch. Since this happened close to the old turtle hole we got Benny to hurry home—get out of there before he yelled at us again.

Over a period of time we used up those extra buggy shafts Dad bought on farm sales. Dad was picking them up for only 50¢, sometimes 75¢. But he thought he had bought enough of them. One day he told us that he was not buying anymore. That meant we had to be much more careful going through the woods.

It went fine for a time, but one ride ended the same old way. About a mile north of our home, where we put up old slough hay, a road went through the woods. It was about directly across from where the Swishers lived.

Our ride took us way back in the woods. After going about as far as we could go, it was time to turn around. Time to head back.

Violet was with us that day. After turning around, she began to beg to let her have the lines. She wanted to drive old Benny on the buggy. In no uncertain terms she was told, NO! It came from a chorus of boys, for no girl was to drive. Her begging and pleading continued. Finally we gave in, she was handed the lines—and away we went! She forced old Benny to pick up his pace, as we rode down this crooked trail.

Then it happened! She did not make the little curve—around a stump! Violet ran smack into a big old stump on the edge of the road. It was one big jolt!

Quick as a flash the shafts came out of the harness. Dropping to the ground, instantly the points were driven into the ground. Benny kept going, which caused the shafts to buckle and break. Good grief!

Together we moaned and groaned. Nobody said it, but all wondered why did we let a girl have the lines? Looking at the broken pieces reminded us we saw the last pair Dad said he'd buy.

After a few minutes we unhitched Benny from the buggy, leading him down the road, while some were pushing it towards Swishers' place.

No matter whose fault it was, they were broken beyond repair. And Dad would not buy anymore. Worst of all, how would we tell Dad?

While we lamented what happened, a relative of the Swisher family, whose name was George offered to help us. He was supposed to be able to do carpentry work.

A couple of us went into the woods to find two straight trees, which we cut down. They had to be about the right size. While we did that others took all the hardware off the broken shafts. Next we stripped off the bark, so we could trim them down to the exact size. But they were so green, it was almost next to impossible to drill holes to attach the single tree. It was hard work, especially with the old tools.

We worked as quickly as we could, but it took much longer than we thought. We couldn't stay any longer, it was pretty late. We had to go home for chores. We quit, leaving the buggy behind. Our unfinished job was left there.

We led old Benny home, walking slowly down that long mile home. All the time we wondered how we could face Dad. Our plan was to take the back driveway to the barn. Hoping, of course, that Dad would not see us coming back—without our buggy.

But he did! First question: "Where's the buggy?" Well, we tried to explain it, which was not going so great. Finally we told him—everything, the whole story!

Once more Dad told us something he said before, "I'm not going to buy anymore." We knew that. So now we knew for sure, we broke the last ones!

The next day we went back for the buggy, and those home-made "green" shafts. They didn't look like much, but they did work. They were good enough to be used the rest of our horse and buggy days. We never broke them either.

We had a lot of good times with the buggy. For a short time we played with just the running gear, the four wheels, plus attachments. It had no seat. We got a long plank, so we could sit on it. Each kid put one leg on one side and hung the other leg on the other—straddling the plank. A lot of riders could sit on that plank. One day, when the Armstrong kids were over, we had 13 riding on it. Here we came riding into the driveway, having a good time. Dad was talking to a salesman at the foot of the hill. The guy took a double-take at all 13 kids in a row. He commented to Dad about so many kids, having doubts, yet asking if they were all Dad's. Dad claiming us all, told the man we were all his! The guy couldn't believe it! (Afterwards Dad got a big laugh out of pulling the salesman's leg—just a little!)

Naturally riding the plank was not the easiest thing. Every once in a while you had to shift from one side to the other to get a little relief. If you got a little off balance you made a quick grab for the kid sitting ahead of you, or fall off!

That could happen! One day we were about two and a half miles from home. In fact we were hoping to make it to Grandpa and Grandma Hoffman's place. During our ride my sister Lois flipped off this plank and sprawled out on the gravel road. As she landed, one leg was directly in front of the back wheel. However, before we could get old Benny to "WHOA!" we rode right over her thigh. Now buggy wheels are narrow, hardly more than an inch wide. Imagine, we rode over her leg on this gravel road! Boy, did she ever cry. Over such pain, anybody would scream.

Fearing we were in trouble, as older ones we tried to convince Lois it didn't hurt. (Something she had heard before from her brothers.) Lois was not convinced. Man, she continued to bawl and howl.

We just couldn't convince her. Lois made it plain to us—it did hurt!

Our plans changed, so we did not get to our grandparents' place. Turning around we headed back home. Hoping, as boys, that in the long ride home she would forget how much it really did hurt.

One day we were riding through the Evans Farm, west of our farm. Benny was taking his time through the fields. Dick Evans and Paul were in the buggy seat. I was sitting on the floor, while my legs were hanging over the edge. It was "boy talk time."

Out of the blue, Red Evans said, "I see your Mom is going to have another kid."

Paul acknowledged that fact. I was stunned! Really? I never knew a whole lot about Mom's pregnancies. She'd several during those years. While I caught on she was going to have a baby, but still I had no idea how to explain it. I was puzzled, how did these guys know so much?

So I asked.

It must have been just as amazing to these younger fellows that I did not know, so they asked me, "Can't you see how big her belly is?"

With that shocking fact facing me, I asked another question, "Okay, you guys know so much, just how do babies come?"

Now it was their turn to be shocked! They wondered, could there be such innocence? Or, is he that dumb?

I heard a snicker. Red and Paul had to laugh a little. They had to chuckle a little at my lack of knowledge about the facts of life! Doesn't he know?

These younger boys would have to teach me the "facts of life" if I were to learn anything. But where do you begin?

Just how would they tell an older boy?

So they first had to test me to find out if I knew much of anything. One asked, "Do you know how a colt is born of a horse? Do you know where they come from?" (One of our mares recently had a little colt. Maybe that was the place to start.)

This was absolutely shocking to me! Nothing short of disgusting, comparing Mom to a horse, especially the way a baby colt is born. Mom was going to have a baby that way!

I promptly told both of them I thought they were so dirty! In total disgust I made it plain I've never wanted to talk to them again!

In silence we rode the rest of the way across the field. I would not talk—period. Perhaps Red and Paul were also shocked into silence. All of us remained silent about those "facts of life."

For some time after that afternoon revelation I had a hard time. I was trying to accept this startling revelation about this gift of life. It was hard.

Mostly I didn't say anything to anybody.

At the time I was nine years old. I silently wondered about this wonder of life.

It was a great experience to have our own Benny and buggy days in Indiana. Old-fashioned, certainly. Life was kept at a slower pace. Maybe we did not have to grow up so fast that way. Yet it helped us to enjoy some of our families' "good old days." For one thing, it helped us to appreciate some of the life of our parents and grandparents. Plus, since times were changing from the buggy to the car, we got to enjoy both.

It gave us plenty of time for needed "boy talk"—maybe that should be "kid talk." What better place for such talk— in the buggy seat while leisurely riding through the countryside of Hoosierland.

Old Benny, God made only one such horse, and some little Hoosier boys enjoying God's world together. That old horse had a good life in front of our buggy. As children we, too, had the good life.

As mentioned, we lived during those Great Depression days. In some ways they were the best of times, in others, the worst of times. Sometimes hard. People worked hard. Dad did. Others had it hard, too. It was not only hard in Indiana, but in the whole country. Really we must not forget, this was world-wide.

At times we had little, but thankful for what we did have. Others we knew had far less than even a little. This caused us to be dependent upon God, our Heavenly Father. But in other ways, we were dependent upon one another in those times. Neighborliness brought all of us closer together. My family, extended family included, had a big influence on my life. But so did our neighbors. I know I was shaped by our many friends in the marsh. Naturally more people had an influence in my life—in the schools and the First Reformed Church at Dutch Corners.

When Dad and Mom got married they had to set up house-keeping with very little. Mom looked through a catalogue to make out her list, as Dad requested. Then he said he had to scratch out about half the things. Dad once mentioned Mom had $400 worth on her list, but he brought it down to nearly $200. With that much they started housekeeping on the home place.

A shopping list had some of these prices: Sofa-$74.50, Phonograph-43.50, Wool Dress-1.95, Leather Shoes-1.79, Man's Shirt-47¢, Double-bed Sheet-67¢, Wool Blanket-1.00, Double Bed & Spring Mattress-14.95, Dining Room Set (8-piece)-46.50, Sirloin (per 1b.)-29¢, Pork Chops-20¢, Sugar-5¢, Bread-5¢, and Corn Flakes-8¢. Pontiac Coupe-$585, Chrysler Sedan-$995, Packard-$2,150, Used '29 Ford-$57.50.

Those prices while the annual earnings were: Farm Hired Hand-$216, Doctor-$3,282, Teacher-$1,227, RN-$936, Steel Worker-$422.87, Railroad Conductor-$2,729, Waitress-$520. Let me add one more, U. S. Congressman-$8,663.00.

Over 25% of the people were out of work.

Yet we never knew about the "homeless" during those times. At least we never heard of them. However, that did not mean people had homes of their own. Some simply moved on property which did not belong to them. I did hear of the term "squatters" when a boy. These did not have a legal right of title, but still moved on the land. They had to have a place to go. After moving on some acreage they put up a small shanty or small house in which to live. For them, that was home, so they did not have to be homeless.

Any number of farmers lost their farms. As a result the big land companies got them back, or banks got them. The Northern Indiana Land Company had a lot of land in the marsh around the year of 1909. Farmers could farm the land. A land agent for the company or bank would oversee the farmer's work. Generally the land was farmed for shares. Dad was in the marsh, on our home place, even before he was married. Dad and his brother Ben farmed the place in those days. They lived in the little shanty, which was on the hills in the middle of the farm, near the old barn and small machine shed. They were south of the present building site.

I can remember a wooden bridge over Cook Ditch. The bridge was a little less than a quarter mile from the Hodge Ditch bridge. You crossed the wooden bridge to reach the hills, where they lived in the shanty. (A few years later they moved the shanty just north of our house on the big hill.)

Dad farmed our home place on shares. He got three-fifths and the land company two-fifths. A man by the name of Hoover was our land agent. (As a kid, I thought he was President Hoover for a time. Never asked questions, just thought he was our agent.) Farming on shares meant both parties shared the expenses of seed and fertilizer. Dad was expected to furnish the horses and machinery, and do the work.

Our farm was in the Kankakee River marsh. Early explorers joked that the river was as wide as it is long. First names for it were Thekiki Huakiki, Seignelay, and several other ones. Finally, the cartographers agreed and adopted the official name Kankakee River. Our home place is 1.8 miles from the bridge on the Old Grade. To the south is the Hodge Ditch with a bridge .7 of a mile from our house. Across the bridge was the Carter farm, 1.2 miles from us. Further south was where the Systmas lived.

Nearest neighbors to the north were the Obenchains and Armstrongs. I also remember the Hilliards, but I do not know where they lived when they worked for Dad. Almost a mile from us were the Swishers and Hancocks. 1.3 miles from our place were the Kruceks. To the east, across Hobbs Ditch, were the Sampsons, while to the west was the Evans farm. The Cook Ditch made its way through our farm, then flowed along the Old Grade.

There was a man who lived northeast of us, not far from the Sampson home place. Every now and then we would visit him. He was about three miles away. This fellow had a sword hanging on his wall. That was pretty fascinating to me. One time we stopped, after he had been killed. Rather frightening to look around. His little shanty had been vandalized when we got there. It was spooky, so we got out of there in a hurry.

The Kruceks family was an interesting place to visit. They raised a lot of potatoes. And they milked goats. There were three sons and a daughter living with their parents. None were married when we were kids. They called my Dad Marty, which sounded strange to me, as if my father was only a boy!

The names of the sons were Jim, John and Frank, while Mary was their sister. All of them would fuss over us whenever we stopped. I liked it when they showed us the goats. I especially liked the little goats, which I felt were so cute. Maybe our interest was enough for them to give us one little goat of our own. That little thing followed Mom all around the yard. A little pen was built in the cow barn for it, where it stayed at night. Our fun with this little pet was short-lived. Our pet died one night. It hurt. We felt very sad over losing that pet.

A large family living across from Sam and Rose Obenchain was the Armstrong family. They had either 12 or 13 children. Charles was the oldest boy. Jeanette was my age, also in my class at school. They were squatters. They built only a small house, which couldn't hold their entire family. So they attached a large green tent for sleeping quarters. Many of the children slept in the tent—even in the cold winters! It was heated, making it rather cozy when you were in it. Near the house they put up a sapling fence, in which they kept their horses and a few cows for milk. This family was very poor, but such good people. I liked them. As a boy I felt for them in all their need.

The Obenchains lived a half mile north of us, the older folks, along with their unmarried children, Buck, Tom and Rosie. Orville was another son, but did not live at home. Burl was married, who lived where Buzz Swart presently lives. As kids we'd stop in to see them every now and then. Burl's wife would greet us with a rag or handkerchief around her head. It looked like a big bandage across her forehead. She told me she had another migraine. The woman suffered a lot with such headaches, for we hardly ever saw her without the rag around her head.

Even though she did not feel well, she treated us so kindly. They didn't have children of their own, so she would make a fuss over us. Almost every time she gave us some special kind of treat before we left.

Since we made the rounds, our visits took us to Sam's place, too. Sometimes we'd go in their house, other times we'd go where the boys spent most of their time. That was in a one room building just behind their home.

In June of 1931 the Swishers moved into the woods about a mile north. Near them lived Mose Hancock, whose wife died in childbirth. So he adopted out his daughter Mabel. Those at home were older children, Elmer, Minnie, and Teddy.

The Hancocks lived in a small tarpaper house off the Old Grade. It looked like it had been there for years. Elmer and Teddy did work at times for Dad, especially during harvest.

But we were closest to the Pete Swisher family, who lived a short distance north of Hancocks.

Pete and Liz were in their late forties when we first became acquainted with them. Several of their children were married. Their children's names were: Ada, Flossie, Anna, Francis, Chuck (Chod), Wesley, and Violet.

Since they moved in the middle of 1931, that meant it was in the heart of the Depression. As Violet put it, "And I know we're ever so poor, but we had a lot of love, and that's most important."

Pete's family lived in a tin home. Poles from the woods were used for the framework, while the sides and roof were covered with black colored sheets of tin. Holes in the tin were filled with tar. Only the good earth-formed the floor in their home. Being as large as it was they sectioned it off with curtains hanging in front of the bedroom areas.

Their heating stove has always been a fascination to me. They were very creative in building their stove. Really it was only a 55 gallon oil drum, a barrel on its side. A hole was cut in the end for a door. Hinges were put on this so it could open and close. On the opposite end was another hole, for the stovepipe. That pipe allowed the smoke to go outside. This barrel stove was bolted to half a tire rim, one on each end. These were the legs of the stove. That stove really heated their home. Remember they did not have any insulation in their home. Yet they lived in this home for several years.

Later they got some secondhand lumber to build another house. It took some time to complete that one. I don't know how long they lived in the newer home. They moved away from their place after the mother died. Liz died when she was 54 years old. Mrs. Swisher died, very suddenly, on October 20, 1937.

A garden patch supplied some of their food. Generally they borrowed our horses and plow each year to get their garden ready for planting. Out of gratitude they gave us a stinking old billy goat. Before it was over we were not that grateful for this old goat. But that's another story I'll share later.

They shared with us some acorn squash, which we called table queens. As a kid I thought those golden-fleshed squash were so delicious! Ever since those days as a boy I've enjoyed them, so I am thankful for that—not for the goat!

Dad said that Pete and his family were always there to help when he really needed them. Dad was good to them, as Violet said, "I know your parents were very good to us." It worked both ways. Dad did appreciate the many times Pete's family came through.

Pete's brother Horace also moved into the same area of the woods, yet closer to the Old Grade. They built a two room home. The lumber for their home looked newer, but it was never painted, so it deteriorated. We knew this brother as Hossie, who was the oldest of the two, at least three or four years older than Pete. His wife was a very short woman, named Evie. They had three children, Kenny, Mary, and Jim. The oldest was three years older than I was, while Mary was a year younger, with Jim four years younger yet.

Living on the little forty acres, which Dad later bought, was Nicholas Homeninski. This was west of the four corners of the Old Grade, toward the main Highway 53. This family fled to the United States. Their flight was caused by Stalin. Josef Stalin was the winner of the power struggle in Russia, after Lenin died in 1924. At once those people faced a police state. The reigns of such leaders as Stalin were gruesome on a scale it's hard for us to imagine—enslavement, terror, oppression, confiscation, corruption and fraud. Unbelievable evils. It is thought that 10 million starved or were executed by Stalin. If any of the people tried to rise in power, they were eliminated by purges. This resulted in more executions of hundreds of thousands, who were "enemies of the State." History records Josef Stalin alone was guilty of the persecution, imprisonment, torture and death of some *fifty million* human beings, even before World War II. Approximately fourteen million peasants died during the Stalin years from 1930-1937.

Nick, providentially escaped with his life, along with members of his family.

I learned this one day when we had been threshing rye for Nick. That's when Nicholas talked with me, I had to be 9 or 10. He simply asked me if I knew Stalin. As a boy, I told him that I had heard of his name. Never to-be-forgotten was this statement of Nicholas Homeninske: "He is a beast!" That was my first lesson in brutal history. Later even worse facts came out about this monster who ruled Russia from the 20s until 1953. Stalin changed his name to the Russian term for "man of steel." And to think some world leaders during the war thought of him as "good old Joe." Nicholas thought of him far differently, which I accept from one who had been through it all, "He is a beast!"

When they moved on that little farm, the family was in desperate need of food. Nick planted grapes. At first he put in a good sized patch of potatoes. When it came time to dig them, Nick brought a truckload of people from Gary. These Russians took a forked-stick to dig his potatoes during the early years of the Depression.

Nick would try to get some wheat, rye or oats for his first crop. Then quickly after it was harvested he had the stubble plowed. Then came the second crop for that season such as buckwheat. He went for two crops in the same year, as often as he could.

You could tell they were people who lived through hard times. Whenever we threshed grain for Nick, he would put a canvas or two under the threshing machine so none of the grain would be wasted. He wanted to catch any grain which fell out of the heads. Afterwards he carefully gathered up all the loose grain.

While we were cleaning up one threshing job in the middle of his field, Dad told me I had better check the oil in our old Dodge truck. Since I couldn't stand next to the fender to open the hood, I stood next to the bottom of the fender. I stepped on the running board to reach it. However, I got into trouble with a flare box mounted at the bottom of the fender, as I stumbled over it. Falling forward I tried to catch myself, but failed. Before I could break my fall I broke off part of my front tooth. A big chunk of the tooth shattered when I fell on the big black headlight. Some of the crushed parts of the tooth remained on the top of the light.

I ran to Dad to have him look at it. Nick came over to see what happened to me too. Naturally I felt very bad about losing part of my front tooth. My tongue confirmed the damage.

I felt sick. Nick, seeing it bothered me, tried to be helpful, by saying, "Don't worry about it. You'll get a new one there."

I turned to him, showing him my teeth, saying, "These are my new ones!" Certainly I couldn't expect new ones when I had some of my permanent teeth.

Daily I see that chipped front tooth, so many times I have a frequent reminder of that traumatic experience on Nick's little farm. I think of Nicholas, too.

He had a cave, where canned fruit and vegetables were stored. I saw potatoes, carrots, cabbage, and other things in it.

Several times I'd eat with them. Not upstairs! No, you did not go upstairs, not with work clothes on.

In their basement Nick had built a stove from brick and parts of an old stove top. His wife did her cooking and baking on it.

One day I was doing some work for them, so I was invited to eat with them in the basement. That day she had a big meal. Mrs. Homeninski had made kolachis, with prune filling. Inside this sweet roll dough she tucked her prune filling. It was delicious! I can't tell you how good they tasted—it was pure joy eating her kolachis. I could have stayed at the table all afternoon eating them. Again and again she pulled those kolachis out of her oven. Each time she would smile as she put more on my plate. Knowing I was enjoying her food, she'd go for more. To this day, I have no idea how many I ate. (If my parents had been there I would have been told that I had enough! But they were not there.)

But Nick and Mrs. Homeninski thought it was fun to feed this hungry boy more of their tasty food. Frankly I can't tell you a thing about the other food we ate. But I'll never forget her prune-patties this dear woman gave to fill my stomach with such a delicious dish. Her kolachis were so good I can't erase from my memory that meal. It ranks among the most tasty food I ever ate in my life.

Nick was really a building contractor by profession. One wouldn't believe it seeing his buildings on his little farm. His barn, sheds, and house were all built from old secondhand lumber, and scraps. These were Depression times. They began

42

with nothing. After all, they had absolutely nothing when they fled to our country, trying to get away from Stalin. They escaped only with their lives!

Later he started doing more construction building in Gary. His oldest son had architectural training. So the two got into the construction business as partners. After things got better for them, he offered to sell his forty acre farm to Dad.

We went to Gary, Indiana, to close the transaction. Nick had to take us around to a few job sites at the time. Looking at the size of these jobs, one had to admit they had come a long way.

Once again we had to eat with them in their home. But not before Nick changed his clothes. First we went down into the basement again with Nick. He got cleaned up. His wardrobe was there, so he put on a suit. While we waited, he gave us a small taste of his wines. After he was all dressed, then we were taken upstairs to the dining room.

His wife and a daughter, with other women of the family had the table spread for a big feast. It was almost like a Thanksgiving table set before us. We were treated to an excellent dinner. It made me feel like we were out of place, in an upper class dining room.

Later all the papers were signed for the little farm. It was the last time I remember seeing our Russian neighbor, Nicholas Homeninski, a very special person. A man whose life was so different in America after his escape from the man he considered a beast, Joe Stalin!

Another Russian had a shack across the fence to the west of Nick's little farm. I only knew him as "Russian John."

John's last name was known by Dad, even though he told me several times, I always forgot it.

Russian John was a squatter. John was another person with nothing. However, before too long he built his shack from wide rough sawmill lumber. There were stories about him, which made him a little mysterious. One story had it he stole all the boards from a mill. This meant he had to go some distance to get the lumber, about three miles one way. Every night he got a few more boards, which he'd carry on his back.

Finally he had enough to build his little shack with rough lumber.

Later John had an old Model T Ford. His was a stripped-down old truck. He sat on the gas tank, with a little wooden box back of him.

Every now and then he'd come to buy a gallon or two of gas. John was a man of few words, which added to the mystery about Russian John.

One time he came for gas when he had pus oozing from wounds on the side of his face. Those festering wounds came from being hit with buckshot.

To the west of John was a family named Bailey. This family came from Kentucky, naturally their pets were some dogs. John had a few chickens. That's when the feud began. Those dogs got after John's chickens. The story was that John set out poison for the dogs. This caused trouble between the men. Bailey used some buckshot on John. Nothing much could be proven. Nobody was saying much either. This was the way they tried to settle things. That's why John had the wounds oozing pus from being hit with buckshot.

Roy Bailey himself had an earlier injury, which happened when he lived in Kentucky. The man had a very crooked neck. The story told about Bailey was he had been in a knife fight in the hills of Kentucky, so for the rest of his life he'd hold his neck crooked.

Russian John himself could handle a knife! John butchered a hog for us. He was there early, even before we got on the bus that morning. John was still there when we got back home again.

He wanted the pig in the open area downhill, near our tool shed. There was a small pile of straw in the driveway. John chased the hog toward the straw. Russian John was running behind the animal with a knife in his hand. With a leap he landed on the back of the pig. While holding on, he reached around the neck—then stuck the animal. The hog bled to death on the pile of straw. Next he set the straw on fire to singe off the hair.

We saw that before getting on the bus. The hog was butchered while we were in school. John was cutting up the meat when we got home from school. The meat was placed in large crocks. Before placing each piece in a crock, Morton's Salt was rubbed into the meat. This was to preserve it. Mom was not too happy with his salting the meat, I remember. She thought he had overdone it. It was too salty.

Let me get back to his knives. I changed my clothes so I could do my chores. I was fascinated with John cutting up the meat, so I watched him for a little while. I looked over his butchering equipment. My interest was drawn to his knives. I picked up one of them. Instantly Russian John yelled at me not to touch anything!

But a moment before he yelled I already had the knife in my hand. Just for a split second it slipped in my hand. When it did, the knife touched a finger on my left hand. That light touch sliced into my finger!

With his yell, naturally I quickly put it down. Looking at me, in his broken language he asked if I had cut myself. He was sure I had. I denied it. Holding my finger to keep it from bleeding anymore, I lied, shooked my head, and said, "No! "

Quickly I left to look at the cut. Deep. It hurt. I wrapped it up. But to this day I recall how razor-sharp he had his knives. Just a little touch—yet it opened up my finger in an instant.

To this day I have the scar. It is the reminder of Russian John. It also reminds me of the day I lied. Now I can not tell a lie, with that scar to tell the truth, I did get cut!

I've wondered, too, what would have happened if Bailey and Russian John would have used knives in their feud?

Roy Bailey lived on 20 acres. Coming from Kentucky he built a small house for his family. The kids were on our school bus. Lula was my age, then came Lola and Sola. Next in the family was the only boy, Ollie. The youngest was Mae.

One year the older girls all had appendicitis. It was so strange how close to each other they had their surgery. Mom thought it was due to the raw pickles and cukes they ate. My Mom always had to soak cucumbers in salt water overnight. After that she felt it was safe to eat them.

Lola, who was the quiet girl, had the most serious case. After a short time she died. It seems she was about 13 or 14 years old. I still remember her funeral, with an open casket at the cemetery. There was so much loud crying at the grave. Pictures were taken before they closed the casket. The graveside service was very long.

Mrs. Bailey took the death of Lola so very hard. The mother and her daughter were close to each other. I guess one would have to say the mother never did get over the death of her daughter.

Some weeks later, as she was walking along Highway 53 she was killed. A mystery surrounds that death. Mrs. Bailey was facing the oncoming traffic, walking towards the river bridge. Suddenly she stepped right in front of a car. When this car hit her, she was instantly killed, about a mile from her home.

The family had another funeral shortly after Lola's.

Lula around the same time was dating a much older man. Not too long afterwards they got married.

Both Ollie and Mae were in school when I was a senior in 1943. Ollie was much older, yet he was only in the 5th grade. That boy almost made it impossible for any teacher in the classroom.

One day Mr. Ewart, our principal, talked to our senior class about Ollie. He requested our class supervise Ollie. Taking turns we helped him with his lessons. Naturally he was no longer with his own class, but sat most of the time in our big assembly hall. We did try to help him, but it was difficult. He could not retain facts very long. One would go over and over common words, but he just did not grasp it. Much of the time Ollie thought it was funny. His idea was to consider it a "fun game" to play with the seniors. The boy was trying everybody, but he was not trying himself!

One day he was cutting up. His disturbance was more than Mr. Ralph Wurzburger could take. It was time for some discipline. Before he could even begin correcting Ollie, the kid jumped out of his seat to attack the teacher. Repeatedly he kicked Mr. Wurzburger in the shins. He was vicious. Frankly it was unbelievable how vicious this boy could be.

Mr. Ewart had a plan, but I doubt it accomplished anything. He tried. We tried. I guess we all failed.

Roy Bailey bought pickles during the early days of World War II. For that summer we got a good price for our pickles. But he stopped buying before the season was over, which meant we had to find other buyers. Naturally the price dropped when we switched buyers.

Afterwards that family moved away. Ollie made the news, every now and then. Later the paper reported his death. It seems it was a tractor accident, where a fire was involved. That was the last I heard of him.

In the spring farmers moved, if they were making a change. When that happened there was a lot of activity.

One spring day I watched this farmer go by, several trips were made. Each time he went by with his team of horses and wagon. Load after load were moved.

Later that day, to my surprise, he turned into our driveway. He stopped his team, "Whoa!" After they stopped, he jumped off the wagon and unhitched the team. As a kid I couldn't figure out what he was doing. His horses were given a drink out of our horse tank, then he headed straight for our barn. Nothing was said to anybody.

Finally, I was very, very curious, so went up to him, asking, "What are you doing?" Here he was, in our barn. He put his horses in the stalls where our horses belonged.

Smiling, he quickly helped me to understand that he had talked with Dad. My father had given permission to put his horses in our barn on the day of his move to a new farm.

The man I found out was Buzz Swart, who was our new neighbor to the north. The big mystery was solved for me.

Buzz had John Deere tractors; we had Farmalls. His tractors had the hand clutch; our Farmalls had the foot clutch.

One of those early years Buzz asked for some help. Before having a hard frost, he wanted to cut some soybeans with a binder. Dad told me to go over and help him. Buzz decided to put me on his tractor, while he ran the binder. That afternoon we cut some beans with the binder for feed.

Everything went all right—well, almost! However, I was not used to the John Deere. Ever since I was about nine I ran a Farmall. A Farmall was my kind of tractor. It was a big switch to use a hand clutch. Actually it wasn't going that bad. Naturally we took it slowly at first, but later we ran the outfit faster.

Then it happened. Soybeans began to pile up on the binder apron. The reel pushed, bent a little in the middle, finally the slat slipped by.

More beans fell on the apron. Buzz spotted trouble, as the pile was getting too big. We had to stop. Buzz yelled from his seat on the binder, "Whoa! Whoa!" Oh, I had to stop in a hurry!

My foot quickly rammed forward to push in the clutch. Nothing happened. The John Deere pop-popped ahead...it didn't stop. Again I pushed. Again. And again!

I heard a sharp crack! Then snap! Pop! Bang! Buzz hollered one more time: **"WHOA!"**

Finally I grabbed the hand clutch! Everything stopped.

Good grief. Now I did it. I felt awful. I sat in silence. As I listened, only the John Deere went pop-pop, pop-pop.

Next I heard laughter. Loud laughter. Buzz laughed, and laughed, and laughed. While he laughed, I died a little more. Slowly I turned around to see the ruins. Half the reel was broken into pieces. It was awful. I felt sick on the inside.

Buzz spoke, half laughing, saying he could tell I drove Farmalls. To him it was so funny watching me stomping and stomping to push in a clutch, which was *not* there.

All my stomping didn't stop that John Deere. To Buzz it was funny. It wasn't funny to me. His acceptance of my mistake helped some. Yet I felt terrible about what had happened. The reel was a mess. Half was shattered into pieces, but the other half was okay.

Buzz and I both got down to look it over. We'd just fix it. We took off the broken parts, then took the good sections—moved them into every other section on the reel.

Dad put us on the tractor at an early age.

Naturally we had only half the normal slats on the reel, but we'd finish the job that way. It worked. Before evening we finished the job cutting his soybeans.

The longer I worked the better I began to feel. No big problems came up the rest of the afternoon.

Buzz made it easier, in being so gentle with me. Oh, for the rest of the day, I did remember I was running a John Deere tractor.

I caught on, the trick was never to forget to *pull back on the hand clutch to STOP!* I got it!

The Marsh

It was called the marsh. Where we lived it was 1.8 miles from the Kankakee River. It had several names before the map-makers settled on Kankakee. The original name had to do with "Wolf Land." That comes from various words such as Thea-kiki, Haukiki, or Kankekiki. These had to do with land inhabited by wolves and river. It appeared first in Jesuit history in 1666. This river was thought of being as wide as long. At one time, I was told, the old river spread all over the marsh. It was a paradise for hunters and trappers in early years. Later it was channeled to follow its present course, as I came to know the Kankakee River.

It has an interesting history. Over three hundred years ago the Kankakee Valley was explored by the first recorded white people. This was the expedition led by Robert Cavelier Sieur de LaSalle. His party found the undrained swamp land and dense tangled woods full of snakes and wild animals. Even so it became known as a hunter's paradise for the birds and fur animals. Migrating birds discovered it to be a special place for them. The marsh was the home to muskrats, mink, fox, wolves, and others. Dad told of going through the marsh when their huts or dens dotted the areas now covered with corn and soybeans. Those huts were thick in some areas, one could almost step from one to the next. Early settlers found this to be the source of income and food for themselves.

LaSalle found various Indian Tribes along the river. Included among these were the Pottawattomie and Iroquois Indians, who were fierce enemies. History tells how these Indians became friendly with the white settlers and trappers.

The French-Canadians were, according to history, reported to be the original settlers in De Motte, which is five miles from our home in the marsh. Its actual founder, for whom the

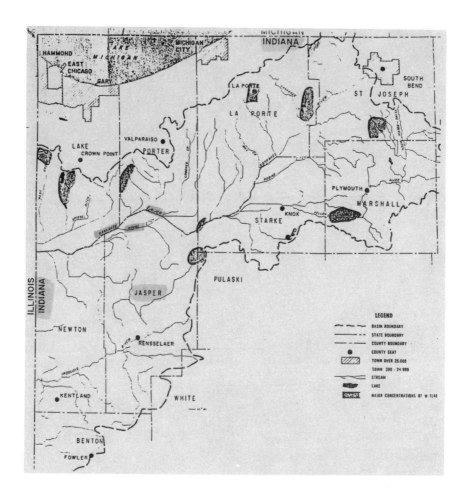

town got its name, was Colonel Mark De Motte. This man was a colonel in the Union Army, a hero of the Civil war. Later he became a Congressman. Founding of De Motte took place around 1882, maybe 1883.

Farmland was not in demand at first. However the swamp grass of the marsh was. It was feed for horses. Others shipped it to Chicago to be sold there.

One big land owner bought about 33,000 acres of the land north of De Motte. He purchased it for $1.00 per acre. South of De Motte land was purchased by Otis from Chicago. Dutch

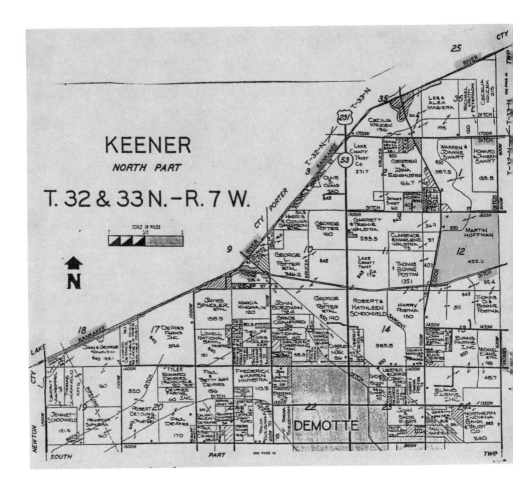

KEENER
NORTH PART
T. 32 & 33 N. – R. 7 W.

SCALE IN MILES
1/2   1

N

DEMOTTE

SOUTH   PART   SEE PAGE 18   TWP

families were sponsored to come to America and settle on the ranches.

Our farm was in the marsh, north of town. On the south-side we had what was known as the Hodge Ditch. Nearly two miles to the north was the Kankakee River. On the westside of our farm was a road, known as the Old Grade. Dad helped when they first built the Old Grade. Actually he worked for a

52

time with the crew. My Dad furnished a team and slip-scrapper. Day in and day out they built up the grade with these small sand scrappers.

Dad did some trapping in our ditches. I still remember Dad running his traps, when I was a small boy. One day he came back having caught a snipe, or jacksnipe, in a trap.

Dad took this bird to Bill Recker, who stuffed it. When we got it back, Mr. Recker had mounted it behind glass. The setting looks like the snipe is in a marshy area. Most of us recall having this stuffed snipe in our home for years. (There is a small label on the back of the mounting. I got it when we disposed of the folks' furnishings. At the time it came into my possession it must have been in our family for over sixty years.)

Many drainage ditches were dug in the marsh. Some were rather large, while others were small. It could get wet in the marsh. There were a number of those wet years. But I well remember the 30s, some awfully dry ones.

We had the Cook Ditch which ran through part of our farm, then along the Old Grade to the Hodge Ditch. However, when I was a boy I remember the small ditch that ran through the center of our farm, about half a mile towards the Hodge. Small willows grew in this little ditch. But that ditch was buried in those dry and dusty years. Later years one could see a ridge of sandy loam going through the field. That ridge replaced the little ditch.

During those dry years some of our country had the Dust Bowl, as it was known. We had plenty of dust, too. I would say we had a Little Dust Bowl. Dad came out of the fields so dirty, covered with the miserable "itch dirt." One year we had rust in the wheat, then Dad would come home covered with a reddish brown dust. My father looked like someone had taken a cinnamon can puffing the dusty stuff all over him.

Dad had such a hard day, which I can still picture in my mind. The grain binder would not tie the bundles, the knotter failed to function properly. Nothing worked. Hot! Miserable day in the rusty wheat. You could tell the kind of day Dad had by the way he drove the truck home. Mom picked it up. It was such a frustrating time—all day long.

Back home Mom had a hard day, too. Mom was concerned about her sick baby. My little sister Lois was very sick. Late that afternoon Dad came home covered with sweat, dust and rust. Mom, turned to me in tears, saying, "Oh, Dad is so mad again."

After looking out the window, watching the truck come flying up the lane, we went into a bedroom. Mom laid my little sister on the bed. Mom and I knelt beside the bed. There we prayed! In tears we prayed. My sister had been taken to the doctor again and again. She was getting no better, only worse. Mom was worried, but so was Dad. Those moments live in my memory. It is one of the most unforgettable boyhood memories I have. My mother and I knelt in prayer to plead with our Heavenly Father.

Likely that was one of the most frustrating year for farmers in the marsh. Yet wet years could be miserable, too.

Naturally we had some special wet spots on our farm. One wet hole we called the Devil's Hole, near the Hodge Ditch. Many times it caused us grief. At one time the hole must have been a burned-out muck spot. Across the Hodge one farm had problems with muck fires in those dry years.

It was too wet in the spring. Always the last place to plow in wet years. It was hard to get it planted. But the weeds liked that hole. They grew like weeds! Big ones! Generally the biggest weeds on the whole farm.

With those big weeds, it was the hardest place to combine. Only a killing frost made it a little easier to harvest. Tough weeds caused trouble to slug the machine. One-single weed could block the soybeans in the feeder. Once the beans piled up, then suddenly fed into the combine, then we'd get the slug. That meant a lot of extra work. A large wrench was used to turn the cylinder back, after that one could dig out the slug. That wrench was bent, even broken. That's how hard we strained to turn back the cylinder on the combine. Later we welded two wrenches together, plus adding an extension of pipe for more leverage. While it made it easier to unplug, yet it was still hard work. Very aggravating!

Since we lived in the marsh, it could be the wettest of years. Some years it was more than wet, that was whenever the farm flooded. The highest I ever saw the water was when we took a boat over the top barb wire on the fence in the field. We had no problem slipping the boat over that top wire. The whole farm was under water that time.

We lost our winter wheat. Crops were lost even on the high ground. We would spear carp in the wheat field.

Once the water went down, then we could still plant a crop that year. Things were late, yet we could still get in the fields to work the land. However, it was a lot of extra work.

Before we got the crop planted, cultivated and harvested we discovered the "itch dirt" was still there. All the flood waters couldn't wash it away. Each year we found it was there.

It was funny, as boys talked together, Paul or I would comment about the old "itch dirt" on our farm. Some wouldn't believe it. They would give us that look, doubting us. We were not telling tall stories. No matter what others thought, we had "itch dirt" on our farm. It tormented a person. It aggravated a person sometime during the summer. It was plain torment when you had a dry, dusty, hot, windy day. Once it got to you, then you did not even want to turn your head, move your neck. It was like it paralyzed a person's movement. You became a stiff figure, the miserable stuff held you in that rigid form.

One hot day Marty came out of the field at noon. Covered with "itch dirt"—stiff, never made one extra move. Mom asked, "Was the *itch dirt* bad, Marty?"

It had to be—he lost it! My brother burst out bawling.

Most of us felt the same way many times. It gave you such a miserable feeling you could just bawl. On a hot summer day, with a slight wind, that stuff floated into the air. This dirt would settle on every exposed part of your body. All the while you dreamed of real cold water washing the miserable stuff away at the end of the day. One could then keep going.

Finally the day was done. Then came the cold water to wash it away.

A person would want to scratch away where you felt the itch, especially on your feet. So before going to bed you had the pleasure of sticking your feet under the cold water faucet. No drying them—just go to bed with wet feet. Relief!

On a bad day, you almost went to bed singing, "Nobody Knows The Trouble I've Seen." Only the person who also worked in the "itch dirt" could feel for you and understand.

When I was a small boy we travelled the best of roads and the worst of roads. Out in the marsh we had good old dirt roads. North of the farm to the river was dirt, so was the nearly two miles south to our mailbox. It was a dirt road to reach the cement road, Highway 53.

Roads were dusty in the summertime. Some spots had soft sugar sand. In those places a driver didn't want to get out of the track, or he would be stuck. Most areas would pack-down to make a hard surface. However these same areas could be muddy in the spring and fall. Especially bad were the times when the frost went out, then a person could get into trouble. A driver had to have skills to get through or around some mud holes.

A Sunday drive was a treat for some families. If they chose a country road, they could end up in a lake of mud.

Some of these people would come walking to our house. Could Dad pull them out? Dad would hitch up a team of horses on Sunday to help them out. Generally they would give Dad something for getting them out of their predicament.

The worst spot was near the four-corners, going west to the highway. Once you got beyond that muddy section, you didn't want to meet someone in that soft, sugar sand. If you did, then keep moving. The back wheels would do some jumping as you gunned it to get back into your track. In a few seconds a driver could work up a sweat.

At times it was nice to have the road grader come by. The grader would get the road smoothed out again. The hard surfaced sections were really nice after being graded. It was like driving on the highway. But there were times you hated to see the grader come. When the operator would drag weeds and grass from the edge of the road it would pile up in the middle of the road. That was another story.

After the road was graded we had to cut a new track in the soft sand. It took a few days before the road got back to normal again. A driver hoped a pile in the middle of the road did not hit your oil pan or gas tank. At times it did, causing trouble.

If the conditions of the road were bad enough, then we had to haul our milk to the highway. There we had to wait until the milk truck came to pick up our cans. We got our empty ones back. It took extra time out of a busy day on the farm.

We were glad when the roads were improved so our milk hauler could pick up our cans from our milk house.

Traffic was not that busy on our country roads. Generally it was pretty safe to travel on those dirt roads with our horse and buggy. As boys we went miles on those old sand roads. Many more miles were travelled through the woods and in the fields. We had a lot of country to cover. Day after day we'd hitch up Benny and the buggy for another ride. We had one big marsh to explore. Just think de LaSalle explored our marsh. So did Indians. So did early trappers and hunters. As did early settlers. We did too! For us it was very interesting and exciting to explore the Kankakee Marsh.

In the marsh were the HOFFMAN FARMS. I always liked to see names on the farms. Whenever we drove through the countryside I liked to see names

I painted HOFFMAN FARMS on the little crib. The big corn crib is in the background.

on the buildings. For me it was special. I especially liked the Potter Farms.

I kept looking around where I could put our name. The silo would have been a good place, but not the best. For it was hidden from the Old Grade. The big barn was in the way. People wouldn't be able to see it.

I thought of the big barn and big crib, but both lacked the visibility desired.

Finally I thought of the western end of the little crib. It was clearly visible from the Old Grade.

Once Dad bought the little farm from Nicholas Homeninske, then we could have "FARMS" on the sign.

It took me a long time to sketch out the markings of the lettering. I made the name "HOFFMAN" the largest, then "FARMS" was slightly smaller in size.

The crib was painted red, trimmed in white. I used white against the red to paint HOFFMAN FARMS on the little crib.

Certain letters were difficult to make. Those made with block-form were the easiest, but those curved ones were much harder. As a boy I was happy with the results after I got it painted.

Now everybody would know that we lived on the farm. I was proud of our farms. I felt a great deal of satisfaction when it was finished.

For years it announced who lived on our farm in the marsh.

Dad first lived on the home place, then he was single. But he lived near the old barn, in the shanty.

The old barn and little machine shed was on that hill, about .4 of a mile south of the present building site. Both buildings had weathered lumber, never were painted. Uncle Ben and Dad lived in the shanty when my father first started farming in the marsh.

After the folks were married they moved into the house on the hill. When the shanty was moved north of the house it was used mainly for sleeping quarters for our hired men. Many men slept in the shanty.

The Little Shanty on the hill. Dad lived in it before he was married. Later our hired men would sleep in the Shanty. Our WPA outhouse is in the back of the house and Shanty.

In early days the Northern Indiana Land Company managed our farm at first. Dad farmed on shares the first years of being on the home place.

When Mr. Hoover was our agent we had to straighten the big crib. They noticed it was shifting to the east. It was a very hot summer day they tackled the job. West of the crib, in the middle of the yard, a dead man was buried. I was very curious about the burial of a "dead man" in our yard!

On this was placed a winch, which was turned by horses. A large cable ran through the crib, anchored to the eastside of the building. Those horses walked in a circle, slowly turning the winch, ever so slowly moving the big crib to the west.

It groaned! Creaked! Moaned! And moved!

Every now and then they'd check their progress. Finally the workers felt it was in plumb again.

Remember this was done on an extremely hot summer day. Before it got finished Mr. Hoover got sick. The man had spent too much time in the sun. The heat got the best of him. Mr. Hoover suffered a heat-stroke.

He collapsed. Everything stopped. He was down. A few men got a mattress out of our house. They carried it downhill, placed it in the driveway of the crib. Mr. Hoover was laid on it. Since he seemed to have the chills afterwards, they kept him covered. A doctor came out to see him.

He had a fast pulse, being flushed. Yet we had to keep him in a cool place. A slight breeze helped keep him in a little fresh air. He was very confused. I went downhill to look at him every chance I got. I thought he was going to die.

He laid there until evening, when he felt well enough to go.

Then the job could be finished. Since the building was plumb, bracing had to hold it in place. 2x6s were nailed to the big studs. The braces went in both directions, so it would not shift again. The Swart brothers put in all the braces. For years afterwards the old crib stood straight. It had recovered. So did Mr. Hoover.

Picture taken from the pig lot in the big timothy field. Sheller is in the cow yard. White building is our milkhouse.

Summer Work

Naturally we had all the usual work on our livestock and grain farm.

Generally each summer, when we got the corn and soybeans cultivated for the last time, we had a lull for a short spell. After a break threshing would come along or having to combine some grain, wheat, rye or oats.

In some of those early years Dad first tried raising some potatoes. About four acres would be planted. A single row planter was purchased. It had a strange clicking sound as the seed was released from the prongs which speared into the potato sets. These had to be cultivated. Also we had to hoe them. They were sprayed by hand for bugs.

We picked up the potatoes in wire baskets. New potatoes were placed in pits, covered with hay, then dirt, and still more hay. One year Dad wanted to dry out the potatoes. He laid them in piled rows in the little timothy field, south of the tool shed. All those potatoes on top got sunburned, which made them turn colors. That was the last time we did that.

When it came time to sell them, we had to uncover them and take them from the pit. Many spoiled, or rotted. These we dumped into the pig lot. The best ones were sorted and sacked. Some stores bought them from Dad. Signs along Highway 53 directed some buyers to our farm. A few buyers came out from Gary to get a load to sell.

A lot of work went into raising potatoes. Dad only did that for a few years. Afterwards we'd raise enough for our own use. Since we ate them at two meals a day, we needed a good sized patch. During the Depression most families used a lot of potatoes in their diets.

Later we had a large garden, which also supplied many other vegetables for our table.

Painting was another summer job. We had plenty of farm buildings to paint. Some were painted one year, then others the following summer. We painted for many days.

Since it was done in the summertime one would stay on the shady side of the building. Early afternoon it could get very hot in the sun. Dad had me put aluminum paint on the roof of the little tool shed downhill. That job was hard on my eyes, the reflection was so bright I almost closed my eyes. That was bad enough, but the heat was almost unbearable. I complained that it was too hot on the tin roof— so I checked how hot it was that day. 107°! That was one hot tin roof, believe me.

Painting had a few hazards. Underneath eaves the wasps had nests. You hoped you spotted them before they spotted you! It was like a war zone. If you were first, you knocked them down or put a big dab of paint on them. If found soon enough, then I'd soak an old rag with fuel oil. It was tied to the end of a long stick. After setting it on fire you could reach up to destroy the nests.

However, if you missed a nest, then you could be in for a big, painful surprise! Wasps did not like to be disturbed. If they didn't like it, you would know immediately. Here you would be—on top of the ladder—zing! You got stung! And, oh brother, it hurt.

They could surprise you at an unexpected time, especially early morning. One such morning, I had the ladder extended to reach the peak of the old corn crib. Half awake I never dreamed any wasps were around. One wasp had a direct hit, right behind my ear. I couldn't jump—not from the top of the ladder. I just dropped my brush in the bucket of paint. I started sliding down the ladder. But I got nailed one more time before I hit the ground. Running across the yard, I headed in the direction of the gas pump. Too slow. One more sting, again near my ear. Finally his attack was over. I got away. But not before that wasp had three direct hits. Wet baking soda was put on each spot where I was stung. The first thing I did was to get my fire rag. Now was my turn to attack them. I did!

After that I inspected more carefully before painting under the eaves.

In the late 30s we began to raise pickles. Each year we had a patch about 3 or 4 acres in size. With the corn planter we'd put fertilizer in every other row. That would be the row in which we planted the pickles.

Since they were spaced by the planter we could cultivate the plants with the tractor. But we still had to hoe them. Also we had to dust the plants to take care of the bugs.

These rows were easy to see when the plants were small. As time went on the vines began to run. Before long the whole patch was covered with pickle vines. A few spots were open, enough to make out the main rows. From the end of the field it would look like vines were everywhere.

When we first started picking we could get over the patch in a reasonably short time. However, if we had plenty of rain and warm weather, then each picking took much more time.

At first we could cover the whole patch in a day. Later it took a couple days, but late in the season it would take a week to pick the whole patch.

When selling the pickles we sometimes took them to a pickle factory. They did not process pickles there, just the storing in large round tanks. Salt and water would be dumped in the tanks, which helped to preserve them. Pickles were graded, so they brought different prices. Very small ones brought the most money, but they did not weigh very much either. While the larger ones, the big cukes, weighed a lot, these were not worth much. The price was way down. It was the average sized pickle which brought the best price, in the long run.

These pickle factories were in De Motte, Virgie, and Kniman. However, many times buyers had stations where you could sell them. Sometimes they bought them by grading them. Some buyers would take them field run. If they took them by field run on an average you got a better price. We got three cents per pound, which was a good price. If some buyer needed more pickles, he would pay a little more than his competition. One summer we were getting 4¢ for field run, which was a very good price. Naturally they got plenty of pickles. Those buyers would get the best of the crop. But later you were in for a shock, for one day you drove up with your day's picking only to find the station closed. You had to find another buyer. When you did, you would hope he'd take your pickles. Generally he would, at his lower price. We were only glad to have him take our pickles, even though we had to take less money.

Most of the time we picked every day, but never on Sunday. That meant an early start every morning. That way we would finish our picking by 4 o'clock. By at least that time you wanted them loaded on the truck so you could go to the factory or buyer. If they were busy, then it would still be late some evenings before we got back home. Generally the chores would still be waiting for us.

The next morning you had to be back in the patch again. In the marsh it meant dew all over the vines, dripping wet! Our hands were wet stirring through the vines looking for pickles. About 9 o'clock it would begin to dry off. But before that you not only had wet hands, but for two or three hours, wet shoes, and feet, plus your pants were wet to your knees. It wasn't too pleasant picking early in the morning. But it was cool, which was much better than the heat of the afternoon.

After picking a bucket full it had to be emptied into a gunnysack. This gave a person a little break from bending over.

Along about 2 o'clock as a kid you felt like your back would break. No longer were you bending over, instead you were down on your knees crawling around looking for those green pickles.

Finally it would get to you. That's when you would yell at the top of your voice. At least it was some relief. Somebody else would join you, groaning, "oh, my aching back!"

Misery liked company. As we talked as kids, one would say that it would be nice to have a magic wand—just wave it over the whole patch. Maybe one would wish the pickles would all jump into the bucket! That never happened. Not once.

The only way those pickles got into the bucket was to pick each one, one by one, then put it there! Pick! My back—my aching back!

It was funny, but it was the same every year. When we first started picking pickles each summer, the first nights you saw pickles when you closed your eyes in bed. Nothing but vines and pickles, even when you crawled in bed at night. As a kid you thought you'd never get away from those pickles!

We got good pay for our work. This kept us busy in that summer lull. This went on for weeks, as long as 6-7-8 weeks. Pickles were picked until the first hard frost, which would kill the vines.

One year they hung on for weeks. After the younger ones had gone back to school, then Dad and I were alone in the patch each day. Dad could pick about ten sacks a day, while I averaged fifteen. During those times I got about $40 each day. This was very good money in those days. Yet it was hard work—back-breaking work.

One year a man came and offered us a cucumber contract. Not the over-sized pickles we used to call cukes. These were the kind one could buy in the store. We put four acres under contract.

The same year we had also four acres of pickles. The price of pickles was very poor that year. Our first month of picking brought two of us only $100, or a few dollars more. That's about all. When I told Dad how much we made— he quit. Dad then told Marty to get the tractor and disc. He ordered the whole patch to be disced under. He felt we had other work to do.

So we spent time painting buildings, until it was time to harvest the cucumbers we contracted.

We were supplied old beer cases for packing the cucumbers. He trucked them in these cases from our field to market.

While the pickle prices were down, we did make good money with the cucumber contract. Our crop was excellent. This man had contracted 39 acres around De Motte. We had four of the 39. One day we had seven tons trucked out of our field. Seven tons was the picking of only one day. Later we were told by our contractor we got more off our four acres than the other 35 acres.

The next year we never saw the man, so we never were offered another contract. We did try to sell a few cases to people going to market around Gary or other places. This was not profitable at all. After that year we did not plant either pickles or cucumbers.

But anybody who ever picked pickles or cucumbers will never forget those days in the old patch.

Those could be some very, very long days for the old aching back!

Chores

Dad was a "dirt farmer" which is a term not heard much today, but that's what Dad was. While we had the grain crops, there had to be a little extra income. The extra would come from eggs and cream. Therefore we had our chores every day.

Each morning it meant rolling out of bed in time to get the chores done.

Generally I would begin with the chickens. My job was to feed and water them. After finishing in the chicken coop I would go to the pigs. I had to scoop corn off the old truck or wagon. For a few years we had a old trailer, which had the ear corn on it. Each week we'd put another jag of corn to be fed to the pigs.

Later I checked the feeders, which had ground feed in them. Each section of the feeder had to be opened to see if the feed was working down. If not, then you got a stick to poke it down. Any junk under the lid would be raked out on the ground. The hogs would go through that again, so it was not wasted.

Watering the pigs was very important. When I first started this chore I had to start the old gas engine to pump the water. When pigs were kept in a wooded area, then I had to pump the water by hand. Most of the time I'd have to prime the pump with water from a tin can. This would soak up the leathers inside the pump so it would pull up the water. Each time I would pump enough to last them for a day.

Water was put in a trough. Later we had a fountain in our tank or the side of a barrel. Sand would get into these, so each watering required cleaning out this sand. Checking the float was necessary, to be sure it was working properly. If the float stuck, either the water would not come out, or keep flowing over. Either way the pigs would not get their water.

When the weather turned cold, the water had to be kept from freezing. A fire was kept in the water heater to prevent freezing.

While I did my chores I had time to think. What does a boy have on his mind? I was thinking about God and eternity. Eternity bothered me, mostly about eternal punishment. Eternity was such a great mystery. After all, I'd reason, everything had a beginning. Therefore there has to be an ending! How could eternity go on and on—forever, forever, and ever and ever? That baffled me!

I'd say to God, "God, there has to be an end. Everything reaches an end! Sometime. I can't understand how eternity goes on forever and ever." How can it? Why? I could not find answers to all my pondering.

Those were some of my first thoughts deepening my own theology. My search would go on for years. But this seemingly endless search all began in the heart of a boy doing his chores in Hoosierland every morning and evening.

After my chores with the chickens and pigs I'd generally go to the cow barn. There were those critters which had to be milked. Our cows were in their stanchions. Behind them was the gutter, with manure and urine, the "perfume" of the barn.

If the weather happened to be rainy it could be a messy job milking the cows. As they came into the barn, sinking in the slop, dragging their udders through the mud, the cows were dirty. I felt those old mudders always had dirty udders. Before we could milk them we had to wash their udders.

Grabbing a stool and bucket I began milking a cow Dad told me to milk. If a cow had a mean-streak, then I had to put on the kickers. Some did kick, either spilling the milk or putting a foot in the bucket. More painful was to have old bossy step on my foot. That's when I had it with the cow. Whack! Whack! with the old stool.

If the cow didn't behave, then some tail-twisting might change her attitude. It also was the way to make the cow move over, if she wanted to push or refused to get over. Cows knew how to use their tails too. Summer was hard on everybody. Cows would be panting due to the hot weather. It was fly time. Flies made it miserable for man and beast. Flies always seemed to be hungry. Bite! Spraying the cows when they got in the barn helped, but those blood-suckers would still bite the cows. When that happened—swish went the tail. Instead of brushing off the flies the cow's tail would be wrapped around your face. That dirty thing! Disgusting.

Really, nothing was more disgusting than a wet tail wrapped around your mouth with one swish! The tail had to be tied to the cow's leg, either with the kickers or some twine.

When I first started milking in an empty bucket I heard these sounds: "twing" "twing" then "twang." Soon it changed and sounded like "twash" "twash" in the foam of milk. If I milked rapidly enough it was fun to see the foam in the pail. Across the gutter would be a cat sitting and waiting. The cat would be licking its whiskers. So I'd squirt a stream of milk right in the cat's face. The cat would gulp down the milk, then clean off its whole face and whiskers. Both of us enjoyed it. Expectantly the cat waited for another squirt.

After dumping the pail of milk into our cream separator or a can, one had to go to the next cow. When all the cows were milked, then we had to separate the milk. Our separator was hand-operated with a crank. First we had to get the speed up, then the milk would flow through the cupped, thin, metal discs. There was the separating the cream from the skim milk. Cream would come out the smaller spout, running into a small cream can. The skim milk was a bluish color coming out the larger spout, going into a big bucket. Skim milk would be fed to our hogs. We shipped our cream to Western Creamery in Chicago.

During school days we had to move along in the morning. There was the school bus we had to catch.

However, before getting on the bus there was plenty to do. It meant cleaning up, changing clothes, eating breakfast and watching for the bus coming down the Old Grade. If somebody else was ready first, then it was that one's job to keep an eye out for the bus.

In my bedroom it could get very cold in the winter. I liked to use Southern Rose hail oil. I'd buy it at Herman's Barber

70

Shop, where Hermie Bunning was the barber. A big bottle cost a quarter. Some cold winter mornings I had a hard time to get it out of the bottle. One morning I remember, after I mixed it with some water, my Southern Rose was frozen in the bottle.

I used hair oil to keep my hair in place, but I liked having a cowlick the way I combed my hair. Better yet, I liked the nice rose smell. Other guys used different kinds, some used Brilliantine, which frankly stunk, I thought. It always reminded me of the cow barn. My rose smell helped me forget the barn and the cows!

When we got to be teenagers, with more responsibilities, Dad gave us boys $5.00 each week. It was our spending money. Yet Dad gave it with his reminder, "That stuff doesn't grow on trees!" A point we were not to forget. I haven't.

Besides, Dad felt we ought to be saving money, too. My first savings came from my chickens. Each year the folks would get five hundred baby chicks. They were raised in the brooder house, back of the big chicken coop.

Since one of my duties was caring for the chickens, Dad said I could have some chicks of my own. My choice had to be different from the White Leghorns the folks always bought. Looking at pictures I liked the looks of Rhode Island Reds, a heavier bird. I ordered 25 little red baby chicks.

Over five hundred fuzzy balls scattered around the brooder house. Leghorns were fuzzy golden chicks. They filled the place with shrill cheeps in unison. They had a smell of their own. With the heat from the brooder stove their smell hung in the air.

I thought God had made such beautiful little chicks. It was fun to watch the little golden wings, plus a few red ones, explode when I opened the door. Once they sensed I was there with feed they would run over the top of my shoes. I'd be surrounded. It was hard to move my feet.

One time I stepped on a little bird. I didn't mean it. But I killed it. It made me sick, as I saw the insides outside the little body. I cried.

It wasn't long before these chicks had half-fuzz and half-feathers. My birds could always be picked out from my par-

71

ents' chickens. In the fall I sold mine. Dad told me that I should put the money in my savings account at the De Motte State Bank. As best I can recall, it seems I had a balance in my account of $24.50 when I sold them.

As we got into World War II our duty was to buy war bonds. Dad gave me encouragement to keep buying them. $18.75 would buy a $25.00 bond. Since these were savings bonds, almost every month I tried to put my allowance into another bond. That still gave me $1.25 spending money. Once in a while I had to skip a week, for more spending money in my pocket. But that didn't happen too often. Dad had put the savings idea deep in my mind.

Most of these bonds were held for maturity, many even longer. I had some in the late 50s.

My father helped me to learn the value of money, which meant to be responsible for it. Besides I was also responsible to get the morning chores done. Everyday it was the race to get ready for school on time. Clean up in a hurry. Clothes had to be changed—quickly!

One day, day I'll never forget, I was in high school at the time, I didn't completely change clothes that morning. I looked down in typing class at my shoes. Holy cow! Cow manure—all over one shoe! Oh, it was awful. I hurried so much to get ready I forgot to take off my work shoes. That was like a terrible dream. No, it wasn't a dream. It was too real. There I sat with those dirty shoes with cow dung all over them. Pee-uu! I tried to smell around my desk— no, nothing I could detect. Maybe I could hide it. So I tried to hide my shoes the best I could, under my chair. My feet felt big! I could not believe it was happening. When will that bell ever ring? Finally...it did. I got out of that classroom in a hurry. I ran for the boys' bathroom.

Grabbing a handful of paper towels I started wiping. It was a big job trying to clean work shoes. My whole break was used to wipe off the cow manure. No matter how much I cleaned, they were not going to look like my school shoes. Clean enough! But after that I had to scrub my hands—with plenty of soap and water. Over and over I smelled around my

72

shoes and my hands. Finally I passed my smell test. I only hoped a classmate didn't flunk me. At least nobody said anything to me. It was still a long day. My shoes were on my mind the rest of the day.

Yes, I did learn my lesson that day. Never again, as long as I attended school, did I ever forget to change my shoes!

Of course, when I got home, I didn't have to change my shoes to do my chores.

Before chores, something came first: tea time. Mom always had bread and tea on the table. Tea time was at its best when Mom had homemade bread or buns. Tea time would last longer whenever she did. Homemade bread always tasted like one more slice. Generally we were told one more time, "You had enough; you better get going." Finally grabbing for our caps and jackets we'd be out the door. Evening chores had to be done.

If we had a ballgame, then we got going without as much reminding. One more question, as we walked out the door, "Mom, how soon will supper be ready?" Then we knew how fast we had to work.

That routine was the same every day. Every day, seven days a week, we had chores to do. Looking back, it wasn't so bad, for we did learn good work habits. Really, for all of us, it was a good thing to have work to do.

When I was smaller, then I'd get my work done so I could listen to the radio. Every evening I hoped the battery wasn't dead on the radio. Sometimes it was, then I'd miss my favorite programs.

I had my favorites. I liked Little Orphan Annie, who was first in the funny pages. Later Annie was on the radio. She was a never-aging red-haired tyke with her mongrel Sandy. Little Orphan Annie would always say, "Leapin' Lizards!" Sandy, her dog, had his bark, "Arf!" Here are the words to her song: "Who's that little chatterbox?/ The one with pretty auburn locks?/ Who do you see? It's Little Orphan Annie.../ Bright eyes, cheeks a rosy glow,/ There's a store of healthiness handy./ Mite-size, always on the go./ And if you want to know—'Arf!' says Sandy..."

She had a secret society. Mystery codes would be given on the radio, but you had to send for a card to decode a message. Those daily adventures were exciting. But every evening the program ended with some cliff-hanger, so I had to be sure to listen the next time. Her program was sponsored by Ovaltine, a chocolate milk mix. Every now and then I'd beg Mom to buy a jar of Ovaltine.

I thought it would help me grow. At least I wanted to dream I could be like Charles Atlas! I wanted his biceps! His ads in the paper told how a 98 pound weakling became the Atlas who could lift the world. As a muscle-man he became my ideal. Maybe there was hope for me, if such a 98 pound skinny kid could become the Charles Atlas in the pictures! Maybe, just maybe, there was some hope for me, a skinny kid.

If there was to be any hope, then I'd better eat my Wheaties. My radio friend, Jack Armstrong, did.

I can almost hear the shout of the radio announcer: "JACK ARMSTRONG! THE ALL-AMERICAN BOY!" Those were magic words. I joined in the latest adventure of brainy, brawny, awesomely pure-in-heart Jack Armstrong. Jack was always leading Hudson High to athletic glory. He beat the bad guys. And he ate his Wheaties! We were told to play fair and love America. Our hearts had to be hearts of gold. If we'd be honest, we could become rich. If we'd be kind, we would save the world from meanness. That program would challenge us: Will you take that message to all the boys and girls of the United States with Jack Armstrong?

Anyway, listening to our old battery radio, my imagination would go to work. I could really dream as a kid, while sitting right in front of our radio in the living room. Those were some fascinating times for me as a kid.

Most of our entertainment came from the radio. However a few times we'd to to the movies. I can recall only a few of them. The little star of those days was Shirley Temple. I was nine years old when this bit of sunshine began to sing and dance at the age of 5, back in 1934. Shirley was "Little Miss Marker." Right in the heart of those hard times as a child actress she made $300,000 annually. Her pictures grossed five million each year for Hollywood, taking them out of the Depression days. Boys loved her sweet smile; girls demanded golden, 56-curled hairdos, just like Shirley's. Well, as a boy, I thought Shirley Temple was a darling.

But I can't forget the Lone Ranger. His friend Tonto was sure to be at his side. One more, Tom Mix was a straight shooter. Cowboy Tom was sponsored by Ralston Wheat Cereal. His wonder horse was Tony. If I happened to catch the program I'd hear: "Reach for the sky! Lawbreakers always lose, straight shooters always win!! It pays to shoot straight!!!"

Later in the evening you heard the real thing: "Gangbusters." For comedy, I listened to Amos 'N' Andy or Edgar Bergen and Charlie McCarthy.

My first favorite singer was the "Songbird of the South," Kate Smith. She sang for all America. I loved to hear her sing "When The Moon Comes Over The Mountain" and the best one of all, "God Bless America."

Once I got a little older, then I had to hear the evening news. Especially when war was brewing across the ocean. That worried me when I heard of world dictators, who were itching for war.

Gabriel Heatter was the greatest newsman in the history of radio. That is not an overstatement. He was the one with the news which reassured millions of Americans. That was needed in the days when the news was rather dark.

Five words were at the beginning of each newscast of Gabriel Heatter, "AH, there's good news tonight!"

He had a way of grabbing the listener with the first sentence of each news item. Heatter thought there must be the answer to the question, "Why?" when reporting the news. "Be prepared!" was essential, he felt, for a radio commentator. Gabriel Heatter was.

Millions heard him in the 1936 broadcast, when households by the millions heard him from a prison in New Jersey. I was eleven, still I followed the Lindbergh kidnapping. Heatter covered the outcome of that sad story. He covered the execution of Bruno Hauptmann, who was convicted and sentenced to death for the crime of kidnapping and killing the Lindbergh child.

Gabriel Heatter kept me glued to the radio when he gave the evening news. If possible, I never wanted to miss his broadcast.

While I mentioned mainly the chores we had as boys, my sisters had some, too. They were younger, but mainly they all had some Saturday work that Mom had them do each week.

It was time to clean the whole house before Sunday. As boys we dreaded it when any one of them got her job done. You discovered what job she had that morning when you came in at noon or tea time. Either Lois or Wilma would be guarding her work probject for the day. (Carolyn and Rita were too small to be guards!) The guard would tell us where we were forbidden to trespass. If a certain "clean" room was off limits, the guard would block the doorway, then sharply give her orders: "YOU can't go in there! It's clean.") Sometimes I got the idea they would guard the room to the death. I never dared push them that far. However, that didn't mean I surrendered, no way.

But I was bugged by it. They acted like they owned that place, all because they did a little cleaning. Good grief!

That's why I dreaded it, when my sisters did their chores on Saturday.

I can't remember once that we were that bossy to them. Not once can I remember it. Again and again we'd clean the gutter in the cow barn or the manure out of the pig pen, but we never stood in the doorway, ordering like a military guard, "YOU can't go in there!" No, I think I can truly say, never did we do it once.

Hired Men

There were many hired men who worked on our farms. When Dad used mostly horses or the old Fordson tractor, then it took a lot of men to get the work done.

As I mentioned, there were *many,* Dad told of having 39 one corn husking season. Much of the corn had blown down that year, which made for backbreaking work. So some didn't stick it out very long. I think my father said only *three* stuck with him from the beginning until they finished the job in April.

As I began to think about hired men a number of names came to mind. Various personalities again move through my memories. Each was different from any of the others, no two alike. Let me share some special memories which made things very interesting when they worked for Dad. Of course, I must also say, I can't recall all the men, for some are moving around faintly in my distant memory.

When I was quite small, then Pete Walstra worked for Dad. We knew him by the name "Fat Pete." He was a nephew, Pete of Uncle Case. Pete was less than three years older than my Mom, which meant he was in his twenties.

I barely remember when he was on the farm. His favorite saying, often repeated by others: "By hoopen!" "Hoop" in Dutch meant heap or pile. Don't know if there was any connection or not.

Our family repeated one story when I was a child, this one was about Fat Pete and the old Fordson tractor.

Pete was doing spring plowing with our old gray Fordson. Since we had long rounds in plowing a land, it would also be a long time listening to the growl of that old tractor. A growl which could be heard a long ways off. As long as it moved, it growled.

The Fordson must have been a little low on water in the radiator. So it was steaming a little. Anyway, Dad noticed Pete was periodically stopping. Every round. It was discovered Pete had parked under a shade tree, at the end of the field. The outfit stood there for a time, then he would go back to plowing.

Dad wandered what was going on. Finally Dad went over to find out for himself. Dad told Pete he wanted to keep the tractor moving. A lot of plowing had to be done that spring, so it had to be moving all the time.

Dad asked him why he was stopping all the time.

Pete said the tractor was hot, so he was giving it a rest. "By hoopen!" said Pete, "It was really getting hot, so I was giving it a rest in the shade."

That might be okay when farming with horses, but tractors could keep moving.

After that our old Fordson made one continuous growl!

One other story had to do with Pete. Dad was a smoker when I was a very small boy. Behind Dad, when he sat at the table, was a shelf on the kitchen wall. On that shelf were three things: Our family Bible, in the middle, our mantle clock, and a carton of cigarettes.

While plowing, Dad was trying to light a cigarette. Since the old Fordson would follow the furrow by itself, Dad ran alongside the tractor. Running beside it, Dad tried to light his smoke off the manifold. He kept trying to get his cigarette going.

Nearby, going down the dirt road, was a car passing by. Those people could see Dad. The driver saw Dad's weird behavior—all to get one cigarette lit. What would those people think? My father began to ask himself questions, too.

Dad came home, announced at the next mealtime, he had quit smoking!

Pete, a smoker, immediately asked Dad for the rest of the carton on the shelf. Dad refused his request. "Just leave them there," Dad told Pete, "until I'm sure I'm through with them."

Every so often during the summer Pete would ask again. Same answer, each time, "No!" They had to be left there.

The summer was over, the fall came, with the carton still on the shelf. Dad never touched it. Pete again asked. That time Dad gave permission, "You can have them. I won't need them anymore."

Dad never smoked after that. I'm so happy my Dad quit. Not only did it spare me from secondhand smoke, but I never had to be tempted as a kid to become a smoker. Dad gave a good example to us, which kept the smoking habit out of our family. I learned that story from Dad himself, as he talked about his former habit.

Before I started school I remember my cousin Neil Tysen worked for us. Neil was in high school, 15 years old. Several incidents of that summer are part of my memory treasure.

As kids we dreamed of having a tent. We got one, well, not exactly, for ours was not a real tent. We had a gunnysack tent.

In those days the only places for our cars were in the big crib or some shed. It was not unusual to find a car completely covered with bird droppings. Dad and Mom came up with draping a car with gunnysacks sewn together. This big thing covered a whole car. But each time you parked it, a person had to cover it. That was more work to keep it clean.

Each driver covered his car at first. However, it wasn't long before that seemed like too much bother. That's when we got our tent. Dad used some secondhand lumber and old fence posts to build the framework. Those car covers where draped over that frame—we had a tent!

Naturally we played in it every day. But our desire was to sleep in it too. Not alone! Paul and I were not going to be out there alone—all night! Nooo!

Anyway Neil got the job, after all he was a hired man. Neil would sleep with us. After supper we took a lantern and headed for our tent. Our night light was a lantern, turned down a little. It hung in the middle of our tent. No wild animals visited us from the big woods. Oh, we did have some visitors! Maybe hundreds, thousands! Noises of their humming and droning sounded like airplanes making raids. Mosquitoes! They liked our tent too. And us.

Certainly it was not a picnic for Neil to be there with a couple of little boys and all those miserable creatures. He stuck it out for several hours. About two o'clock in the morning he reached his limit of endurance. Our visitors were driving us nuts.

In the worse way I wanted to stay *all* night. But it wasn't to be that night. Our hired man told us to get up. I can remember scrabbling up and heading for the house—and our own beds. Neil went into the shanty to sleep. All of us found it more peaceful to sleep indoors rather than outdoors in a gunnysack tent.

Day after day we played in our tent. That was fun. Never again did we try to spend a night in it.

Before planting we had to clean seed. For that job the fanning mill would be hauled out of the haymow. While we cleaned seed it remained on the truck. When the job was finished, then we'd store it again in the haymow.

The old Dodge truck had to go uphill and around to the barn. Neil had to hold the fanning mill steady while going up the hill. Dad drove around the back of the big wood-pile. However, one thing was forgotten, nobody raised the clothesline by the cob shed. It was just high enough to clear the cab of the truck. Neil was standing up. That meant the line caught Neil right under his nose, while at the same time, catching the top of the fanning mill. Both went flying off the back of the truck. Neil was hurt, thankfully not seriously. The old fanning mill was a wreck. It did not survive. Dad replaced it with a new one the next season.

Neil recovered from the fall. Neil had another accident, which took longer for him to recover.

I still remember him walking up the hill white as a sheet. Paul was with him. Neil was holding his arm.

Dad had sent Neil to get the old Fordson tractor from the field. He came back without it. The Fordson kicked him. Neil lost; the Fordson won again. Neil became another victim of those old tractors. They could *kick!* Hard! When you would crank them, they would kick back. The crank would recoil violently and unexpectedly, kick back, striking a person's arm before you could get it out of the way. Generally the arm would be broken. Neil broke his arm. Dad took him to Dr. E. E. Leeson in De Motte to set it. Splints were made from wooden shingles to hold his arm in place. Naturally he came back from the doctor with his arm in a sling.

Neil stayed on, later taking me to school for my first day. That's another story.

Richard Grevenstuk worked for Dad in the early 30s, when he was still a teenager. We knew him as Tootsie. He had a black Chevy coupe, which was new in 1930. I was five.

Tootsie was 21 years old when he married Dena July 12, 1933. She was 20 when they married. The newlyweds stopped at our place right after they were married. Both of them wanted to talk with Mom and Dad. For me, eight at that time, I thought she was so young, but really a beautiful bride.

Before Dena came into the picture, he was dating another girl. One afternoon Tootsie was in a hurry with his chores. The night of the date, he had to keep moving, since she lived around Monticello.

However, he had a problem. I was his problem. I started teasing him. In a way I thought it was funny that he had a date with a girl. As a kid I started my teasing.

I got into trouble when he was feeding the pigs. The corn came from the big crib. Tootsie would fill a bushel basket with corn, set it over the gate in the pig lot. After crawling over the gate he would dump out the corn. After the corn was scattered out for the pigs, he'd toss the basket over the gate. But while he was crawling over the gate, I'd grab his basket—drag it away from him. He had to go extra steps to get it back. He yelled at me for doing that. It was fun, I thought. Each time I got more daring, dragging the basket farther away than before.

He was getting very upset with me, but I kept it up. My ornery behavior made so much extra work. With such delays, he'd never get to his date on time.

To further frustrate him, I next tossed it over the big gate going down the lane to the bridge. He was mad. I was told in no uncertain terms to bring his basket back. Instead of listening I drug it farther down the lane. Then I ran for my life—

clear to the bridge, where I felt safe. Each time he threatened me, but I'd sneak back—grab it and run. Each time I would let the basket set, then escape. Every time I got away with it, so I got bolder.

By this time I was dragging it near the bridge. Tootsie was extremely angry by that time. I made my last dash for safety. Instead of stopping for the basket Tootsie ran right by it—after me! As I stepped on the bridge I got caught.

I was in big trouble. I was going to get blistered for this. He was furious with me. He stammered as I was given a tongue-lashing. Moments later he was pulling my overalls *tight!!!* Very tight, over my bottom. Bent over his knee the hired man proceeded to blister my butt!

To this day I can tell you my seater was hot! That likely was one of the hottest spankings any Hoosierland boy could get. After a couple of whacks I whimpered. Then yelled. Cried. Loudly I voiced my agony. Whack! Whack! Whack! Finally he quit. He stood me solidly on my feet. Tootsie continued to mutter as he walked back down the lane with his basket. He was determined to finish his chores.

I whimpered and snickered my way back to our house. It was a slow walk up the hill. My butt felt like it was on fire.

Nursing my wounds, I found Mom sewing in front of the south window in the sitting room. Through tears and snickers I told her Tootsie had spanked me—hard. She turned to inspect the damage, I had to drop my overalls. She told me it was red. Leaning forward, upon closer inspection she informed me that I had blisters on my butt. It continued to feel like it was on fire.

I got blistered for my mischievous behavior. I was wiser after that, I knew better than to tease Tootsie when he had a heavy date. It was the best way to avoid his hot and heavy hand.

After that I gave the hired man plenty of room.

Yet we couldn't always dodge his hand. One day Dad was helping with wallpapering at Grandpa and Grandma's place. Their place was over four miles from our farm. Early afternoon Mom was busy putting my little sister down for a nap.

Paul and I hatched a plan of walking to our grandparents' place and riding back with Dad. So two small boys got on the Old Grade and headed south.

We never got there. Back home Mom started calling for two boys, but never got an answer. After a search, it dawned upon Mom where we had gone. So she sent Tootsie to the rescue. His black Chevy came flying down the road. We got caught, within a half mile of our destination—and Dad.

He skidded to a stop. Throwing open a door, Tootsie ordered us to get in the car. Paul got in the middle of the coupe, while I was by the door. Once in the car he started to slap us. Both of us caught it, but Paul got it worse than I. I hugged my door, ducked each swing he made in my direction.

His whacks hurt, but I think I was more hurt that we never did get to Grandpa and Grandma's house. What disappointed me the most was he didn't drive the short distance so we could be with Dad, or even tell him. I wanted Dad to know we almost made it—walking the whole way.

Of course we were told how worried Mom was. Besides Mom and Dad would be very concerned if they couldn't find us. Don't do it again, especially without telling where we were going. We understood that more clearly.

Tootsie worked several years for Dad. After getting married they lived in the house built by Russian Nick on the forty. Also they lived in a place owned by Auggie Johnson in the marsh. Later he was our school bus driver for a number of years. During some of the same times he trapped our ditches. One season Tootsie and Dena helped us picking pickles after school started in the fall. We were short on pickers, so they helped for a week or so. Dena came over when her children were small. The attraction was to listen to a radio soap opera, "Amanda of Honeymoon Hill." The women never missed too many days listening to their program.

He came walking on our farm yard. He found Dad behind the big crib. To us he looked like a tramp. We soon found out his name was Ralph Fayette.

Ralph had been walking the Monon Railroad tracks, when he spotted Pete Mak's place. So he went there to ask for work.

Pete sent him to Dad. How Pete found out, I don't know, but he told Ralph Dad was looking for a hired man. Ralph walked about three miles to our farm and asked for a job.

The guy was different. No initiative whatsoever. Most of the time he had to be told everything. Never did he begin a job on his own, even if he knew what had to be done.

Dad wasn't fooled by his lack of initiative. When he had only been with us for a short time, Dad gave him a big hint how he felt about him. At evening milking time Ralph was standing and staring out the south doors of the cow barn. As the sun was setting, he happened to look east. There he spotted all the beehives on the hill, all 140 hives Frank Roorda had there. Through the trees he thought it might be a cemetery. All those white hives looked like gravestones. So he turned to Dad, asking if it were a cemetery. Dad answered in the affirmative, "That's where I bury all my lazy hired men!" I don't know if the man caught on or not. I doubt it, for he never changed his space or work habits.

Since we generally went to town on Wednesday and Saturday evenings Ralph asked to go with our family. Since he got paid by Dad, the first thing he did was buy new clothes. As small boys, Paul and I tagged along. Like small puppies, we followed the guy from one store to the next. Later he headed for the poolhall in De Motte. While we did not go in we watched him by peeking through the windows. Our behavior was disturbing to him, so he came out to talk to us. After giving us each a nickel he told us to leave. We did.

He never came home with us that night. Dad mentioned to Mom how Ralph had found all the old cronies the first night in town. Wondering about it, he asked, "How do those kind find each other so easily?" One of those fellows gave him a ride home.

Dad had sold his corn. The corn was shelled by the cribs, then hauled to town. Dad rode one afternoon to De Motte with one of the truckers. Once in town, they parted ways. Dad had errands, while the trucker got rid of the load of corn at the elevator. Dad had to cross the main highway to reach the bank.

That's when Dad got hit by a car. He stepped out from between cars, only to see at the last moment this car coming. Dad stuck out his hand, which caused him to be pitched on the hood, then knocked back down to the pavement.

Dad was taken to the doctor's office in De Motte. The trucker came back alone. However, the man didn't tell our family what happened. Oh, he told the corn shelling crew. Also Ralph Fayette knew it. Things came to a stand-still. The crew sat on the roof of the truck just to talk. All their whispering and talking in low tones caused me to suspect something was wrong.

Even though Ralph knew Dad was injured, he never moved a muscle to get started with the chores. Instead he sat with the others on top of a truck cab talking and wasting time. Everybody seemed to be waiting for Dad.

Over an hour or more later Aunt Bess Hoffman drove on the yard. Dad was sitting in the front seat next to her. He got out of the car with a cane. One arm was in a sling. After we gathered around Dad and Aunt Bess, we talked for a short time, then she left.

Dad turned to ask if the chores had been started. All the men shook their heads "No!" Dad next turned to Ralph, who still did not move until Dad got after him. Since Dad couldn't help, he told me to get the Swishers.

I went the mile north to tell them Dad got hit by a car. They came immediately in full force to help out—the cows milked and the other chores done. Dad commented that he could always depend on them. Once again they did not let Dad down.

Ralph could run! In fact he turned out to be a streaker one morning. Dad had given him the job to herd cows along the Old Grade. Some good grazing could be found along the the roadside. Ralph was to keep an eye on the cows.

As the morning got closer to noon, it became quite hot. So Ralph decided to go skinny-dipping in the ditch. Great idea for a hot summer day! However, that's not watching the cows. Those critters seemed to know that. They broke through the fence getting into Evans' cornfield. So Ralph was soon running down the ditchbank in his birthday suit. That's all, well, he did grab a tumbleweed to hold in front of him. My Mom happened to drive by to see the nature-boy giving his tumbleweed show on top of the ditch bank.

Mom reported to Dad on Ralph. Dad paid for Ralph's strip and dip in the ditch. It cost Dad $75 for the damage to the corn. Harv Evans demanded that amount for the damage, which Dad thought was too much. Yet Dad paid it.

As I think about this humorous experience, Ralph was way ahead of his time as a "streaker" with his tumbleweed.

Ralph stayed in the old shanty. As kids we'd go in there to visit with our hired men. They had our old phonograph for music. Many times I'd put records on it and play the music. The men would be lying on the bed. I got to play my favorites. "The Old Rugged Cross" was one I played often. After playing if over several times, Ralph told me he didn't like that record. Naturally I asked, "Why?" Bluntly he told me of his distaste for it. As a kid I tried to convince him the record was a nice song. He ordered me not to play it.

As a kid, I wasn't going to give up that easily. Tell me why you don't like it. I pushed for a reason. Because they played it at my brother's funeral. Then I had a new question, "How did your brother die?" Bluntly he said, "Because he robbed a bank!" His brother was killed by the police.

That's the reason he didn't want me to play it.

About a week later, when I was going to play more records, I found the record had been broken. I immediately challenged Ralph about breaking it. He claimed he had no idea how it got broken. As a boy, I didn't believe him. In fact, even to this day, I am sure I know who broke the record.

One morning Dad told Ralph to get his stuff together. It was the day to ship cream out of the De Motte depot. Four of us were there together on the station platform, Ralph, Dad, Paul and I, gathered in a small group. Dad simply told Ralph that this was the end of the line. The guy knew what that meant. He took off his dirty cap and fired it towards the fence behind the depot. Then he turned and walked away. Later somebody picked up his dirty old work cap and hung it on a post. For weeks it hung there, we saw it again and again, every time we shipped cream. Each time we were reminded again of Ralph Fayette.

I often wondered if he caught a freight train out of town. In a way I think he did. I can almost see him sitting in the open door of a box car, as it hit the rails in rural Indiana. That pictures him as picking up again right where he left off the morning he walked from the Monon Railroad tracks to ask Dad for a job. So I see him as "on the road again."

Ed Timmons was one more hired man on the Hoffman Farms. He was hard of hearing. Often we had to yell instructions to Ed. He drove a big, old car. Since he had relatives around Kersey and Wheatfield he would drive over there some evenings. I'd go along now and then. Ed also smoked a pipe. I tried his old pipe once, taking a few puffs on it. I still picture Ed cleaning his pipe while sitting in the shanty. That was an evening routine with him.

Dad noticed I was trotting to the shanty too often after supper. So he questioned what I was doing with Ed. I told him Ed promised to teach me to play cards.

Each evening I was getting more anxious to get out to the shanty after supper. I could hardly wait to get started playing. Ed sat by the white dresser, while I stood beside it. An old kerosene lamp was on the dresser.

It was exciting to me. Dad began to ask more and more questions about my nightly visits. Proudly I told Dad that Ed was really teaching me how to play cards.

In no uncertain terms Dad told me he wanted me to stop it. Firmly Dad ordered, "I don't want you to go out there. I don't want you to learn to play cards."

As I generally did, I asked the same question, "Why?" But it was only in my mind, I just listened. I accepted it; I never went back. Ed asked why I wasn't coming back, so I told him the reason.

It has had a major influence in my life, for I've never wanted to play cards since. Cards games today, which I could play, but none are inviting. So I almost always refused to play.

87

Many find it hard to understand my lack of interest, I know. But frankly, I just don't care to play. Period.

Later I was to find why Dad made me quit. It was a day of a father-son talk, while hoeing thistles. Dad got to talking about playing cards in France during World War I. He was a good player. A number of servicemen owed Dad money for their gambling debts.

What sticks with me are the comments he made afterwards. The men were returning from France. They were soon to be back on the soil of America. As Dad caught a glimpse of the Statue of Liberty, he silently vowed his card playing days were over! He wanted to forget what the other guys owed him. He promised himself that he would never play cards in civilian life. I'm certain he spared himself problems with gambling by his Statue of Liberty decision.

No doubt, he likely spared his son problems, too. I must admit I was getting pretty hooked on playing with Ed. I know my Dad was wise enough to pick up on that. Today I'm glad he nipped it in the bud while I was a kid. I'm not sorry Dad made me stop.

One thing more, Dad never wanted people asking to use his gun. Yet Ed wanted to go hunting. Over and over he begged to use Dad's 16 gauge shotgun. "No!" was Dad's answer, each time. But Ed kept asking. Finally Dad gave him permission. However it was to be according to Dad's rules. Ed promised to unload the gun in the field—never on the yard!

As Dad feared, Ed forgot. Upon returning home from hunting Ed came very close to the backdoor. His gun was still loaded! There he stopped, only some 15 to 20 feet from our porch and summer kitchen. Ed proceeded to break the gun and unload the shells. I was watching him from porch. Paul was near the washing machine, looking out that window.

The gun went off! BOOM!!!

The shot went through the outside wall of the house. It was only inches from Paul's head. Just as high as he was standing, just a little to his left. A hole, about two inches, was blown in the siding. Once through the board the shot spread going into a 2 x 4 stud and the wringer of Mom's washing machine.

Dad rushed out and took the gun away from Ed. Our hired man stood in shock from the blast. All of us realized later how sad it could have been, had the bullet fired been inches closer to Paul's head.

Dad's concern was always having a loaded gun! Such a gun is too dangerous. A person who forgets that may not realize he had a killer-potential in his hands. A person should never be careless or thoughtless for even one moment with a loaded gun in his hands.

Ed never got his hands on Dad's gun again.

Certainly our hired men had to take a lot, especially from us kids. We would tease. Sometimes we thought of ways to aggravate them. Ed Timmons did not like cinnamon. He hated the stuff with a passion.

But there it was on our table. Every week. Mom gave us rice at least once a week. When we had it, there came out that big can of cinnamon. During the meal it had to be passed around the table, which meant Ed had to handle it. At our table my place was next to Ed. Even though I knew better, I always asked if he wanted the cinnamon. (I knew his answer, before I asked the question.) But each time I had to bring the can down hard on the table, right next to his plate. At the same time giving the can a slight squeeze! Puff! A little rusty cloud arose up from the can. Ed would grunt, my antics would drive him crazy.

One day when things were slack on the farm, nothing much was going on that afternoon, Ed, Paul and I were talking in the shanty. Somehow the subject turned to escaping from ropes. Ed boasted to us boys he could not be tied up. No matter who tied him up, he'd escape!

What did he say? Don't challenge boys who had nothing to do. Ed boasted once too often. We told him we could tie him so he'd never get away. Ed boasted once more time. Okay, we accepted his challenge.

Running out of the shanty we searched the barn for all kinds of ropes, long and short pieces. Soon we were back with our arms full of ropes. We dumped one big pile on the floor of the little shanty.

Ed got on the floor. We roped him like a mummy! Round and round we wrapped Ed with ropes. Pausing every now and then to tie another knot. No way was Ed going to escape, not if we could help it. Finally we tied the last knot.

It was Ed's turn. We challenged him, "Okay, Ed, get loose." Ed grunted. Ed groaned! Ed twisted. And turned. Of course we cheered him on. But there was just no escaping that mass of ropes around our mummy. Again we shouted, "Come on, Ed, get out of there!"

Nothing helped. So I got a bright idea! Maybe he needed some encouragement. I told him that I'd get the cinnamon can if he didn't hurry. Ed struggled harder. The more I thought about it, the cinnamon can sounded like a great idea.

To a naughty farm boy on a lazy afternoon the temptation was overpowering. I weakened—Ed needed my encouragement or he'd never escape. I slipped into the house. Getting into Mom's cabinet, I found that big can—I grabbed it and ran. Once in the shanty I held it up for Ed to see. He could see it from his struggle on the floor. The sight almost sent the man into a panic. Being next to helpless, the best he could do was threaten me with words. Ed continued to grunt, groan, twist and turn. With all the energy spent he did not make any progress in his escape. Since nothing was happening, I gave him a few puffs. But those were followed by many more puffs. It wasn't long he was changing color. Our roped-mummy was turning a slight shade of reddish-brown. More and more he was looking like a mummy, yet with a little life.

Of course, by that time a couple of boys knew we had gone too far. Another color was in the air—the air was turning blue. Ed gave us a cursing, plus one final warning that we better untie the ropes. NOW!

We did. Well, not all the ropes. After all, we had to be sure of an escape! Ed was left with enough rope to slow him down, but still could finally make his escape. Then we beat it. We got out of there—fast!

I ran with my cinnamon can, and for my life.

Ed got untangled for his great escape. Never again did he challenge us.

It was not all one-sided. Ed could do things too, and have his laugh. He could throw back his head and have a big guffaw.

One day a fertilizer salesman drove on our yard. A farmer generally was offered something, such as a cigar or candy. This time Dad was given a cigar. Marty was standing by Dad. He was about four years old at the time. Dad handed it to Marty telling him to bring it to Ed, who smoked. Ed was in the barn, cleaning out the gutter.

When Marty got in the barn he unwrapped the cigar, but kept it instead of offering it to Ed. Marty asked for a light. Ed laughed, then struck a match to get Marty's big cigar going. The young smoker puffed away. Ed got a big kick out of watching him.

Finally it was a little more than Marty could take, so he headed for the house. Once in the kitchen Mom mentioned that Marty pushed several chairs together along one wall. Next he belly-flopped across them, with his arm dangling over the side—with his cigar held between two fingers. About half of it was left. About that time he announced to Mom that he was sick!

Later Marty got rid of some "green stuff"—the small smoker was sick!

Ed only laughed, when asked why he did that. It is not hard to picture Ed throwing his head back and having a big laugh. Ed enjoyed pulling off something like that.

Mom hated it when Ed would spit in the sink in the summer kitchen. There was a pump by the sink, where he would wash up before supper.

If it had been a dusty day Ed would have heavy drainage. While he was cleaning up he'd start coughing, trying to clear his throat. Before he was through he'd gag over the stringy mucus phlegm. Ed would hawk to get rid of it. Soon he'd get rid of it, by expectorating in the sink. Lying in the sink was his greenish gob! But he never tried to pump water over it, so it

91

would wash down the drain. He left that for the next person coming to the sink. It was enough to turn a person's stomach.

Every evening Mom knew it was coming. She'd grumble in the kitchen—to us, not to Ed. One evening she had had it. She gave me orders to go in there and bawl him out for his "dirty habit of spitting in the sink"—as she put it.

Since it was getting dark in the room, it enabled me to confront him in the semi-darkness. I told him to quit spitting in the sink. As a kid I told Ed we were very disgusted about his habit.

Those in the kitchen were listening to us. I came in being greeted by grins on their faces. That made it hard for me to keep a straight face when I walked in for supper. Everybody wiped off their grins before Ed walked over to the table.

After that he hardly ever spit in the sink. However, if he did, then he pumped water on it to clean the sink for the next person.

The Swishers did a lot of work for Dad. Dad felt he could depend on them when needed. Those who worked for us were Pete, the father, Francis and Wes, his sons, and Basil Hall, a nephew of Pete.

My first recollection of Pete was bringing his lunch along to eat at noon. On one cold day he was invited to come in the house. Pete sat next to the chimney, in the corner of our kitchen. He was also near the cook stove. It was a perfect spot to put a chair and warm up.

As kids we watched him eat, constantly turning from the table to see him. Naturally we wondered what he had to eat for lunch. Sitting on the floor in front of him was a quart jar of peppers. While he ate his sandwich he'd reach down for another pepper. Finally we began to ask Dad and Mom why couldn't we have one of Pete's peppers. Our parents told us to turn around and eat our food.

But we couldn't keep our eyes off him. The more we watched, the more we wondered why we could not at least have one. Pete noticed our longing, so he spoke up, "Do the boys want a pepper? Sure, you can have one, come over."

In a moment we were off our chairs, standing in front of Pete, eagerly waiting for a pepper. Each one got one—and much more! Those babies were hot, hot!!!

Never eating anything like that before, we quickly decided that would be our last request for Pete's peppers. Never again. He could eat the whole jar by himself.

Another time we were threshing grain. We had the rig in our cow yard. Even though I was only a boy at the time, yet Dad put me in charge of the threshing machine. At the same time I was to watch the grain in the wagon. Every now and then I leveled out the grain, watching it didn't spill over the edge.

When the guys would come up with a load of bundles they had a wait for their turn to unload. Generally each one would crawl down from the hayrack and take a break. Some needed a drink. Others would find shade, a tree or under the rack. Maybe they would go talk to somebody else waiting. If interested in the yield, they would check on how much grain there was in the wagon or truck. By climbing up the side they would look over the edge of the box.

Pete was standing on the side of the wagon. As I leveled off the grain, he spoke to me. However, due to the noise of the tractor and threshing machine, I could not hear a thing he said. Leaning over, I got right up to his face so we could talk and hear each other. Pete had garlic smell on his breath. Wow! To me, the odor was so strong.

I frankly asked him, "Pete, have you been eating garbage again?"

Pete roared with laughter. Years later, while visiting Mom and Dad he brought up that incident again, "Remember when Bill thought I had been eating *garbage?*"

Pete worked a lot for Dad through the years. The man pitched a lot of hay into our old stationary hay press. Plenty of sweat went into that job on the hot July and August days. His clothes would be dripping wet with honest sweat from that hard work. Some days he had a different job, then he would be bounced around the hay field riding our mower.

A nephew of Pete, little Basil Hall, also worked for us. He was the little guy who could walk! Basil could leave most people behind in the dust. I had to trot at times to keep up when he was on the move. Due to his fast-pace we gave him the nickname "Speed." Other times we called him "Ace" or "Acey."

Back to his quick-step, there is a story about how fast he could walk. One morning he came tired to work, after all, he had returned home from South Bend, Indiana. His plan was to hitch-hike, which was done quite often in those days. But Speed had problems that day, he did not get one ride. Not one. So Speed walked all the way back from South Bend. In one day! In one day he covered seventy miles or more in order to get back home in a single day.

Ace had one good eye, the other was blind. You could see the scar on his eyeball. As he told it, his eye was stabbed by the point of a knife. Basil was trying to cut a slit in a strap of leather, which he attempted by pulling the knife towards himself. Cutting the slit, the knife slipped, then stabbed him in his eye. In time the scar tissue built up. The injury was very visible every time you looked Basil in the eye.

Basil pitched a lot of manure, hay, and bundles on our farms. Besides he swung the paint brush summer after summer. His clothes were spattered with red and white paint. But so was his face, hands and arms. Not to forget his shoes! They had so much paint splattered on them Basil decided to give them one coat of solid red barn paint! With his speed and red shoes he could walk a red streak.

One morning, just before school, I met him downhill by the little toolshed. He motioned for me to come over to him. He brought a small bottle of gin to work. While talking, he wanted to show me the bottle. That gave him a reason to take a good swig. After he wiped his mouth, he offered me a drink. I hesitated, not knowing if I should do it. But he encouraged me to try it. I took a drink. Oh, it had a flavor of an aromatic, giving it the spicy, pungent aroma—something I never smelled before. The stuff burned all the way down to my belly. Basil tipped the gin bottle once more. Again he made me another offer. I took it. With that funny smell in my nose, strange taste in my mouth, and burning in my belly I got on the bus. That was the only time I did that. I felt very guilty the whole day in school.

Basil was a speedy, hard working man.

While Pete was in his fifties, his nephew, Basil, was in his early forties, in all about 15 years younger.

Francis was older than I, eleven years, while Wess was six years older. While in grade school I attempted to be Francis' teacher.

Francis was pitching manure into the spreader. It was springtime. When I got home from school, I was sent to help him haul some manure.

My last class of the day was the health class. Harry Jarrett, our school coach, was my teacher. That specific day he warned us of the hazards of smoking. It was bad for you, besides it was costly. Mr. Jarrett had given us all the facts and figures.

While we stood by the spreader, Francis was going to take a break, so the first thing he did was light up his cigarette. Francis didn't know it, but I was ready for him. I repeated my lesson while it was still fresh in my mind. I told him how bad it was for his health, but how expensive his bad habit was. I capped it off by telling Francis how much money he could have, if he did not smoke.

He smiled at me, then told me I was all wrong with my figures. With a grin, he told me that it would be twice that much: "My wife also smokes!"

When he was younger, sometimes he had Mom order things for him out of a catalog. Mom had a hard time getting the sizes needed in making out the orders. This was comical when he wanted to buy a dress for a lady friend. What size is she? But he give some general comments about her size, not helping at all. Finally Mom asked, "What is her bust measurement?" It was funny to see this young man explaining with gestures the size of her bust. Mom got some idea, then sent off the order. An order was sent either to Sears, Roebuck and Co. or Montgomery Ward. The cost of his order would be deducted from his pay that week. Francis felt it was an easy way to do his shopping. But it did cause problems for Mom when she made out an order.

About the same time he came to work one day with his head shaved. He showed off his head, pulling off his stocking cap. Francis stood there with his big grin. At a Saturday Night Dance someone had grabbed his cap. The cap-snatcher proceeded to wear it on his own head. Before the evening was over, Francis got more than his cap back. What he got back was his cap—plus cooties!

Francis had head lice. So with the help of his mother he got rid of them, by cutting off all his hair.

Another time he came over with an injury to his face.

This injury was one deep cut between his eyes. In fact, it ran down his forehead and then down the middle of his nose. He got it while chopping wood with a double-bladed ax. His ax was stuck, after a chop, so when he went to pull it out—it came out with such force he was hit in his face. Francis had a severe injury, plus a scar to wear. As I recall, it was asked why he didn't go to the doctor to take care of it. But that would cost too much, he commented. Adding he could wear a scar for that much. He did.

Francis and I plowed together one year. I was plowing with our F-30 Farmall, with a three bottom plow. That year we had a rough time turning under the corn stalks. Two of us worked together to get the job done. A board was put across the plow frame, where Francis would ride while kneeling, then with one foot he could stomp on the stalks. If it started to plug up, then he'd stomp down. The wad would go through and be covered up with the soil.

It was a cold day in the field. We'd stop for a few breaks. It was hard and boring for Francis. Also he wanted to warm up, which he did by the tractor's exhaust pipe. In those days the Farmall did not have a muffler. It just had an elbow, which shot the fumes out to one side. I had the F-30 idling, while he stood there. Francis said that he could kill the engine. Never! Not my F-30! For me that tractor was *the* tractor. It was a big engined tractor in those days. Anyway Francis claimed he could stop the motor.

My response to him was he would never be able to do it. He was positive he could. So he took his fuzzy winter cap from his head, which he wadded into a ball. Quickly he put his cap into that exhaust pipe. He stuffed it into the hole while my tractor idled slowly. Result: Kill the engine.

Just as quickly as he stuffed it into the pipe...I pulled the throttle back! I opened it wide open! The F-30 belched out a ball of fire. His cap blew right back into his face. However, that fire ball burned a round hole in his cap. Francis pulled it back on his head, with his hair sticking through the hole. We laughed and laughed.

We went back to our plowing. Naturally, when we came out of the field later, somebody asked what happened to his cap. Francis pointed to me, saying, "That darn Bill burned a hole in my cap!" With a grin he had to admit how he did challenge me by saying he'd kill the engine, but he got burned when I gave her the gas. We had a number of laughs over that experience.

Wess was about six years older than I was. Even so, we had some good times together. Old Benny and our buggy rides were a lot of fun. Later we took rides in old cars and trucks.

If we didn't have some shafts on the buggy, then we'd push it to the top of the hill for a ride to the bottom. The person up front had to steer it with his feet. Those rides could be exciting by the time we reached the bottom. Wess had the problem of hitting a tree—too often! But it was fun. As kids we many times made our own fun.

Wess was good at riding the bullrake. That was when we would be baling the old slough hay up north. It was nearly a mile from our home place to the hayfield. Yet it was across the Old Grade from where the Swishers lived.

My job was to windrow the hay. Wess then would take the bullrake to pick up a load of hay. Gathering a load from a long windrow, Wess would move it to the baler.

On one run Wess got into a nest of bumblebees. A colony of some 10 to 50 bees lived in one nest. Bumblebees liked the thick, slough grass. But those bees did not like us to disturb their nest.

Wess disturbed them. How he paid for it! They nailed him between the eyes. So his face, especially around his eyes, was very swollen. But that was nothing as to how he looked the next morning. Then he came to work with just slits for his open eyes—barely able to see out of them. Yet he still had a big grin when we looked at him. It was just another interesting experience in a hayfield.

One summer Fat Bumgardner worked on our farms. His own family worked for years on Uncle Jake Hoffman's ranch. Fat brought his dog along. Dusty would ride on his bike. Fastened to the back of his bike was this lid of a bushel basket. His dog liked to ride behind Fat. He bought my guitar. After buying my guitar he had to find a place for it on his bike. He rode down the back driveway to hit the road again. Fat loaded all his possessions, then rode away.

I remember him lying on the bed in the shanty, while lying there, he told his interesting stories. Fat had many fascinating ones.

This is a true story. Many find it hard to believe. It's true! I was 10 years old when I went on my first honeymoon! I really did. What's more, I went with our hired man and his bride.

Harry Baker was the hired man. He was living in southern Indiana before coming to work for us. Lucille Root, who lived north of us, told Dad she knew of someone who could work for him. She named Harry, adding quickly she'd have to contact him. She did.

Shortly after that he came from southern Indiana to be our hired man. It wasn't too long before he got cleaned up each evening to go away. He would visit the Roots. More and more evenings were spent this way.

Not surprising to us, an announcement was made: Harry and Lucille were going to get married.

They did. Naturally time would have to be taken off to go on a honeymoon. Harry requested it, which Dad granted. They told us they were going "back home" for their honeymoon.

When I knew of their plans—I asked Harry to go along. Honestly, I asked him, "Can I go with you?"

It stunned him at first. Shocked by my asking, Harry put me off by saying he'd have to ask Lucille.

Harry didn't know any other way to handle my request. The groom and bride talked it over. One morning I asked Harry for their answer. Once again I asked him, "Can I go along, Harry?" His answer thrilled me, "Yes." I thought it was wonderful, I was going on a trip—a honeymoon!

I packed my own clothes. Then came the day, I was ready. Harry had some relatives picking us up. They were Uncle Harry and Aunt Opal Mahlone from South Bend. When I got in the car, I saw their Bible on the front seat.

Our things were packed in the trunk. Three of us got in the back seat. My spot was behind the driver. Our destination was Bedford and Medora, Indiana. I recall a comment about our trip would be over 200 miles.

Our first stop was by Harry's grandfather. His little farm was out in the countryside. I soon found out I'd be staying there while on my first honeymoon. My sleeping partner was Grandpa. With him I had my first experience of sleeping in a featherbed. Maybe it would be better to say I was buried in feathers each night. Never before or since in my life did I ever sink into bed at night. That bed was soft-soft, very soft.

Grandpa had a few cows, along with a few other animals. Buildings on his place were made from rough sawmill lumber. Plenty of space between the boards. His type of farming was very easy going, a laid-back style.

All the relatives and old neighbors heard about the wedding of Harry and Lucille. Several parties were thrown for the newlyweds. One was called a shivaree. Each get-together had plenty of homemade ice cream. Pop on ice was found in wash-tubs. All the people had a good time laughing, singing and visiting. As kids we did a lot of running around the yards, near the older people.

One morning we went to visit at the home of Harry's mother. He had a couple of sisters older than I was, by a few years. I had another "first" at their place. His sisters' bright red nail polish, not only on their fingernails, but on their toenails! I had never seen painted toenails before in my life.

The girls were not well that morning. Their mother was trying to get them to take something, which they refused. It was a dose of castor oil!

An awful lot of time was spent running after the girls. The mother had a spoon in one hand and a bottle of castor oil in the other. She chased those girls all over the inside of the house and porch. Finally they surrendered, on the condition they would get an orange after the dose of castor oil. With a shiver each girl took a spoonful of castor oil.

Most of my time was spent on the farm. The bride and groom, along with Harry's uncle and aunt did a lot of visiting. Finally it was time for this young honeymooner to go back home to northern Indiana. After a half day on the road we were back home again.

I had gone on my first honeymoon trip.

I've often wondered if I happen to be the youngest Hoosier farm boy to go on a honeymoon with the hired man and his bride. 10 years old!

It was back to work. The honeymoon was over. Dad and I were in the cornfields cultivating the tallest corn. Harry was in the next field running a weeder over smaller corn. The wind was blowing hard that day. We were all trying to stir the ground so as to prevent too much damage to the very young corn.

Dad had given orders to Harry how to do the weeding. A steady pace, keep moving, but not to chase the horses.

Dad and I were coming back on our rows. Harry could be seen as we cultivated towards the west. Harry was headed south, after just turning on the end, ready for another round. Heading for the Hodge...he was moving—fast!

Dad and I both couldn't believe what we saw. Both of us stopped to watch.

Off to the west was this huge cloud of dust. We could hardly see the team or Harry on the seat of the weeder. They were streaking across the cornfield.

Dad and I talked, asking why he was going so fast. My Dad was pretty upset with him for going so fast. Just as quickly the cloud of dust stopped. Dead still. After a few moments, the wind blew the dust away. Harry could be seen picking himself up and rubbing the dust from his eyes.

The back end of the weeder was up in the air, completely off the ground. The tongue was rammed into the ground, buried over half-way.

Those crazy horses got a runaway notion, so they took off. Harry only went along for the ride.

Dad and I walked across the field to see what really happened. When the tongue had fallen out of the neck yoke, then dropped down, with all the speed they had it was driven into the sandy soil, between the rows. Three of us could not pull it out. Dad, then, told me to get the tractor. We hooked a chain on the weeder axle, then pulled it out.

Harry was introduced to our tricky team, who without any horse sense, would get the nutty notion to runaway. They could do that at a moment's notice.

After a little time Harry was back to weeding the corn again. At a much slower speed, once the team got its good horse sense back again.

It was harvest season.

We either were working in the field with the grain binder or we may have been threshing grain. All the men had come in from the field for the evening.

We still had the chores to do, which included milking the cows. Naturally we headed for the barn to get that work done, then we could come in for supper. The other fellows, of course, were through for the day and free to go home.

One fellow did not go home.

He came in the barn, walking back and forth behind the cows. All of a sudden he blurted out to Dad, "I want my money, Mart."

Dad listened, then tried to explain to Teddy Hancock he paid all the men on Friday night. So he assured him that he'd get his check then.

But Teddy was not satisfied at all. So he persisted, "Mart, I want my money. I worked in the buckwheat today!"

Dad tried again to get him to wait until payday. Nevertheless Teddy still insisted, "I want my money. I worked in the
buckwheat today!"

Dad discovered today was payday for Teddy. He was not
going to leave or wait, so Dad unsnapped the pocket on the
top of his overalls. That's where Dad kept his pocketbook.
Opening it, he pulled out a bill, handing it to Teddy.

Teddy had his one dollar for working in the buckwheat
that day. Content, with his pay in his pocket, Teddy headed
down the Old Grade for home. He had about a mile to go.

Our family recalled that incident many times. It seems like
I can still hear Teddy's plea for instant payday ring in my ears.

Dad had two men working for him who were the odd couple. They would come to work in a Model T Ford coupe.

One of the men must have weighed well over 300 pounds.
Not the other fellow, with all his clothes on he must have been

Left to right, Bill, Paul and Dick (Red) Evans, a neighbor. Picture was
taken in 1940 on the yard by Hermie Belstra.

125 pounds, hardly any more. Criswell, the heavy man, tipped the coupe sideways. Spurgeon, the much smaller man, rode high on his side. Yet it looked like it was going to tip over, a strange sight as it came down the road.

They found a way to level out the car, by putting a chunk of wood between the front spring. There was no bounce in the spring, nor anything to absorb the shock of a bump in the road. It may have rode like a lumber wagon, but at least it didn't look like it would soon tip over.

They had solved their problem, making up the enormous difference in the weight of these two hired men. At least they both had a solid ride back and forth to work each day.

They were a great team of workers. Those two men could really pitch bundles when we were threshing grain. They helped us when they pitched hay while baling slough hay.

Hard workers, should I say they both carried their own weight when pitching hay or bundles?

Boys Can Get Into Trouble

Summertime was a good time for boys to get into trouble. We spotted this big hornets' nest. There it hung, from the underside of the roof, on the southside of the little crib. This was when it was a single crib, so the front side was open. Corn could be scooped into it, or it could be filled with an elevator.

Their nest was about 12 to 14 inches in size, attached to the tin roof. Hornets were buzzing around it, in the warm sunlight.

Three of us talked about it. At the time, Red Evans, Paul and I were standing by the three steel bins on the ditch bank. These were near the bridge, which crossed the Cook Ditch and went into our fields.

Cement slabs were laid, on which the steel grain bins were setting. Off to one side, nearest the bridge, was some left over gravel in a little pile. Small stones were in this pile. We decided to try hitting the nest. Each would have a turn. Each of us picked out some of the best stones, then waited for a turn to throw.

At first we all missed, still trying to get our range. If a stone hit the steel roof, that made a lot of racket. But it also made the hornets very angry. For a few moments they would fly around, then settle down again.

But they didn't get much peace, for another stone was soon fired. Finally a new round of throws came up. Red was first. Bang! Missed the nest, but hit the roof. Second to throw was Paul. He threw. Bang! Missed the mark again. Third, my turn. I threw. No racket...only a soft plunk... Bull's-eye!

Within a few seconds—pow! Another bull's-eye! Paul's eye! An angry hornet scored a direct hit, close to his eye.

Now a hornet is a large wasp whose sting is very severe. Paul got that kind of sting.

I fired the stone; Paul took the hit. Next there came a debate about what happened. It was not fair. I threw the stone, but Paul got stung. Red and Paul felt it was not fair at all.

Still don't know how the angry hornet felt. Could he tell who threw it? Maybe he felt any one of the three stone-throwing boys was a fair target. I know one thing, the bomber didn't debate the fairness. Boys had messed with their nest! Some boy was going to pay. Paul paid. One other thing was certain, it didn't take two attempts to hit his target. One try was enough. That hornet got Paul's eye the first try!

Neither Red or Paul, nor I was ready for another try. We walked away to find something else to do that summer afternoon.

One day it was my turn to grind feed for the cows. We had the grinder on the east end of the big corn crib. The tractor used for grinding was parked in the cow yard. After the job was finished, then I parked it again by the toolshed.

Billy Binge, as I knew him, came over. Billy wanted to drive the tractor, so he started begging. At first I told he could not. Our F-30 Farmall had a strong clutch spring, which I felt he couldn't push in when he had to stop. Billy begged and begged. Finally he came up with the idea that I could help him.

I gave him permission. He drove it out of the cow yard, through the gate, then towards the toolshed. The farther he drove, the more confident he felt—I was not needed.

I told Billy to get ready to stop. Now! He tried. His foot slipped. Again, he tried, but he was not strong enough to keep it pushed in. At the last moment, I yelled, "Try harder. Push!" But there was the fence—right in front of us.

We hit it. All the slack was taken out of the fence. By the time I got my foot on the clutch we had made a big "v" in the fence line!

Billy apologized all over the place. He kept repeating that he didn't mean to do it. He patted me on the shoulder, saying it one more time, he didn't mean it.

I knew that he didn't. But Billy did not realize how hard it was to stop our F-30 tractor. Generally I would grip with both hands on the steering wheel, scoot forward on the seat, then push on the clutch with all my strength. That's the only way I could get it stopped.

Again, it was easy for boys to get into trouble.

Back of the big crib was our water tank in the cow yard. The pump jack was fenced off, next to the crib. A gas engine ran the pump.

Most of the time we'd have the tank full when the cattle came from the pasture. On a hot day we'd have it pumping while we did the milking. The cows coming from the barn could have plenty of fresh water.

A pump jack would move up and down run by gears at the bottom. Two small gears, meshed with the teeth on the two larger gears, went round and round. Going up and down it pumped the water.

When the engine was going, those gears turned around very fast. It was not unusual to be around there. We played in the water at times. One evening kids were by the pump, while the tank was getting filled. Two boys sitting on the platform were Marty and Jim Swisher.

Marty was rather small at the time. Jim was about three years older. In fascination they watched those gears whirling around. After a little while Jim dared Marty, saying, he bet Marty was afraid to put his finger between those gears.

Almost instantly Marty stuck his finger between the gears. Within a split second it rolled his index finger between meshing teeth. His finger was smashed to the first joint.

It happened in a moment, yet it took months to heal. The bone was damaged. More injury was done to the nail and tissue on the end of the finger. Grease and grim were ground into the finger, so an infection set in. It caused a felon. Later, part of the bone festered out. His finger was deformed even after healing took place.

The dare made to a small boy caused some big trouble.

Boys can get into scuffles. Before doing our chores after school, Paul and I got to scuffling around. It took place on the little porch, one of the first porches. It was very narrow, enough room for the wood box and a place to hang up our clothes. On the east wall were two large storm windows and the door leading to outdoors.

Anyway we got into our struggle in those close quarters. There was pushing and shoving. Before we both knew what happened I was head-first through a storm window. Glass went flying outside by the front steps. I hung from my waist through the broken window. No cuts at all.

Two boys stood there in total silence. Both of us could be thankful no injuries resulted from our horseplay.

Uncle Ben Hoffman wanted to use a team of horses. His brother-in-law was sent to get the team and hayrack.

Since we had recently shelled corn, there was a huge pile of corncobs, at the foot of the big hill.

Dad got the team out of the barn, hitched them to the wagon. So he stood by the gate, ready to open it. However, at the same time he warned the young man this team might want to get away from him. "Watch them!" Dad warned. He hardly paid any attention to Dad's words, as he crawled on the hayrack, yelling, "Giddiup!" They did! It was one fast start. They went flying through the gate as he laid flat on his back on the rack, while the horses went up and over the huge pile of cobs. Up one side, over the top, down the other side! After a few big gallops they were into the timothy field fence, west of the toolshed. That's where they got hung up.

As Dad ran over there, the young guy said he guessed Dad wasn't kidding. Dad didn't have to repeat his warning. After getting them away from the fence, they were ready to go down the Old Grade. The fellow was not near so cocky as he headed for Uncle Ben's place. There were ditches around much of our farm. The Cook Ditch ran through part of it, and along the north and west sides of the farm. On the east was the Hobbs Ditch, while the big old Hodge Ditch was on the southside.

A few mink were in these ditches, but many more muskrats. Various men through the years would trap these animals for their fur.

Dad did for a few years. Later Pete Mak trapped our ditches. One morning he found something unexpected in a trap. He caught a fox. That trap was set near the old wooden bridge, west of the old barn.

Tootsie Grevenstuck wanted the same trap-line.

During this time Tootsie was our bus driver, so he suggested that we take some of Pete's traps, or at least snap the set traps.

Saturday morning early we followed the ditch, where we discovered a few traps. We pulled the traps out of the ditch, then headed across the field to the old barn. At the same time Pete Mak came by to run his trap-line. Immediately he noticed a few traps missing, that's when he spotted us on the run. Pete started yelling and running after us.

We made it over the hill. Quickly we threw the traps into the little shed. A board was off the side, so we tossed them through that hole. Next we ran to hide. But we weren't fast enough. We got caught!

Both of us stood by the old barn while Pete scolded us. After that he wanted to know what we did with his traps. We told him where he could find them. He wasn't through with us yet, as his parting words were, "I'm going to tell your Dad!" With that parting shot, he turned, lumbering over the hill with his recovered traps.

Brother, he was going to tell Dad! That could mean trouble. Paul and I took off for home, about a half mile away. Pete took his car, so he got there first. The closer we got voices could be heard. Man, Pete was talking so loud to Dad. He blamed Dad for sending us out there to take his traps. Dad denied it, saying he had nothing to do with it.

Later we decided to give our excuse to Dad, Tootsie told us to do it. It didn't sound very good at all. We knew better than to listen to Tootsie. We also knew better than to take Pete's traps and hide them.

Pete continued to hunt and trap. After he gave it up, Tootsie did get to trap our ditches for himself.

Later another incident happened. As kids we thought it was funny, even more, we were glad it happened to Pete.

Pete was a big man. He had a lumbering walk all his own. It was easy to spot his walk, even from a distance.

While hunting he was crossing our fields carrying his gun. He was in our pasture, which was fenced in. Pete did not spot something, all those little white spools on our fence posts. He missed seeing them.

In order to get out of the pasture, Pete had to crawl through the fence, in between the wires. Remember now, Pete was a big man. He moved slowly. So he took his time getting between the wires. Placing his gun barrel on the wire, then he proceeded to crawl through. As he got half-way through—he got it!

Zap! Pete got a solid jolt! And another! One more! It just kept pulsating giving out one charge after another. This was our new electric fence.

Once he escaped, Pete lumbered to our barn. Finding Dad, Pete bawled out Dad for having an electric fence. Dad told him he didn't tell him to crawl through the fence. Anyway Pete was still charged up about it when he talked to Dad.

Afterwards we all laughed. We could picture Pete getting one jolt after another. It was a little funny.

Years later, when I was visiting in Pete's home, then he brought up the time he got a big charge from our electric fence. But then he began bragging about his own electric fence, claiming his had a bigger kick than ours did. I took his word for it. I was not going to test it, in order to compare it with ours. Grabbing our fence—five or six pulsating jolts were enough—I was ready to let go.

I can't recall how old I was at the time, but I had a goal in mind. My goal was to help dry dishes for Mom for a whole year. I challenged myself to do it each night after supper.

One night I got into trouble.

At school the boys were into snapping towels when taking showers after gym class. Boy, the right distance, a damp towel, one could give a smarting snap! It could almost cut a kid when you connected.

109

This one night I was way ahead of Mom. My drying towel was wet. I was waiting—with nothing much to do. I backed off, snapped Mom as she stood by the sink.

Several times I made some contact. Mom told me it hurt. Naturally as a kid I denied that; it couldn't hurt that much. So I kept it up.

The snaps got harder. I would dry a few things, then snap the towel again.

One more try, I got off a "perfect snap"—right on target. It cracked like a small bullwhip!

Mom left out a muffled cry. It had to hurt! Scared, I knew I had gone too far that time.

Mom turned to me with tears streaming down her cheeks. I felt awful. Rotten!

It frightened me so much, quickly I threw down the towel, ran into the summer kitchen to hide.

It was dark in that place. Only a little reflected light came under the door. Feeling my way through the dark, I got behind the black stove, where I hid. Every now and then I moved, trying to find another place to hide. I was quiet, listening for voices in the kitchen. My greatest fear was that Mom had gone to tell Dad. I didn't know what was happening on the other side of that door. The unknown made it much worse. The night was passing slowly. I was chilly.

I have no idea how long I stayed in hiding. It was a long time, so it seemed to me as a boy. Finally I made up my mind to go back in the kitchen again, not knowing what I would get.

Mom was waiting. I went straight to her and told her how sorry I was. She forgave me, but let me know it hurt her. I knew that, that part I could not take back.

I still continued to dry her dishes each evening, no more snapping the towel. I did reach my goal, every night for a whole year.

After that, I figured my sisters could dry the dishes.

This next incident happened while in grade school. Paul and I were getting ready to do our chores. Time to change shoes after school. Generally we did that in the kitchen. Both of us had high tops. Now our father wore the genuine high tops, which almost reached to his knees. My brother and I each had a pair, but ours reached about the middle of our calf. This allowed us to tuck-in our pants at the bottom, then lace up our boots.

This particular day, for some reason, Paul and I got into it.

I was sitting by the door that went out to the porch. Paul was across the kitchen. We were exchanging some strong words. Things got worse. Paul picked up one of his high top boots, firing it at me. It went alongside my head—hitting the wall next to the light switch. The heel of the boot broke through the sheetrock. It left a small semi-circle impression of the heel.

Whatever was bothering us ended right there. Both of us were pretty sober. Such damage to the kitchen wall, next to the light switch was bound to be seen.

It was time to get busy. We finished dressing in a hurry and got going on the chores—before we got into more trouble.

Kids in Conflict

As kids, we got into it. Many times. Yes, we did fight. We had our battles. Like all families we were kids in conflict while growing up.

Naturally we used words. Also our hands and feet. Sometimes, as Dad would suggest to the smaller ones, "Pick up something and make up the difference!" The younger ones had the "difference" and Dad on their side.

My brother Paul and I got into it a lot of times. Paul was 18 months younger. Yet Paul had a bigger build than I, so he had an advantage.

One day we were punching out each other. Our battleground was the little timothy field between the toolshed and the ditch. After reaching the bottom of the hill we crawled through the fence, then began our battle. In the middle of our scrap, somebody drove on the yard. We were spotted fighting. As boys, we wondered who came over. Time out! Both us went to see what our visitors wanted. We stood around and listened until they left.

As they drove away, we crawled through the fence to fight again. Round #2. I still remember coming out on the short end, which led to tears between punches. I was too stubborn to stop. My brother was not about to quit, for he was winning.

Paul would get in a good poke, then hold me off with one arm outstretched. This was so frustrating to me. Angry, yet I could not get back at him.

Finally, in desperation, I grabbed his arm—wound up a full swing with my free arm—a haymaker, as it was called. My fist struck him over the heart. Just for a second or two Paul stood stunned.

I landed my best hit. More likely, it would be the only one I would land in the whole fight. So I quit. I walked away. I left the battlefield, crawled through the fence and headed for the house.

Later Paul admitted he felt my blow. As a kid, I felt some satisfaction for once. Other fights Paul landed the best punches.

Not too often did we take punches at each other. Paul knew how to use a wrestling-tactic far better. That was his best method against me. But it was so frustrating for me, leaving me very angry after it was over. I couldn't win. If he moved in—it was all over!

With one move he'd grab the back of my neck, pull down on my head. Then with his free arm, Paul came across my stomach, with my head down it was pressed against his stomach. With his arm he made a quick lift. My neck would crack! A few fast moves, the simple snap of my neck—I was finished. It was over.

Next, he'd push me away from him. Shoved backwards, defeated, I stood still with deep-seated anger. Most of the times in tears, too.

Knowing my own size, I had to admit I was helpless to fight back. However, there was another battle, inside I was waging a war. I was totally consumed with hatred.

Again, Paul was the winner; I was the same born loser.

My fighting back could only be an empty threat. Most of the time I kept it under my breath, I made a silent vow. Some day! I'd give my brother the licking of his life!

As a kid in conflict, in anger, I wanted to do just that— once. But it never happened. Long, long ago I gave up on that, by the grace of God. God had to do it for me. For my old nature wanted to hurt him, really hurt him. Paul hurt me; I wanted to hurt him.

First God had to help me with my inner conflict, which was my greatest battle. I had to let go of the grip this passion for vengeance had on my heart. God broke that grip. My Heavenly Father's grace is amazing! Praise Him for His miracles of grace in my heart. Jesus cut the malignant cancer out of my sinful soul. He touched me, set me free!

Lois had to take plenty from her brothers. There was some hitting. Mostly she had to take our aggravating teasing. It had to be enough to frustrate her to no end. Boys, at times, don't give up.

Every now and then she reported us to Dad. He'd patiently listen to her complaint about Bill or Paul, then offer his advice. It was simple advice, "Pick up a piece of stove wood, make up the difference!"

(Man, she had Dad's permission to fire firewood!) Even knowing that didn't stop me. My favorite way of escape from conflict was to run for the barn or woods. No sense to stick around for any of her fireworks.

One day I was back to my teasing. Lois had all she was going to take. After all, Dad gave permission to use a practical plan to fight her own battles. Lois picked up a piece of split wood.

When I saw the look in her eye, while reaching for the split wood, I took off! She held the difference high over her head.

Since I was older, and a boy, I felt confident I could out run her. I headed toward the barn. The only trouble was trying to get the little gate by the milkhouse open. Up until then, I was way ahead of her— but she was coming. My brief pause at the gate gave Lois enough time to get closer and throw the wood. She let it fly!

Direct hit! Right on my crazy bone! Oh, I thought she killed me. Oh, I had

Left, Paul, Lois, myself in back. Younger members of the family in the center.

114

I'm on Paul's bike. Our house before we remodeled it, when my bedroom was added, also the entrance was changed.

no feeling in my arm. Maybe I would live. Wounded, I worried about my whole arm being numb. I stayed away for a long time. As I nursed my wounds I wondered if I had gone too far.

It would do me absolutely no good to tell Dad. After all, Lois got her battle plan from him. Good Grief! I could picture the two having a victory parade!

This one I suffered in silence. I walked alone, rubbing my numb elbow. I was not going to let on, for sure I wasn't going to let them do any flag waving. A little wiser, don't do it again, now that Lois knows how to make up the difference. Getting hit that way, a kid could get hurt. I knew she would not hesitate a moment to do the same thing.

Marty got teased, too. One evening, just before supper, he and I were half way between the house and the barn. He had the BB gun. This little air rifle shot small BBs, 0.18 inch in diameter.

In our exchange he threatened to shoot me. He wasn't going to give a threat like that, I grabbed the gun away from him. I held it up, shooting it in the air. With that I handed it back to him. Before he could shoot it again, he'd have to cock it. Since he was rather small, I felt safe, regardless of his threat. It would take time for him to cock it, aim and fire! In the meantime, I would not stand around!

I intended to run for my life. I had two directions to run: barn or house. Pick one. My choice was the house. My plan: run for the porch, open the door, duck in out of the firing range. Move!

While I was running away, I heard Marty cocking the gun. Only a moment more, I'd be home safe.

Door open, one foot in—he fired. The shot rang out!

Bull's-eye! The BB hit the calf of my leg.

I yelled. Oh, he killed me. Not really—but that BB shot stung! It burned.

Wilma, our kid sister, witnessed the war between brothers. Later she told me she thought he really had killed me.

Marty later told me that he was aiming for my butt. While he aimed for the seat of my pants, the BB kept dropping as it got nearer the target. Gravity helped change the strike-zone, but he still hit his marked brother.

I knew then that I was not faster than a speeding bullet. Well, not faster than a flying BB!

When Lois was small we had a nickname for her, "Little Miss Muffet." It wasn't too bad when we called her Muffet. Yet it seemed to irritate her when we had to quote the nursery rhyme—

> Little Miss Muffet
> She sat on a tuffet,
> Eating of curds and whey;
> There came a great spider,
> Who sat down beside her,
> And frightened Miss Muffet away.

About that time she wanted teasing brothers to go away! While we didn't always aggravate her that way, there were enough times to make life miserable for our Little Miss Muffet.

One afternoon Marty and Wilma were kids in conflict. I have no idea what started it. However, they did not wait too

My younger sisters, Wilma, Carolyn, and Rita, with Aunt Ricca Tysen.

long after getting off the bus. Their fight began by a big bush alongside the south driveway. Now, just beyond the bush, along the edge of the drive, is one big sand-burr patch.

First a few swings took place. Wilma next got hold of Marty's blonde hair—and held on. Down they went, into that miserable patch of bristly burrs. They rolled. They struggled. It was one big conflict.

Since it was tea time, some of us would glance out the kitchen window. Reports were given to Dad. After a little while Dad felt it had gone on long enough. So orders were given that it had to stop!

Both quit. Both got up. Both were covered with one sticky mess of sandburrs clinging to their school clothes. Marty got up with some blonde hair missing!

Coming toward the house, both were picking off those clinging sandburrs, for they were covered with them. Their conflict was over, for now.

More to follow, for all of us kids.

I'm in the seventh grade.

117

It's Funny Now!

Before school, one of my jobs was to feed the chickens. Near the chicken coop was an old feed house. Feed was stored in this black tarpaper building. I had to get mash out of there, by using a coal hod. With it I'd fill the feeders each morning. Next I had to water the chickens. Each time I watered the chickens, I first had to prime the pump. Enough buckets of water were pumped to fill all the water troughs and pans. Once filled they had enough water for all day.

Two funny things happened. Early one frosty morning I did a very dumb thing. Maybe you have guessed what it was by this time. Yes, I did! I put my tongue on the pump handle. It stuck!

I didn't know what to do. My heart began to jump in my chest. I panicked! So I jerked backwards—ripping my tongue off the handle. That was a horrible experience for a kid. My tongue was so sore for a long time. Don't ask, I'll never know why. I don't know what possessed me to stick out my tongue to touch the pump handle.

Now it's funny, but it certainly wasn't on that frosty morning in Indiana.

Another funny thing happened while feeding the chickens. Mash was kept in sacks in the feed house. Generally I would empty the sack into the coal hod. Once empty, I'd hang up the empty sack. Other creatures wanted that tasty feed. Plenty of mice and rats got into the feed. I hated both of them. But of the two, I hated rats the most. Rats chewed big holes in the sacks. Many times the sack was then useless.

Feed companies were using print sacks. In order to sell their brand, their gimmick was to appeal to the women on the farm. Mom used this print material for sewing dresses. So we had to be careful not to snag the sack on a nail or rip a hole in it. We had to be careful to avoid tearing the sacks. Those miserable rats didn't care about the nice material. To get at the feed, they chewed a big hole in every sack.

Dad decided to dump the feed into some old water tanks. When a truck brought more chicken feed, we emptied the sacks into the tanks. No more holes in Mom's print sacks.

However, the rat tracks were all over the top of the feed. Rats just jumped into the tank. When the tanks were nearly full they could get in and out very easily. But once the steel tank was almost empty, to get in was easy, but many times they could not make it out again. Dad told me to put rat traps in the tanks to catch them. So early winter mornings meant checking traps. I had to throw out the dead ones I caught in the night. After feeding the chickens, I'd reset the traps.

I hated it when it was rather dark. Without lights in the feed house, I'd have to feel my way around.

One morning, in the darkness, I dipped into the tank for mash. Oh, something was in the tank! No more—ran up my sleeve! I felt it run up my arm inside my jacket—then moving around in my armpit! A vision flashed in my mind—a rat could bite me! Oh, yew!!! Screams in the dark of the early morning...I cried for help!

I stumbled out of the old feed house...running towards the house.., yelling at the top of my lungs! I held out my arms, holding them up in the air in front of me. Terrorized, I cried for fear, "Oh, help me! Help me!"

Halfway to the house, it moved, away from my armpit. Then I felt it running up my arm, then jumping out of the sleeve of my jacket—a little mouse. As he hit the ground he ran for his life.

My heart was nearly jumping out of my chest. I felt so weak. But it was over. Unable to move, I stood by the big gate going out of the chicken yard.

Mom came out of the house, running towards me in the semidarkness. She'd heard my screams, "What's the matter, kid?"

I told her what happened, explaining, "Mom, I thought I had a rat up my sleeve!" Well, what was it? I have to confess—only a little mouse.

Now it's funny. Not that dark morning!

One day we were in the field, near the Hodge Ditch. The grain had been cut with the binder. Bundles had been dumped in piles. We were there to shock the bundles, in neat rows.

Marty was out in the field with us, even though he was quite small. He was wearing a little pair of overalls. As a bundle was picked up a mouse ran towards Marty, then right up his leg. On the inside of his overalls!

The little guy went into shock. He trembled.

I ran to him, flipped the straps on his overalls loose, dropping down the bib. Out jumped a little field mouse. Marty was nearly paralyzed, unable to move from the spot. His heart was racing wide open! It was beating so hard it was moving his clothes. I placed my hand of his heart, it felt like a rapid-fire machine gun.

Since then, I have wondered, a child being so frightened, could a little guy have a heart attack? He didn't. But maybe he wasn't far from having one.

Once I had my other chores completed, I was supposed to help out with the milking. This was before we had milking machines. Dad had a few easy cows for me to milk by hand.

On that particular morning I was told to milk a cow at the north end of the barn. It was cold there.

Dad checked how I was getting along. I was very slow. He wondered why I was taking so long. After he checked a couple more times, I still wasn't finished.

Finally he walked over to see for himself. Why was I so terribly slow? Dad discovered the problem, "Bill, you have to take off your gloves if you are ever going to milk that cow."

He was right, it did go faster when I took off my work gloves!

Another morning I was still half asleep when I walked into the cow barn. The cow I was to milk was at the other end of the line. I pressed my head against the cow, leaning on her, half sleeping, trying to milk her.

Since this cow was rather unpredictable, I had kickers on her. This made her unstable on her feet, especially when she tried to lift her leg to kick. Several times she was swaying.

I kept on milking. Half dreaming, I had a picture come to mind: How horrible it would be to have a cow fall on you.

No more than the thought flashed through my mind—I was under the cow. She lost her balance; she toppled over. Old bossy was lying on top of me. I started yelling, so Dad came running. It wasn't very long before Dad had the cow up and off of me. I scrambled out of there in a big hurry.

I was wide awake as I finished milking that morning. The old cow didn't lay down on the job, but neither did I. I milked faster, too.

Animals can be funny, at times.

Pete Swisher needed a truck to haul some melons and other vegetables to Gary. Dad gave him permission to take our Model T Ford truck to the market.

Later he wanted to show his appreciation for the use of the truck. Dad told him he didn't care to have anything. After all, Pete had helped Dad out many times. However Pete still wanted to do something.

He did. The something was to give us a stinking old billy goat!

They brought over this old goat. What a miserable animal! He had to explore everything. One never knew what he'd do next.

To our amazement we couldn't believe what we saw out the kitchen windows. We ran outside to see for certain. There this goat was, standing on the roof of our GMC truck. He'd jumped on the fender, then the hood, finally hopping on the top of the roof.

That egotistical critter acted like he was king of our farm. I think he took great pride looking over his conquered kingdom.

One evening he paraded around back of the barn, at the same time the cows were coming into the barn. His timing was perfect. The old goat cocked his head staring at the cows. Our cows panicked. Half of them tried to flee from that strange creature. They tried to go back out the south doors—all at the same time.

With fear in their eyes, they acted like they had to run for their lives. They had to get away from that goofy monster. Down the hill they ran. In wild fear they ran through the barb wire fence. Naturally the cows cut up their teats and utters. By that time the old goat cost us much more than he was ever worth. He had to go.

Dad told us to go to Pete and tell him to come and get his old goat. That stinking billy goat got our goat!

Afterwards, it was funny. But it wasn't then. However, do you suppose that old goat pulled one over on all of us? For sure, he knew how to get our goat!

On the school bus we began talking about what we would do that night. It was Halloween; we found ourselves by the Swishers. We had some big ideas, especially about tricks we intended to pull off. Big talk, mostly.

Mose Hancock, who lived about a mile from our place, but was a close neighbor to Swishers, was going to get a visit from us. Mose and Teddy, his son, had an old buggy. Our plan was to take the buggy all apart. Piece by piece it was going up on his roof, where it would be put together again. Of course, the next morning he'd search for his buggy. Only to discover it on the peak of his house roof. (I have no idea what we were thinking. After all, Mose and Teddy would hear us running around on the roof! But as kids, we were dreamers.)

We got there early, the Swisher family were still eating. So we sat around while they ate. Pete, turning to us, asked what we were up to. Were we going out that night? All of us giggled. Pete again tried, asking, "What have you guys got up your sleeve?"

A few comments were made, followed by more laughter. Finally we spilled the beans, telling of the buggy on the roof. It sounded like a lot of fun for us kids.

Pete calmly said, "You guys better watch out. Old Mose has a gun."

No more laughter. Within a few minutes all our grand plans for Halloween night fell apart. Maybe it was time for us to head back home, we did have a mile to walk. It was pretty dark.

And it was Halloween!

Pete encouraged Wess to walk us part of the way. First they got a kerosene lantern lit. Together we walked through the sandhills. After being about halfway home, Wess had to go back. We'd have to go the rest of the way alone. We took the lantern. Paul and I quietly walked in the sugar sand on the Old Grade.

One place we had to pass belonged to Sam Obenchain. Stopping on the road, we turned down the lantern. It was barely high enough to see if it were still lit. Slowly we walked on. Our fear was their dog. Would the dog hear us? Would the dog come tearing out on the road and chase us?

Finally we made it passed their driveway. By then we thought we had it made. In the eerie silence of Halloween night we timidly took each step. It was so quiet.

Out of that still night came: BANG! BANG!

Paul voiced our worse fears, "They are shooting at us!" Paul took off!

I was left in the dust. I'm certain he made it home in record-setting time for a half mile.

I got moving, but not nearly so fast. I had to lug the lantern. Paul was home some time before I got in the house. He was sitting on a chair inside the kitchen door. Breathing heavily, I stood in the middle of the kitchen.

While Mom and Dad looked at Paul, he quickly blurted out, "I'm not scared!"

I was. In fact, I felt I had good reason to be, they shot at us!

The next day we had big stories to tell. Obenchains shot at us! Really? Yes! We had good proof, for we heard the bullets whiz by our ears.

A few days later Dad and Sam Obenchain were talking. Sam thought it was funny, laughing he told Dad about Halloween night. They had been watching us walk by. Once we got beyond their drive, they shot off a couple of firecrackers.

It was funny for them. It wasn't funny to us.

Those two firecrackers propelled two boys home Halloween night in record time in Indiana!

A wheel spinner on the steering wheel was the "in" thing in the 30s. My dream was to get one for my tractor.

You could grip the spinner—whipping the steering wheel around. Turns at the end of the fields could be made so easily.

I kept looking at them in catalogs or stores. The price was very reasonable, about one dollar. But a dollar was quite a bit at the time. Yet I still wanted one on our 1935 F-20 Farmall.

That tractor had steel wheels, front and back. Maybe I could put a homemade spinner on the tractor. The steering wheel had holes through it. Spotting those holes, I put a small bolt through the center of a spool, then bolted it to the steering wheel.

I had my own spinner. The spool would not turn, but I could let it slip in my hand as I whipped it around while driving the tractor.

It worked great. All day long I enjoyed making the turns. Late afternoon I was discing some new ground. Stumps had been recently cleared out. I had to watch for small pieces of stumps and roots.

Since it was a new piece of ground I went over it several times with the disc. Unnoticed was a small rooted stump in front of me. The stump caught the rim on the front steel wheel. Suddenly it jerked the front wheels—I lost control of the steering wheel. The front wheels turned cross-ways! My steering wheel spun, whirling in a circle. I made a grab for it. Missing it, I got hit on my crazy bone of my elbow by my spool.

The tractor's motor died. Everything stopped. My arm went totally numb. I just sat still for a long time.

I waited for feeling to come back—it didn't.

That night it didn't change. Even the next morning I still had some numbness. Oh, this is serious, I thought. I removed my homemade spinner, never to put it back on again.

It just wasn't funny to get hit so hard on my funny bone.

Slowly the feeling returned. That was a relief, for I had fears and worries about having been permanently injured.

Never again did I ask for a spinning knob. Maybe they were neat on cars, but not on steel wheeled tractors.

I learned one thing, that thing did not tickle my funny bone!

I still remember Mom's delicious yellow cakes. Such a cake was the best. Sometimes Mom made them three layers high. What a treat! Mom sometimes sliced bananas with white frosting between the layers.

A kid had to take his time eating that kind of cake.

There even was a special way to take your piece of cake apart. All the frosting was removed very carefully. There was a special order to eat it. Start at the bottom, then work your way to the top. Save your frosting for the last, again from the bottom to the top.

One Sunday morning we had company over. Uncle Fred and Aunt Bess and family were there. Mom had a special yellow three layer cake. Every kid got a big piece of cake.

Before we ate it, each kid carefully prepared for the feast. Quietly we ate, enjoying every bite. Then Babe, about three years older than I was, left out a yell, "Holy Moses!"

Everybody stopped eating. We wondered what happened. Soon she gave us her shocking news, "I thought I was eating the bottom and I'm eating the top!"

Without realizing it, she was eating her special treat, the wrong way. She had eaten the best part, while thinking it was only the bottom. In other words, she ate the best, but was not enjoying it as the best.

As a kid you had better pay more attention as to how to eat your cake. Otherwise you could eat the best, but get very little satisfaction from the most delicious part.

Funny things can happen with dogs on the farm. One of our neighbor's dog came over to pester our pigs. He'd get into the pig pen and chase after them until the pigs would nearly drop.

Once they get started with something like that it can get destructive. It is far worse if a couple of dogs get together. It goes beyond injuring the animals, sometimes killing them.

This dog had been back several times. He was a pest. It was suggested we ought to turpentine the dog. So the dog was caught, then kept in the horse barn. After breakfast one morning, the time had come. Turpentine was splashed under his tail. Afterwards he was rubbed vigorously with a rough corn cob. The dog must have felt like "the seat of his pants was on fire." He shot out of the barn. Downhill he streaked, with his burning bottom. He was headed for home, yelping as he was leaving.

Harry Sigler, a carpenter, was coming around the wood pile. The dog was coming directly at Harry. So Harry started to move one way...then the other...back again. The dog was coming full-speed towards him. Harry didn't know which way to move at last. Harry stopped, while the dog ran between the man's bowlegs.

Before he could turn around to look the dog was on the Old Grade. The whole thing was very confusing to Harry.

Not as confused as Harv Evans was when his dog came home that morning. Later he mentioned how his dog acted. He told how the dog sat in the grass, pulling himself along with his front legs. Likely he was trying to cool off his hot-seat. I don't know if he got the "fire" out that way, or not.

That dog never returned to bother our pigs. Perhaps he guessed there was something left in that turpentine bottle.

That was one Indiana dog who must have burned all his bridges behind him.

However, another dog decided to visit our farm. This one was a big bulldog. Evidently well-kept, with his neat appearance and fancy harness. Nevertheless he, too, proved to be a nuisance around the farm.

Dad told me to a few tin cans together. Mom would never completely cut off the lid when she opened a can. She bent the lid back. After putting small stones in each can, I bent the lid back to close the can. Using a piece of baling wire, I attached it to the dog's fancy harness. Once he took off the racket would cause enough clattering noise to make him run home much faster. Since he was harnessed up, he had to be ready to pull his trailing tin cans.

Dad had on his hightop boots, with them he made a kicking gesture, as if to boot him on his way. Just to give a little encouragement to get going.

This bulldog turned on Dad, instantly, "GGRRR... UMMM..."

The bulldog marched directly towards Dad, "GGRRR... UMMM...GGGRRRR...!" Dad was backed up flat against the northside of our house. There Dad stood holding his breath. The bulldog was not going to budge one inch! He stared at Dad with an evil eye.

After catching his breath, Dad softly said, "Go away... get out of here..."

Once more Mr. Bulldog let it be know he wasn't about to be booted off the farm. Only after looking Dad in the eye once more, then he turned around, walked very slowly down the back driveway.

The only sound we heard—clink...clank...clunk...clink... clank...clank...clunk!

After reaching the Old Grade the bulldog turned north. Those tins can never made him change his pace. It was a slow, leisurely walk home. No way was he going to run with those tin cans in tow. His pace was the same, as he disappeared out of sight. Boss bulldog was having his day. Nobody, I mean, nobody was going to run him off.

However, he must have gotten the message that he was not welcomed at our place. Maybe his owner made him stay if he was going to drag so much junk home. Anyway, he never came back.

It was funny seeing Dad backed up flat against the house. Dad didn't think it was so funny—for a few moments—when he was eye-to-eye with Mr. Boss Bulldog.

Once we were threshing grain at Blake Morrow's Dairy Farm. Dad and Marty were keeping an eye on the machine. Both were standing by our tractor, while hanging around nearby was a bulldog. He was the kind who could never win a beauty contest, even at a dog show. Marty began to call the dog names. The dog just stared at him. Since he had that look, Dad told Marty he better watch out.

A few moments later Marty called him another name: "Bootlegger!"

That did it! Being called a bootlegger was more than the dog was going to take. He took after Marty. Knowing he meant business, Marty quickly ran for a safe place, climbing on the tractor.

Dad laughed, saying to Marty, "I told you not to call him names." Dad was right. Especially that name. Especially that bulldog!

Another experience was funny, now—and another bulldog.

During World War II it was hard to find certain things needed. A lot of things were rationed. No new trucks or cars were coming off the assembly lines in factories. Plants for a number of years were geared up to manufacture war equipment. After all we had a world at war on two fronts: Europe and in the Pacific.

Our old GMC truck was not getting any newer. It had seen better years. Dad had been watching the ads, if possible, to find another truck for sale.

It was rather fruitless checking these out. Some were in no better condition than our own truck. If one was in good condition, generally it would be sold by the time we got there.

Anyway, we still were looking. This day we were checking one for sale on the outskirts of Le Roy. As we drove up, Dad told me I had to go to the door this time, "This is your turn, Bill."

After knocking, a woman and her dog answered the door. She greeted me far more friendly than her dog. There he was, to my right, looking me over. A bulldog! His comments were always the same, over and over, "GGRRR...UMMM...GGGRRR...!" (I got the feeling he didn't like me.) She and I talked. Then her bulldog had his say. Same old thing. But he had that look in his eye, I was glad the door was only open a few inches.

Anyway, I found out the truck had been sold. Thanking her, I turned to go back to the car. Dad and one of my brothers were watching and waiting for me.

I cut across their lawn. About halfway back to our car, I heard the door open...and close! I next heard stampeding feet hitting the ground. That crazy dog was coming after after me—those pounding feet sounded nearer than I wanted. So as to not take me by surprise, the bulldog decided to announce his coming, "GGRRR...GGGRRR!" (The very same thing he said to me by the house.)

By that time my heart was beating faster than his footsteps were pounding the ground. I felt, by that time, he had to be almost at my heels!

I froze! Totally paralyzed, my legs refused to move.

I was stiff as a frozen fence post in a winter storm.

The dog hit me. But his head slipped between my stiff legs—and then stuck!

He first tried to back up. But he could not get his big head freed from between my legs. Leaning backwards, pushing with his feet, he kept trying to pull his big head free. Didn't work. So he decided to grunt, then added a little, "GGGRRR...GGGR-RRR...!" (He said that before, can't he say anything else?)

With his grunt and words, shaking his head, he tried again to move in reverse. By this time, I guess, he was stuck with me. Neither of us could move.

Coming to my rescue was the woman of the house, calling her beast off. I can't recall the endearing name, some

Three friends, Howard Hoffman, Mel Koster and myself.

129

sweet name, was given to him. She called a second time. By this time I was so weak I couldn't hold him any longer. Finally his big fat head slipped out. The woman scolded him. Sulking and grumbling the old bulldog walked back towards the house.

With the little strength I had left, most of it suddenly drained from my body, I managed to get back to our car. I then discovered my Dad and brother were laughing. Jokers, it must have been funny to them.

I could barely open the car door. But I crawled in, so glad to sit down. I was weak! How weak was I? As weak as a cat with that same bulldog after it!

Those guys in the front were still breaking up. It took several miles down the road before I began to recover from that weak feeling.

As I look back, it must have been a funny sight. A bulldog having his head stuck between my legs, vigorously shaking his big head, but unable to get it in reverse. I never had any sweet name for that creature. If I would have had a stick, I think he would have gotten a lump on his big head!

Afterwards I could laugh about it. Yes, it's funny now.

That Old Dummy

Each year we hoped to finish all cultivating before the 4th of July. We were going to make it in time. Thoughts crossed our minds as to how we would celebrate the 4th. We did some daydreaming while cultivating.

As boys, we stopped several times to talk in the fields. I had an idea! Make a dummy, to fool people. After supper we got to work on making this dummy. First we searched in Mom's rag bag. Things we needed: old shirt, pants, cap, gloves, and old shoes. The stuffing would be straw. So we went to the haymow for our creation. A white seedcorn sack would be the head, with some coloring.

Finally the dummy was stuffed, fully dressed. Up close, anyone would know it was a plain old dummy, looking like a scarecrow.

The trunk of my '37 Plymouth was where we first put it. Face-down, then he looked far more real. Laid out in the trunk that way, it appeared to be a person lying face down. Next we had to test it out.

We drove to Uncle Ben and Aunt Ed. They were still milking, which wasn't unusual. Going into the cowbarn, we had to talk to our cousins about it. Taking them to my Plymouth we let them have a peek. Next we had to try it out on our aunt, so she had to have a look. However, we had to give her a big story, in order to get her to take a look. Our question to her was, "What do you do when you find some fellow lying alongside the road?" But we added, we had found such a fellow beside the road.

She told us to stop joking. Well, if she felt that way, come and see for yourself. While she was very skeptical, still she had to check it out. Opening the trunk, she took a step or two backwards...then she didn't know what ought to be done.

Quickly we closed the lid. The rest of the family were curious enough they wanted to see for themselves. Feeling it passed the test, we'd use it on the 4th.

The next day was our annual Sunday School 4th of July Picnic. It was mainly the Picnic of the First Reformed and American Reformed churches, but people of other churches came, too. I was anxious to show off my dummy. I left home rather early, so I could stop at Harry's Shell Station in De Motte. Generally a number of young guys would gather there. So I went there, hoping to meet a few friends. How would I get someone to look in my trunk?

Sam Douma was one working that day. I told Sam I had a tire in my trunk that had to be fixed. Sam went out to get it and fix it. The moment he spotted the dummy facedown—he slammed the lid shut. Immediately he was back in the station. He giggled, very nervously. It shook him. Grabbing for a smoke, Sam lit up. Sam did not want to talk about it.

Other kids wondered what happened. I offered them 25¢ if they would get the tire out, so it could be fixed. Being skeptical, they had to go take a look. The lid would go up, then down part way.

After a few moments, they'd open it again, just to get a better look. They all came back laughing.

Afterwards I went to the picnic. Smaller kids found out about it, so they started talking people into seeing this. Off and on through the morning, they would convince somebody else to take a look. People had a good laugh, however, nobody would touch the dummy. They'd just look.

Late afternoon most people left the picnic, most had to go home to do chores. A few of us decided to go to Crown Point for a celebration there. My car was too small, since there were four of us we took Mel Koster's car. Really there were five, two in the front, while three of us were in the back seat. We made the dummy sit in the middle. His arms were around the two of us guys, one on either side of him. We had to pay to get into the fairgrounds. By then, it was dusk, as the fellow bent over, asking how many we had in the car. Four. Again he looked in—"No, five," he said. We told him that one in the middle was only a "Dummy"—we didn't have to pay for him. The man wouldn't buy it. Before he'd let us go in, we had to pay for the dummy too.

The old dummy sat alone in the car the whole evening. Later we ran into some girls we knew. This was just great, Mel wanted a date for the night. For a date he was offering his "right arm." Most of the time, that would be his usual offer. Of course, only certain girls were worth his "right arm"—he'd name them. We knew who qualified.

Alberdena, Evelyn, and Thelma wanted a ride back to De Motte. Some other fellows had given them a ride to Crown Point, but they said they did not want to go back with those fellows. They talked to me about a ride. I'd ask the other guys, but that would make a full carload with the dummy, making eight.

The girls could ride back with us. Back at the car, we had to figure out just where the dummy would sit. The front fender. His feet were tied to the bumper, with one hand tied to the headlight. Then three sat in the front and four in the back seat.

Upon getting to Hebron we decided to stop at a restaurant for something to eat. Before we went in, it was time for a little fun. Our dummy was laid next to the highway, about fifty feet from the stop and go light. The streets were rather deserted, as many were going home, rather bushed after a big day. Once their eyes caught the dummy lying there—the sight woke them up! Some went through the light, only to turn around for one more look. They would slowly drive by.

After our stop in Hebron, we had to get going, too. But we had one more stop before De Motte—the Kankakee River bridge. A painting project was giving the bridge a new paint job. Painters left ropes on the bridge over the 4th.

Mel Koster ran up the girder of the river bridge. A rope was dropped, which we tied around the dummy's neck. Pulling him up, the dummy was swinging in the breeze. Cars were coming, so we had to get out of there. We ran along the gravel road along the bank of the river. I stumbled, then fell, sprawled in the gravel. Because we were running hard, it was a very painful fall as I skidded in the loose gravel.

Cars whizzed by. Nobody was noticing the dummy, he was too high. He had to be lowered, after that the headlights caught the figure swaying in the night. His shoes actually hit the roof of a car or two. It was July, so car windows were down, we could hear women scream. Drivers braked hard, tires squealed. A few stopped. By that time we decided to get out of there.

The dummy was taken down and we headed south for town.

One fellow left his car unlocked by the Shell station. Cousin wild Bill put the dummy behind the steering wheel. The owner, trying to see in the semi-darkness, tried to get him out of the car. John was pretty upset, he tossed the dummy out in the street. Someone pitched the dummy on the railroad tracks.

It had been a long day, so all of us headed for home.

Later we heard a train cut off his legs. A section crew discovered the victim lying on the tracks. Bert Struble stopped his handcar, so he could investigate the "victim" hit by the train. Some of the summer crew told how he slowly walked towards the dummy. Once he was close enough to see the straw stuffing, Bert gave it a big swift kick. Straw went flying.

The crew threw the remains next to tracks, where it was set on fire.

A few nights later I was back in town, stopping at Harry's Station. Naturally, among the younger guys, there was a lot of talking and laughing about the dummy. Harry listened for a little while, then he took me aside. After he got me in the back, Harry warned me, "I wouldn't talk too much about that dummy. Today the sheriff was in town asking a lot of questions." Enough said.

Some travellers had gotten very frightened by the "victim" on the Kankakee River bridge. Calls were made to the sheriff's office. Reports were that a man hung himself. So the sheriff had to go to the northern part of the county to ask questions.

By that time we discovered our fun could have caused a lot of trouble.

I recognized I'd be in more trouble than anyone. I came up with the idea. As a young person I thought it was pretty cool.

To this day I'm glad nobody was hurt.

I did make another discovery. One of the girls asked if I hurt myself, when I fell on the gravel road. I thought she showed concern for *me*. That caught my attention!

Oh, she was Alberdena Dykhuizen.

It Hurts

I liked him. Nevertheless that big police dog decided to bite me. We were at Grandma Walstra's house, on the back porch. It was Uncle Garret's dog.

I was standing on one side; brother Paul was on the other side of the dog. He was big, for we could barely see over his back. We began to pet the dog. It seemed he liked it, letting us stroke his back and pet him. Nobody had told us to leave him alone. The dog acted like he wanted us to play with him.

Without any warning, the dog jerked his head around, making a snarl and snap! Instantly my arm was in his mouth—he was sinking his teeth into my arm. One large fang tooth went through my arm a few inches below my elbow. (The scar it left still remains on my arm.) Nobody could explain why he turned vicious. People at Grandma's house were asking about the sudden change in the dog's behavior. Nobody knew the answer.

I wasn't taken to a doctor. In fact, nobody there even talked about going to a doctor. I can remember Grandma Walstra and a few others looked at it. A white rag was wrapped around my arm, that was all. Of course, after that happened, Paul and I were told not to get close to the dog.

However, each time I see my scar, I still remember the big police dog biting me, when I was only petting him.

Another time, I got hurt on a mudboat when I was a boy. This mudboat had two large runners with some 2x6 cross boards. Old Benny would be hitched up in front of it. We'd be on our knees when taking a ride. One day, as we came up the back driveway, I grabbed on a board to hold on. My fingers were on the bottom of the board. buried in the sand was a sharp stick, which caught my finger. It nearly ripped my fingernail off the index finger of my left hand.

At first I never realized anything happened. However, by the time we reached the top of the hill I felt it. Boy, it really hurt! By that time it was bleeding. Once I discovered how badly I injured it, I ran to Mom. Mom wrapped a cloth around it, then took me downhill to show Dad. He had the Model T Ford truck by the cow yard gate. Dad took me around the truck, opened the door so I could get in. Mom was told to open the gate, while Dad drove through. We went straight for the doctor in De Motte. Dr. Leesen cut off the nail and wrapped it up. It took a long time to heal. Mom mentioned later, her knees were so weak she hardly could get the gate opened and closed.

This injury left a scar on the end of my finger. It changed my finger print. My nail is shaped differently than any of the others. If I snag it on something, it hurts. My finger is very tender.

As a kid I had a hard time telling my right hand from my left. Since the injury, I glance down, looking at that finger—that's my left hand! I've checked directions to the right or left by looking at that pointer finger on my left hand.

Nothing hurts like a boil.

The Bible tells of all the boils Job had. The poor man had them from the top of his head to the bottom of his feet. I never had that many, but I did have 89 one year. That's the year I was in sixth grade.

Before that Dad had a carbuncle or two on his neck. They were large, very severe boils. Dad suffered with them, for they are so painful.

Any number of times I had 13 boils at the same time. That happened often that year. A boil would start as a red, tender lump, which would throb. In a day or two it would get much larger, and more painful. As pus collected, it began to form a yellow head or center. Pressure from the pus made the skin tight, which caused constant pain. Finally it would come to a head, then burst through the skin. Once the pus drained out, it relieved the pain. Healing could begin after that.

Boils made me feel miserable. At first they seemed like an oversized ripe pimple. I couldn't help but bump it a little now and then. That was just the beginning. A knot formed inside the red swelling. I could tell when it was coming to a head by the white point, which stuck up out of that angry swelling.

It would be stiff with poison. Before it got any better it had to explode! Some reddish and yellow matter would come out, leaving a hole in the middle. It was a big relief for the boil to drain out all the poisonous pus.

There were days I could not sit in school. On those miserable days my teacher permitted me to do my work by a window and a heat register. Believe me, I liked her for being so kind when I had such pain.

Other times I couldn't go to the bathroom because I had boils around my "seater." A few of those bad times I stood against a tree in the yard, trying to go to the bathroom. I'd cry and cry, for it hurt so much.

One day we were playing in the pasture, just over the bridge. While I couldn't play, I did stand watching the other kids. A big dog ran between my legs and bumped the boil-heads! I cried that time, too. A bump would be enough to break them open, so I'd have to wipe away the pus.

Most people thought it was bad blood that caused boils. (A few said it was due to my orneriness. It was trying to come out of me. That wasn't funny. Was it true?) Whatever the cause, my parents had all kinds of suggestions as to what they ought to do. Since I had bad blood, then I needed iron, they'd say. For that I was supposed to eat RAISINS! I ate all the raisins the IGA Store had. As a kid, I claimed Bill Swart wanted to get rid of his supply on hand, so I ate them for him. All of them! I can't believe I ate them all. (For years I could not stare a raisin in the face, much less eat it!)

Next I had to take sulfa powder. I remember it was so very soft. Yellow. It was mixed with honey, then I would swallow the dose. The stuff didn't always mix with honey, as a result I had to be careful not to breathe in the powder, otherwise I'd choke. I took many, many doses of sulfa, can't say I liked it either. More homemade remedies were suggested that year. Our family said we would try them.

One day Dad was in Hebron to see his doctor. Dad mentioned to Dr. Buteman that I had all these boils. He told Dad to have me come in so he could give me a shot.

Mom took me in for the shot. Belly-down I got my first shot of a new drug, oil-based penicillin! Doc shot me! I thought the doctor killed me!

I limped—wounded—to the car! I moaned and groaned. For a time I could not tell which was the worst—a boil or that shot. But I lived.

Best of all, I didn't have any more boils.

During the year, as a kid in sixth grade, I learned to feel for Job, who had all those boils. As I said, he had them from the top of his head to the bottom of his feet. I just had most of mine on my bottom. That was more than enough.

Even as a boy, I discovered life can test your faith, but so can boils. Thank God for His healing blessing.

When I was a kid we used many homemade remedies.

If I had an upset stomach, Dad had a remedy. Dad felt it would do the trick, as he offered, "This ought to warm up your stomach a little." That remedy was to put a little ginger in a glass, adding fairly hot water. "Here, drink this," I'd be told.

It felt warm, all the way down, even including my stomach. That remedy had to be a great cure-all handed down from one generation to another.

One evening Mom and Dad were going to a turkey supper. As I recall farmers had been invited. I can only remember Marty and I were left alone. The others were not around that evening. I know Mom had left some supper for us two boys. Before leaving she also gave us a large can of fruit cocktail. That was our dessert.

She offered us the whole can. So naturally, we quickly asked how much we could have from that big can. "As much as you want," Mom suggested.

What an offer! Well, we feasted on the fruit cocktail. Two boys managed to put away the whole thing. It proved to be too much of a good thing. I know, as it brought me plenty of misery.

Before the folks got home I was vomiting my dessert. There I was, on my knees by the stool, when the folks came home. They found me in the bathroom—in plain misery! I 'fessed up—we ate the whole things (Would I die?)

Dad looked at me by the stool, "You better have a little ginger." So he mixed my next cocktail. I shivered as I drank it. Again it warmed me up.

As I jokingly said, "It was Dad's cure-all." It must have been.

Believe it or not, I never vomited again from that teenage experience until 1989, just short of 50 years!

Maybe there was something to Dad's special ginger warmer-upper.

Mom had some special stuff too. She began this when we were small. Mom gave us cod-liver oil. What a taste! The fishy oil taste stayed with you. Every time, for a long time after taking a dose.

Mom's cure-all had to be castor-oil. I never would swallow that stuff without a battle. She'd force the awful stuff on Paul and me. However, I must admit, we tried every trick in the book to escape taking our dose of castor-oil.

She had a remedy for that. Take it with coffee! Coffee? Plenty of sugar. Then, of all things, with plenty of cream. At first it was hot coffee, with one large dose of castor-oil added. There we would sit watching that oil-slick floating on top.

Next came her orders, "Drink it right down—now!" (Could that have been child abuse?)

Now was not now for two boys. More time was needed. Stall. Just wait, we'll drink it, we promised. Plea after plea, just wait.

Our medicine was cooling off, as we waited. In fact, it was cold by the time we got through waiting.

Mom, standing over us, gave her instructions once more, stir it and drink it. Yuk! So we would stir the cold cup of coffee and cream, with the swirl of castor-oil slick! It was some sight. No wonder we didn't feel well.

After our "stall time" Mom countered with "threat time."

For some reason she was determined we had to take our medicine. Sooner or later, mostly later, we had to surrender. One more last stir, held our breath, and drank the horrible, yukky-stuff.

The taste stayed with me for another half hour. My mouth was oily, so were my lips.

I can't say it cured any thing. But it was enough to give any kid nightmares of the oily slick swirling on top of a cold cup of creamy coffee. If I close my eyes I can almost be hypnotized by a vision of the swirling slick! No wonder I never liked coffee! People ask, "Don't you like coffee?" Can't understand that, a Dutchman not liking coffee. I know they mean to be gracious, but who would believe me if I told my story?

My mind wonders, while they try one more time, "Sure you won't have a cup of coffee anyway? Glad to get you a cup."

Then for old-time's sake, I may say, "Thanks, maybe I will. ...yes, a little sugar, and cream. Cold coffee is fine. Oh, you wouldn't happen to have a little castor-oil."

Only in my dreams. Thanks anyway.

As kids we had our usual childhood diseases. One of the first I remember was having measles. Shades were down in the middle bedroom. Naturally the light hurt our eyes. To avoid any damage to our eyes we had to stay in the semi-darkened room. Bored. Dena took care of us for a few days. She showed us how to place a piece of paper over a comb to hum to give us music—at least we had our own entertainment.

Mumps! I had them on only one side. Painful! My jaw hurt, especially around my ear. It was most painful to be jiggled while sitting on Dad's lap. If he bounced me around, then I'd grab my neck and hold my jaw in my hands. There was talk about mumps going down, so I had to be careful.

Once was not enough. Afterwards I had them them for the second, on the other side.

That was enough!

Chickenpox. One child after another got the chickenpox. They were very itchy, so it was hard to keep from scratching.

141

We got plenty of warnings about that. Yet each one of us got a pox mark or two.

When I was in the lower grades our school had one case of diphtheria. The little Marshall girl died from it. I remember her. A few days before she got sick, during recess, she sat in a window. I was playing nearby. A few days later school was closed. We heard the news that she died. That really hit me, to think a little girl died from that dreaded disease!

A few days later we were all picked up by the school bus. Everyone got a shot. We went into a basement room of school to get it. The whole student body was immunized the same day.

For weeks I'd look at the window where she sat. It was a constant reminder every time I'd play outside during recess. Nobody was sitting in the window then. Yet in my mind, I could still see her sitting in that same window.

I was saddened because a little girl died from diphtheria.

The Whooping Cough Gang: Back left, Paul, George Roorda, and myself. Front, Marty J., George's cousin, and Lois. We are standing by the hayrake, which I ran during haying time each summer.

One more contagious disease was whooping cough. Boy, we had some bouts of coughing that summer. Our biggest problem was trying to play—hard. Especially when we wanted to run, it kicked off that whooping cough. One had to stop! One of us had to bend over to whoop. Whenever I'd whoop I could not breathe. My face would turn red, almost blue at times. Exhausted I'd gasp for air—making a *whooping* noise. Since this could last from two to ten weeks, well, we spent the summer whooping it up.

George Roorda and his cousin would come with Frank to take care of the bees in the woods. It was a summer of playing and whooping together.

Later we were told not to run or play so hard. That helped some, if we listened.

Dad and Mom decided we'd go to Hebron for some celebration, instead of De Motte. It may have been the 4th, as I remember we had firecrackers. If we started coughing, we'd be told to go away from people. It wasn't necessary, most of the time they got away from us. The mother grabbed her kids to run, avoiding us "like the plague."

Paul and I played with firecrackers, away from the crowd. Since it was very dry on the grounds, we started a grass fire. When we threw a firecracker it caused the fire. It happened where all the cars were parked. Dad and other firefighters had a big job to put it out before it reached the cars. Paul and I stood back watching the men stomping out the burning grass. They looked like some natives dancing in the fire and smoke.

At last the summer was over, so was our whooping cough.

As a child I knew our doctor had his black bag. Either he was carrying it or looking in it. It seemed like he had all kinds of things in that bag. Generally he pulled out his stethoscope, so he could *listen*. Boy, it was always cold! His bag was full of bottles and tiny boxes of pills, syrups and salves. All these were stashed neatly inside his black bag. Most bottles had corks. Our doctor would scribble on the label on the side of the bottle, maybe, "Take one teaspoonful every 4 hours." Those small boxes generally had tiny pills inside. His doctor's office had a smell of medicine. A few times our doctor would make a house-call. We'd be very quiet when he walked through the door with his black bag.

One felt secure to have a doctor come to help someone who was really under the weather, as we used to say.

Well, when I was born, our doctor himself was under the weather. People said that when he had been drinking too much that day. He had the day I was born on the old home place.

As a result, he neglected a few things when I was born. Today they'd say I had "phimosis" I imagine. Frankly I can't remember how it later came to the attention of my parents. But it did, about the time I was becoming a teenager. Dad and I talked. I know what Dad suggested. It was wrong. Medical people say the procedure could badly damage the tissues of a boy. That time, Dad's home remedy was the incorrect medical method of handling the problem. Most of the time this corrects itself by the time a boy is five. It didn't. So by the time I was a teenager, I had to have medical help. Circumcision was necessary.

I was 14 when Dad and I again talked about it. During the Thanksgiving vacation we went to Renssalear, where we saw Dr. C. E. Johnson. The man was a good doctor, even though he had a few rough edges.

He examined me, then immediately picked up the telephone to call the hospital. He talked about surgery, as he informed them, get prepared for a "radical circumcision!" That sounded scary. I didn't say anything. Quietly I kept all my thoughts to myself. But not for long, in a few moments we walked out the back door of his office over to the hospital. We talked a little as we took our short walk.

Everything was happening so fast, I hardly had time to take things in. In the operating room I remember them strapping me down. Instantly a mask was over my face! Next I heard, "Breathe deeply." Again they repeated it. I refused! I was not about to breathe deeply, instead I held my breath. I kept shaking my head—NO! NO! ...still refusing to breathe in the ether, which had such a horrible smell and taste. But I could only hold it so long——I had to breathe!!!

Suddenly it all happened. I took one big gasp to get some air. Within seconds things began to whirl. I was going into another world, just as quickly I was out.

They operated. I knew that when I woke up. When I did, I was lying on a little cot in the room. A nurse and the doctor were talking to me. It wasn't long before I got up. I soon dis-

144

covered the only comfortable way to walk was bent over. Oh, my clothes really irritated me, I held out the front of my pants. Oh, it felt so tender and sore. Nothing was going to touch me, if I could help it.

Doctor Johnson told me how he wanted me to dress my wounds. After that Dad and I got back in the car for the ride home.

Around home I wore only a big pair of long johns. I had no pajamas. That old fashioned underwear was the most comfortable way to go.

Naturally I missed some school. Nine days, in fact. Those nine days were the only ones I missed during my four years of high school.

People were asking questions, so I'd just say, "I had to have minor surgery."

That's the way books today even put it, "This is a relatively minor operation." That's what they say! Maybe it is. However, for me, it was not when I was 14 years old!

One neighbor woman had to come over, after hearing about my surgery. She wanted to know more. Embarrassing! It seemed she had to know, so she kept asking more questions. Finally sitting around our kitchen table, while in my long johns, with Mom, we told her. Her questions went on and on, so embarrassing.

When Dad came in, I mentioned to him how many questions she had. Dad teased me a little about it, in a way it bothered me.

Back at school, I did tell our coach about it. During my freshman year I was student manager for our first team in basketball. Doctor's orders were no lifting. So I was unable to carry the equipment before and after games.

I still remember one out-of-town game, likely at Kouts. Anyway the coach told some players to carry the equipment back to the bus. My job was to see that everything got picked up. Casey, an older student, began to ask why I couldn't carry the stuff to the bus. I had to explain that I had had surgery. His next question, "What kind?" Together, on the way to the bus, I frankly told him, "I was circumcised."

Casey stopped, looked at me, "Why?" However he did not wait for any answer, but blurted out, "Are you a Jew or something?"

And then another, "Was this for a religious reason?" Some way or other I managed to simply tell Casey "NO" was the answer to his questions. By then we had reached the bus, so we both stopped talking, we both got on the bus.

The hard part was to put on new dressings daily. Since it was the end of November and into December, it was cold in our house each morning. I'd get up early to start a fire in the old wood cookstove. With the oven door open, there I would change the dressings.

Every morning I was all alone. But one morning a few other kids decided to get up early. There they stood, watching me when Dad walked in.

Dad was upset with me. I thought he'd tell the others to go back to bed for a little while. He didn't, instead he bawled me out for changing my dressings before the younger kids. I tried to explain that I was there first. Dad didn't accept my explanation. Right in the middle of my procedure I was told to pick up everything and get in the bedroom.

I felt Dad was very unfair with his decision. I was one angry boy who grumbled as I finished in the ice cold bedroom. After all, Doctor Johnson told me to warm up my bandages and salve by a hot stove. As stitches worked their way out over the weeks it was hard to remove bandages in such a cold room. Daily I was upset with my father.

I must admit, Dad's orders were hard for me to accept. While I obeyed, I felt he was not very understanding or fair.

Anyway for me, at 14, it was an unforgettable experience!

Scars and Scares

As we were growing up I remember our old cookstove in the kitchen. It was a big black stove with white enamel. Enamel was only on the warming closet and oven door. Our black range had a reservoir to warm water. Our stove was trimmed with some nickel. But that was only nickel plated, nothing elaborate. My parents bought the stove when they were first married.

On the oven door was a pock star, very noticeable. Looking at the stove, the star stuck out like a sore thumb. Dad had damaged the door with one swift kick. He had on his big high top boots when he kicked it.

Around our house it was not unusual to have the oven door open. To help heat the kitchen Mom would have it open. She had it open, while I was running around the room. I had learned to walk shortly before an accident took place. When I stumbled, I hit the corner of the stove near my eyebrow. It was a horrible looking cut, causing blood to run down my face.

The sight so upset Dad he gave the oven door a big boot. The oven door slammed shut! That's when his kick starred the white enamel. That pock mark remained through all the years we had the old black range.

The warming closet was such a nice place to dry wet gloves. Not too close to the stovepipe, otherwise they'd get scorched. We knew from the smell when that happened. Water in the reservoir was used for washing up.

The cookstove had its scar to the day we got rid of it. My eye injury gave me a scar, which I still have in my eyebrow.

One summer evening Dad, Paul and I headed for the Hodge Ditch and the old swimming hole. Other men and boys were also there. After a hot day, the farmers and boys were ready for a good swim. Nobody had a swimsuit. All of us went skinny dipping.

I begged Dad to teach me to swim. Dad had his hands under me, then let me kick and paddle. That was the way I splashed around—trying to swim. (I was also trying to drink the ditch dry!)

Dad never noticed. All the men were too busy talking. While they talked I was having my first swimming lesson. However, Dad was paying more attention to their conversation than to my lesson. No longer balanced on his hands, my bottom was higher than my head. Since my mouth and nose was under water, I could not yell for help. But I could drink ditch water.

I struggled. I tried to fall off Dad's hands—anything. But Dad held on tight. After Dad finally looked, my head was lifted out of the water—I gasped for air. I could only spit, sputter, choke, and cough. Naturally I recovered. Glad my first swimming lesson was over.

About the same time a sudden summer storm came up. All of us got out of the water. In the distance, towards home, we could hear thunder rumble and see flashes of lightning. It wasn't safe to be around water, so all the swimmers ran for their cars. As we left the Hodge bridge we could see it storming back home. Mom and Lois were home alone.

I quickly ran to tell Mom what happened. I was excited about my experience in the water. Right under Dad's nose I thought I was drowning.

But I was stopped short before I even told my story. Mom was sitting on the bed crying hard. Her whole body was shaking. She was holding my little sister while she cried.

When the storm suddenly came up Mom thought of our little chicks by the brooder house. She wanted them in the brooder house, then close the windows and door. Mom ran out there with baby Lois in her arms. Once she took care of that, they hurried towards the house again.

By that time it was a severe electrical storm. As she reached the big gate going out of the chicken yard a flash of lightning struck. That bolt dropped Mom to her knees near the gate. What was so frightening for her was how hard she held the baby. Her arms pressed Lois to her breast with such force it was scary. At first she wondered if she hadn't crushed the life out of the baby. After being stunned, later, she was able to get to the house. She went to the bedroom to cry. I found her there.

Of course I got to tell her my story. Mom said that she felt funny before we left. She had a premonition something was going to happen. It did. Both at home and at the old swimming hole.

Another scary experience for me was the runaway with the hayrake. Each summer, late in July and into August, we'd put up the slough hay. Almost a month or more would be spent baling hay in the marsh.

Earlier times some farmer tried to break the ground in those hayfields. While trying to plow the sod, some sod turned over, but some only flopped back. There were no problems when it turned over neatly in the furrow. But those chunks which fell back left the ground so uneven, extremely bumpy in a number of places.

Each year the slough hay continued to grow. Even with the uneven lay of the land we could cut and bale the hay.

My job was to run the hayrake. I would put the hay in windrows. After turning it, then it could dry out some more. However, the main reason for the windrow was so the bull-rake could pick it up. Our bullrake had long wooden teeth on it. Two horses pulled it, one pulled on one side of the rake and the one from the other side. Pushing into the windrow of hay, a whole load could be gathered up. The huge pile would then be moved to the baler.

Two men would pitch it on the platform by the baler. Another man, standing on the platform, would feed the hay-press. It would press the hay into bales.

Wess Swisher was our man on the bullrack. Generally he had that job each year. One trip to the press Wess had his eyes nearly shut. He ran into a nest of bumblebees. Those angry bees nailed him between his eyes.

He must have hit a colony of them. There can be from 10 to 50 bumblebees in a colony. Those bees like to nest in thick grass. The slough grass would be a perfect place to nest. If they find a hole in the ground, they use it. Now bumblebees have many enemies, but man is considered the worse enemy. For that, we can, and do, catch it.

Wess did. The following morning Wess came to the field with small slits for eyes, barely able to see out of them. Whenever Wess would grin or smile that day, then his eyes would be completely closed.

Later it was my turn with the bumblebees. Another nest of them were disturbed. As I was raking the hay around a brush patch my team of horses stopped. Then stomped. Snorted a few times. They bucked. They kicked. They vigorously stomped the ground some more. There they stood—having a strange behavior change. I could not get them to move. I couldn't understand what made them behave this way.

All the time those bumblebees were stinging the horses in the belly. After a few more stings, they were not going to stay there. They got another notion in their heads. Before I could get it all figured out I was in for the fastest ride of my life across a hayfield!

My team took off, taking me along for the ride. They were wild! I was up in the air, then down again. I hit bump after bump. A hard landing would cause the rake to trip. It caused the rake to release, then dump. Every time it dumped, the rake teeth would slam under my seat. The force would jar me. Immediately the teeth would fall to the ground and drag until the next bump.

During my wild ride I had all I could do to hang on to my seat. I held on with one hand, while the lines of the harness were in the other hand. I gripped the reins with all my strength, but with all my might I held on with my fingers through the holes of the seat on the rake. If I could help it, no bump was going to bounce me off. My greatest fear was of falling forward, then the rake would drag me along. That meant being rolled over and over in the hayfield, until the rake tripped again. That awful fear made me hold on for dear life!

Pete Swisher was on the platform by the haypress. He yelled, "RUNAWAY!" He had spotted my team coming. Dad was behind the baler, piling bales of hay, so he glanced around the bale pile to see. I was headed in his direction. Dad quickly jumped in front of my team—waving his arms.

These horses were running blind—not even seeing him. They were coming at full speed. Dad jumped out of the way, just in time. If he hadn't, they would have run over him.

Dad yelled.

My team galloped wildly across the field towards the road toward home. As we rushed by I was unable to hear what my Dad yelled. I was going too fast; the noise kept me from hearing him. Those teeth of the rake rattled across the rough field, then another clashing into the bottom of my seat would ring out. (Later I learned what Dad yelled: "Drop a line! Drop a line!" By that, he wanted me to pull on only one line to make them run in a circle, which would head them in the direction of our corn field. He felt the tall corn would stop them.)

As this runaway team raced on, my thoughts were also racing. Faster and faster my thoughts raced during the ride. Would I fall off? If we got on dirt road, the Old Grade, would I meet a car? Would a driver come over a hill and we hit each other head-on? Would the team run over the gate by the big corn crib? Would both horses try to go into the barn through the same door—at the same time? Who might get in the way? How would it all end?

But first, we had to get out of the hayfield. How would we go around the edge of the cornfield? Suddenly we were coming to the first curve, would we make it? Could we make it through the opening to the road since it was surrounded by all kinds of trees? Just as quickly, the team was going so fast they completely missed that opening. Missed by fifty, or more, as much as one hundred feet. They ran right into a lot of trees in the woods. Noise everywhere—one moment. CRASH! Everything became silent...still.

151

Only the horses were panting. I had fallen off the seat. In my fall, I dropped between the double trees and the front framework of the rake. The double tree against my stomach, while the steel frame was pressing against my back. Both horses stood among the trees trembling. Their whole bodies quivered! I spoke quietly, "Whoa...Whoa..." Quickly I slipped out from between my pinned position after the crash.

I walked near the one wheel, the one which hit a big tree. It was totally flat on one side.

I ran away from there, starting back towards the men baling. Dad met me, being the first one. Running up to him, "Dad, I'm all right!"

Dad, with a blank look, ran right by me. I followed him back to the runaway team and rake. He looked all around the mess. After a few moments, he spotted me. He was relieved.

Pete Swisher had jumped in the old truck, so he was the next one there. He shook his head when he saw I was okay. Later Pete said to me, "Billy, they ought to give you a medal the way you rode that thing." I didn't feel that way, for I was only hanging on for dear life!

Dad told me to take off part of the day. Then he gave other orders, "Go home, get the car, then go to Dick Morrow, ask if we can use his rake."

Dad then unhitched the team from the rake. Next the team was put on the mower, which was hard work. Hot, too. Dad gave strict instructions not to let them have any rest. A few hours later those sorrel horses were white. White with lather! Dad wanted them to get those runaway notions out of their heads.

So often I have thought of the Lord's sparing mercy. Honestly, I don't know why. It is one of those things a person can't explain. Only experience! I do know His Providential care was caring for even me. God had been so good. That very thought humbles me.

How can I say that? As a boy, and many times since those days, my Heavenly Father took care of me through such scary experiences. I know He had to take care of me. I thank Him, for all His goodness and grace.

Some years we could have high water in the marsh. It was hard work when we had to deal with a flood. We got stuck in the mud so often, especially once the water had gone down and we were anxious to get back in the fields again. Sometimes we got in too much of a hurry.

While we were trying to plow some soup-holes were a grief to us. Dad's tractor went down near the Hodge.

Only after unhitching the plow did we get it out. Dad pulled out of the hole, then wanted to back in, to hitch up to the plow again. Dad backed up. I was standing behind the tractor, in front of the plow. It was the spot I'd drop the plow hitch into the clevis. His tractor rolled back so quickly that it was almost on top of me before I could even think. It got away from Dad somehow. By the grace of God I made one fast move, getting me into the only safe place. Otherwise I certainly would have been crushed between the plow and the tractor. Dad and I were both very quiet. Again God was so good.

The fall after getting out of high school I did some custom work. This time we had some work of picking corn for farmers north of us.

Dad did run the picker for a few days; I did all the chores.

One morning he told me to go to Orin Bell's farm to pick corn. Before I left, Dad gave me special instructions on what he wanted me to do. Mainly it had to do with greasing the 22-B International cornpicker. On some shafts Dad wanted the grease fittings removed and put in the tool box. After I got the grease job finished, those zerks were placed in the box, as he instructed me. Those specific ones were his concern, being close to the operator. These were on the side delivery elevators of the two-row picker.

It was a frosty morning. White frost was all over the cornstalks. Neither was it clearing up very quickly that morning, which made the picking very difficult. While the going was slow, at least I did not have much left to pick. Only eighteen rows were left in the field. I had counted the rows before Howard Bell took the last two wagons to his farm, where he was unloading them. Since his farm was over a mile or more, he wouldn't be back very soon. It was no problem, for I had enough empty wagons to finish the field.

But those frosty stalks were causing all kinds of problems. They were not feeding through the rollers. Before I knew it, the machine was all plugged up on the right side.

Therefore I had to stop to clean it out. I idled the tractor down. The picker was still running. After getting off the mounted picker I reached under the rollers yanking at those broken off stalks. With a big yank, most of the time, the rollers would grab the stalks and feed them through. After some yanking I had cleaned out all the plugged stalks.

I got up, to crawl back on the picker. To do that, I stepped back on the wheel and tire, taking hold of the elevator as I pulled myself up. Once on top of the tire I would step over the elevator, onto the tractor seat. But I never got there, not that time.

As I was pulling myself up, I suddenly found myself slapped against the side of the elevator! My big sheepskin overcoat got caught on an outside grease fitting. A hole in my coat touched this tumbling shaft. This little hole, an inch or less, dropped with precise accuracy on top of this whirling zerk.

As the shaft turned, it wrapped my coat around it. It happened in a split-second, I hardly knew what was going on. Next, I heard the slip-clutch slipping. For a brief time the shaft stopped turning. But by then I could hardly breathe— my coat was so tight! While the clutch slipped, I tried to pull myself up enough to shut the tractor off. Only my fingernail could reach it. It slipped off. I tried again. I couldn't reach it. Just then, the clutch grabbed for one more turn. One more twist—then it slipped again. I couldn't breathe! I couldn't breathe! By then I was getting light-headed. I feared passing out.

How could I shut it off?

I was so close, fingertip close. I only needed a little more at my fingertip to shut it off. My cap! I grabbed for my black cap, folded it. Putting it over the end of my fingers— reached— pushed—the engine clicked a few more times. Turning over a couple more revolutions, then it died.

No longer was it tightening its grip on my coat. But what was I to do next? Howard, likely, would not be back for an hour. I was on top of the tractor tire, unable to get out of the grip of this suffocating monster.

Maybe I could wiggle out of my coat. So I moved around, only to end up off the tire. There I was, hanging in the air, alongside of the corn picker. My feet were at least a foot from the ground. There I hung.

However, I soon discovered I had gained a little freedom inside my straight-jacket. I wiggled all the more. I felt I must continue my struggle in order to get out of my straightjacket. I felt movement, then I fell to the ground.

Without my coat, I ran away from the cornpicker. Some distance away, I turned to look at the monster! I cried. I just stood in the middle of the field on a cold day crying hot tears. It was frightening.

I cried for fear, relief, joy, and pain. I knew I had to go back, right away. If I didn't I would not go back. So I slowly walked back. First I unwrapped my twisted sheepskin coat from the shaft. I put it on again. Even with it on, I shivered. Next I had to start the tractor again. It started. I crawled on. When the machinery started again, after I put it in gear, I was one little shrivelled up farmer. I was not going to get close to any moving part.

I finished the last rows without any more trouble. Really I did not have too many rounds to do. Once finished, that job was done.

There was even enough time for me to get home before noon. I asked Orin Bell to help me get my line of wagons hooked up behind the picker. I wanted to be on my way home.

No way! Orin was not going to let me go before I had dinner. I had to stay for dinner. Besides, he said, his wife had prepared a big meal that day. Adding another thing, he needed help, the electric company had brought out a light pole for a yard light. After dinner we had to put that pole up.

I was in no condition to help with that job. My back was killing me. It hurt. I was getting more stiff by the hour. But I didn't want to tell him what happened that morning in his field. (I never did tell him. Years later, I understand, he did find out.)

We had a delicious dinner cooked by Mrs. Bell.

After dinner Orin had that job for all of us. I was not much help in putting up his security light. More than anything, I went through the actions. While "we" got it up, I did very little.

In an hour or so I got on the road with my equipment, heading home.

Once I got home, I asked Mom to wash my sheepskin coat. It was very dirty, greasy—but I never explained it to Mom. I wanted to know where Dad was. He was out in the barn, according to Mom. That's where I found him doing the chores.

The first thing I did was tell him about getting caught in the picker. The first question asked, "Why didn't you remove those zerks?" I did, I told him, just like he told me. Then I explained how it was an outside fitting which caught my clothing. Dad stared, without saying anything. Then Dad told me his story, he got caught earlier in the week. (Neither did he tell anybody, until that moment.) It ripped his old army coat right off his back! Dad was standing up running the machine when a gust of wind blew the tail of his coat towards the shaft. It got caught! Dad braced himself as it tugged away, only the sleeves of the coat were left on his arms. The rest of his old World War I army coat was wrapped tightly around the inside shaft on the side-delivery elevator.

That's why Dad would not go back to finish the job. Instead he sent me.

While I have had back problems from that experience for years, off and on, God did graciously spare my life. I'm thankful to Him.

Across the Hobbs Ditch, to the east of our farm, Harris Sampson was caught in his picker that same year. However, his was a pull-type picker. His brother had warned him about not having a guard-shield in place. Still he did not replace it. When Harris got caught in the power-take-off shaft, it stripped all the clothes off him. That was the way he came walking up to his crib, where his hired man, Harry, was unloading corn. The injured man had only his socks, shoes and cap on. He was naked. A large ball of clothing was wrapped around that shaft. Later I saw Dad take the clothes off the shaft.

Dad and I went to see for ourselves. We crossed the ice on the Hobbs Ditch between our farms. We found the spot where Harris fought for his life. It was almost unbelievable, but we saw it with our own eyes. Harris had stomped down frozen earth in the corn field some six to eight inches. He was fighting for his life! His struggle was to keep out of that death trap. He won.

Yet our neighbor still lost. His internal injuries, eventually, proved too much to fight off. Later complications took his life.

Working on a farm can be very dangerous at times. If a farmer drops his guard for even a moment, it can end in a tragedy. Nobody knows what it is like to fight for your life when caught in some farm equipment. Only one knows, the one who was caught in such a life/death struggle! Nobody else can even begin to imagine the horror of what it is like. When spared, however, that same individual can be deeply grateful to God, like no other person.

Fun with firecrackers can turn into a frightening experience for a boy. It did for me. When I was a boy it was legal to have firecrackers in Indiana.

Each kid got a quota, when divided in our family. Of course, the size made a difference. Ladycrackers were little ones. Hundreds were in each package. Naturally they only made a small pop when they exploded. Sometimes I could light a whole string at once. One explosion after another was then heard: pop! pop! pop! pop!

They were rather safe for kids. It was not too likely a child could get injured with one of them. Still each one had to be careful.

The next size was about as big around as a lead pencil in size. Such a firecracker was about an inch long, maybe a little more. The explosion was bigger. When the fuse was lit it began to spit sparks—throw it! Get rid of it at once. *Now!*

Every now and then, a kid would hold it too long. Bang! That hurt! It caused an awful sting to the finger and thumb. The skin would feel so tight. A throbbing sensation could be felt for hours afterwards. I had it happen to me a couple of times.

As boys we liked to put a firecracker under a tin can, then light the fuse. When it went off the tin can went flying in the air. For us it was fun to see how high it would go. Sometimes even larger firecrackers were bought. Those were powerful! But since they cost quite a bit, few were bought. If we had these, it meant we had to be very, very careful. This kind had a big BANG!

I would bury the pencil size in the sand. I would dig a small hole, place the firecracker in it, then cover it with a small pile of sand. Only the end of the fuse would be sticking out. I would light it, run, and wait for it to explode! It would blow the sand away, leaving a little hole in the ground.

One day we were expecting company. That day we were going to have fun with firecrackers. I buried one in the sand, behind the old summer kitchen. I lit the fuse; it spit a little. Nothing happened. I waited a little longer. Nothing. So I decided to dig the firecracker out of the sand. Carefully I began to brush away the sand—BANG! It exploded—right in my face. Sand was blown into my eyes. The pain was awful.

I couldn't see! I couldn't see anything—even with my eyes opened. My eyes stung. They burned. I tried to see again—everything was hazy. Oh, did it ever hurt! I was so afraid, kneeling in the sand. Crying, I thought I might not see again, would I be blind?

I cried. Seeing a little, I got into the house. They tried to wash them out. I tried to look in a mirror, both eyes were terribly bloodshot.

The longer they bothered, the more fear I had. I talked about how much it hurt, but never said anything about my real fears. The thought of going blind was kept to myself.

Even though I was excited about having company, I did not enjoy the rest of the day. I traded off the rest of my firecrackers for some of those little ladycrackers. I had enough of those miserable fun-makers.

Even though we were very careful, injuries still happened. Really, I had waited a reasonable length of time before I checked out that buried firecracker. Yet there was the smallest of spark in the fuse which set it off. That took all the excitement out of playing with fireworks.

After several days my eyes began to improve. I was so thankful I could still see. I realized fireworks could be extremely dangerous. It is much safer for kids to leave them alone.

Sparklers were fun. So were our cap guns. Yet large firecrackers under a can, much worse, under a bottle, could cause severe injuries. All the children's excitement and fun can turn pleasure into pain with one powerful explosion! More than just a firecracker blows up then.

I enjoy fireworks at a big celebration, exploding into showers of beautiful colored sparks in the sky. I still like a big BOOM! But I'll let professional people handle all those fireworks. That's less scary, much safer.

As a boy I was fascinated by the Indian motorcycle the Evers boys had. They would really roll out of town on their Indian.

One story was that one took off so fast he unseated his brother. He slipped the seat right from under him. The one brother ended up sitting on the road.

After World War II we talked about getting a motorcycle. To do that we went up north to buy a Harley-Davidson. The cost was somewhere between $600 and $700. It was a small one compared to the bigger bikes, only a 45, as compared to a 74. Dad, Paul and I all had a share in it.

I used it a few times to go to the First Reformed Church for midweek meetings. Also for a night out I'd go to De Motte or Hebron. Paul used it to go to work one summer. In the fall, as I recall, it got pretty chilly some nights on our motorcycle.

Later Paul traded it. He bought a bigger one, which was a 74 Harley-Davidson. While the first one we had could be compared to a small car, not having too much get up and go.

The second one was more like a high-powered car with a big engine, which could take off and move.

One ride I'll never forget was the one of June 22, 1947. Sunday. In fact, it was the week of our wedding.

Paul had taken it for a ride. When he came back, I wanted to take a spin. I had finished the morning chores, so I had some spare time before getting ready for an afternoon church service. I was dressed in an army coverall. Dad and Mom were in church, attending the morning service.

After Paul parked it, I got on it. I rode off the yard, headed for the main road, Highway 53. What I didn't know was the adjustment Paul made on the front end, which made it a little easier to ride on our dirt roads. Once on the highway, as I crossed the tar ribs on the pavement, I noticed it had far more bounce than ever before.

The road was busy with Sunday traffic. I got behind one car and couldn't pass. Every time I'd check, if it were safe to pass, more oncoming traffic prevented it. I'd let up, pull in behind the car again. Again and again I tried to pass.

By the time I got to the Kankakee River bridge I still didn't have a chance to pass, nor could I pass by Ted Hanaway's place, north of the bridge. Finally, near Bert Hanaway's place, I had a chance to pass, nothing was coming. I rolled open the throttle. Wide open! The big Harley-Davidson roared down the highway. With plenty of speed, I was passing Gabe Musch and his family. They were coming from church at First De Motte.

As I glanced down, I remember seeing 65 mph as I reached his front fender. Instantly I heard squeals from my front tire. I had a speed-wobble! It was shaking the daylights out of me. The sway was causing me to lose it!

Gabe slowed, pulled over to the cabled-fence along the highway. I tried to hold on! With all my strength I grasped the handlebars. I tried to pull it out of the wobble. It shook so violently things began to blur, even the large billboard next to the road! Flashing through my mind: "You'll never see a wedding this week!"

160

Just as quickly the motorcycle went from under me— I landed in the middle of the pavement. I was sliding, skidding over the cement, across the passing lane. On the edge of the road I skidded through the gravel. Finally I stopped sliding. My body was lying still. I was lying under the cables next to a ditch. My cap was gone. One shoe was missing.

The motorcycle slid farther down the road. It spun on its side—in a circle! It roared. Belched smoke. Then it died. It lay quietly next to the big tree by Dick Morrow's pig lot.

Gabe was outside his car, hanging on his open car door. His wife and girls were crying in the car.

I got up, looked around. My shoe was spotted down the bank, next to the water in the ditch. Scampering down the bank I got it back, putting it on my foot. I limped down the highway to where my cap was lying on the center white line.

By that time, I felt pain. I had hurts everywhere. My skinned spots were smarting.

I managed to get back to Gabe's car. His whole body was shaking. He hung on the door as we talked. Gabe asked what he could do for me. I told him he could help me pick up the bike. However, he was so shook up, I had it up before he could walk over to me. I sat straddle of it, ready to kick it, to get it started again. Gabe grabbed the handlebars, pleaded with me to leave it. They would take me home.

I protested his plan. I told him I had to get it back home. His next plea was that I would not go fast, "Bill, promise me!" I told him he didn't have to have a promise, for I was not going to go fast. Period.

(Later I heard, in the afternoon, Gabe had a spell. He was that bothered by what had happened. Mrs. Musch told me, over 46 years later, she was reminded of it every time she saw a motorcycle on the road. She never wanted to get close to one while going down the highway. Some time after that Sunday, I also learned, the Morrows heard and saw what happened. Dick told his wife he was not going out here. Their son Merrit had been hit by a car on the same road a few months earlier. After such a traumatic family experience he could not take another. Besides, he told his wife, that fellow would not be

161

living after that. Dick later found out I was the one who had been injured. Then he felt bad he didn't come and offer help. Dick felt sorry about it, but he explained why he felt the way he did. I told him I understood.)

I rode the bike slowly home. I was hurting.

I had holes in my coveralls. When I got home I asked Lois and Marty to help me. Someone got water in the bathtub. Lois gave me black coffee to drink as I sat in the tub.

The gravel scraped some "hide" off. One bad spot was on my right hip. All the sliding on the cement went through those layers of material on the pocket of my coveralls.

Even with my injuries, I still went to church that afternoon. How I felt, that was something else. I told some it felt like somebody took a softball bat and hit me on both knees. I was hurting everywhere. Some of my injuries seeped out some fluids.

Later I had to go to my doctor for my hip. He gave me the ugliest black medication. The stuff stained my clothes. Finally I had to use a rubber tire off a toy to protect my sore. It kept my belt from rubbing the scab. Eventually it healed.

(Yet as I write this more than 46 years later, I still have trouble with this tender spot of skin. Winter months are the worst, then it is constantly irritated by my belt or shorts.)

Almost daily, I still have a constant reminder of what happened one Sunday in June. I did, by the kind Providence of my Heavenly Father, see our wedding day that week.

Stranger still, during the wedding ceremony at First De Motte, a few motorcycles stopped at the crossroads by church, then roared off. That evening I had to have a reminder.

Thinking back over this story, God must want me to remember His grace. Recall how busy I said the traffic was that Sunday morning? I couldn't find a place to pass for a couple of miles. When I could pass, only Gabe Musch's car was on the road. No other car came down Highway 53 for ten minutes, at least that long.

That, I believe, was due to God's Providence, not by chance. My Father in Heaven must be given the credit and

162

glory for directing traffic during those minutes on Sunday morning. Praise His Name!

After that happened to me I had very little desire to get on a motorcycle again. I know, I did ride it home. I did not get back on it again, except when Dad asked me to get it out of the field. Dad rode it out into a field one day, but had trouble turning around on the edge of plowed ground. Once the engine died, Dad simply walked away from it. I got it out of the field for him.

One other time I got on it. Marty asked me to go for a little ride with him. Frankly I was very skeptical. But he promised me not to go fast. So I crawled on behind him. Together we rode off the yard by the folks. Just passed the back driveway he opened it up!

Old fears swept over me—instantly. I made some excuse, getting him to stop. Once he almost stopped, I planted my feet on the ground, so the bike went from under me. Once I was off, he completely stopped.

Marty wanted me to get back on, again he promised not to go fast. I told him to forget it—I'd walk. I did.

That was my last ride.

The Day De Motte Burned

I was in the fifth grade when we had the big fire in De Motte. Our classroom was on the southside of the school. Mrs. Wolff was across the hallway with her class. She came knocking excitedly on our door. Quickly she told us about the fire. With that she invited our class to come to her room, "You better come to our room. The whole town is on fire!" Our class was shocked.

It was Wednesday, April 15, 1936, near the end of the school day. Wisely they kept us in school a little longer that day. It was the safest thing to do. None of the students living in town were allowed to go near the fire.

As we went across the hall, the first things we saw were flames leaping high into the sky. Black clouds of smoke rolled and tossed upwards. Out the school windows we could see most of downtown was on fire.

There was no official cause known as to how the fire got started. One report suggested it may have been caused by a large trash fire which spread when it became quite windy. Another cause suggested a spark from a train started the fire.

De Motte did not have a fire department. There was a pump in front of Cheever's Garage, so they formed some kind of bucket brigade. Other fire departments came from nearby towns in response to the alarm. However, they had no water with which to put out the flames. Tanks had to be filled from ditches, then the units hurried back to the fire. They fought a losing battle with the raging fire.

Every now and then trucks and pickups would be parked on school property. Merchandise and equipment taken out of stores and business places had been loaded on trucks, then parked away from the fire.

Little did I realize it, but Dad was there with his truck. He had gone to town with Marty in the Dodge truck. Marty was four years old.

Dad first backed up to Osting's Store. Herman wanted Dad to take a load of shoes out of the store. They were getting ready to load when flames came leaping over the edge of the roof. It was like a big angry red-orange flag waving over the front of the store. Flames were over Dad's truck. The heat was very intense. That did it for my Dad, so he jumped back into the truck and drove away. From there Dad drove around the northend of the business district, where he stopped at Konovsky's Lumber Yard. Men quickly loaded our truck with window frames, doors, lumber, and roofing materials. Once loaded, Dad immediately drove away from that part of town, away from the fire.

Later Dad came home with his load. He parked it in the big corn crib. After a few days, he took it back, when they had a place to store it again.

Since we were home from school, we watched Dad go in the crib. All of us were talking about the fire. Dad had his story. We had all kinds of questions.

But Mom had one more for Dad, "Where's Marty?"

He wasn't home, that was for sure!

Dad then remembered he had Marty with him in the truck in front of Osting's Store—even when he went to the lumber yard. But after that? Marty was gone!

Later we found out where he had gone. Evidently frightened by the fire, the four year old got out of the truck. He ran to the westside of De Motte. (That meant he was running away from the fire.) As he was running down a street he was spotted by two women. They got to talking about that little boy. Within a few moments it dawned upon them that he looked like one of Mart and Sena's children. They decided to take him to some of our relatives. First they took him to Uncle Dick Tysen's home, from there he was taken to Uncle Ben's. Finally they got him home again.

The fire was terrible. Many of us were frightened by that destructive fire. It left De Motte in rubble. There were three homes and a total of 14 businesses destroyed. Some of those who lost places were: Konovskys, Swarts, DeKocks, De Youngs, Ostings, Starkeys, and others.

All kinds of stories were told afterwards. Many I thought, as a kid, were so interesting.

I saw a pickup with the front end up in the air, while the tailgate almost touched the street. It was a wonder the tires did not blow out or the springs break. A marbletop soda fountain was in the back. And it was heavy! That long fountain hung way over the tailgate.

One of our teachers told us that two men loaded it from Curtain's Cafe. Two very excited men carried it out during the fire. Later they had to put it back in the cafe. Then they had a hard time getting enough men around the fountain to carry it in. I thought they said some 14 or 15 men lugged it back in the restaurant.

Business places started sharing space after the fire. A few old unused buildings were cleaned up for a temporary business. They did this until the downtown could be rebuilt.

There was one more story, I recall. One man, a total stranger, came to town with a truck. He offered to help. They worked furiously to load it. Some person told him how to get to the school yard, where he could park.

Since he was a stranger they wondered if he understood the directions, so they watched as he drove south.

However, as the people watched—to their surprise and horror the man drove by the school yard. In fact, he kept right on going, around the curve, completely out of town.

He never returned. He proved to be one without morals, willing to profit from the great loss of others. Such people took advantage of those who needed his help most. The stranger didn't gain that much. Being a thief he made a little gain from what was stolen, but for how long?

As God is just, there will be payday—someday!

The Bible truthfully tells of fire with that judgment, too.

166

School Days

The first day of school will always be in my memory. Engraved on my memory was Billy standing in front of Mrs. Rapp.

According to a note in my school record is the date: September 6, 1931. Neil took me to the bus and brought me to my room. Neil Tysen was my older cousin. He was fif-

One of my ear-liest school pictures.

My first teacher, Mrs. Rapp.

teen when I was in first grade. During the summer he worked on our farm, so my folks had him stay on for a few weeks when school started in the fall. Mom and Dad wanted him to take care of me during those first days.

I sat with him on the bus. When we got to the De Motte School Neil took me to my first grade room. Mrs. Rapp was waiting for her new pupils who would be starting school that year. Neil introduced me to her, giving my name Billy.

I remember looking up at her. It was so interesting, as she talked to me. She had my complete attention. Just looking at her helped, for I was away from home. Yet fear was in my heart, I was afraid. About that time I decided to get some assurance from my big cousin, so I turned around to look at him. Neil was gone!

I raced out of the room, into the hallway. Right outside the door was the stairs to the high school. Out of the corner of my eye I spotted Neil running up the stairs. In a hurry, he was taking the steps two at a time. Just as quickly, he was almost out of sight, I saw his legs vanish out of sight.

I was alone! I trusted Neil; he deserted me. A funny feeling hit my stomach. Mrs. Rapp did all she could to get me settled in my room and at my desk.

My teacher did settle some fears. Yet the *first* day will always be part of my memory. While that fear left, then I had another one. That one had to do with the *last* day of school each year, would I pass? But I still get constant flashbacks of those early days. To this day the smell of new crayons, chalks, books and paper, all those things flood me with old memories. The smell can cause that same old feeling to go through me. In an instant, I can be back there again, even though it is over sixty years later.

I think I had Mrs. Rapp for my second grade, too. For my first few years we had two grades in one room.

When I entered third grade I moved across the hall. It was the room next to the school offices. Our school principal had his office there. Mr. William M. May was our principal. Naturally, older boys had scary stories about being sent to his office. Mr. May had a big paddle to punish the bad boys. I didn't want to get into trouble and visit that place. I liked my new teacher, Miss Angie De Haan. I had her for the next two years.

I remember Miss Angie, as we called her. To me as a boy, Miss Angie was so pretty. She was the one who came to celebrate my eighth birthday. I talked about it at home, where Mom tried to prepare me for her not coming. Mom didn't want me to be disappointed. Yet I still invited my teacher. She said she would, so excitedly I told Mom my teacher was coming over for birthday cake. Still not wanting me to be disappointed, Mom mentioned that likely Miss Angie would not be coming. After supper I kept looking out the window—she would be there. I trusted my teacher. She gave me a promise. Soon I saw the car lights come up our hill, my teacher did come. She didn't disappoint me. Coming along was her sister.

Oh boy, I was really proud. I sat as close to her as I could. Most of the time we sat around the kitchen table. Together we had cake and tea. Before they left, they told us they had such a nice time visiting. Miss Angie mentioned she was so glad Billy invited her.

Since I stayed in the same room for my fourth grade, I again had Miss Angie for my teacher.

A few experiences of that year really stand out. The first had to do with speeches which had to be given in front of our class. While I remember being in front of the class, I can't remember my first speech. However, I do remember the one Jeanette Armstrong gave. Jeanette lived about a half a mile north of our farm. She came from a large, poor family. Jeanette was so shy. While she stood in front of our class she fussed with her stockings. Girls wore stockings over their knees. An elastic garter would hold them up. Generally that worked, unless the elastic got weak. If the garter was old, then the stockings would sag. Girls would have to keep pulling them up, fixing the garter to hold them in place. Whenever a girl was nervous, she would tug at her stockings and garters.

This shy girl had such a hard time in front of our class. Being extremely nervous she forgot what she wanted to say, that's when Jeanette would lift up her dress and pull up on her stockings. Over and over she did this. Her time in front of the class was so hard on her. Our class felt for her, too. But we all felt so bad because Miss Angie scolded her afterwards. She was corrected for repeatedly lifting up her dress and tugging at her stockings. Nice girls, she was told, were not supposed to do such a thing in front of the class.

It was an awful experience. Once Jeanette got started, the poor girl couldn't stop herself. Forgetting her speech she had to do something. She tired so hard, but couldn't help herself. I was sorry that she had to be reminded of what she did wrong. The girl blushed, and dropped her head, when scolded. While it felt like a horrible day for me, certainly it must have been far worse for my little neighbor friend.

Another thing I remember happened in English class. Miss Angie wanted to teach us to drop the word "ain't" from our vocabulary. We'd work at it every day during our English lessons.

She tore off the cardboard back of our yellow paper tablet. In the upper two corners holes were punched, with white string threaded through each hole and knotted. We hung this

169

cardboard around our necks. Miss Angie demonstrated how it would work. If a student said, "Ain't!"—whoever heard it first would punch a hole through the cardboard. Our teacher jabbed a hole with a pencil. The scar was the bad mark for saying the bad word "ain't." But now Miss Angie had a hole in her card! She reached into her desk for a sticker, a bright red circle which she used to cover her bad mark. During each class she would wear her card with the red circle.

Each day we had a class time for wearing our cards. Soon holes were showing up. That bad word was repeatedly spoken in class. Each time it was heard some student got up to poke another hole. Another bad mark on somebody's card.

A few of us had none. We watched ourselves very carefully. Others slipped. They got caught. Holes were jabbed again and again. One of my friends, Charles Rathburn, got caught a lot of times. Naturally it bothered him. Poor Chuck was frustrated as day after day he got poke after poke.

Chuck talked a lot in class. It wasn't long before he got his first poke. He said it again, another poke. Again, another one. That was a very bad day for him. Soon he was caught a couple more times. More holes. It was too much! Chuck lost it!

Chuck looked up, slightly cross-eyed, then said in utter frustration: "AIN'T!" Naturally some kid quickly poked his card one more time. After that totally losing it: "AIN'T! AIN'T! AIN'T! AIN'T! AIN'T! AIN'T! AIN'T! AIN'T! AIN'T!" Can't say when he quit. Soon he was silent.

Soon classmates were surrounding Chuck—punching more holes all over his card. Chuck's card looked like it got hit with big buckshot from a gun. Holes everywhere!

For a few moments it was very quiet. Afterwards the tension broke. The whole class broke out in laughter. Even Chuck had to laugh about it.

As I remember it, I slipped once, but nobody caught it. So my card didn't have a hole in it. To this day, that word: "AIN'T!" sticks out like a sore thumb whenever I hear people use it.

One more thing is remembered about my fourth grade year in school, I took notice of girls! Several of us got into some serious romances. A few of us fellows in my grade fell for girls in the third grade.

We played together at recess time. We paired off, spending our time as couples. But we felt that we didn't have enough time together. At night we'd write notes at home, then pass them around the next day. Couples were doing this together, one writing to another couple. We would pass our notes early the next morning as we played by the giant strides.

After gathering together, we passed these notes after getting off the bus. Shortly the bell rang; we had to run. All of us stuck the notes in our pockets and went to our rooms.

Our classroom was near the giant strides. Miss Angie was able to see us out the window of our room. We didn't know it, but she was watching one of our early-morning exchanges.

That particular morning, once we got to our seats, Miss Angie spoke to me, "Billy, where is the note you got?"

Her question startled me. Suddenly I felt so warm. Out of fear I immediately confessed it was in my jacket in the hall. I was told to get it. Then the others were instructed to get their notes out of the hallway.

I got mine. Once I was back in the room, my teacher told me to give it to her. It was awful. My fear was she would read it aloud to the whole class. If she would have, I would have died! She gathered up all the notes. Then we were firmly instructed not to pass notes!

Our confiscated notes were never mentioned. Nothing more was ever said to us.

It scared me enough that I didn't pass another note in school, until I got in the eighth grade.

It didn't stop our romances. We still got together as couples at recess time. Before the year was over, in the spring, we got pretty serious. We decided to get married.

Our big wedding was held during the noon hour. It took place by the northeast corner of the old schoolhouse. In the corner of the building was a good hideout. No teacher could spot us there. It was a perfect place to have our big wedding.

Alice Hamstra and I decided to get married. She was in third grade; I was in the fourth. We didn't bother to get our parents' consent. Nor were we finished with our education. We decided to go through with it.

Lois Lageveen was the preacher who performed the ceremony. Some of our friends were our witnesses.

Other kids may not have been interested in girl-boy relationship, but we were. We talked to others about being married. In fact we did a lot of bragging to the other kids. Our puppy love romance had taken us to the altar—we really got married!

Another emotional experience happened while Miss Angie was my teacher. It was about the time of Holy Week. She read from the Bible about the Crucifixion and Easter story.

Part of the Gospel she read dealt with Jesus before Pilate. Pilate gave the choice of Barabbas or Jesus. Then the crowd cried out with one voice, "Away with this man! Release Barabbas to us!"

Pilate was cornered. Wanting to release Jesus, he made an appeal to the people again. But they cruelly cried, "Crucify Him! Crucify Him!"

Echoes of that cry was to be heard for days around our school. The first time was after hearing the story. We were going to our buses that day. We went out the front of the school building.

One boy started screaming as he ran down the steps. Shouting his cry, we heard, "Crucify Him! Crucify Him!" Again he repeated it.

All of us stopped walking, turned to look at him. Stunned, we couldn't believe what was happening. Waving his arms in the air, he cried again, "Crucify Him! Crucify Him!" Most of us stood in silence in front of school, while our classmate continued this frenzy. He was still screaming when we got on the bus. Yet we could still hear the echoes of his cry.

As a boy, I felt sorry for Jesus. Even more, I felt sorry for my classmate, too. Why would he do this? A few of us tried to talk to him in the next few days, telling him it wasn't nice to do that.

Once or twice, he totally ignored us. He would start to run, wave his arms, cry out, "Crucify Him! Crucify Him!" It was

172

like the boy was possessed. I was haunted by his demands for Jesus to be crucified again.

After all these years, when those passages of Scripture are read I can almost hear the cries of my boyhood classmate. It goes through my whole being. Tears come to my eyes.

I don't think I'll ever be able to explain what possessed that boy to do it. Yet this may be a solemn reminder that all of us were there when they crucified Jesus on Good Friday! We were there!

And likely, we, too, would have cried with the cruel crowds for His crucifixion! We'd be no different. Yes, we were there!

My fifth grade teacher was Mrs. Fern Bauman. For me she was one of the greatest teachers. I really liked her.

I can remember the "coldest" and "hottest" experiences while in her class.

One afternoon the temperature unexpectantly dropped to -24°. It caught everybody off guard. That far below zero in Indiana, with fierce winds, meant conditions were serious. School had to be dismissed early that day. Since the sudden change was not expected, many of us were not dressed for such bad weather. Those of us from the country could be in trouble if buses could not get us home.

Mrs. Bauman asked each of us to show what kind of coats and gloves we had to wear. I remember I didn't have heavy clothes along that day. Other students didn't have enough to wear either. Our teacher called her husband. He ran the feed-mill in town. She asked him to get all the extra coats, jackets, pants, shirts, etc. around their house, just empty the closets of anything they could spare. Go to the basement too, he was told, more clothes could be found there. But before he brought them, he was told to make another stop, at Marie Osting's Store for large safety pins.

It wasn't long before he brought everything he gathered. Personally each of us was bundled up, pinned up, before we got on the bus that frigid afternoon in 1936.

I had on a big man's jacket, but it kept me very warm.

It was cold! I checked the temperature before going to the barn— -24° below zero! We were in for a terribly cold night. The cattle were given extra straw to help keep them a little warm for the night. I know that made me feel good to be able to do that for them.

Also we had to get in plenty of wood for the night. All our stoves would have to be fired through the entire night.

Now for the hottest time. That was in April of 1936, the day De Motte burned. Most of downtown burned with that fire.

We watched from Mrs. Wolff's room. Our class joined the sixth grade, after she excitedly announced, "You better come to our room. The whole town is on fire!"

Main street from the Coffee Shop to the Lumber Yard burned, plus a few places on the other side of the street. Three homes and fourteen business places were destroyed by the fire. As those flames leaped into the air, we witnessed a very hot fire.

Mrs. Bauman would have us exercise in class. We would stand in the aisle, beside our desks. Most of them were not that bad, except bending over to touch our toes. Not that it was hard to touch my toes, that wasn't it. It was okay, except when the girl in front of me didn't change her bloomers for almost a week. Touching my toes on those days—bothered me! Indeed it was time for a change—to another exercise.

The next year I went across the hall, where Mrs. Wolff was my sixth grade teacher. Naturally kids had a lot of things to say about her name—Wolff.

I thought she was a good teacher, except for the time she would not give me my report card.

At the end of a school day, we had tea time when we got home. Dad would be sitting at his usual place, at the end of the table. When we got our report cards, we all gathered around him. One by one the report cards were shown to him. He'd comment; after which he'd sign them.

I went by the cabinet in the kitchen, for nothing better to do, looking out the window. I didn't have a report card to show Dad anyway. Mrs. Wolff did not give me mine for that grading period.

One assignment we had that month was to paint a picture. It had to be done with water colors. That's when I discovered how few talents I had as an artist. Very, very few. My biggest problem was using too much water. Colors ran all directions. My paper was waterlogged! The surface of the paper was more like a small lake—waves everywhere. Each day I tried a little more. I was not making any headway in getting it finished. Until finished, Mrs. Wolff told all of us budding painters, there would be no report cards. So I didn't have one to show Dad .

Dad looked over all the others. Looking in my direction, I was pointedly asked, "Willie, where's yours?"

Defensively I sputtered, "Oh, that old lady Wolff..." No chance was given for me to say anything more.

Dad quickly interrupted me, "Hey, hey, I am on your teacher's side!" (That was it—two against one.) Again he asked about my report card.

I told him about my unmastered unfinished painting. Dad showed little understanding, water colors or not. He just told me to get busy and get my card.

Further, he told me to get busy by changing my clothes and get outside to do my chores.

I got out of there in a hurry. My clothes changed, immediately I walked over to the woodpile to chop wood. By then I was feeling pretty sorry for myself. So I decided to talk to myself.

While chopping wood, I swung the ax each time in frustration. With each swing I told somebody what I thought. I had something to say to my teacher—chop! The chunk flew apart. More said—chop! More wood went flying. Next, I had a big heater chunk to split. Time to tell Dad off. I had my say— chop! That one split in two. This big conversation was going on for some time—talking aloud to myself about Dad. Split wood went in all directions. My frustrations were exploding!

I had quite a talk with myself. Or did I?

For some reason I turned. There was my Dad right behind me. One hand holding a small branch on a maple tree; the other resting on his hip. He had been listening!

To this day, I swear, I came off the ground several inches. I know I left the ground. Dad had heard it all. I stood stunned. Dad looked at me. What was going to happen now? I didn't dare ask that aloud. Dad waved his hand, firmly saying, "Get busy!"

I did!

After that, if I still had to talk with myself, I would, but very quietly.

Also, I got busy in school, in a few days I had my painting finished. Mrs. Wolff gave me my report card, which I took home to show to Dad.

(Mrs. Wolff was really a nice teacher. One who was so understanding, especially since that year I had so many boils. By then I was on my teacher's side, too, with Dad!)

Dale Schwanke was my best friend. Dale and I both got Eversharp pencils as Christmas gifts. Dale liked mine better than his. I felt mine was the nicest pencil.

Mine had a cap over the eraser. One habit I got into was to remove it, suck on it. I'd get it to stick to my tongue. With my mouth open, I'd wiggle it around. It became a bad habit. Once, however, I almost swallowed it.

Dale kept looking at my pencil. One day he asked if I'd trade. Even though his was not as nice, compared to mine, maybe I should get rid of mine. After all, I might accidently swallow the cap. Also, I'd rid myself of the habit of sucking on the cap. We traded.

Dale was in a desk across the aisle from mine. Sure enough, one day Dale had that cap on the end of his tongue. Later, I looked at him, only to see Dale's Adam's apple make a big move. He turned white. Dale did! He swallowed that dumb cap!

I can still see him raise his hand. Mrs. Wolff asked what he wanted. Holding up his new pencil, Dale explained, "I swallowed the top off this."

She came to his desk, trying to find out if he had bread in his lunch. He did, in the back of the room. They got his lunch. Dale ate early that day. Mrs. Wolff helped him pull all the crusts off his bread. He gulped them down.

Next she gave instructions to Dale, saying he had to tell his parents. They were to watch for the evidence in a few days.

Later Dale and I laughed about what happened. (I thought: That could have been me!)

I'm glad we made a trade, otherwise, sooner or later, I would have swallowed the evidence.

I had a couple of very embarrassing moments in school. The first one, which stands out, was while I was in the seventh grade. It happened in music class. Our seating arrangement was to have girls in the front row and boys in the back. Alice Sytsma was directly in front of me that day. Her dress was white, with some red dots, with a long belt. The belt made a huge bow, with long tails hanging out the back of her chair.

I put my foot on her chair, which bothered Alice. I pressed my toe against her belt, as it hung down. Alice tried to change her position, only to find out she could not move. Trying to reach back, she pushed at my foot, wanting me to move it. I didn't. Frustrated, she turned around looking at me, but I still would not take my shoe away.

Of course, by that time, the teacher noticed something was going on. A few glances came our way, but nothing was done by the teacher.

Finally Alice felt she had to move, so she gestured for me to get my foot away. That time the teacher asked what was going on over there.

Alice told on me. She said I had my foot on the belt of her dress, and I wouldn't take my foot away.

At that point the teacher took action, saying, "Since Bill doesn't know how to behave he will have to leave the class." Further, I was told to please go back to the main assembly hall. I could go there to do other school work.

I felt so humiliated for being kicked out of class. Most embarrassing for me was to have it happen in front of girls! Guys would understand, I thought.

But I had no idea what would be done by the teacher in charge of the assembly hall. So I did not report in, I simply went straight to my desk to study. Hoping, of course, I would not be asked why I was there.

However, I was very uneasy about it. Several times I got up to sharpen my pencils. Then I'd go back to my desk again. I found it hard to study.

One of the older students across the aisle asked why I was there. Putting on a front, I bragged about getting kicked out of class.

While I tried to act big, I felt so rotten inside. Alice felt bad about it, for she came up to talk about it after school. But the whole thing was my own fault, I had it coming.

Maybe I learned far more that day than I would have if I stayed in music class. Without question, this was the best lesson for me.

About the same time, we had our math class in the main assembly. Our class sat in the front rows, near the blackboard. Mr. May was our teacher. Each day, right after lunch, we had this class.

My seat was in the middle of the front row; girls were seated on both sides of me.

One day I glanced down to discover my fly was open! My pants had buttons, but the buttonholes were too big from wear. I glanced both ways, checked to see if the girls near me were looking, quickly I buttoned my fly. Next, better check it out—so I tugged on the front of my pants. It popped open!

Over and over I'd try again. I was not getting it buttoned properly, so the fly would pop open every time.

Off and on, through the entire math class, I did my best to get my fly closed. Each time, I only found my pants wide open in front!

Finally, the bell rang, quickly I put my notebook in front of me and headed for the restrooms. It was so embarrassing to me. I made sure of two things: my pants were buttoned prop-

178

erly and my fly was closed. It was—so I headed for my next class.

Was I ever glad when they put zippers on our pants!

That was a whole new day for boys.

With zippers, it was less likely to have the fly open. Nor could ornery guys rip it open, then laugh, saying, "Hey, your fly is open!" But we didn't have to worry about losing a button, then be in big trouble for the day.

I was very happy to have my first pants with a zipper.

Another embarrassing moment happened when I was in the eighth grade. Another Alice. This one was Alice Hamstra, a seventh grader. She was the one I married four years before. Alice and I were together again.

Earlier we got into trouble with writing notes. But then we got started writing letters to each other. Sometime during the day we'd manage to exchange our letters. One of us would walk near the other's desk, drop our letter. The other one would bend over and pick it up off the floor.

During this same time Art Walstra, my cousin, was dating her sister, Gertie. Art and Gertie were engaged to be married. Alice had been spying on them, watching them necking on their davenport.

Anyway she mentioned some of her spy information in her letters. In this letter to me she told that she was only able to hug her pillow when she got to bed at night. She also commented on my blue eyes. When I made eyes at her, that got to her.

This all comes back to me, on this embarrassing day I did not get her letter *first*.

As she made her drop, I was not aware another guy watched us making our exchange. He knew our pattern. Big Sam Kingma, who was in her grade, jumped out of his desk, dashed down the aisle, swooped down to grab the letter. Sam had it before I had a chance to pick it up off the floor.

Terrible! It was awful. (Even though we tried to throw people off by having pen names. Bill = Melvin; Alice = Betty. Now these guys broke the code with this specific letter.)

When the bell rang, big Sam ran out of the assembly waving the letter. On his way down the stairs he gathered other guys, who ran after him. He bragged and blabbed about Bill's letter from Alice!

Running after him, I tried helplessly to get it back. I fought. I punched. They pushed me back. I was outnumbered. Sam, being protected by the fellows, continued to read my letter aloud. Everybody around him could hear him. Special parts were read over and over for emphasis. Especially about hugging her pillow and my making eyes at her. "Betty" told how she felt! Naturally they knew me as "Melvin."

They had a big time at my expense. Those seventh grade guys teased and teased. It was a lot of fun—for them!

It made me angry at Sam for doing this to us. But Sam was so much bigger than I there wasn't much I could do about it. If fact, I could do nothing, except take it. Being rather a cocky bunch, it was a lot of fun to read our "love letters" and laugh. I found it very hard to take from them.

Finally, after they had their fun, Sam gave it to me. However, it was very embarrassing for me that the boys knew what we were writing in our letters.

After that, Alice and I were more careful when notes or letters were exchanged. None of those fellows could be around at the time.

When I got into the seventh and eighth grades we had courses in agriculture. John Borman was my teacher. One of the things he challenged us to do was to have a pest control drive. He made it a contest between the boys. Points were given for various pests.

Evidence had to be brought to class. Each day we came with a brown paper bag. Inside the bags were our catches of the day or night before. Our bagged evidence was either heads or tails: sparrow heads, mouse tails, rat tails, etc.

A sparrow head was worth so many points. Naturally the tail of a mouse was not worth as many points as the tail of a rat.

This contest kept us busy trapping the mice and rats. Our BB air rifles were used after supper each night. The chicken coop was a good place to find sparrows. But other places, too, the barn, crib, or tool shed. With a flashlight we shone where the sparrows roosted for the night. One would shine the light; the other one would shoot the spatsie, as we called a sparrow. The dead sparrow's head would be pulled off, then put in our bag. The next day at school we collected our points. Our cats on the farm got the rest of the spatsie for a bedtime snack. We went from one place to another for our spatsie hunting until we were through for the night. Our traps also had to be checked for mice or rats.

Later we got to include muskrats in our contest. A muskrat has a good-sized tail, so we could fill a bag rather quickly. Of course, trappings from our ditches made it easier to bring in these tails. My friend, Walt Mak, since his father was a big trapper, had a lot of points from muskrat tails alone. I got a lot of points this way, too.

In 1937 I won this trophy with my ten-ear corn sample.

This pest drive put us into a keen competitive spirit in school. One good result was getting rid of a lot of pests on our farms.

Mr. Borman was the one who encouraged me to get involved in the corn show. After school he came to the farm, where he helped me pick out my ten-ear corn samples. I won trophies in 1937 and 1938.

He took us to the Armory in Rensselaer where we were awarded our trophies. The roads were so icy that night. But we had a strange experience, after we brought Al Bosma home. My cousin Bill, of Uncle Jake, and Susie Bosma were sitting in his car on the yard. They had a date that night. They saw us drop Al off, then drive off the yard. How-

181

This was after I won my second trophy in the year 1938. Our old wood-pile is in the background.

ever, as we got on the road, Mr. Borman's car spun around, so we drove back on the yard again. Bill and Sue looked at us. They must have wondered what was going on, but we turned around, then drove off the yard one more time. We made it that time.

When we were in grade school, my class had more boys than girls. A few boys were older, having failed a year or two. However, when we got into high school our class size changed, from year to year. Some dropped out, when they quit, after reaching the age of sixteen. When we were sophomores we ended up with only five boys. Later, by our senior year, we were down to three boys, Walt Mak, Dale Schwanke, and myself. Even some girls dropped out. One more girl was added to our class in the last half of our senior year, for Bertha had enough credits to graduate with our class. In our graduating class we had nine girls and three boys in the Class of 1943. We started high school with twenty-four the freshman year, but by graduation we were down to a dozen.

Teachers, naturally, had problems with students. Classroom teachers identified the greatest threats to the educational process, listed in order: 1. talking out of turn, 2. chewing gum, 3. making noise, 4. running in the halls, 5. getting out of line.

Those were the big problems teachers faced when I started my high school days. I remember the shock in school when a teacher caught two athletes sneaking a smoke during the noon hour, while uptown. They were expelled for three days and not permitted to play in a basketball game that week.

Since we had only five boys in class during our sophomore year, it was hard to participate in any competitive sports with other classes. After that year we lost tall Sam Kingma and Kenny Sekema.

We had a team to play basketball. Five boys. No subs. So we got into a tournament that year. Lost our first game!

We played a class team which had a good press. After they scored, we had an awful time getting the ball in. So often that team got the ball back, only to score another basket.

It was more than frustrating. It was humiliating. Besides they had no mercy on us. If we did get it down the floor, which happened a few times, we got just *one* shot. No more. With a fast break they were down to the other end to score on us again.

We lost, as I mentioned. But before it was over, we were hoping against hope to find a way out of our helpless predicament. There was none. We had to take it, until the game was finished.

The score, well, I'll never forget the score of that game, as long as I live. 100 to 5! (Final) So when the final buzzer sounded, it was a sound of mercy. Finally it was over. Oh, the agony of defeat!

While in high school I got into long distance running. School had gotten a new cinder track. Also they built the obstacle course, because it was World War II. There was a big push for national fitness at the time.

I spent a lot of time on the cinder track, a quarter mile track. At noon I'd hurry to eat my lunch, then practice on the track. I'd run around and around during the rest of the noon hour.

One of the older athletes talked with me, because he paid attention to me, an underclassman, I liked him. He was Clarence Boezeman. Most of the time we called his last name "Bushman." His nickname, which most of us used, was "Buddha."

Buddha gave me a lot of encouragement. Certainly I never had the speed nor endurance to become a winner. Buddha joked with me, hardly ever calling me by my own name, instead I was called "Glenn Cunningham." Glenn was a great miler. Today you find him listed in the Hall of Fame for Track and Field. Buddha told me to keep running, which was like a push to reach for my greatest potential.

The only race I remember in my first year was one at the end of the season. The whole field in the mile had gone after Settner, who held all the records. Instead of going after him, I set my own pace. Finally I caught up with Bill Longstreth from Wheatfield. Most of the field was finished, but Bill and I had half of our last lap to complete. We were very even during the last lap. Around the last 220 we both started to sprint. But by that time spectators started walking out on the track. Seeing us coming, they tried to clear the track for our finish, not everybody got off in time. I hit some girl, spun her around, as she stepped out in front of us. We both kept on running. I edged out Bill at the finish line.

Settner had the record for the whole county in those days, nobody could outrun him. He told us he ran to school each day, and back home again after school. It was about five miles, so he was in excellent condition. He continued to be an outstanding winner during all of high school.

Settner was the best miler, who attended another school. De Motte School, however, had the best half miler, Leonard Story. Nobody could catch him when he gave his kick on the last lap. He was like a machine, always a winner. It was sad news for all of us when Story lost his life during World War II. After graduation Leonard enlisted in the Navy. When they were making a landing in the European Theater he was killed.

The last race during my senior year was one when I tried my best, trying to keep within striking distance of Settner. There was no way any runner would beat him. Yet I had my best finish. I was coming out of the last curve when Settner crossed the finish line. That was the hardest I ever tried. The rest of the meet that day I tasted blood. The same taste was still there a few days later. I felt I tried my best, nothing more could have been given.

But my best meet was in Crown Point. Our school had a duel meet with them. It was open competition, so we were not limited to how many events we could enter. My best was in the broad jump, the mile and half mile. We also took first place in the mile relay, which I also ran. We won the meet by a big lopsided score. Our team really had fun that day!

Teachers in high school I remember were Ewart, Ely, Ruck, Stephens, Cook, Rainwater, Flick, Venable, Wurzburger, Murphy, along with some others. Especially I remember Miss Keever, who was our class sponsor a couple of years. During our sophomore year I was our class president. During our senior year I was class vice president.

Mr. Ely did a lot of work with 4-H. In the classroom the man had to have a yardstick in his hand. It was a pointer, and more. You never knew when it was going to break. Mr. Ely did break one over a student who got to him one day. That kid got bopped, but had it coming.

Most of the time he'd put one end on his shoe, with the other end in the palm of his hand. Mr. Ely would then press down, so the yardstick would bow one way, then the other.

Harder and harder he'd press. How far could he make one bend?

Sure enough, in some class, he'd pop it. Snap in right in two! However, it would be replaced the next day. It stood the stress so long—then it snapped too!

Ruck and Stephens were coaches. I got along with both of them. Mr. Ruck helped me so much with typing. When I needed practice in typing, Mr. Ruck offered to get a new portable typewriter for me. I think I paid $50.00 for it. In class he only accepted perfectly typed papers, no eraser marks. He'd rather have a perfect paper than one with mistakes, yet typed with speed. Yes, he would hold them to the light, every eraser mark could be spotted!

Afterwards Mr. Stephens helped me with advanced typing. Both of these teachers taught business classes which I took. Mr. Stephens was our class sponsor in our senior year when we took a trip to Chicago. I also worked as student manager under both coaches. Both trusted me, so that I would run a few errands, such as doing banking for them, depositing their checks and getting cash.

I had one teacher, Mr. S. Bert Llewellyn, who also taught my Mom. A few boys in my class, including me, were such poor spellers. Tall Sam Kingma, Claude Mosier, and I were in that group. Mr. Llewellyn felt we were trying to see who had the most misspelled words on our tests. Maybe he thought so, but the truth was, we were trying to be better spellers. Again and again, it only proved we needed to study our spelling words in order to get better grades.

Some teachers wanted reports written in ink. A person had to be careful with his work, for a mistake made a mess.

One day a dark face was in front of me!

I was acquainted with the old fashioned fountain pen. New pens came out about that time. That type had a plunger, working much like a syringe, by pushing the plunger down, then drawing ink into the barrel.

I had borrowed one of those new pens to write a paper. However, I had problems, evidently it was running low on ink. After looking it over, I turned around, asking for help to fill it with ink. Alberta Greathouse was sitting behind me, so I asked her. I held up the pen, with my thumb on the plunger, "Do you just push this down?"

I pushed! A big gob of ink exploded out of the pen—flying into her face. Suddenly I was looking into a very dark face! She glared back out of eyes with fire. Her penetrating-glare went right through me. Shocked, I stared back, not knowing what to do.

As I recall, she left her seat immediately and went to the restroom.

Then I noticed my cousin, Florence Hoffman, who saw the whole thing. To her it was so funny. She was splitting over it. The whole thing was not that funny for me, I was doing a slow die. I'm not too certain how Alberta really felt. And I wasn't going to bother to ask.

Really, no need to ask her, for that look said it all!

I don't recall how the paper ever turned out.

During our junior year we gave our class play, the sensation of the year, "The Campbells Are Coming." It turned out super. That play was one of the really fun experiences of high school.

But not that much fun in rehearsal! A few nights before we gave the play, our dress rehearsal was a disaster. We were fighting. I got slapped in the face by one of the girls. She claimed my look made her forget her lines. However, according to the play book, I was suppose to give her such a look! Anyway she let me have it! I was angry! We had trouble.

Our principal happened to drop in to watch that dress rehearsal, which by then was in chaos. Well, he proceeded to give us one good dressing down! We got his message. Afterwards he encouraged us to get in there and give the best performance ever!

The following night we gave the performance of our lives! As we sometimes say, we had the people eating out of our hands and rolling in the aisles. Mrs. Steunenberg, the minister's wife, of the American Reformed Church, told us the next morning, "You kids were *superb!*"

The plot was that we were an educated family from the hills. However, my sister went off to a snob-college, where she met a Campbell. He was from a high class family, super sophisticated. So when she was bringing home her new man, we decided to act like hillbillies, which the Campbells thought we were.

I would eat fishworms and wild lettuce sandwiches. When our sophisticated visitors came into the house, I'd jump on the table to eat the worms. (Worms were pink macaroni tubes.) I'd hold these "worms" above my mouth, wiggle my fingers ever so slightly, which made it look like struggling fishworms were being swallowed! The stage floodlights made the pink wiggling worms all too real. People could laugh or gag in the audience, they had a choice. We were having great fun. That night we pulled it off. The audience loved it.

Of course, those Campbells could never have their son marrying into such a hillbilly family. My sister came to her senses, too. Her snobbery act was dropped.

It was a play to be remembered. After such a horrible fight the night of dress rehearsal, we had the extreme opposite when giving the performance.

During our senior year we gave another play, but could not begin to match our junior class play. In the fall, "Aunt Abby Answers An Ad" was presented. A good play, but not as clever a plot or story compared with the accomplishment of our junior play.

I watched the upperclassmen, when I first got into high school. Bill Rowen was one who was willing to talk to some of us younger fellows. But Bill had his ego too. Bill had a special line he used from time to time, which was, "I'm a self-made man!"

One day we gathered just outside the assembly in the hall. Bill was talking to some of us, when the subject turned to shaving. Each guy had his story. Since I had been shaving for a short time, I still wanted the other guys to know about it.

While I was proud of it, Bill Rowen gave me a put-down I've never forgotten, "Oh, Hoffman, you only have peach-fuzz

188

anyway." The whole group laughed. At the moment, I felt crushed by his comment. It hurt. After all, I was just trying to be accepted by them. And I never had any self-made man image of myself. It made me withdraw after his put-down.

During the first years of attending De Motte Grade School I had one friendly face I saw often. It helped when I could see Uncle Al Roorda, who was the janitor.

Every now and then I'd go see him in his workroom. Since the school was rather small, he had some spare time. I found him making kites. I checked in on him quite often that year.

My interest in those kites was personal. My Dad had ordered those kites. It was a big job assembling those kites, all different styles. There were at least six, maybe seven of them. Each one was a new challenge. One was very fascinating to me, the big box kite, open in the middle, while two boxed covered areas were on the ends.

After months of work, Uncle Al brought them out to the farm. His car was full of kites.

The best place to fly our kites was in the cow pasture, just over the bridge. All of them were fun to fly. It was that big box kite that amazed me. It flew so high. As it danced around in the air, that box kite really captured my heart. How could a box fly?

A few needed tails, so we had to experiment to find the best way to fly them. We had hours of fun with those kites. Eventually what happened to all those kites, I don't recall.

There were times when I stayed overnight at the Tysen's home. Uncle Dick and Aunt Ricca were expecting me one day after school. However, I didn't go directly to their home. Instead I went to Jim Bahler's home. My friend Jim told me his mother often had pea soup ready for them after they came home from school. Since it was cold that day, Jim expected his mother would have soup ready for them. That sounded so good to me, I invited myself to his house.

No pea soup! Both of us sat in their kitchen—waiting and waiting, but two boys were not served soup that day.

After playing and talking with them for a long time, I knew I had better cross the railroad tracks and go a couple of blocks to my relatives. Aunt Ricca wanted to know what happened to me and where I had been. As a kid I made some flimsy excuse, saying I visited Jim. I never told her of my hopes for a bowl of pea soup. But Aunt Ricca had food ready for me on the table! I also spent the night with them.

When I was in the grades there were large roadside billboards on school property. Those were located directly across the highway from the American Reformed Church.

Often we played around them. During nice weather in the fall or spring we'd eat our lunches by those billboards.

Leaning against the wooden skirts on the bottom, we'd sit back and eat whatever our mothers had packed in our lunch buckets. Dale Schwanke and I would slowly eat and talk.

Since we had the whole noon hour, sometimes we played before we ate our lunches. One day Dale suggested we throw stones at the trucks going by. After the stones were thrown, we had to quickly duck behind the billboard to hide. Traffic generally slowed when hit, but then drove on.

Dale hit one big truck. Quickly we ran behind the sign, hoping nobody would know where we were. However, this trucker stopped—we heard him coming. He was yelling! Boy, were we ever afraid he'd discover where we were. He found us!

The trucker continued to yell! The man fired questions at us. Yelled some more. Trembling, nearly frightened to death, we finally admitted we were throwing stones. After a time he got it out of Dale that he was indeed the guilty culprit. That mad trucker gave Dale one stern lecture. By the time he finished, two boys nearly had the daylights scared out of them. Finally he finished bawling us out, he got into his truck and drove away.

Dale and I knew better. That was our first and last stone throwing prank. We learned a different lesson at school that day, after that trucker got through with us.

Many times we played softball at recess time. We'd choose up sides, or play work-up.

Our play changed when people began moving into Pondville. Many coming from Gary or Chicago, or another area up North. A few of these kids changed things for us.

One boy moved in who was known only by the slang name "Dago." He was Italian, all of us kids called him by that name. The kid was rough. Many of us were hurt by him. While we played he did things to get attention or hurt somebody. One of his mean tricks was to jump on our backs. As we waited to bat or watched the softball game, he had to jump on our backs. Dago would yell, then leap on your back. Naturally we would cave in, falling to the ground. He dared do it to the smaller boys. He was mean. It hurt us. After several days of this, we were all getting very sick of his meanness.

Gradually he began jumping on the backs of fellows who were a little bigger. Most of the time, however, he was pretty careful. Yet, as time went on, he got bolder. One of the boys he did not bother; Cooper, the biggest kid in class, he never touched.

I talked to "Coop" about Dago. One of these times, I felt, he would dare to jump on Cooper's back. My plan was to have Coop suddenly fall backwards and sit down hard on Dago. Sure enough, he did decide to jump on him. Cooper sat down hard on Dago! Dago got hurt! The big bully got up howling how much he got hurt. All of us cheered Cooper. Finally Dago got what he had coming. Personally, I thanked Cooper.

That ended Dago's dirty, back-jumping, malicious trick.

A couple of brothers also moved to De Motte from the North. What they brought to school changed things by what they showed some of us.

Before I saw a few a funny papers. The comics had Popeye the Sailor-Man. But these boys showed me a different Popeye. This was in a "dirty" little, fat book. I'd never seen anything like it before. Oh, I saw some of these books, but they were clean comics or storybooks.

The pictures of Popeye were not funny, yet boys were laughing. The group was standing near the Standard Oil filling station, close to school. Boys were howling, as they looked at this little book, about four by four inches, two thick. It was a dirty book. Pictures of Popeye were pornographic. A couple of us were invited to see, "You ought to see what's in this book!" After that invitation I did look, at only a few pages.

That was all, just a few pictures were seen. My innocence was gone. Those dirty pictures became images on my mind. Like a clear photo, I can always see them. The Devil used them to put sin in my heart and mind. He used the eye-gate, with only a few dirty pictures. Satan used my eyes to stimulate sinful desires in my heart, which I knew were wrong, but I suddenly found a strange delight awakened in me. It was a desire for something forbidden by God. Those pictures were tempting to see.

I discovered my imagination could be used to sin against God and myself. Suddenly sin twisted Popeye of the funny papers to be something so filthy and dirty. Yet I wanted to see more. The bell rang, so we all went into school. Never again did I see the book, nor another picture.

While I did not look again, I never saw it with my eyes— yet I still see those pictures! They never left my mind in all the years since that morning. No, I don't think about them on purpose, but if something suggests the thought, then it all comes back. Then I can see the pictures!

I learned that books, pictures, plays, even advertisements can awaken and stimulate desires which are forbidden by God. I must be careful what my eyes see, somethings I must not look at. God wants my heart pure. Dirty stuff is sin, which can be so bad it brings forth death in the end.

My Heavenly Father will forgive my sin, as I confess to Him my sins. He will cleanse my heart and mind. I hear the words of Jesus, "Blessed are the pure in heart, for they will see God."

When I was in school, I guess I'd call De Motte School a country-school, more or less. Boys and girls did get in trouble at times. A few fellows would use rubber bands to shoot paper wads. With paper tightly wadded together, it would sting if you got hit. Some made a spit-wad. They would stick the paper in their mouth, chew on it, then make the wad. A spit-wad really stung.

But boys shooting paper-wads wasn't a big problem. Some kid may start it, with a few joining in, but they'd quit after a few days.

The one I hated was getting stuck with a pin. A few fellows pushed a pin into the eraser on a pencil. While walking the halls or in groups, between classes, these guys would tap people with a pin. You felt the chill, after getting stuck with a pin. Most of the time the guy would walk innocently down the hall. A few acted pretty cocky about it, those watched and grinned after you looked around. It was a big thing to see girls get very upset by being stuck. Naturally they were bolder to hit guys harder, those times were extremely painful.

It got to be a real problem, after a few days. One day it came to a halt! One boy hit another fellow in the elbow. He drove the pin in far enough that it stuck! That pin was almost buried into the fellow's elbow.

Our principal put an immediate stop to such a twisted type of fun. I was very glad he came down as hard as he did on that group of guys. While a few of them thought it was so smart, frankly it was very foolish. And dangerous to our health. We all had a few days of danger in the halls of our school. I know some thought they were just giving a tap. Really they did not know how far the pin was sticking the person. Proof of that was sadly discovered when a pin was buried in the student's elbow.

For certain reports and papers we had to use ink. So we had to have ink bottles, blotters and ink pens.

On one particular day a girl could not get her ink bottle open. I was across the aisle, but she didn't ask me.

Instead she went to the football players. Several took his turn, but not one of them could open it. Finally in frustration she threw up her hands. Her report wasn't going to get written that day. Coming back to her desk, she threw herself into her seat—defeated. I asked for the ink bottle. The girl must have thought I had to be kidding. Why bother? After all, I was about the smallest guy in high school. Anyway, she handed it to me. I bent over the bottle, locked a grip on it—turned it—it popped loose!

I handed it across the aisle to her. She had to be totally mystified that I got it opened. Those big football players couldn't do it, how could this weakling ever open it?

I'm certain milking cows by hand helped me with my grip! Maybe she didn't realize that. Anyway, it helped her out. Likely it helped me even more. It gave a good boost to my self-esteem! That afternoon, even for a few moments, I was in the league with the big boys. Well, at least, I felt like I was.

There was some stealing in school. Some money was stolen out of lockers. This happened while we had basketball practices. During a practice several people would ask to go get a drink or go to the bathroom. They had to leave the gym. Some players gave me their pocketbooks for safe-keeping. When I was student manager I'd do that for them.

For a number of weeks we had the same problem. After a practice, some player would tell the coach he lost money. It would be taken from their clothes in the locker or from a bill-fold. A few times the stolen billfold would be found uptown. The coach and I would try to check it out. I'd be sent to the locker room off and on to check. One evening I was handed several ropes, with the instruction to tie all doors shut. Plus I had to check all windows on the lower level of the building. They were all locked. This way the coach wanted to see if it was an inside or outside job.

One night the coach left the gym. He was gone for a long time. Nobody knew where he was, I didn't either. His plan worked. He caught the person.

The coach hid in a little room for plumbers, where they could work on water and heat pipes. He was in the dark. While he could not see, only hear, it was enough. Someone came into the shower room. The lockers began banging away, open and shut! open and shut! Bang! Bang! The coach suddenly jumped out—catching him in the act! When he later told me who he caught, I couldn't believe it. One of the star players. I don't know what he said to him, but that put a stop to the business of stolen money during basketball practice.

Every year pictures had to be taken for the *Keen Keener,* our school annual. All kinds of sports pictures would be taken, one after another—football, basketball, track, etc. Athletes would be changing for one picture, then for the next. I was in a few, but not in others. So the guys asked me to take care of their billfolds. More and more guys gave them to me. However, a few did not come back to claim theirs. I hid them, so I could have my picture taken with a group. When I got back to the locker room one was missing. So I reported it immediately to the coach. He was furious, so he ordered, "Everybody stay! Nobody leaves."

We were all searched. Each person had to show how much money they had in their billfold. This was done on purpose, for we knew the exact bills in the stolen one. One by one each player was searched.

My brother Paul's turn came up. It happened he had the exact same bills in his billfold. This looked strange for a few minutes, both, for him and for me. It made me uneasy.

However, Red Evans had grabbed Paul's pocketbook at a gas station during the noon hour, asking, "How much money do you have, Hoffy?" Red looked; he'd seen those exact bills. Red then testified they belonged to Paul.

We failed to find it in the locker room. Before school was left out that day, every student was searched. Each desk was checked. A boy in a lower grade had it. The kid stuffed it behind his books, in the back of his desk. Besides, he took a pencil to disfigure all the faces of the pictures in the billfold. The exact money was there, too. Authorities were called in, even though he was quite young.

The boy did not come back to school. The court sentenced him to a special boys' school. I felt bad for the boy, but he did this to himself.

Naturally, I felt much better after the whole thing was cleared up. After all, I had hidden those billfolds in a very good place, so I knew they were not out in the open to tempt the boy. He had to be looking to steal something, otherwise he could not have found them. Frankly he was a thief. I agree with the decision of the authorities, who held him responsible for his stealing.

Living five miles from town. I had to ride the bus.

However, the ride was longer than that, for we took a few side roads to pick up other kids. It must have been a ride of nine or ten miles each bus ride.

Gerrit Woudema was my first bus driver. Seats were along each side of the bus, with one row of seats down the middle. Those center seats faced the front. Early years I sat on the side, right behind the driver, to his left. He and I would talk a little from time to time. Gerrit was a very quiet person, so few words were exchanged. At times he'd turn and smile at me.

I was embarrassed one time when we hit some pussy willows along the edge of the road. They really smacked the windows. My impulse was to say something. I did, calling him, "Daddy" when I did. Oh, that was awful for me as a small boy. Mr. Woudema turned his head, gave me a smile. That made it easier.

Some high school girls would sit in front, while the bigger boys went to the back. If I looked at the high school girls, many times we'd smile at each other. Dorothy Akers would tease me, calling me "Dimples." While I liked it; I would also blush.

A few years later I moved to the back of the bus. One day we picked up the Maks. The high school boys were all excited that morning, as they talked in the back of the bus. One said, "Today is the start of the World Series!"

My first thought—that has to be something awful! All day long I wondered what was going to happen. How terrible would it be? I was in sheer misery the whole day. I wanted to go home. Whatever this "World Series" turned out to be—I knew I wanted to be home and close to my parents when this horrible thing happened. Later I discovered this bogeyman for one Hoosierland boy had to do with nothing more than baseball!

In later years Tootsie Grevenstuk became our bus driver. There were changes over the years, different kids and different routes. This made it hard for any driver to maintain discipline.

On the last day of the year he got set-up by some older students. Windows were broken, three in all I believe. While he did stop to get order restored, only to have the student begin a struggle with him, then purposely put an elbow through the window.

Once Tootsie got shot in the back of his neck (close range) with a spit-wad. Tootsie's neck turned dead-white, then bright red. That had to sting as badly as any bee.

Generally he had his way to keep kids in line, as he approached them, grabbing both hands, he'd bring them down and punch them into the pit of the stomach. With the wind knocked out of them, most kids would sit very quietly after his discipline.

As Paul and I got older we took a car to school, if we had something to do after school. If we were late with chores in the morning, then we'd take a car, too. But even in our junior and senior years we mostly took the bus. Those were the early years of World War II. Gas was being rationed, so it was patriotic to ride the bus.

I didn't want to miss school if I could help it. In the seventh grade I missed nine days. Only three were missed in the eighth grade. When I had surgery in the ninth grade I was absent nine days. However, in the last three years of high school I had perfect attendance. I had to wait until then to get my perfect attendance awards.

My grades were the following in the years for which I have my report cards:

7th...26-A,	31-B,	12-C	
8th...26-A,	16-B,	8-C,	1-D
9th...11-A,	15-B,	19-C	
10th...13-A,	19-B,	7-C,	1-D
11th...6-A,	14-B,	11-C,	1-D
12th...3-A,	27-B,	10-C	

Our Class of 1943 graduated on April 19th. Only twelve received diplomas. Only three of us were boys, while there were nine girls.

I received two awards that night. I was given a Holy Bible by my pastor, the Rev. Raymond Schaap, for clean sportsman-

SENIOR CLASS

SENIOR CLASS OF 1943: Top row: Anne E. Klip, Cordelia Kooy, Ruth K. Moolenaar. 2nd row: Hazel L. Punter, Delpha N. Heimlich, Bernice Vander Ploeg. 3rd row: Florence M. Hoffman, Alice Sytsma, Bertha Vander Molen. Bottom row: Dale W. Schwanke, Walter J. Mak, Bill M. Hoffman.

ship. The other one was the American Legion School Award for courage, honor, service, leadership and scholarship.

Mrs. Herman Vander Ploeg reminded me that I should never forget the Bible. While she congratulated me, immediately followed it with encouragement to read my Bible. Of all the people who came through the line that night, her words alone are the ones I remember. Nor have I forgotten my Bible, for it is God's Word.

I have to thank my parents for helping me through school. Since my father only got to the fifth grade, education to him was so important. It was one thing he wanted his children to have—a good education.

Years later I was given a couple of my books from grade school. Some interesting things were found, as I paged through these books. In my *Arithmetics Second Book,* I wrote on the back cover:

"When you live in a dog house
   consider me as a pup."

"It was Billy in the summer
   It was Billy in the fall
But when I went to see him
   It was not Billy at all.
It was WM."

"She was dumb in the summer
   She was dumb in the fall
But when I went to see her
   She was not dumb at all.
She got smart."

Inside the front cover I had written:
   "You love..."   on page 175
   On that page it says,   "Go to 181..."
                             "Go to 200..."
   Then on page 200:   "You are a fool for looking."

Once I graduated, I considered my days in the classroom were over. But when I reflect back, I think of my dreams for life. One summer afternoon I had to meet with principal Al Ewart. Before starting high school he wanted to talk about some courses I ought to take in the years ahead. Dad went along with me.

Mr. Ewart was seated in a swivel chair. He was turning around in different directions as we talked. Only small talk at first, he had to break the ice.

After that, it then was time to get down to business. So Mr. Ewart asked what I wanted to do in life. Asking me, "If you could do anything, what do you want to be?"

At fourteen I shared my dreams. First, I told him, I'd really like to be a race car driver at the Indy "500"—I was serious. But Al Ewart pushed his swivel chair back, then roared with laughter! It was a wonder he didn't dump himself over backwards. After he got that out of his system, he next asked what else I'd like to be.

Second, I said, I wanted to own a fleet of semitrailers, doing over the road long distance hauling. That one didn't seem so funny to him. By this time he had his doubts, not sure about my dreams and ambitions for life. Just to be sure, "You don't want to get into farming?" I told him I did like farming, but that isn't what I'm dreaming about.

Skipping over the Indy "500" race car career, he felt that I better take some commercial courses if I wanted to get into the trucking business.

That afternoon he signed me up for commercial subjects, suggesting typing, bookkeeping, business math courses, etc. One thing he felt was necessary that I should take all the typing I could get in high school. I did.

Mr. Ruck got me that first typewriter, so I could get in far more practice in typing. I bought a portable Royal typewriter. I did a lot of assignments at home, in order to get perfect papers for Mr. Ruck. Those were the only kind he accepted. No eraser marks were acceptable with him. None. Not one! Just to be sure, he held papers up to the light. Be sure your sin would find you out.

All the typing gave me a skill, not so much with speed, but of typing without mistakes.

I remember the final exam for him. His speed test put a lot of fear in my heart. Many girls, some played the piano, could type with speed. During that test, with all their typewriters pecking away, I got nervous. I pecked away. Mr. Ruck walked around the room during the speed test. Spotting me, he walked over, whispered in my ear, "Be calm; type your speed. You can do it." With his words of assurance, I settled down and finished the speed test. I never got nearly as far as the girls. Take ten words off for every mistake, he said. Circle the mistakes. I had none. Once they averaged out the number of words, we all came out with the same number of words per minute.

I had learned a valuable skill in high school. The other commercial courses helped in life, too. I know, as I now reflect on it well over fifty years later, Mr. Ewart did laugh. Yet as a boy, I dared to share my dreams and ambitions, the Lord was going to use that time to direct my life. God in His kind Providence was urging me to take those commercial courses.

No, I never did race in the Indy "500," nor own a fleet of semis, but my course was set by my Heavenly Father's hand. His Providence provides, so that nothing is by chance! I have to respond to my reflection, "Thank You, Father. Praise Your Name."

Unknown then, life in the classroom was still ahead of me. In 1947 I took a winter short course at Purdue University in Lafayette, Indiana.

But many more hours were ahead, in fact, years—seven years in Hope College and Western Theological Seminary. Many reports, papers, letters, and manuscripts were typed. Dr. John R. Mulder who was a professor at the seminary urged to write full manuscripts. Each sermon a full manuscript. Further Dr. Mulder challenged that we should continue doing it for the first ten years in the ministry. I accepted his challenge, which was practiced my entire ministry. It meant I literally wrote thousands of manuscripts of sermons and Bible studies and lessons.

My education continued in October of 1949, when I began my studies at Hope College, Holland, Michigan. Four years later, June 3, 1953, ten years after high school graduation, I received a degree from Hope. I graduated magna cum laude with a Bachelor of Arts Degree. My major was in History.

In my senior year I wrote a paper in Senior Bible, "The Christian Conception of the Meaning of History." In the contest my pen name was Mark, used so the judges would not discover the student who was the author. While it was among the final papers, I did not win.

However, my motivation was much greater to study in college, especially when I compare my accomplishments with with those in high school. Of the 45 courses taken at Hope College I earned the following grades as my final marks: 33-A and 12-B.

Three years later, May 23, 1956, I graduated from Western Theological Seminary, Holland, Michigan, with a Bachelor of Divinity Degree.

When I was in the Middle Class I wrote a paper for Church History. This one was entered into The Vander Ploeg Church History Contest, under the pen name of The Catechism Kid. The subject was "A Comparison of the Heidelberg Catechism with the Westminister Confession and the Augsburg Confession." My paper was awarded first prize. The next year I was awarded first prize for Sermon Delivery, with my sermon, "The All-Sufficient Accomplishment" based on the text John 19:30b, "It is finished!" Our Savior's wondrous claim for sinners!

Life ought to be a searching for His Truth, in Christ. As a wise man said, "The fear of the Lord is the beginning of wisdom, the knowledge of the Holy One is understanding." As a sinner I turn to the Holy God, Who gave me a Savior and the guidance of His Holy Spirit through revelation, "But these are written (recorded) in order that you may believe that Jesus is the Christ, the Anointed One, the Son of God, and that through believing and cleaving to and trusting in and relying upon Him you may have life through (in) His Name." (John 20:31)

There is a truth found in *The Shorter Catechism,* one of the most well-known, which is this:

Question: What is the chief end of man?
Answer: Man's chief end is to glorify God and to enjoy Him forever.

Indeed, the pinnacle of wisdom and learning any person needs to have is for God's glory and that God is for that one's enjoyment. Both, glorifying God and man's enjoyment, go together. To God alone be the glory, both now and forever!

My class in the early years in De Motte School. I'm on the right, leaning against the brick pillar. Our teacher, Mrs. Fern Bauman.

Old First Reformed Church of De Motte

I can still remember the old church. The one built in 1900. It was placed on an acre of land at Dutch Corners.

First Reformed Church at Dutch Corners was organized "with thanksgiving to God" by twenty-three Dutch Immigrant members on January 25, 1893. Meetings, led by the Founding Brothers, were first held in a school north of De Motte. The first church, parsonage, and horse barns were built on that site in 1900 at a cost of $600 on the one acre donated by Jacob Groet. That information is on the Centennial Historic Marker.

My Christian baptism took place on June 7, 1925, in that church. This puts emphasis on the wonder of the Covenant of our Heavenly Father with the Family of God. My parents had me baptized as a child.

The First Reformed Church, Dutch Corners, De Motte, Indiana. Parsonage is beside the church.

Family dressed for church on Sunday afternoon. Back, Dad, Mom, and Paul. Marty J. is holding onto Rita Jo, Lois has Carolyn in front of her, and then Wilma.

The great revelation Scripture affords us from the ancient time of Abraham onwards is precisely that God, in His great grace and incomprehensible mercy, chose from all the sinful, fallen humanity one family, one people, one nation to be and remain His own people, to establish a Covenant with them and their children, to communicate to them the Gospel of His grace and salvation, which is His way of revealing to His children His own glory.

As it has been said with truth, "this Covenant is a relationship which God imposes in His sovereignty." Abraham, nor any other believer, chose this by themselves. It pleased God to make such a Covenant. God said to us, "You are *My* people and I am *your* God." To His promise we must respond. We must respond by faith. The pledge of the Holy Spirit is given as assurance of His promise. His promise is explicit:

"Believe in the Lord Jesus Christ and thou shalt be saved, thou *and thy family.*" (Acts 16:31)

205

That message of our Heavenly Father of His salvation and grace was diligently preached and taught in the First Reformed Church. I heard the wonder of the Gospel call, so by the faithfulness of God I responded by faith to confirm that I was in the gracious Covenant of my Heavenly Father. Through the grace promised I was able to respond with faith.

I took this step at the age of twenty. I had wanted to do it before that in my life, but was very reluctant to do so. I felt I ought to be much better than I was. However, more and more I gained an understanding that it was all by the amazing grace of God. Indeed it was only by grace alone! Nothing in my hands could be brought, nothing but my sinful self.

I have a Bible given to me by Pastor Raymond Schaap when I graduated from high school in 1943. It was dated April 19, 1943. However, there are two more dates in the back cover: Oct. 8, 1945 (a Monday) Oct. 14, 1945 (a Sunday) .

That Monday evening I attended a Consistory meeting. Also, waiting in his car by church was Andy Hamstra. He and I both came to confess our faith in Jesus Christ as our personal Lord and Savior. Neither had any idea the other was going to be there.

The second date was the following Sunday, when both of us stood before the Family of God in the First Reformed Church. That was our public reception before the entire congregation.

I'm so grateful that I was so led by the Holy Spirit to confess Jesus Christ as *my* personal Lord and Savior. I know for sure, there have been many times since then I've disappointed Him, but there has never been any disappointment in Jesus! Never, never! Praise His Name, all glory to God.

At various times the Holy Spirit has given new assurance to me that I am His child and in His Covenant. One stands out, which was in the early days of our marriage, in 1947, while I was home alone reading Christian literature. That experience made it so solid that I *knew* by His grace and through His Holy Spirit that Jesus Christ was *my* Lord and Savior, being in His Covenant of promise. I just lift up my heart in praise and adoration to glorify His Name. Amen!

I do remember things about the old church. I also remember the names of ministers, Rev. Koster, Rev. Swart, and Rev. Oosterhoff. But the first minister I remember was the Rev. Louis Benes, Sr. He was our Pastor from 1924-1934. Dominee Benes preached in Dutch in the morning and English in the afternoon. When I was nine he retired. There was some pressure for him to retire, which he did at the age of 69. He served 30 years in the Gospel ministry, which he entered when he was 39. Three of his sons became ministers and a daughter married a preacher. Even as a boy of nine I know my Dad felt sorry for him. One Sunday my folks talked, Dad told Mom a letter ought to be sent to him and also give him something. I knew something was happening in our church, as I listened carefully when my parents talked.

When I was ten a promise of a Call was given to a student who graduated from Western Theological Seminary in Holland, Michigan. Our candidate was 32. I remember this new minister, the Rev. Raymond Schaap, who touched my life as a teenager. Few attended the Dutch services in the morning. Mostly older people came. The largest attendance came at the 2 o'clock service. I never understood the Dutch language, yet I attended with my Dad at a few Dutch services. One unforgettable experience happened at one of those services. Rev. Schaap was preaching with enthusiasm—stopped! He was at a loss for words. He couldn't think of the Dutch word he needed. He was stuck! Rev. Benes, then retired, was attending church that morning. He spoke up, aloud, giving Rev. Schaap the word needed. Pastor Schaap thanked him, used the word, then finished his sermon without anymore trouble at all. (As a boy, I didn't know about Dominee Benes talking aloud in church!)

My Dad always took his Psalm book from which he sang, everybody had their personal copy. Those Psalms were sung very slowly—my Dad would point to the words. He wanted me to help sing along. It seemed so slow to me. One morning, as we were going home I asked Dad, "Why do you sing so long in one place?"

207

Most of the time Dad would take my little Grandma Hoffman to the Dutch services. Little Grandma was little—even with her hat on. Like the other women in those days, she wore her black hat to church. Even with her hat on she barely could be seen above the pew. Sitting besides her was my Dad, who weighed well over two hundred pounds. It was quite a sight to see Dad hold his little mother's arm and walk her down the aisle to their pew. My Grandma liked it when Dad took her to church, as I recall her saying as a small boy, "Your Dad remembers me when I am old."

In the old church sometimes men sat on one side while the women with children would sit on the other side. When I was small, I knew a few families who still did this. It seemed so strange to me to see a father come to church, only to sit on his side, away from his own family. Only to notice, across the aisle or in another section would be his wife. (As a kid I thought at first that they were not getting along with each other. The whole thing didn't look good to me, but it was their old custom.)

We had an old black potbellied stove in the main part of church. The pulpit was in the corner of the old church. I thought the old pipe organ looked so nice. Each service some boy had to go behind a curtain to pump the organ bellows, to have air to play it. We had velvet collection bags. These, I thought, looked like an old floppy cap, in it you placed your offering. I could hardly see anything in that bag, as I tried to look. Never did I get a good peek in one of those bags.

In the back part of church was a large room, called the Consistory room. I just thought it was the name of the room, never realizing Elders and Deacons, along with the minister, made up the Consistory. A big door could be closed to separate it from the main sanctuary. That's the room I had for Sunday School. There was a small organ back in that room. It was the kind that had to be pumped with your feet as you played it. This organ was used when we sang in Sunday School.

Mrs. Zylstra was in charge of Sunday School and played the organ when we sang. One of her fingers was crooked, sticking out as she played. As kids we watched that finger.

There was no messing around, for she'd get after you. We were very careful about our behavior.

However, we still had a big problem while singing. It had to do with this one boy. This little boy with a round-face, who would sit in our pew—he bothered us. While we tried to stay away from him, he kept coming, moving slowly down the bench. Closer. And closer. When he could reach you, he'd slip his hand down the pew and give one of us kids a hard pinch! It hurt! I knew we would be in for more trouble when he slowly inched nearer to us.

While he came closer, we tried to move away. But finally we could not move away from him any more. He was there—right next to me—and then, the pinch! He did it again!

One Sunday I went home from Sunday School telling Mom that I did not like that naughty boy. This kid was four years younger than I. I wasn't going back any more. He was too mean to us. (That boy, I found out, was little Kenny De Vries, known to us as the pincher! And we didn't like him when he was so naughty to us.)

However, we went back, but stayed away from him whenever possible.

One of my first teachers was Rose Hamstra. I liked her, as a little boy I thought she was so pretty and nice. We had our class in the little church kitchen in the corner of that back room.

One of the first men I had as a teacher was Mr. Klienblossom. Our class met next to the pulpit platform, close to the curtain a boy would have to go behind to pump the organ. One Christmas Mr. Klienblossom gave me a little red and white pen knife. I've kept it through the years. As a teacher he made a strong impression on me, even though he wasn't always easy to understand with his brogue. I still thought a lot of him.

Later he was our church janitor. One particular Sunday we had a bad smell in church. A woman turned around, blaming him for that strange smell. It was getting worse, this smell of fumes. It was bothering all of us. She finally turned to him, asking if he were trying to kill us! Mr. Klienblossom was upset with her, too. He even threatened to quit.

After the service Bill T. Hamstra and I went down to the furnace room, where we discovered the problem. We found smoldering smoke and fumes coming out of a closed garbage can. The janitor had thrown clinkers, plus some live coals, into the can. But it was Sunday. Since it was, he did not want anybody to see him carrying them out. So he slapped the lid on the old can, which only made the matter much worse. It was funny to Bill and myself. Immediately we knew what had to be done, so we grabbed the can—carried it out and dumped it—with the other ashes on a pile behind church. Yes, we did, even on Sunday!

The old outdoor toilets were behind church, too. Between church and Sunday School it was the place where the guys would go and talk. I still remember being there when Wilbur Hoffman, my cousin, roared away from church. Bill really floored it, as he headed towards town. His brother, Albert, was with us, knowing by that sound it was his brother. Al said to us, "If I ever do that, I hope they shoot me."

Young fellows could be extremely hard on their cars. Only, sometimes that car was Dad's car!

Rev. Schaap liked his cars, too. He had a heavy foot. Sometimes he attended sports events at our school. One time he came to a track meet at Mt. Ayr High School. For some reason or other, a couple of us had to leave the meet early, so we were invited to ride with him. He, too, was in a hurry to get back. So he drove very fast. About that same time he traded for several cars. The car we rode in was one he had recently purchased, so he was still finding out how fast it would go. I can still remember the ride we had after going through Roselawn, heading for De Motte. We took those hills! The car would shoot up the hill, then over the top! Every hill felt like you lost your stomach—almost like flying. He kept telling us that he didn't know how fast it would go. So he stepped on it a little harder. I sat in the middle, while Casey sat on the outside. We watched the speedometer. Casey would poke me in the side, then nod his head. Both of us had grins, as we watched in wide-eyed wonder as we took each hill a little faster than the last one. Rev. Schaap commented about his speed, then stepped on the gas to get a little more out of the car.

We went over some of those hills at 75 to 80 miles per hour. Each time we got that sensation in our stomachs. Casey would poke me each time. The last hill we went over better than 85, that time we almost floated for a second or two. Pastor Schaap said that this car can really go. After that he slowed down a little. But it didn't take that long to go from Mt. Ayr to De Motte that afternoon.

Rev. Schaap could drive with a heavy foot. He did that day. Rev. Schaap could really preach. He touched my heart, with his sermons. I listened. I have to say he was my favorite preacher. As we got to be teenagers, many of us boys would go sit up front. A whole row of us would be sitting together. We did that when we got the new church built in 1940. I was fifteen then. They tore down the old church, which was forty years old. During the building of the new church we held our services in the De Motte High School. We sat in school desks in the big assembly hall.

Since we lived seven miles from Dutch Corners, we did not go at night to catechism. Instead Rev. Schaap would come to school, at the noon hour, when we had our catechism lesson. The groups were small, but we had a good time with him.

There was a time when some young fellows liked to stay out of church and talk. That way they could stay out until the last minute before church started in the afternoon. Many hoped most of the pews would be filled, so chairs would be put up along the back wall. Some of the guys really liked that. Back there they could talk during the service. If they didn't do that, their chairs would be tipped back and they'd try to sleep. A few of my close friends liked to talk. Talking during church always bothered me. I didn't like it at all. It was disturbing, so I couldn't listen to Rev. Schaap's sermons. Several times I attempted to talk to them about their habit. My only solution was in going up front, so I told them I was going up front so the minister could watch us. So in order to do that, I had to lead the bunch in or tell the usher to take us right up to the front. At first we had a few grumbles. But they got used to it.

No longer were we in the back, where we could get into trouble. Instead we were known as the young men who sat up front. We also were known by the seminary students who came to preach at our church. They told each other that they would have a group of boys sitting in the front row!

I liked that much better than sitting in the back. For some of my friends it was too big a temptation to talk. Or sleep. We all could share in the worship service much better while up front.

At times I'd complain to Dad about the conduct of some guys in church. He felt things were not that bad. Then he gave me a few stories out of the horse and buggy days. At the time they had the old church and the barns behind church.

After a number of years being away, my Dad returned to De Motte. He came dressed up, with a hat and topcoat. He came to a Christian Endeavor meeting.

Dad sat down, placing his hat in the pew ahead of him, while he hung his coat over the pew. He was eyed by some young fellows. Jake Walstra challenged Dad with a question, after picking up his nice hat, which Jake held up, then asked, "Is this yours?" Dad told him it was.

Jake doubled up his fist—Pow! He knocked in the top of Dad's hat. As if that was not enough, daring Dad, Jake said, "We'll see you out in the horse barn afterwards."

So after the C.E. meeting, the guys headed for the barn out back, waiting for the dressed up guy. Jake, however, stayed behind, waiting outside the door for Dad to come out. Once again, Jake dared Dad to come to the barn to settle things. He was really itching for trouble. "They" were going to have some fun that Sunday night, at Dad's expense. To go to the barn would have been no good. It would have been a no-win night for Dad.

Dad had another plan. Instead of going there, to settle it, Dad wasted no time. So he challenged Jake, "Why wait that long? Let's settle it right here!" With that, Dad gave Jake a punch in the face. He staggered backwards, right up against the side of the church. It all happened before Jake knew what hit him.

It was settled, then and there. Dad mentioned that he and Jake became the best of friends after that. Had Dad gone to the horse barn, Dad would never had had a chance. Then strangely, a few years later, Jake and Dad became brothers-in-law.

Some fellows could be ornery. One evening, while they had their C.E. meeting, a few girls were walking around church. As they walked, it wasn't long when the boys spotted them through the window. One opened the window, wide. One by one they jumped on the pew and out the window. They left the meeting to join the girls.

Some were rude to the preacher. Naturally they sat in the back. Since services could be long, even the sermon could be 50 minutes, if not an hour long. When it got too long, then the young men pulled out their gold watches. They would hold them up by the chain. These watches would swing back and forth. So many pendulums were moving above the heads of the congregation. The minister could not help but spot their rude reminders.

Dad also mentioned their being invited to the minister's home after church. They sang, as the minister's wife played the organ or piano. However, a few were bold enough to make suggestive remarks about her.

My Uncle Ben Hoffman shared a story with me. He and a friend were caught doing something in church. An Elder, Uncle Case Walstra, saw them. So he stopped them at the door after the service. Uncle Case told both of them to be at his house Monday night. He also gave them the exact time.

They were a couple of frightened young men. As an elder of the church he was calling them on the carpet. Fears made for a restless night. And the whole next day. They dared not be late, therefore they were on time at his door.

He invited them in. Immediately Uncle Case started a conversation with them, but not a word about their conduct. Naturally all evening they worried when he was going to talk about it. But as an elder, Uncle Case said nothing. Nothing!

Later they were served lunch. In a way, they still enjoyed the evening. Afterwards he said good-bye to them. It remained a total mystery to two young men. But Uncle Ben said never again did they pull anything in church.

Uncle Ben told me how he had the greatest respect for my Uncle Case Walstra. He was one of the outstanding Elders in his eyes.

Another story told by Uncle Ben had to deal with catechism on Saturday. This was when he was younger than the other incident. The Dominee taught all the classes himself, taking one group at a time. So there was plenty of free time. Others had to wait their turn. After all classes were finished, then they could get in the buggy to go home.

Involved in this experience were some of the De Kock boys and uncle Ben. They had two in each buggy. One drove the buggy, while the other had the buggy whip.

Two buggies and four boys left Dutch Corners after their catechism. They drove side-by-side down the road. They would get close enough to get into a buggy-whip battle. One boy would whip the boys in the other buggy. When they couldn't take it any longer, then they would pull apart for some relief. They cried, for it hurt so much. Yet they did not stop. With all the smarting pain, only to return for another whipping.

As if that were not enough, they started bumping into each other's buggy. Finally they tried to hook the hub of the wheel into the spokes of the wheels on the enemy chariot. One attack after another, until spokes began to fall on the road. The final ramming completely knocked out a couple of wheels. No longer would they roll! The war was over. Both buggies were broken down.

The catechism kids were in trouble. However, they decided to join forces to get one buggy running again. They fixed one buggy, so it would roll again. Together they went for help. I have no idea how they explained it. I don't recall how Grandpa Hoffman heard the story. I got the feeling he, nor Mr. De Kock, ever heard the rest of the story.

214

Not every Sunday did we attend church. Especially this was true in the winter. There were some very severe winters in the thirties. Besides we did not have the best of roads in those years. Nor was there highway equipment to keep them open. Cars were not warm either.

It was not often, but we did miss church. At least we did not go to First Reformed Church. We did have church, at home.

As kids we held the service. The living room, where we had our big heater stove, was the place for our worship. Chairs were set in rows. Mom had a flower pedestal, which was tall, but I could look over it. That was my pulpit. It was in front of our pews. On my pulpit was our Children's Bible. It was the Bible story book my folks read for us.

Everybody had to attend church. Mom and Dad generally sat in the middle of the chairs. Some of the smallest kids were with them. The older ones sat in the front pews.

I would get the order of service together. We sang, I know, but I don't know the choice of hymns. I would imagine we sang from memory, so we knew "Jesus Loves Me." We sang other familiar Sunday School songs or hymns.

The sermon was my part. I'd use a very familiar Bible story. I had watched our preacher enough, so I'd try to preach like he did. I told them!

What was my favorite Bible story? The Nebuchadnezzar story. A picture of him was in our book. It clearly pointed out God's judgment upon the king. While he was on the roof of the Royal Palace of Babylon, he said, "Is not this the great Babylon I have built as the royal residence, by my mighty power and for the glory of my majesty?"

For robbing God of His glory, this all was taken away from him. And God didn't wait!

The Bible says, "Immediately what had been said about Nebuchadnezzar was fulfilled. He was driven away from the people and ate grass like cattle. His body was drenched with the dew of the heaven until his hair grew like the feathers of an eagle and his nails like the claws of a bird." That's the picture I still can see in my mind, as in our book.

I also remember Jacob's ladder, as well as the wise and foolish virgins.

I know when I preached I gave exhortations to my family. I preached like our preacher would preach. My family was told from my pulpit.

We prayed, and had an offering. This was the way our service at home went, whenever we could not get to the Dutch Corners church.

In my teen years I got involved in more work at church. Bob Hamstra asked me to help him with collecting and counting money in Sunday School, also passing out the papers. But before long I was teaching a class of young boys. Alberdena Dykhuizen also began teaching about the same time.

Later she became our president of Christian Endeavor. I became vice president the same year. My main job was to line up topic leaders for our meetings. Generally this was set-up for an entire year, but some of those scheduled would make some kind of an excuse to get out of it when it was their turn. Most of the time, it was last-minute backing out. So if I couldn't get a replacement I led the topic for that evening. One year I took care of the topic for eight Sunday evenings. The following year I was elected president.

Pastor Schaap had accepted another Call after I graduated from high school. The next year the Rev. Fredric Dolfin became our new minister. He was a recent graduate from seminary. His age was 24 when accepting the promise of our Call. Both of these ministers made a great impression on my life.

As time went on I got more and more into our church and her ministry. God's Call was becoming more clear to me as time went on, with Pastor Dolfin helping me to see it more clearly.

Let me share how this unfolded in my life. My Call became my vision, which through the years has been before me. God spoke His Word to confirm my Call. Mine was crystallized by His Word. The specific passage is Matthew 28:19, 20.

Long before it was being written on my heart, God called. I say that because I believe with all my heart that God called me from my mother's womb. That's the way our God works. With absolute certainty I know He did just that in my life.

Now He works it out through His people, His Word, His Holy Spirit, and through life's circumstances. He's in control of all. All helping to confirm my Call.

One childhood experience still stands out in my mind and heart. It still goes through me, each time I think about what happened. The minister near to my heart as a boy was the Rev. Raymond Schaap. One Sunday, as he was greeting us at the door, this happened. My brother Paul, eighteen months younger than I, and I came to the door at the same time. Instead of shaking hands, he placed his hands on our heads. One placed on mine, the other on Paul's, asking, "Which boy is going to be the preacher?" His question penetrated to the depths of my heart. I've *never* forgotten that sacred experience as a boy.

From time to time Pastor Dolfin urged me to consider going into the ministry. I felt that I'd continue to be a Christian engaged in farming and serving the Lord in His Church. All the busy activity helped me to avoid accepting God's Call into the Gospel Ministry. The first year of our marriage I was elected as the youngest Deacon of our church at Dutch Corners. I served on a committee for Temple Time, a Reformed Church in America radio broadcast. Also our church began a Men's Brotherhood that same year. I was asked by our minister to lead the first Bible study. That evening, in the organizational meeting, I was elected as president of the Brotherhood.

During those years I asked Rev. Dolfin to suggest Bible study materials. He even ordered some of these for me, in this way I began to build my own library.

God continued to touch my heart to answer His Call. Finally, around the midnight hour, October 1, 1949, God spoke His Holy Word, from the Sacred Page, which confirmed His Call. I had returned home from a Sunday school Teachers and Officers meeting. One item of business had to deal with making a choice of a new missionary to support. During the discussion a comment was made as to how long it was since a son of the church had gone into full-time service—Benes boys,

M. Tysen, and H. Zylstra. Strange, but my heart almost stood still. Fearful. Would I have to say, "Lord, here am I, send me?" I was quiet. I stared under the table, almost fearful that my name would be spoken.

Afterwards I lingered to talk with our pastor. Rev. Dolfin, personally, was struggling with a Call from another church. We talked about such a struggle. Finally I opened my heart to share my feelings, admitting maybe I should go to a Bible school. However, he advised flatly against that. Then he pointed out to me that our Savior deserves the very best, you should think of college and seminary. To such an idea I protested: "But seven years!" I rebelled at the very thought. Much less even considering the thought of Greek and Hebrew! As we were parting, he told me to pray. Adding that he and Mrs. Dolfin would be praying, too.

I travelled a rough seven miles home. My rebel spirit put up a battle. Why had I even talked to him about it? I told Allie about it, as she was waiting up for me. Our second daughter had been born a month before, so Martha Jane was only four weeks old. Karen Ann, our oldest, was thirteen months older than our newborn. Both children were sleeping, but before we went to bed, we had to have our devotions. We read the passage from Matthew 28. There it was, His Call in verses 19 and 20, Part of the Great Commission.

God didn't need neon lights in the heavens. His marching orders were before us on the sacred page. My Savior Jesus Christ spoke those words! Now they were meant for me!

The next morning our devotional booklet spoke again. The theme mentioned people will pray and give, so that others may go, but they will not go themselves. At the bottom of the page was this question: "How about you, reader?"

I talked with my father, Dad said in effect, "You go, we'll take care of things on this end." Once again I talked with Pastor Dolfin. This was on Sunday morning. He had a busy schedule, likely some time later he could talk. So I took it to mean God was closing the door. However, that afternoon he approached me, saying his schedule had completely cleared of every conflict. My family was invited over Sunday evening. In a positive way, he talked of going to Hope College. He wanted to go the next morning, but I had to get someone to help Dad with the harvest. Tuesday we visited the college. At a special meeting, rules were set aside, I was to begin college the next morning. A home to rent became available that Tuesday afternoon. Allie and Pastor Dolfin returned home.

I stayed in the seminary dormitory that night. Once they left, I returned to my room. I dropped to my knees next to the bed to pray. Fearfully, I said, "Heavenly Father, I don't know all I promised You. I don't know what is before me in school. But You did promise to be with me, I want You to remember that. I need You to be there. I need your help, for Jesus' sake. Amen."

A knock was heard at my door. There stood two seminary students, when I opened the door. There was Bob Schuller, along with his closest friend, Warren Hietbrink. They introduced themselves, then Bob asked about my being there. I told them of my Call, as simply as I could. Schuller turned to Warren, saying, "That's amazing. I never heard anything like that, have you, Warren?" They gave me encouragement, which was very supportive.

Wednesday morning I attended the first chapel service, then my first day of classes. Thursday we moved from our new home on the farm to Holland, Michigan.

God opened all doors. I had to listen to His Call and obey. My Heavenly Father had lined up all things: First, His people, and His Word, also the Holy Spirit's urging, and last, life's circumstances. God, through all of these, assured me of His Call to preach the glorious Good News of His Gospel of Jesus Christ.

I left the old home place to go for Jesus. I left the farm in faith. For seven years I trusted my Lord, all by faith. After my studies, at Hope College and Western Theological Seminary, then came three promises of Calls extended to me. Then the Church of Jesus Christ recognized my gifts, following those promises I still went by faith, but I could go also by sight.

God gave solid assurance of my Call. That doesn't mean Satan didn't try to get me to doubt God's assurance. Each time

I reminded our old enemy that I had a vision of my Father in Heaven, Who gave me His Call. Praise His Name for the solid reality of His blessed assurance.

All glory to His Name. He alone is worthy.

I remain so thankful for those years being part of the Body of Christ in the First Reformed Church of De Motte, Indiana.

Isn't it just amazing? Another boy from Hoosierland was called into His service.

To think I had the privilege of lifting up on high the Name of Jesus! "O Lord, our Lord, how majestic is Your Name in all the earth." It is also majestic in Heaven. Some glorious day it will be majestic forever and ever!

A boy from Hoosierland was called to serve his Lord. That Call took him to various places in our country. I was student pastor for two summers. The seminary sent me to two Presbyterian churches in 1954. They were seven miles apart from each other in the small communities of Kunkle and West Unity, Ohio. The following summer, in 1955, I was the student pastor in the First Reformed Church of Ireton, Iowa. The date of my ordination was on June 19, 1956, which was held in the Carmel Reformed Church. Carmel is a small community near Sioux Center, Rock Valley, and Hull, Iowa.

I served the following pastorates:

Carmel Reformed Church, Rock Valley, Iowa
June 1956 to January 1960

Trinity Reformed Church, Battle Creek, Michigan
February 1960 to September 1965

Hollandale Reformed Church, Hollandale, Minnesota
October 1965 to June 1969

First Reformed Church, Fulton, Illinois
July 1969 to October 1973

American Reformed Church, Luverne, Minnesota
November 1973 to September 1985

Bayshore Gardens Reformed Church, Bradenton, Florida
October 1985 to September 1990

I retired on September 30, 1990, after preaching my farewell message. During my ministry I had preached 3,704 sermons.

To God alone be the glory!

"Dutch Corners" Church as I remember it when a boy. Generally it is known as our second church building—1914.

The Old Outhouse

As a boy I well remember our old outhouse. Ours was a "two holer" toilet, in our backyard, just behind the little shanty.

During the winter it could be really cold to go out there. On a cold day or night, the visit to the toilet was made in a hurry. I know it was cold on a kid's poopet. If it was subzero weather, then you could use the pot, called the old American vessel in our house. You hoped somebody had emptied it. Nothing worse than finding it full. Pee-uu, it smelled when the lid was taken off. You also hoped you didn't bump it to spill some of it. Of course, it was a disaster if it got tipped over—with yellow stuff all over the floor. To a Dutchman an old pot could be *vies*.

In the summertime, it was different. Never had to be in such a hurry. One could sit out there in peace for a little while.

My memory as a kid was that of Mom and Dad sitting out there in the outhouse after breakfast. Both there at the same time, Dad on one side, Mom on the other. We'd play around in the yard while they sat in the toilet. If their stay got too long, then I'd peek in the door. I'd ask how much longer they were going to be in there. Generally I was told to close the door.

There wasn't any toilet paper in the privy. Next to you on the seat was an old catalog, either Sears or Wards. Sometimes it was on the floor. Every visit you looked through it, but eventually you had to use some paper out of it. Not those slick pages. Maybe they had the nicest pictures, but those kind were not the best for toilet paper. A plain page was picked out, then wadded up to be used. Whenever it was nice weather, most of us took time to page through the catalog. I liked to look at the toys, or clothes. I always hoped nobody would take my favorite pages for toilet paper.

Most of the outhouses generally got dumped over one time in the year. If yours got tipped over, then you knew some big boys had visited your place at Halloween. It was great fun to dump one over. Naturally most families would look out the window the next morning, to see if some boys had pushed over their old outhouse. Setting it back up again was the first job of the morning.

Each outhouse had a pit. Sometimes it was only about two feet deep, maybe three. But then, others could be very deep, up to seven or eight feet.

If a farmer had his dumped over enough, then he might move it ahead a few feet. It was ready for any mischievous night visitors. In the dark they may slip or fall into the pit. Right into the pee-uu-wie mess! Many old stories could be told about fellows falling into those pits during those nights of outhouse dumping. For a fellow to get into such a filthy or dirty mess, everybody else would be *vies* of him! People got a kick out of such news—serves him right!

As a boy I can remember seeing our outhouse dumped over. I wondered what boys would do that to us. Dad talked about it one year, so he decided to do something about it. Big fence posts were put around it, one on each side. It must have been too much work for pranksters, for it was never dumped after that.

When I was seven years old Grandpa and Grandma Walstra had their 50th Wedding Anniversary. The celebration for Hijt and Mem was at the school. It was there, probably, because Uncle Al Roorda was the janitor at school.

Anyway, I still remember that night! I had to go to the toilet. That meant I had to visit the big outhouse behind school. This one was a "four holer" with plenty of space between holes. You could lay your clothes in that space or there was paper setting there. I took off my vest when I sat down on the seat. These toilets had deep pits. I happened to brush my vest when I got up—down through the hole it fell! Right into the pit!

I ran into school bawling my head off. All the people turned, wondering, what happened to Billy? Between heart-

223

break cries, I managed to tell them. Uncle Al and several other men when out there with a flashlight. Uncle Al had his long pole, which had a hook on the end. This pole was used to open those high windows in school. With that pole he hooked my vest and pulled it from the bottom of the pit. Fortunately it landed on nothing but paper. It wasn't even dirty. I put it on again and ran into school—a happy seven-year-old ready to celebrate with Grandpa and Grandma on their anniversary.

I never did figure out the number business: one or two. What was it, do you have to pick a number? What difference did it make anyway? Why did some adult have to know what you were going to do? Besides I never understood why one was one or two was two. Frankly I never felt like I wanted to tell anybody that my visit was going to be one or two, nor one-two! (Once I think about this number stuff, that's probably where it all got started. Everything since has been a number. I'm even a number. It was never so complicated during the old outhouse days!)

Many times on the farm we didn't have the luxury of the privy or pot. Both might be clear across the farm. Whenever that happened, then the whole out-of-doors became an out-house. You stepped behind a bush or tree, or behind the tractor tire or the wagon. Maybe some tall weeds were found, or a cornfield was just as handy. Out in the woods or grove, you sometimes had to sit down over a fallen tree. Should it turn out that I was in the great outdoors, I sat on the tractor draw-bar or the wagon tongue.

While on the yard, then more choices were possible. The choices included going behind the house, barn, crib, shed, or even a strawstack. However, it was much better in the barn, there were the horse stalls or the gutter behind the cows.

Only trouble was that you never had a catalog along out in the field or woods. Many times you had to use leaves, grass or weeds, instead of a page out of the catalog. That could be a little disturbing or dangerous, for most boys could tell a story about using the wrong weeds. The worst pick would be to grab a handful of nettles, with those prickly, stinging hairs. Any boy who decided to use those nettles had to be prepared

224

to live with more than a slight irritation for several hours. Instead he should have used his handkerchief, only to say it got "lost" somehow. Around the barn, perhaps in the field too, an old sack was a good substitute for a page out of the Sears catalog.

Away from home a public restroom could be a smelly place. I felt many were very *vies* places to go, which had to be the Dutch in me. I never enjoyed standing by those tin troughs which stunk and splattered. Most disturbing, really disgusting, were the fellows who had to pee all over the toilet seats. A few were ornery enough to do this on purpose. While they thought it was smart, I thought it was dumb.

In those "Good Old Days" of the outhouse, sometimes one had to be very creative. Regardless of one, two, or one-two.

During the Depression our government was looking for ways to get people to work. One of the work projects was to build new outhouses. Some official came to our farm; Dad bought one. As I recall, the price was about $22.50 or $25.00.

It was painted grey. They dug a four-foot deep pit. The floor was cement, one solid slab, with the seat formed also from cement. A varnished seat and lid was fastened to the cement stool. Coming out of the back of the seat was a vent pipe. It was vented through the roof.

That was such an improvement in eliminating odors. This was one neat outhouse, I felt, as a kid.

We used the new one until we got our indoor bathroom. Even then, when we were outdoors, we still frequently used it.

As our family grew, our house was remodeled from time to time. When we got our bathroom, part of the old summer kitchen was used for that purpose. Far from modern, by today's standards, but it was indoors. We really liked it.

I still remember the door to the bathroom was open, when company walked in. Our visitors were Dad's cousins, Lommie Barsema from Maywood and his brother, John, from the Oak Park area near Chicago. They couldn't believe we had a bathroom on the farm. Standing in the kitchen, one pointed to the stool and bathtub, saying, "Get a load of that—they have a bathroom!" For them, it was hard to believe. I guess those city-cousins felt farmers wouldn't have the luxuries of the big city. This was so unexpected, weren't farms to have only outhouses? City cousins, not anymore!

Yet I still recall, after supper, in the dark, Dad, Lommie, and us boys still stepped behind the house to go to the bathroom. Even with a new bathroom, old habits were hard to break. It was much easier to go behind the house. I can still remember the jokes and laughter of Lommie and Dad, while they were behind the house.

But the passing of the old outhouse on the farm eventually changed our whole lifestyle.

Our outhouses on the farm in Hoosierland still have a special place in my memories. After all, the outhouse was an institution of all its own. How could all our modern fixtures and decor ever replace it?

The Old Wood Pile

There was always that old wood pile on the hill. It was a big pile at times, but much smaller at times, especially after a long, hard winter. But in the spring, we'd buzz wood again. Then the big pile would be back.

Our wood pile was on the crown of the hill. It was surrounded by the shanty and house on the west, the old black cob shed on the northside, with the barn to the east. Other buildings were to the south, but downhill.

When trees were cleared off a patch of land they would be brought to the hill on the running gear of a wagon. If possible the tree was left whole, only trimming off branches. Some were long ones piled under the clotheslines. However, if it were an older tree, quite large, then it would be cut up so it could be loaded. From those large logs we would get big heater chunks.

At times a ditch bank had to be cleared, so it could be cleaned out.

Wherever we found the wood, it would be hauled by wagon to the pile on the hill. It would take weeks, maybe a month to get all the wood needed for another year.

This pile started at the big oak, where we had our swing. Going north, it covered the crown of the hill, reaching the drive near the cob shed. The whole hill was covered with logs.

We started buzzing from the north end, working to the south, until we reached the oak tree with our swing. Our saw was staked down. A belt from the pulley of the tractor ran the saw.

First of all, the buzz saw was sharpened, so we could cut through the hard wood. Once you started the saw, it would whirl so fast that it would "sing" as it turned. It would put a ringing in your ears all the time you were buzzing wood.

227

One person would push the logs into the saw. Another person would hold the end, maybe with the help of another person. Then one person held the end to be cut off. He caught that piece or chunk. It would be tossed on the pile. Piece after piece was cut off, hundreds, thousands, until it was finished—the whole pile. All day long we worked at buzzing wood. The pile of logs had to grow smaller, as the pile of chunks grew larger. Some years it took more than one day to cut all the wood. Eventually the last log would be cut up.

After it was done, then we'd walk around the pile to pick up the strays. Some chunks tumbled too far. Others were tossed too far. Finally the big pile was ready for another winter. Looking at that huge pile, one could hardly imagine, but eventually every piece of wood had to be carried into the house. Some of the smaller pieces were burned in Mom's cook stove. A lot had to be burned in the big heater in the living room. That was a big pile of warmth for the next winter as we gathered around our stoves.

I'd sort out the smaller pieces of wood for the cook stove. I had to split some of it, small enough to fit in the fire box of her stove. Other pieces would be big chunks. They were burned in the heater, which had a much larger door and fire box. If a chunk had a big knot, which made it difficult to split, you tried to toss the whole thing in the heater. Our heater could get hot! On a windy day, with the draft open, it could burn very hard. Red spots could be seen on the stove. A "red hot" stove was HOT!

Those big chunks were placed on a big mat or on newspapers by the heater. Depending on how cold it was, but I made sure plenty was brought in for the whole night. On the porch was our wood box. That's where we kept the split wood. Some would be put by the stove in the kitchen, so you didn't have to get it from the porch every time. Once gone, then you had to go to the wood box.

If they predicted very bad weather, frigid cold or heavy snow, then more wood was stacked on the porch. Most of the time I had plenty piled on the porch, which meant we had dry wood to burn. Of course, if the weather did change for the worst, then enough wood was indoors for that storm. If I could help it, I never cared to get wood when the weather was so miserable.

After the wood was in, I still had to get a bucket of cobs. Dry cobs were good for starting a fire. Maybe the fire went out during the night, cobs were then handy for that chore in the morning. Most of the time a fire could get going much faster with dry cobs, then add wood. We kept a good supply of dry cobs in the old black cob shed.

Many times our red wagon was used to carry wood to the house. I'd pull the load to the porch door, where I unloaded it. From there I'd take it to the heater or wood box. Any extra would be piled high in the corner of the porch.

Sometimes I'd put a big chunk in front of the porch door. It held the door open, so I could carry the wood into the house in a hurry. With the door open, I could carry a bigger armful each trip. The whole armful would be dumped when I reached the wood box, or the place where I was cording it. If two of us worked at it, one would load the arms of the other. That person could carry a much bigger load, who would then trot or run to the house to get it dumped.

It was a lot of work to get enough in the house, if a cold spell was expected. I liked to be prepared for bad weather. With the wood indoors and piled high, I got a nice warm feeling as a boy. Knowing we'd be warm on a bitter cold winter night gave me a feeling of satisfaction. A big pile in the house gave me a lot of assurance.

Maybe a good feeling came from the wood pile itself. One of my first toys came from our wood pile. A piece of wood was my "baby" when I played. Mom told how I'd play with a stick of split wood, wrapped in a little blanket, for hours. That was my first doll. Just a plain piece of wood was one of my first playthings when I was very small. Mom claimed I had a lot of fun with my wooden doll.

One specific day is tucked away in my memory. We were buzzing wood on April 12, 1945. Perhaps one third of the pile was left. We had stopped for a break, since the saw had to be sharpened. I ran into the house for a drink. Quickly, I turned

229

my little radio on for a minute or two. A news flash was being given: "President Franklin Delano Roosevelt died in Warm Springs, Georgia." I was shocked, stunned!

A few more details were given, but I dared not listen any longer. I shut the radio off. The crew was ready to buzz wood again. They started before I got back. Over the noise of the noise of the saw, I yelled the news of our President's death to Dad.

It wasn't news my father liked. His first comment, "Now we are going to have that old Truman for our President."

Dad was a reader. He had read some stories about Truman, which caused him to wonder about our vice president. Those stories were about him as he got into big time politics, which sent him to Washington, D. C. Dad plainly was not fond of Harry S. Truman.

Deep in our thoughts over hearing the shocking news, we mostly went through the motions of buzzing more wood. Each one of the crew was alone with his thoughts. What was ahead for our nation? We were still fighting a World War!

So that day still lives with me, seems like it happened only yesterday. I could show any person the exact spot where we pondered the news of the death of our President Roosevelt.

Our Pump and Power Plant

Changes eventually came to our home. We had some changes in our house with a new pump and Delco power plant. Remodeling of our kitchen not only made it larger, but we got a pump by the kitchen sink.

At the same time our summer kitchen was extended, to the east. Also the entrance to our house was changed, with a small porch. It had a door and two large windows.

Another pump was put in the summer kitchen, where Mom did her washing. That room was also our storage room. Our work clothes were hung in there. There was also a large gunny sack hanging on a nail, which was our rag bag. Useful and interesting things were in that bag. But those rags came in handy many times.

A sink and pump were in the summer kitchen. After chores our hired men and family members cleaned up there, before we ate. A wash basin was in the sink. Naturally, only cold water could be pumped into the basin for washing up.

When we remodeled a new pump was put on the end of the kitchen sink. Dad had driven down a sand point, which did not have to go very deep. It was always easy to reach water on our sandhill. No longer did we have to carry water. Under the pump was a bucket in the sink. The bucket had a dipper in it, which was used for drinking. Besides you used the dipper to put water in the basin.

One could pump a dipperful of fresh water, for drinking. Other times a person just dipped out some water from the galvanized bucket. After a drink, then it was put back in the bucket. The next person would use it. Nobody thought too much about using the same dipper. It was reused many times.

This was a big help to have new pumps. It would be a few years before we got running water in our home.

When I was small we had Aladdin lamps. These were gas lamps with mantles, which helped the flame to burn brightly. However, those mantles were extremely fragile. Naturally a child's temptation was to touch those cute little white mantles. That was the wrong thing to do. Instantly it would disintegrate in tiny white ashes. The times I touched them was enough to dissolve them into worthless ash. At times a small hole would be found in the mantle. Generally it did not have to be replaced, for it would still burn that way.

Each evening these lamps had to be checked. Gas was checked, then pressure had to be pumped into the tank. In lighting an Aladdin lamp, one had to wait for the lamp to generate. Afterwards adjustments would be made for a full flame and brightest light.

Normally we had kerosene lamps around the house. They were rather simple to use. But they didn't produce the light an Aladdin did. The flame was a yellow glow. Then, too, if you turned the kerosene lamp up too high, one ended up with a dirty chimney. Even a black one, in a hurry. One had to carefully adjust how high you wanted it to burn. A black chimney meant it was a poor light for the room.

When we went outside a kerosene lantern was used. As one walked after dark, generally it gave enough light around your feet. We'd use a couple of them in the barn after dark. In the winter it would get dark early, so we had to use them in the horse barn and calf pen. A couple were used while milking cows. One hung it up wherever you were working. Generally a nail was nearby, where a person hung the lantern. Even though they gave a poor light, one was thankful to have light when it got dark.

One could get the chores finished.

The biggest change took place when Dad bought a Delco plant to generate our own power. Dad got it at a farm sale. It was secondhand, but in good shape. We only got the large generator, without batteries.

Dad ordered the sixteen large storage batteries. Both the Delco engine and set of batteries were placed in our cellar. A trap door had to be opened to get into our cellar. Others had to be warned when we had that door open. Many times we'd close it behind us, to prevent somebody else from falling down the steps.

Our cellar was mainly under the old summer kitchen. It was a single room for a fruit and vegetable storage area. The walls were made from cement blocks, while the floor had soft, dry yellow sand. A cement block-base was poured for the generator. The engine was bolted to the base. An exhaust pipe went through the wall outside. Against the west wall we placed the two rows of batteries, eight on top, plus eight more below on the bottom shelf. Rods were so positioned so all the batteries were connected. However, when they were installed, Ivan Cheever made a mistake. One row was lined up incorrectly, so all the rods had to be bent, while the other row had straight rods. He could have saved himself a lot of work had both rows been lined up properly. His mistake did not cause any problems as to how the system functioned, for it worked all right.

The end battery, at the bottom, had three colored bulbs. If the batteries were holding full charge, all floated to the top. But as the charge dropped, the green one went down first, then the yellow, finally the red one hit the bottom. You could tell by the lights when the batteries were low. It was time to put gas in the tank and start the Delco engine. With dim lights, it was time for a recharge.

Our lights were never very bright anyway, for we used only light bulbs of 25, 40 and 50 watts. Very seldom did we use larger ones.

We had just a couple of bulbs in the horse barn and cow barn. Each room had a bulb, generally in the center of the ceiling. At first we had only a few lamps in our house.

Whenever Mom was going to iron clothes, then she told me to start the Delco. Her iron would really draw down the lights, making them dim. The power plant had to run all the time Mom did her ironing each week.

The Delco motor had a sound all its own. While outside, one could easily tell the motor was running.

If we had it running to recharge the batteries, then one had to check it every now and then. The red ball, or bulb, would float up first, then the yellow, after it ran for some time, finally the green one was back on top. Once the green ball floated to the top, we knew those sixteen batteries had full charge again. We could shut off the Delco.

We had "electric" on our farm, something most farmers did not have in those days. We did, which helped us out so much. After all, during those Depression days more than 89% of the farms in our country did *not* have electricity. It was dark in the countryside!

However, something was soon to happen on many farms. Farms were to get their own electric power. The new program was called REA, Rural Electric Association.

Most of the buildings had to be wired for this change. It meant we could use more bulbs, and much larger ones, too. We got more electric appliances and motors. This was a big change in the lives of all farm families.

The early beginning of REA happened on May 11, 1935, when I was ten. Our President signed the bill, with his signature, Franklin D. Roosevelt brought the Rural Electrification Administration into being.

Times were tough. The year 1934 had a disastrous drought, with 1936 not being any better. Some naturally thought it was the worse of times to think about putting electric on farms. Some sneered at it. Some even said it was a "lot of foolishness" to put electricity in rural America. Costs were expected to be four times more in the country than in the city. Utility companies often refused to sell wholesale power at reasonable rates. They scoffed at the very idea of REA, commenting that a bunch of farmers would never be able to run such a system.

They were wrong! With the backing of President Roosevelt, Congress, and those determined people in rural America—it worked! Bright lights were soon shinning in that dark countryside!

While it didn't reach us in those very early days, that didn't bother us, for we had our Delco system. Jasper county did get it, but it took a couple of years. Our own electric system was one big improvement over the lanterns, and gas and kerosene lamps. Lights may have been rather dim, but our farm was not in the dark! Once the REA came through we had another big change. We had even a yard light on the end of our house.

This was just the beginning of big changes for us, and for all farmers, with many more to changes to come.

The Insect World

God put many insects on our farm in the marsh. Our old sand hill was full of fleas.

During the dry years of the Depression we had no shortage of sand fleas. Those miserable pests could bite!

Dad tried to control them by covering our yard with buckwheat straw. The idea was for the flea to crawl inside the straw through the joint-hole, once in there, the flea would not be able to get out. During those times Dad had our yard covered each year. We walked on buckwheat straw the whole summer.

While it helped, it didn't take care of the problem. At night they would bite us in bed. Mom had a nightly ritual before all of us kids fell asleep. It was her evening flea-search. She could spot them on the white sheets. While flea hunting, she used a flashlight. She'd spit on her finger and thumb, then nail 'em. She moved fast enough to pick them off one by one. Once caught, the flea got her squeeze play. As it was hung up in her wet spit, she'd place the flea on her thumbnail, then crush it by rubbing it out with the other thumbnail. Each captive flea got the same treatment. Once each bed had been cleared of all the fleas, then we could try to get some sleep on a hot summer night.

Play could be pestered by the fleas. Cousin Bill of George and I had our bellies covered black with them after playing in an old pig shed. We had to strip and run for relief. Once we began running free in the breeze, we were flea-free. But even nature boys on the farm eventually have to put clean clothes back on.

We also had plenty of flies. Houseflies were aggravating pests. During the summertime we had sticky fly strips hanging around the house, summer kitchen and porch. We'd also go after them with a hand sprayer, in which we used a fly spray. Now and then we'd spray the house. It was used every day before milking our cows. It seemed that a coming storm made them bigger pests than ever. At least their bite was more painful, it seemed.

Once you had seen them in the cow yard landing on the manure piles or in the gutter, then you hated them on the food or table. You just were *vies* of every one of them!

During the summer and fall those dirty things were all over. They would bother the animals. Many times they were bothered by the deer fly and black horse fly. Deer flies would be so hard on the cows while resting in the shade. But they bothered the horses too. A big black horse fly was about a full inch long, which could give such a severe bite. Animals constantly shivered to shake their hide, or switched their tails. If we had a chance to slap one of them with our hand, we'd give them a good smack. Generally blood would splatter.

Now and then a person would get bit by a deer fly. Man, it was an awful bite, very painful.

Lice. Those lousy creatures would make your skin crawl. Our chickens sometimes had lice. We'd use a powder to dust each bird. But if we really wanted to go after them, that took Black Leaf 40. All the roasts would be painted. Talk about stout stuff! It stunk! It was so hard to breathe while doing the job. It was almost impossible to stay in the chicken coop very long. How the chickens stood it, I'll never know. But Black Leaf 40 took care of the lousy lice!

While doing the chickens at times I'd discover a louse crawling on me. After such a discovery, I felt like lice were all over me. I would imagine lice everywhere—in my hair, over my body, in my clothes. I itched all over. I had an imagination that ran wild; I felt really lousy.

The most horrible time for me was when a louse from a dead chicken crawled on me. All the time I carried the dead bird, I'd constantly spit. That really bothered me.

Stink bugs stunk! The odor of a stink bug fascinated us boys. You could smell it a long time after you handled it. Stag and horn beetles were interesting, too.

Those huge black bugs were known to us as pinching bugs. It was fun to get on your knees or bellyflop to watch them. It was fun to see them pinch a stick or straw.

I think the greatest pleasure of a summer night was to see fireflies. In the evening they were busy flashing their lights. At the bottom of the hill and all the way to the Cook Ditch we could see their little lights flashing everywhere. They would fly all over the little timothy field. It wasn't long before we'd be running after them. It was fun to catch them. We'd cup them in our hands, then peek to watch them flash their lights. Most of the time we put some in a bottle, so we could watch them better. It always amazed us that God gave them such marvelous lights to flash. Fireflies added one more pleasure of a summer's night in Hoosierland. An evening on the farm would give us a beautiful display. Any boy was fascinated to watch the action of this light display for a while in the evening.

Another beautiful creature made by God was the butterfly. These painted beauties had breathtaking colors. We had many of the common, attractive monarch. It was like they had a flight pattern all their own. At times it was like they would do a dance from one flower to another, or from weed to weed, or bush to bush. It was like a waltz while in flight. As these butterflies usually would fly by day, their multi-colored wings flashed colors no person could match. Some painted with blacks, others oranges, or greens, reds, yellows, purples, maybe a thousand other shades. Butterflies were so beautiful on a bright day in Indiana. In the warmth of the early morning sun they were like a symphony over the landscape of the fields. They actually declared the glory of God.

Nights were filled with the flight of moths. Especially darting around a light. Many were not as colorful as some butterflies, yet they had a beauty all their own. Once in a while we'd discover a cecropia moth, a sight to see!

Closely related to these creatures were the many caterpillars seen on the farm. There were the cocoons and larva. The special ones were the woollybears. It was fun to hold one in your hand. I always thought the woollybear had fur. It must have been a scary thing for them, each one would tuck itself in a tight, little ball.

One common pest was the corn earworm and borers. I came to know this new visitor as the European corn borer. During the Depression we had our car stopped one night. These officials were checking every car for corn. That was the first time I heard of the European corn borer. They requested to look inside the car and trunk. Using a flashlight for their search, one found himself shinning his light right on our old American vessel. While on our trips, we always had a pot on a trip. He was taken aback by the evidence discovered. Our family had a good laugh after we drove away, joking about his search for the European corn borer.

One more pest showed up during those dry years. It was the chinch bug. They overran the grain fields. They destroyed the grain as they fed on plant juices. They were a plague during the days of the Chicago World's Fair. In order to get in free at the fair, farmers were to bring a quart jar of chinch bugs. Now these were very small, almost minute, but two or three generations could be born each season. Some farmers plowed a furrow around the grain fields. In the furrow the farmer dug postholes, into which they poured creosote. The idea was that the traveling chinch bugs would tumble into the hole to their death, falling in the creosote.

We had to dust or spray for the potato bug. Another one we had to watch out for was the striped and spotted cucumber beetle. We called them pickle bugs. Once spotted on our plants, we dusted the field with lime. It was the same kind of lime we used in the cow barn. We'd dump some lime in a loose knit sack, in which we bought binder twine. This sack would be shook up and down as we walked down the rows of pickle plants. The dust would drift down on the plants.

Since our farms were in the marsh, I must not forget those pesky mosquitoes. During a wet season we had so many of those creatures. Their constant buzz was enough to drive a person goofy. This was especially true when a mosquito got into the bedroom at night. About the time I wanted to go to sleep, I got buzzed! Swatting didn't help much. It seemed one of those pesky creatures always managed to escape. In the stillness of the night, the drone of its return flight would be heard. Sooner or later it came in for a safe landing. Before I knew it, a beak pierced into my body to draw blood. The itch afterwards was miserable.

It didn't help much to know the male mosquitoes were the harmless ones. Their beaks are not fitted for piercing into a person. Females bite, and pass on disease. Also, they are the only ones which buzz.

It seems easy for them to find a person. It was extremely aggravating when I had to work in a shady or wooded area, then they seem to know just where to find me. They did their best to keep me and others from work. As if that were not enough, later at night, they tried to keep me from getting sleep. They were pesky! It was a pleasure to catch them in the act—then bop them!

God indeed had many creatures on our farms. A summer's evening was not complete without the katydid call. These were so green, with leaf-like wings. Another one adding to the night's songs was the cricket. It seemed like their shrill musical night song came from all kinds of hiding places. It was enough to keep you from going to sleep. A night search could be so difficult when trying to locate its hiding place. Many times the black cricket would be found almost right in front of you. Once found, you did not tell the cricket it had had its swan song! Its night song had been sung.

Not only were the crops damaged by the crickets, but so could your clothing. Crickets eat clothes. One day while picking pickles it got so hot, I took off my undershirt. I tossed it on a plant, intending to pick it up later. But I forgot to go after it at the end of the day. The next morning I went to get it. It was full of holes! Overnight they riddled it. Unbelievable! After looking it over, I hung it on the lane fence. Our young black stallion took it off the fence with his mouth. Next, I saw him lower his head, so he could put his foot on my undershirt. After that he lifted his head, ripping it to shreds. several times he repeated it, then walked away.

Between the black crickets and the black stallion my undershirt was ready for the old rag bag.

We had plenty of grasshoppers, more some years, than others. But we always had plenty of them. They could be destructive too. As a kid I was always fascinated by the way they could "spit tobacco." Once we'd catch one, then we'd make it spit tobacco juice. Generally spitting on our hands, but that could be wiped off on our pants. It felt very strange when a grasshopper landed on your bare arm in the summer. It was also fun to watch them take a big hop. Chasing them, I'd watch how far they could leap.

In a more painful way we learned about blue mud dauber wasps. We had plenty of the common paper wasps, who had nests under eaves, or in the barn or crib. I recall some yellow jackets which nailed me while preparing to unload grain with our elevator. I was unfolding a canvas when these yellow jackets decided I had to be paid back for disturbing them. That was very painful when they repeatedly stung me.

Ants were found in many places on our sand hills or under dead logs or wood. They were always such busy little creatures. When I was a boy I enjoyed watching ants with all their energy. I could learn a lot of lessons from those energetic little insects. Bumble bees could cause plenty of trouble, if a person bothered them. Generally I gave them plenty of room, when I knew they were around.

Bumble bees were always in our hay fields. More than one story could be told for knowingly or unknowingly messing with them.

The bumble bee had a way of getting your attention, so you paid much closer attention next time.

There was honey in the woods. If you went over the big hill east of the farm yard, you could spot them. Beehives. Near the Cook Ditch, 140 hives were in the woods.

Frank Roorda had all those bees in our woods. If you did not know any better, one might think it was a cemetery. All those beehives on the hill looked like so many white headstones in a graveyard.

241

Believe me, they were very much alive. Frank had honey bees tucked away in our woods.

His little shanty was built out of boxcar lumber, from a yellow car. It was only a one room shanty. Frank built it upon a slab of cement. A few windows were along the front, the southside, with a workbench under the windows. A door was on the eastside.

In one corner was a strange looking machine. This was used to render or extract honey from the honeycomb. One was very unique, with all those hexagonal cells of wax built by the bees. Wax would be put on wooden frames, which were placed inside the beehives.

Inside the hive would be found a colony of a queen, workers, and drones. Those little bees would work the entire area on and around our farm. Frank felt this was one of the best places to have his bees.

For one pound of honey it takes 550 bees working. They had to make 2.5 million visits to flowers—all for one single pound of honey. They took the flower nectar back to the hive bees. Those bees then converted it into honey, which was stored inside the beewax honeycombs.

Clover makes for a light colored honey, while buckwheat flowers produces a darker honey. A good hive could make 15 pounds in a day, according to one source. That means the 80,000 bees in one colony really had to be busy.

As boys we liked visiting the shanty, liking better the taste of honey. On our way through the woods we saw many red honeysuckle plants. They would give us a little taste of honey. Down at the bottom of those flowers were four little bulbs with honey. We'd nip these off to taste the honey.

But that was nothing. The real taste was given to us in the shanty. Frank would hand us each a big chunk of honey still in the honeycomb. Sweet! That was sweet!

You know in the Bible Samson had a riddle about something sweet. In the answer, coming in the form of a question, "What is sweeter than honey?"

I think the Psalmist knew something about honey, too. When talking about the Bible, he said, "How sweet are your promises to taste, sweeter than honey in my mouth!" (Psalm 119:103) The precious promises of God are so compared: "They are sweeter than honey, than honey from the comb." (Psalm 19) As kids we found out how sweet was honey from the honeycomb! Very, very sweet!

As boys we got our sweet treat in the old shanty. Frank would watch us, looking over his glasses. Most of the time they had slipped down on his nose, so he'd drop his head to see over the top of them.

Well, nothing could be sweeter. Nothing was stickier! It would be dripping from our hands, from between our fingers. It took a lot of licking and slicking.

Bees were everywhere. They were busy, for he had all kinds of honey stored in his shanty. 4,500 bees weigh a pound. 550 bees would have to make 2.5 million visits for one pound of honey. Now 80,000 working in a hive brought in fifteen pounds each day, on a good day.

How much did Frank have stored there? Plenty, I'm sure. Frank told me one day that he shipped out all his cans and drums of honey. A truck had been back there to haul it away.

Just think, little honey bees had hauled all that honey to the hives, storing it in those 140 hives on the hill. But it took a truck to haul it away!

Somewhere we have to be reminded that a bee can sting. As kids we made that painful discovery too often. The bee has a stinger for self-defense. There are barbs, or hooks, on the stinger. A sting causes sudden pain as poison is injected.

Over and over I remember seeing Frank brush the stinger off. When a bee sank its stinger in me, then I ran to Mom to pull out the stinger.

It would still hurt, but we always had good news. What gave us comfort was the death of the bee. When a worker bee stings it dies soon after losing its sting.

The Bible tells of the greatest comfort of all in Jesus Christ. Believers trust in Jesus Christ, the Resurrection and the Life. Our Savior took the stinger for us. We have a deadly enemy, death! We have to face the grave. Jesus Christ pulled the stinger for each Christian.

The Bible challenges with these questions: "O death, where is your victory? O death, where is your sting?" The Bible then reminds us that the sting of death is sin. Also the strength of sin is the Law.

But Christ pulled the stinger! The sting was taken out of death because sin is cancelled, and the strength of the Law to condemn us was removed, because it has been fulfilled in the Savior. We have been forgiven by the grace of God. Jesus paid it all, the complete debt of our sin.

The Christian, therefore, can challenge death, the last enemy. Christ pulled the stinger, as He brushed it off. He died to do this for us. But He rose again on Easter! In Christ death is swallowed up in victory. As Paul said, "Thanks be to God Who gives us the victory through the Lord Jesus Christ!" That's the glorious news of the Resurrection.

Christ died for our sins, but on the third day He arose again. Now we have a victorious Savior! He pulled the stinger out of sin and death, so He gives us the victory. He is the all-sufficient Savior. Nothing shall ever separate us from His love and grace, from Him. The victory all believers possess in Jesus Christ can never be lost. We are more than conquerors through Christ Who loved us. (Read the solid assurance given in Romans 8 and I Corinthians 15.) We can place unshakable confidence in our Savior. I praise Him, for He pulled the stinger for me!

Death could not keep his prey. Jesus my Lord had one mighty triumph over His foes. Our Easter Master arose a Victor from the darkest domain. Hallelujah! Christ arose!

The little honey bee with the sweetness of honey and its stinger gives us a wonderful reminder of the Gospel of Jesus Christ. May all the glory be given to the King of Kings and Lord of Lords! He is worthy of all glory forever and ever.

Dad's False Teeth

After Dad got into a problem with his teeth, then it wasn't long before he got false teeth. They could always be found in one of two places. Either in his mouth, but most likely his set would be in his shirt pocket.

Evidently, Dad did not get a good fit. His set bothered him a lot. It was not an unusual sight to see Dad downhill early in

Dad and Mom by the lilac bushes.

the morning. The toolshed door would be rolled open. Next, Dad would reach around a pole, to take a rasp or file off the shelf. The big horse rasp was one used on the horse's hoof. It was a rough and rugged old file.

Standing still, Dad would be testing how his teeth felt in his mouth. Next, he'd slip out a plate into his hand. Looking at them carefully, he'd find the exact spot causing a problem. With the rasp, that spot would get the works. A few times he'd use the smaller file. After a few moments, he'd clean off his teeth, replacing them in his mouth. He'd work on his false teeth until they felt more comfortable in his mouth.

For years Dad would rasp away on his set of false teeth.

It was no wonder the dentist didn't know what happened to them. He'd attempt to adjust them for a better fit. But there came a day when the dentist was astonished to discover how much wear and tear Dad had on his set. Little did the man know that Dad has his own Dental Clinic in the old toolshed.

If they bothered too much, Dad simply slipped them out of his mouth and put them into his shirt pocket.

One day they found a new place to be kept.

Dad was plowing, with his teeth in his pocket.

Leaning back to adjust the levers on the plow, he lost them. Those choppers slipped out of that pocket, right under the plow. Within a few seconds they were turned under, buried in one of the furrows. But where?

Dad searched in the sandy loam of the field. It was hopeless. All the scratching around in the soil never came up with his set of false teeth.

Those old teeth never knew it could be so gritty. Just to think about it is enough to send a shiver up my spine.

I have no idea if they will ever be discovered again. Suppose, just suppose, they were found "some day" in the field. Let the imagination of the future farmer run a little wild. Could he imagine—? Maybe early Indians had false teeth! Maybe some old trapper drowned in the old river bottom, as he was going under for the third time, he spit out his teeth. Why—maybe there was some foul play in that field. So a search would be started, digging in the whole area. Here are the teeth. Where are the bones from the body which go with them? As I say, speculation could run wild, unrestrained!

Maybe some scholars would write a paper about their find. All because Dad did not keep his teeth in his mouth.

Dad's old teeth caused a lot of problems. But those old false teeth finally bit the dust! Oh, well, Dad never did like them very much anyway.

Smell of Homemade Bread

Nothing could match the aroma of freshly baked home-made bread! Saturday afternoon was special on the farm in Indiana. That was the day Mom baked bread. Nothing tasted better than warm bread and buns.

Coming in the house at noon, a glance at the cook stove told the story. There was Mom's big bread pan on the warming closet of the cook stove.

When we were smaller we liked to watch Mom make bread. On the table would be flour, baking powder, yeast, plus other ingredients. This would be kneaded, worked and pressed into a big mass of bread dough. After this was done, then it would be placed in her big pan. The pan was wrapped in towels and placed on top of the stove. It had to rise. It was fun to watch it push the lid up, lifting it way above the rim of the pan.

Later it was ready to be put into the greased tins. Mom would be plumping the bread dough. We liked that; we'd be right on top of her. Every now and then this soft dough for a loaf would hit one of us kids right on the cheek! Mom, of course, did it on purpose. Pow! Again the bread dough, so soft, would hit its mark. The sides of our faces would have flour on our cheeks. It was fun. We liked it, so we begged for more.

But she had to get the dough in the tins. She had a number of loaves each week, but some dough was kept for biscuits. Those little round balls were put into pie pans. When they were ready, she put them into the hot oven.

After a short while there was a smell...a wonderful aroma in the kitchen. Later the smell drifted into other parts of the house.

When we were older a whiff of baking of bread would draw us like a magnet to the house. Saturday afternoon we could hardly wait until tea time. That special time was pure enjoyment before the chores. The kids in our house weren't the only ones who felt that pull of freshly baked bread. It wasn't hard to find other kids coming to our place on Saturday afternoon. Other kids got to know, firsthand, about Mom's homemade bread. It was so interesting how other kids "happened" to be there to play or come over to talk—on Saturday. I must confess, freshly baked bread would be inviting to me, too.

Mom had on the table the tea, biscuits, butter and brown sugar for our feast. Oh, boy, they were really good. To this day those experiences are part of the fondest memories I have of my boyhood. Really, nothing tasted better than Mom's homemade bread and hot biscuits with brown sugar. Especially when it came fresh, and hot, right out of the oven. Sometimes they just got out of the oven—hot! Almost too hot to handle. I'd toss a hot one back and forth, until I could hold it.

Over and over as kids we had a question for Mom, "Can I have just one more, please?"

When it was that fresh, so soft, we could hardly cut it. Only one bad thing about it, homemade bread didn't last very long around our house. It tasted too good.

Of course, we took some of this bread to school for our lunch. After we butchered a hog, then we'd have cracklings on the bread. Cracklings were from the crisp rind of the pork. The fat had been melted down so we'd have lard. With the lard removed, those crisp cracklings were left. Still a little greasy, but they tasted good on fresh bread.

Every now and then some friend would want to trade bread with you. Most of the time, when a trade was made, it was trading homemade bread for store bread. It depended upon what the other kid had on his bread. I made very few trades, because I liked my own lunch much better.

We made our own butter when I was a boy. Since we had a cream separator, we did separate the cream and skim milk. We used the cream in our churn. As a kid I thought churning butter took a long time. But, if we kept at it, we always got butter. It was homemade butter.

I still remember in the third grade we were talking about butter in class. One student said that he didn't like "cow butter" but he sure liked "store butter." All of us kids from the farm had a big laugh about that one.

Whenever we churned butter, we got buttermilk. Mom would use some of the buttermilk in which she cooked barley. Some called it "karnemelkse pop." But in our home it was something like "soep-n-brea." For me it was a little sour tasting, so I'd sprinkle sugar over it. A swirl would be floating on top until I got it mixed. I thought the barley tasted the best, but the sour tasting buttermilk was not as delicious. But it was nice to have soep-n-brea every now and then.

Some of the dishes served had to have a Frisian origin, as Mom's family brought them along from the Old Country.

Even so, I think Mom had her own special days for cooking some meals. On wash days the meals were always a repeat of all other wash days. Rice. A big plate of rice had to have plenty of butter cover it, melting over the hot rice. I liked to sprinkle white or brown sugar over top of it, along with a little

Wash day on the farm, with the clothesline on the hill towards the barn.

Our house after we added to it. Our hill has gravel on the drive and some grass is beginning to grow in the sand. Mom is in front of the kitchen windows.

cinnamon. Besides rice, I liked a slice of homemade bread and a glass of milk.

Saturday had it specials, too. We could count on tomatoes and macaroni. Once again, Mom had her own way of fixing that dish. Once the macaroni was cooked canned tomatoes were dumped into it, adding some sugar and a chunk of butter. Mom knew the correct amount of sugar to be added. For me that was one of the best meals of the week, I never got tired of having tomatoes and macaroni as a boy. It was delicious! How does good food taste? "Smaakt lekker!"

Before we ate, we all bowed our heads for prayer. Dad and Mom had silent prayers. Often I wondered as a boy what my folks were praying, yet I never asked. As the oldest, I would pick up on the signal, when Dad was finished, then I was to start my prayer, "Lord, bless this food, for Jesus' sake. Amen." Paul was next, then the others, from the oldest to youngest.

Many times we had a Bible story after the meal. It was read from a Children's Bible Story book. Afterwards, I started, first of the kids, in thanking the Lord for our food, "Lord, thank you for this food, for Jesus' sake. Amen." The rest of my brothers and sisters again followed with their prayers.

Most of our meals were very simple. During the Depression we always had food on the farm. Milk, for sure. Bread, along with potatoes and gravy, and meat, were there for dinner at noon. Mom served some home-canned vegetable. Meat was usually pork, as we butchered hogs quite often. Of course we had plenty of eggs from our chickens. Every now and then we had chicken for dinner. That was the time I'd chop the head off a rooster. Mom always cooked extra potatoes, so for supper we'd have fried spuds.

I liked fried potatoes, fixed my own special way. Generally, I was given the same reminder each time I fixed my own specialty. On my plate was a good helping of fried potatoes. Taking a soft boiled egg, or two, which I put on top of the potatoes, adding salt and pepper. Most of the family could accept that, but I was not finished yet. Next, I put catsup all over it, last of all, pour plenty of honey over all of it. That was it. Others had been watching, then came the same reminder, "Now you better eat that, too!" And I did, every time. Because I liked it!

What others thought, I'm not too sure, but it was a colorful dish I had in front of me. Just think about that for a few moments—brown, crisp potatoes, the white of eggs, adding the soft yellow yolks, red catsup, golden honey, plus the black specks of pepper. I'd say that was very inviting, just waiting to be eaten by a Hoosier boy! You know, nobody else ever tried it, that I know of. Maybe I was the only kid in the whole State of Indiana who had that delicious dish for supper. Every time it was good, and every time I ate the whole thing.

Mom from time to time had home-canned vegetables and fruit for our meals. Our folks did a lot of canning during the hard time of the Depression. I liked fresh vegetables from the garden, too. In fact, I liked most of the food we had on our table.

A few other memories linger now, as I think about food. Dad was great at spotting ads. Once he found a special deal on fish. The order was shipped in a large wooden crate, packed in ice. Since it was in the dead of the winter, it was still frozen when it arrived by train.

A variety of fish came in this special deal. Included was a small tub of pickled herring. After bringing it home from the depot, we had to find a place to keep it, so we put the crate in the little shanty. We did not heat it, so it stayed frozen for the winter.

As fish were needed, we'd get some for a meal. But I just loved those pickled herring. Quite often I had the craving, so I'd slip into the shanty for some herring. We had some on the table now and then. I must admit, in all honesty, I had more than my share. Nobody checked it out, as to why I went into the shanty. And frankly, I wasn't going to tell anybody about my craving for pickled herring. If somebody did, I would have been caught with my hand in the pickled herring tub. I'm so glad Dad discovered that ad for fish. But, most of all, the contents of that little tub tickled my craving—often!

I liked sponge mushrooms. They were the only edible ones, our family felt. We considered others to be poisonous, which was not true. Others ate them. I still remember seeing Nick Homoninski and his wife picking all kinds. That day they had some Russian friends from around Gary, who were all out mushroom hunting. They had baskets filled with all kinds. They were so excited about how many they found. They were telling me how delicious they were, but I was not as excited as they were—I felt some would be deadly poisonous.

However, I could get excited about the morel mushrooms, sponge ones, we called them. We found many in small groves on the farm. A small patch in the woods could fill a whole milk bucket.

Mom would cut them in two, roll them in flour, and fry. They were so good. I could always go for seconds. Those morel mushrooms were a delicacy, pure pleasure to eat. They were eaten generally for supper. Rich tasting, but I enjoyed them.

Some foods we just never ate before, an unknown in our house would have been squash. Not until the Swishers gave us some. That family had a large garden. They introduced our family to the acorn squash, table queens, as we called them.

Mom cut them in half, placing them in the oven to bake. They had a bright golden-orange color. After being seasoned, they had a nutty flavor to them. We would add plenty of butter, then seasoning. Other times we would sprinkle brown sugar over the buttered squash.

Table queens were good. I liked them with plenty of butter and pepper. Ever since I was a boy, I've enjoyed those tasty little squash. I still think of how nice it was for the Swishers to give us our very first acorn squash, table queens. We have them to thank.

One unforgettable experience happened on one Sunday evening. Dad was late getting the chores done. Paul and I were busy playing on the swing by the big oak. That tree was on the path to the barn.

Since we would be eating much later, it was far too long for two boys to wait. We were hungry. Going into the house, we asked Mom for something to eat. She had fixed jello for supper. Besides she had whipped cream. That was offered to us, jello with plenty of whipped cream. We ate it.

Then, back to the swing to play.

We decided to take turns of getting "wound up" on the swing. One would twist the swing until the one in the seat was wrapped tightly in the swing. By that time, the seat was lifted up in the air. The swing rope was a mass of twists! Tight!

No more twists—let it go! Around and around one of us would spin. I would unwind in one whirl. Each of us had several turns.

Finally we whipped the cream and jello too much! I started upchucking the whole mess on the hillside. My supper was spoiled for that evening.

Even since then I've a certain distaste for whipped cream. Too much whipping of the cream on the old swing was too much for a small Hoosier boy. No thanks, no, no whipped cream, please!

Special Treats

Some things were special treats for me as a kid. It was a treat to get a 5¢ ice cream cone. Generally I felt I got my money's worth. Most of the time we got big dips.

However, if you discovered the place of the biggest dips, then they got your 5¢ for the larger cone. That I got at Schlosser's Creamery, but that was in Rensselaer. So we had to go there first. Once there, I knew my way to their creamery for that big cone.

All day long, especially on a hot summer day, I thought about going to town that night. I looked forward to my treat. I never spent my nickel very quickly. It took time, trying to make up my mind about the flavor to choose.

People in those places had to have patience. Kids could stand there a long time picking out the flavor to buy. Once decided, it took me even longer to slick my cone. It had to last. I worked at that, slick by slick. More times than I want to recall, I would discover a drip on the bottom. Maybe a friend would say, "Hey, your cone is dripping on the bottom." Naturally, by then, it was soft and soggy on the end.

Lifting it up, I'd catch the next drip on the end of my tongue. But, too often, I was tempted to bite the end off. Once I bit it off, then I had to go to work—on both ends!

Only clever maneuvering helped me to manage the rest of my cone on a hot night. But then I had another problem, walking around town with sticky hands the rest of the night.

On a very hot day, I would dream about an ice cold bottle of pop. I could picture it, under those floating chunks of ice. Man, it was cold searching around in that icy water. Among the different kinds in the cooler, I tried to find my favorite.

I liked root beer. But I had two others as my favorites: cream soda and Pepsi Cola. Both were so good. My first choice for a number of years was the cream soda. Its tang was tops. I liked the smell. Those crackled bubbles spit in my face. Sometimes the soda would fizz, then I felt it bubble up with a smell going through my nose. Small sips were taken. It would sting my tongue, so I swilled it around from one cheek to the other. That was one way to get every last bit of sweetness out of the sip.

While cream soda was first choice for years my taste changed to Pepsi.

A filling station was a good place to get a bottle of pop. There we would stand around talking to friends. Slowly I'd drink my pop. Matt Musch's Standard Station was a favorite place around De Motte. Matt didn't seem to mind boys hanging around. I liked to talk with him. It was fun to watch him change a tire and patch the inner tube. Matt would "talk to the tire" as he did his work. If he ever got frustrated with a tire, then he'd use his favorite slang expressions, while talking to the tire—"Hot diggiddy dogs!" "Pie face!" "Jenny wren!" As boys we'd say those were Matt's cuss words. But Matt never used any bad words, that we heard. He was a nice fellow. I enjoyed getting my treat at his filling station.

Every now and then I wanted something besides an ice cream cone or cream soda. Everything sold mostly for a nickel: pop, cones, Cracker Jack, gum, big all-day suckers, candy bars.

My treat had to taste good, but I wanted my money's worth, too. Two candy bars I generally bought were O'Henry or Pay Day. I guess I'd say Pay Day was the one I liked best, especially for the taste in the center of the bar.

No matter what I would buy, it took a long, long time to make up my mind. In that way, I held on to my nickel longer. But I didn't want to regret spending it quickly on something I really didn't want at all.

In the last couple years of high school I had another special treat. Walt Mak and I had a different kind. Walt got us started. After eating lunch, then we'd go uptown to buy bananas. We could get a big bunch for about 19¢. A brown paper sack was almost stuffed full. At times we'd sit in his car eating bananas until the whole sack was empty. All the time we ate, we'd swap stories. With another story we'd peel back the skin on another banana. It was repeated until the last banana was gone. Walt would eat the most of them. But both of us enjoyed the special times together and a special treat at the same time.

As three senior boys we were pictured in the *Keen Keener* as the "Three Blind Mice." Left to right: Bill, Walt, and Dale. Walt became a farmer, Dale a lawyer, and I answered the Call to the ministry.

Play in Indiana

I liked to roll an old tire. With one hand I'd push it, once rolling, then I ran after it all over the yard. It was fun to get it rolling down our big hill, but very hard to keep up with it.

One morning I was rolling a tire by the big barn. It was very sandy on the hill, during the dry years of the 30s. As I rolled it near a few big oaks, something on the ground caught my attention. It was an Indian sandstone pipe. I bent over, picked it up and put it inside my tire. The rest of the morning I played with the pipe inside the tire. At noon I brought it in the house to show what I had found.

At that time I was told it was a special find. Word about the Indian sandstone pipe reached August Johnson, who lived by the Kankakee River bridge on Highway 53. He was a collector of Indian relics.

Mr. Johnson came over to talk to me about buying it. At the time I was eight or nine years old. His offer was $25, which was a lot of money in the Depression. I refused to sell it. At various times he'd come back, still trying to buy my pipe. I simply would not let go of it.

Each time he wanted to handle it, looking it all over. I had to take him to the place where I found it. He asked a lot of questions. As he continued to persist in wanting to buy it; I persisted in resisting his every offer.

The man had a lot of knowledge about Indians, so I found it interesting to talk with him. I told him how I thought we had a lot of Indian burial sites on our farm. These were behind our chicken coops. I pointed north, below the big hill, into a bottom area. He wanted to know why I thought those were graves. I mentioned the piles of earth, which looked like mounds over graves. Little trees had grown on each mound, about eight to ten feet long and a few feet wide. To me they looked like graves. Of course, with my boyish imagination, I concluded they had to be Indian graves.

August told me I was wrong, for Indians always put their graves on hills or mounds, never in bottom land. Then he pointed out the sandridge which runs through the entire marsh. Anyone knowing the area, knows the ridge, which runs for miles and miles from the northeast to the southwest, cutting across country. Then he said those were the hills on which burial sites would be found.

Years later, as we were hauling yellow sand from the big hill on the north property line, between the Hoffman and Swart properties, I found two axes in the hillside. They were neatly lying side by side, two axheads, plus one more stone which was being made into another axhead. It was far from finished. I dug all around the area, as we loaded several truckloads of sand, but never found any other relics. Just those three stones in a perfect row were found.

I have kept my Indian sandstone pipe and those two axheads. I've added arrowheads to my collection, which started while I was playing.

While walking through the big woods, east of the barn, we discovered a mystery. It was along the road to Frank Roorda's bee shanty. A few feet from the road, somebody had been digging. Only part of the dirt was replaced in the hole again. Some leaves had been raked over it.

It was one big mystery. Our imaginations ran wild, in all different directions. One thing was certain, some people had been in that secluded part of the woods. We had no facts, but we *knew* what happened. A person had been killed; the hole was dug to bury the victim.

Our mystery was as good as solved. Only evidence was needed, which we were going to get. Running back home, we returned with shovels for the dig. We dug and dug, soon we had a hole big enough to bury a big horse. Deeper and deeper we dug, all the time our mystery grew. Finally we were way over our heads—it was a deep hole. Still no body! Finally we had to give up our search for a body in that mystery grave! We thought we were getting close to China.

258

A body was never to be discovered.

But weeks later the mystery was solved. The De Motte school district had dug up some trees to landscape around the new school building. Trees were taken from our woods. Our school had someone from Purdue University help find trees in our woods. (Dad had given permission.) Our woods had one of the greatest variety of trees in all of Northern Indiana. The expert from Purdue had shared that fact with our township trustee, Ivan Cheever, who shared it with us. Some of the trees and plants used to landscape around school came from our farm.

So the baffling mystery was solved. Not the way some boys would have liked. While digging we knew we'd make all the papers when the body was found! But we never made the news. Even on a sandhill, a hole in the ground really played on the fertile imagination of boys in Indiana.

In the summertime it was fun swimming in the old Hodge Ditch. Several places over the years were known as the old swimming hole. Generally it had to be a sandy area. Other spots in the ditch were too muddy at the bottom. We wanted to stay away from those places. If some sand from the bank had been pushed into the ditch, such a place was a good place to swim. It wasn't too deep, but was clean at the bottom.

In the early days we went "skinny-dipping" in the Hodge. Dads and boys alike took a dip after work was done. All swam naked.

Piles of clothes were scattered around on the ditchbank, or tossed on some bushes.

Depending on how warm the water was, a person had to decide how he was going in. The best way was to jump in, if it was a little cold. Yow! It took your breath away, if you were gradually walking into the water. As a kid I held my breath as I stepped into the cold water. Once in, it didn't seem so bad.

It was noisy. Kids didn't talk, most of the time it was yelling. But it was fun leaping into the Hodge. Holding one's nose with one hand, waving the other one in the air— running down the bank and leaping into the water with one big splash! We did bury a plank in the ditch bank, then we had a diving board. Some guys got to be good divers, but I never was very good at it. Even my best swimming was the old "dog paddle" style.

Plenty of shouting went on, especially during our water fights. It was done by skimming the heel of your hand across the water, with your fingers curved away from you. This way you could shoot a spray of water at other swimmers. When some ganged up, then one could be picked on. You tried to defend yourself by holding up your hand in front of your face, while fighting back with the other. But you could not duck every time. Having enough of the fight might mean getting away from the gang altogether.

My diving ended in total failure at first. My first tries proved painful. Belly-flops! Landing with a big plop in the water—on my belly. A bad one took the nerve out of me I found it safer to take a flying leap, landing bottom down. That was a good way to splash others with plenty of water.

At one swimming hole we had a long rope on a limb which reached over the ditch. Swinging over the water, then dropping in the ditch meant you had a super splash!

Skinny-dipping in the good old summertime was a lot of fun for boys in the marsh.

Later, when girls wanted to join us, all the boys had to buy swimming suits. When we got older, we worked on a more fancy spot on the Evans' Farm. The big tree on the south bank was used in which to put our diving board. Our dressing rooms were on the north bank. Rooms were made in the middle of the high weeds. We'd spend hours there on a hot afternoon or evening. An afternoon swim would get interrupted by chore time. We'd hurry with them, so we could get back for another dip in the evening.

Mostly the old swimming hole was for kids from the farms in the marsh. Later, kids from town, hearing about it, joined us at the Hodge Ditch.

My cousin Bill and I didn't go skinny-dipping, but we did run around in the buff. Bill of Uncle George came over for a visit for a few days. One afternoon we played in old hog sheds. Those sheds were built in the side of the hill, the large hill east of the cow lot. Those sheds were built out of logs and rough lumber. Bill and I spent a whole afternoon in those old sheds. Once we got back to the house, we kept rubbing our stomachs and itching ourselves. Grabbing our clothes we kept twisting them. Finally we lifted up our shirts, only to discover our bellies covered black with fleas! Mom quickly chased us away from the house towards the shanty. Next she had us strip! Handing us a five gallon bucket of water, she told us to put our clothes in the water. For a few minutes we were two flea-free boys. We also were free to run around the hill naked as nature boys. Both of us were laughing, having a high old time, until we got hollered at. Somebody drove on the yard, so we hid behind a couple of big trees. Our freedom didn't last too long, for we were told to go and get some clean clothes on!

Hide-and-go-seek was a barrel of fun. One of us had to be "it" in the game. That one had to count high enough so everyone had time to get to some secret hiding place. There were plenty of places to hide, around the barn, cribs, cob shed, shanty, chicken coops, steel bins, or woodpile. When you spotted the person looking for you getting too far from base, then you ran to get home free! We played this game with cousins or neighbor kids who came over to play. I remember playing it at times with cousins, but it would be at night in the house. We'd hide under the beds. Coming out of our hiding place meant we brought dust and cobwebs with us. When we got older we played it under the yard light. We discovered some neat hiding places. At times they would be only inches away from us. We had to be very quiet, hardly breathing. If they did see us a lot of yelling took place—as you both raced for home base. Sometimes we got home free; many times we were caught!

As boys we liked to play with a slingshot. First we had to find a forked stick, shaped like a big "Y." Generally, we found one in a young tree. The bark had to be stripped off. The handle had to be long enough to grip it in your hand, while the upper part of the "Y" had to be big enough for a stone to be shot through the opening. To those prongs we tied strips cut from an old inner tube. One on each side. On the ends of these strips we tied a piece of leather, usually cut from a shoe tongue. The leather made a little pouch to hold the stone we would shoot. Pulling back on the rubber bands or straps until taut—then let go. The stone went flying through the air. We'd generally aim at old pail or a tree. At times we tried to hit a bird in a tree or bush. Missed every time. At times we aimed at the side of a steel bin. Man! an empty bin made a lot of racket. We never played over a long period of time with slingshots. A few days was enough, we quickly lost interest. Then we tossed it on a shelf or in the corner, for the newness wore off.

We liked to explore things around the old barn, which was a little less than half a mile from home. Stored in the barn was a big rusty barrel, which had tar in it. It took an ax to chip chunks of tar out of that barrel. Once heated, the tar was used to coat roofs. But the biggest part of that barrel was never used. However, as boys, we'd manage to chip off a small piece of tar. It was hard stuff!

Even though it tasted awful, we'd stick it in our mouths. It had to get warm, then it was soft enough to chew. That was our black gum.

We also made our own corncob pipes. On the farm we had no trouble finding a cob. A big cob would make a good-sized bowl on the pipe. Cobs had a soft center, which we dug out, then with a knife we made a hole in the side of the cob. Certain sticks also had soft centers. A piece of baling wire would be pushed through it. Once we got it open, we could suck air through it. It looked, a little, like a real corncob pipe our hired men would smoke. We'd walk around with our homemade pipes in our mouths, acting like we were smoking.

One hired man had one, which was the filthiest thing. Yet one night I tried to smoke it in the shanty. Just two or three puffs was all I could take. A couple times before that I tried a newspaper and corn silk smoke. This happened behind the barn. I wrapped my smoke, trying to make my own cigarette. From the size, perhaps it was more like a cigar. Anyway, rolling my own, I tried to smoke it. Everything went up in flames, two puffs was more than enough. Good grief! I nearly choked to death on Billy's Own Brand. That was the extent of my experiments with smoking. Those few puffs—I was through for life!

However, one Saturday night, while we were uptown, I was challenged to smoke by some cousins.

Five of us were riding with Bill of Uncle Jake. Bill is about seven years older than I. By then he had his own car. I must have been twelve. One of the older boys took out cigarettes and passed them around the car. Everyone took one, except me, I wouldn't take one. They started to make fun of me. They smoked, and kept after me, for being a coward. I was told I was chicken, as I got teased for not smoking. Finally, I felt I had to defend myself, so I shot back, "You know what, I'm the only man in this car!"

I can't tell you how they felt after I had my say. We continued to ride around in cousin Bill's Chevy, but those fellows never bothered me after that.

Hours were spent as boys playing in the Indiana sand on our big hill. Dry sand, almost tan in color, was dusty stuff. But I thought it was like brown sugar when it was wet. When it was a little wet it was better to play with. Boys could build roads, farms, yards, fields, almost anything. Just let a boy's imagination work. During the Depression I remember the trucks and cars we got from the IGA Store in De Motte. We'd go to that store to shop, a twice-a-week event for our family.

It happened on a Wednesday or Saturday night they had a special. I spotted it immediately when we walked through the front door. Toys filled the bottom shelf, a whole line of trucks and cars. Wow! They were big, not small toys. Near the toys were large piles of OK laundry soap. Each bar of soap had a red label, about nickel-size, pressed into the corner of the bar. Of course, there was a special sale on this soap. Buy five bars, plus 25¢, you got one of those toys. Wow! We couldn't believe it. Bill Swart talked to Dad about his sale. Dad walked out of the store with a toy for each of us kids. Mom had plenty of soap, enough to wash dishes and clothes for months. I can still remember playing near the barn under the big oak trees with our new toys. One was a green dump truck. I hauled sand to make a road extending from those trees to the oak tree by our swing. We really talked big as we played in the sand. It didn't matter at all how dirty we got. Mom had plenty of OK soap to wash our dirty clothes!

We played by our back driveway, behind the shanty and toilet. A tile drain came out by the drive. Since it was always wet around that drain bees came there. Bees were there daily. One day we got an empty medicine bottle from the house, so we could capture a bee in it. We caught one. Once we got the bee inside, we stuffed a cork in the bottle. Then two boys had another great idea! Our kid sister, Lois, was watching us. Paul and I decided to pull the cork, then place the open bottle against her bare foot. Lois protested! It was scary for her, but big brothers tried to convince her the bee would not hurt her. But the bee did! She was stung under her foot. Lois limped to the house with howls from the pain. After much more howling the stinger was pulled out by Mom. A couple of sheepish boys got a good talking to for their ornery prank.

Sometimes I wanted to be all alone. One hide-away I enjoyed was in the attic of our house. I had to climb a ladder in the summer kitchen to get into the loft area. It overlooked the summer kitchen. A wall about twenty inches high protected us from falling out of the loft. I liked to play above the kitchen area. Later an opening was cut through a wall, so we could get in the attic over the old part of our house. I put some loose boards in there. Crawling through a small opening I could get to my secret hiding place. My imagination could work in my secret place. It was my office. I ran a radio station up there. I can't say I played with any other brother or sister up there. It was my place. I kept special things in my own little world.

In the haymow of the big barn was another place we all spent hours. The floor was slick, which they said was due to waxing, when it was used for square dancing during World War I times. I can't verify the story, but I heard it a number of times.

When I was a small boy the haymow would be full. It was stacked high with loose hay. While threshing we also blew straw into the mow. The only place to play then was on top of the hay or straw. Later we used bales, so it wasn't piled so high.

There is a track in the top of the barn, which was used to put loose hay in the mow. We made a swing in the haymow, by using the big hay rope. It reached to the peak of the barn. A board was put at one end, so we had a swing seat. Bracing on the ends of the barn was used from which to take off. Some times we'd jump off the bale pile, taking a big swing ride. All of us did a lot of swinging on that big rope!

Probably the most hours were spent playing basketball in the haymow. When there was too much hay or straw in the mow, then we had an outdoor court. Our rim was bolted to the end of the barn. Many times the weather kept us from playing basketball outside.

But we could play in all kinds of weather in the haymow. Our basketball rim was bolted to one half of an old barn door. When the net wore out, we put a gunny sack on the rim for our net. An electric cord was used to give us a light. The bulb was hung high on one of the rafters, so we had enough light to play.

Many times we would get a quick game in—one on one, to 21. We'd challenge each other to just one game. Before we had to milk or go in for supper, just one game, we'd say. Hundreds of times we had to play a game to 21!

When other kids came over we'd play sides. It was a nice basketball court, while protected from the weather, it gave us no protection from the cold. We played some games at very low temperatures.

We loved our basketball in Hoosierland. But we liked soft-ball when summertime came around. We played softball in the timothy fields. Small calves were in those fields at times, but the short grass made it a good place to play ball.

If we were going to play catch we used the toolshed or the crib doors for our backstop. I pitched when we played in a league uptown. I practiced with a backstop, so my catcher did not have to run so far after the ball.

Just west of the toolshed we had our track. I practiced my long distance running on the grass. We had our high jump in the middle of the area. The scissor-method was used by most high jumpers. A few were beginning to use the roll, which I tried to use. My best record as a boy was three feet nine inches. Over and over I would go for that, my limit.

We also pole-vaulted there. We got an old bamboo pole from school, which we kept in the toolshed. The pole had been used at school for years, but then it was replaced. It was nice enough for our play at home. And much safer than our old pole. Before the bamboo pole we used a boat paddle. (Thinking about that now, that was very dangerous, extremely dangerous, for it could have broken and one of us fallen on the splintered end. Come to think of it, one paddle did break on us. Some boy in Indiana did get severely injured when his pole broke at his home.) The bamboo was much safer. And we could get much higher by using it.

During track season we enjoyed hours on our little track by the toolshed.

Every year we had one large pile of corncobs. Our big crib held 5,000 bushels of corn, so when we shelled corn, the pile of cobs was again on our yard. Naturally, one game we liked was "King of the Hill." The King was on top, pushing others off his hill. If you got pushed off, you did your best to crawl back up and knock the King off the hill. It soon had a flat-top. All the vigorous playing flattened the pile in a hurry. But it was fun while it lasted.

I have no idea how old I was when we first talked about getting bikes, maybe nine or ten. As I can recall we went either to Hammond or Gary to buy secondhand bikes. "American Flyer" was the name of my bike. Red. Skinny tires. Of course, with all the sand on our place, balloon tires would have been the best to have. But I was excited to have my own red bike. I was one happy kid. I gladly settled for it, even if it was far from being what most boys would have wanted.

Learning to ride it was another thing, for it was not easy in our loose sand. So we tried the lane to the pasture, south of the bridge. With our cows going up and down that lane, they packed down the cow path. Pushing the bike near a fence post, I would crawl on, then push off. Paul was doing the same thing. However Paul got too close to the barb wire, it got him. He had a nasty cut...in a most unusual place.

For me, the red bike was special. One time I really cried over it. I had it in the big corn crib, leaning against the side of the driveway. That way it was out of the way of machinery or trucks parked in the crib. On this particular evening, one cow got into the crib. It jumped up into the north side of the crib, to eat some corn. I was told to chase her out of there. Instead of going out the same door, this old bossy decided to go out the other door—leaping right on top of my American Flyer! There was no way that cow could ride my bike. Yet she tried, the poor wheels buckled into the shape of horseshoes. I cried.

Many of the spokes were broken out of those bent wheels. My bike was useless. Dad bought two new rims and enough spokes, which the Swishers put together. While it was fixed, never again did it ride very good after that. It was a second-hand wreck. The wheels, at best, wobbled as I rode it.

One day I was taking it out to the field at the noon hour. Dad wanted the cultivator to keep going, right through the dinner hour. So Dad sent me to relieve the person on the tractor. Riding my bike, at break-neck speed—I nearly did! I was standing up pumping as hard as I could go, when my front wheel hit a mole track, across the road. My wheel turned sharply—sideways. I stopped, short! I flew over the handlebars, landing in the buckwheat patch besides the road. Even though the doctor later said my collarbone was not broken, I hardly believe he was right. (To this day I have a knot there. Besides, when fitting on new clothes in any store, the salesperson will mention how my shoulders are not the same. One is higher than the other.) I know that. I also know that I had a miserable time that noon hour. Each time I tried to put the cultivator in or out of the ground I sat there and cried from the pain. No matter how I attempted to do it, the pain shot through my neck and shoulders.

Dad always joked about it. For years he'd tease that I cut the yield of his buckwheat crop that year. I had knocked down too much buckwheat when I went over the handlebars. It was

267

like I got pitched off a bucking bronco. Not really, but I did go flying off my American Flyer!

Wintertime gave us a chance to enjoy other kinds of play. Snow, if it packed just right, allowed us to have a snowball fight. While it was fun, sooner or later somebody got hurt. Somebody always ended up crying.

If water was put in the snowball, likely some kid would be hurt by such an iceball. Getting smacked with one of those could cause tears.

It was far more fun to make huge snowballs, making a snowman.

Since we had the big hill we had fun with our sleds. My first sled was a wooden sled, named "Rocket Racer." Rather small, only thirty inches long, but solidly built. After all these years, it is still in excellent shape. There are hand-holds on the runners, where I could hold on while going downhill. With some ruts at the bottom of the hill, one had to hang on when bouncing across them. Later we got bigger sleds, so we could belly-flop on them while sliding down our hill. It was big fun going down the hill, but it was less fun walking back to the top again. Finally, it got old, so we would quit when we got tired. It still was a lot of fun.

What I liked most of all in the wintertime was to go ice skating. We only had to go to the Cook Ditch to do our skating. Our skates were the kind which clamped to our shoes. On the back of the skate was a strap, which went over the ankle. We always had to have a key with us, so we could tighten the skates on our shoes.

When it was cold enough we skated around the turtle hole area. I'm not sure why it got the name. Yet we did see turtles there, especially in the summertime. But Dad told of having to stop his car one day on the Old Grade to allow a huge turtle to cross the road. No, it was not a herd of turtles which stopped traffic. Only one. Yet it was the largest Dad ever saw. Dad claimed it was larger around than a big washtub, and about knee-high. Dad came home to tell us about it. The dimensions described were far larger than any other turtles we'd ever seen.

Anyway, the turtle hole, as we knew it, was on the west side of the Old Grade, on the Evans' Farm. It had a thick growth of willows around the pond. That gave us good protection from the harsh winter winds.

While we skated there often, still our favorite spot was on our side. The Cook Ditch had a wider spot where we could skate. Once it froze over the ice was solid, we never had to worry about falling through.

But we did fall! We fell hard on that hard ice. I know I went down—many times. If my skates shot from under me, I would land on the back of my head. Those were awful falls which I've never forgotten. I'd hit so hard at times, for a time afterwards—strange smells would be sensed. Boy, something got jarred loose! It made me more careful for a while. Generally, that happened when I tried some fancy move or jump. When I did try that, I paid for it.

At times we'd skate south towards the Hodge, getting as close as we dared. There was some open water, especially where reeds and weeds were sticking up through the ice. Carefully we had to work our way around those areas. With open spots there would be moving water and very thin ice. Those places had to be avoided.

Other times we would venture east on the Cook Ditch. We'd go as far as the bridge near Sampson's Farm. We'd be gone several hours if we went there. As long was we kept skating we'd keep warm. Our feet would get cold after skating for a couple of hours. If the weather was really cold it was best to skate closer to home. It was easier to get back home to warm up our cold feet.

When we were in grade school we had good times on the ice in the wintertime.

A Boy's Imagination

I played just east of the old cob shed. A big oak tree stood there. After we got our new outhouse, the old white two seater was moved there. I removed the two seater section. This gave me a special place to store things.

During that time I built my own wagon. The front wheels came off a broken red wagon. Also our old family baby buggy wore out, so I took a set of wheels off of it. Those were wire wheels with spokes, while the wagon had disc wheels.

I found an orange crate, the same size as a 30-dozen egg crate. Heavier lumber was used to replace the thin boards on the side of the orange crate. I wanted a top on my wagon, but I didn't want it to leak. Dad had some leftover roofing materials, which were used to cover the roof on our Dodge truck. I got the scrap pieces. One strip was almost enough to cover the top. A few inches did have to be added to one end. That was a patch-job. With hinges, I could open the top. Those rear wheels of the buggy were lower, while the wagon wheels on the front made that end higher. My wagon was not level, the front was several inches higher than the back. But the rain could run off the top.

I found a big steel rod, about 30 inches long. Dad had a large vice mounted on a stump by the barn. I started a fire on the yard, so I could heat the rod until it was red hot. I had watched our blacksmith, Hansen in Hebron, enough to know what I had to do. After it was red hot, I hammered away on the rod. My biggest problem was keeping the iron hot enough. Only a few hits were made by the anvil after each heating. So it took me a long time to bend hooks on each end. It was finally shaped like this: ⌒ Here is a rough drawing of the way my wagon looked.

An old pulley was found in the barn. I hung it on a limb of the big oak. It was about 8 to 10 feet high. I had a long rope through the pulley. The rope was attached to one of the hooks on the rod. I hooked the other one to the handle of my wagon. Then I would pull my wagon off the ground and up in the air. At times it was three or four feet off the ground. In my imagination I was unloading grain at an elevator. Just like the front of a truck was lifted up to unload corn, wheat, or oats when we took it to an elevator.

Later I painted the roof with red barn paint. I played with my homemade wagon for years. However, I can't remember what happened to it.

I made other things, too. I used up scraps of lumber found after something new was constructed on the farm. For my storage chest I used lumber from the little crib. That chest was used for my county fair grain samples. After I had a sample cleaned and ready for showing at the fair I put it in there. That was the way I kept it away from mice. The chest was kept in my bedroom. Later I put casters under it so I could move it easily.

When I had the bedroom on the east end of our house, I wanted some of my own things in the room. Time was spent looking through catalogs so I could order furniture. I then purchased unfinished and unassembled furniture.

I bought twin beds, a desk, and two night stands. I had to assemble each piece. Yellow shellac was often used at the time, I decided to use that finish on the woodwork. I finished the twin beds first. It took much more time to put together the desk and night stands. The wide top on the desk wanted to warp out of shape, so I had a hard time to keep the top flat. That wasn't my only problem, the shellac was sticky at first. Finally it dried completely, so paper and books didn't stick to the surface.

With all that furniture in my small bedroom, it was crowded.

One day while combining wheat I ran into a mother pheasant on her nest. She half flew and half limped across the stubble. The cutter bar ripped into her back while she sat on her nest. It was sad, unable to stop in time, nor could she get away in time to avoid getting injured. The saddest part was she could not live with her injuries. And here she was sitting on a nest of eggs.

I gathered up the eggs, before they were broken or damaged. I took them home. Every year we seemed to have enough broody hens which wanted to set on eggs. They wanted chicks of their own. I put the eggs under a broody hen. I put her in the old white outhouse, which I used for storage. That's the place where she sat on her nest.

Finally, I heard tiny shrill cheeps one morning. I had baby pheasants. Thirteen hatched. Oh, they were so tiny, so cute. These tiny creatures had to be fenced in. I got wire with very small openings for their little yard. Those little things got out, as they could wiggle through the smallest hole. When they escaped their little yard, the mother hen was very upset. They would dart around the yard. Most of the time the mother got them to stay close to her.

It wasn't long before they were half-fuzz and half-feathers. They were growing. Our gas man, Harry Mockler, raised pheasants in Hebron. Harry delivered fuel for Mobil. One day I showed him my little pheasants. At that time Harry told me that a person had to have a permit to raise wild birds, like my pheasants. That was news to me. After all they would not even be alive if I hadn't saved the eggs when the mother pheasant got injured. Anyway his news changed everything. For sure, I did not have a permit. A few weeks later we talked again. Harry said that he'd buy them from me. So I sold my thirteen little pheasant friends to him. I knew he would take good care of them, for he knew all about raising wild birds. Besides I was beginning to wonder what would happen to them when they grew up. This took care of that future problem. One day he brought out some gas to the farm, then we caught them and he took them home.

I took the money he paid me and put it in my savings account in the De Motte State Bank.

I enjoyed my solitude on the farm. My imagination was constantly working while I did my chores. But the best times were when I was alone in the big fields on the farms. It gave me time to myself. Alone it gave me time to think, meditate, dream, pray.

It depended on the kind of work I was doing. Certain work gave me more time to myself. It was easiest when I was plowing, discing, or cultivating. Not so much concentration was required, so I used those moments of freedom to enjoy life on our farm.

On the long trips from one end of the field to the other, I thought about so many things. I had questions, too. While in my teens I really had an inner struggle with myself. I had a very low self-esteem, as I look back. One question haunted me, hounded me, the same one repeatedly came back to me: Will anybody truly love me?

I wondered if I even had any right to expect love from any other person in the world. My size bothered me. I was a puny weakling in my own eyes. Compared to other boys, I did not have any ability to be good in sports. As I played games with other guys, most of the time I was chosen last for a team. Those picking players finally had no other choice, except to pick me. So I came out second-best, or at the bottom of the pile, as I thought about it.

But I still had a longing deep inside, I still wanted to be loved. I wanted someone to care for me as a person, to love *me.* In all my soul-searching I could not discover any reason why another person would want to give love to me, to share with me.

Yet that did not keep me from dreaming. I would imagine how it could be. My dreams allowed me to escape from my hurts.

I thought about what I wanted to accomplish in life. I had dreams about what I wanted to be. I dreamed of many things. Out in the big fields there was time to meditate. So many times I talked out loud with God. I spoke directly to Him. During such talks with God I uncovered my soul in prayer. As I look back, some of those experiences were some of the best times in prayer. Some of the fondest of my memories cherish those special times of prayer.

In Hoosierland I could not have asked for a more pleasant place in God's world to spend my solitude. God was with me in those big fields. He was so great! I seemed so small. But I knew He cared for *me*.

I know, at times, those struggles inside were so painful. Yet so much of my life was shaped by those times alone with One Who cared personally for me, for He is my Heavenly Father.

I shall remain humbly thankful for such a privilege and opportunity. The Psalmist in the Holy Land had such experiences, but the same God gave me mine in Hoosierland. I lift my voice and heart to say, "Thank You, Father, for being so good to me. I love You. I adore You. I praise You."

My heart swells with praise to this moment. For those times as a boy on the farm God was helping me in those sacred moments to keep eternity in view.

It is one thing to be alone. But life has to do with others, with relationships. It starts with the family, right at home. Later in my teenage years, I had to show my spirit. Before that I would pout. As a teenager a rebel-spirit came out at times. I was not alone feeling this way.

Dad would give us orders to do some job. Often, under our breath, as boys, we questioned it. If one of us told the other what had to be done, our protest would be: How come we have to do that? Who said we had to?

Referring to Dad, one of us would say, "That's what the 'Boss' said!" (That pretty well settled it.)

It was the spirit in which we would mention it among us boys. Mostly that came up when we had to do a job we did not like. If one got an unpleasant job, why did the other get the good job? Be as upset as we wanted to be, the comment would be made, "But that is what the 'Boss' said!"

This was very true in my life when I reached the age that I s certain I knew as much, or more, than Dad or Mom. But ew better than to question it, really, for Dad was "The "

ould grumble, complain, sulk, bellyache, moan and l the time I did the job, mostly under my breath. The I didn't keep it to myself I got into big trouble. No

274

matter how I felt about the job or decision, my Dad was still my boss.

As a young person my strong-will wanted control. Rather than get into an all-out power-struggle, I knew it was best not to challenge Dad. I wanted to be free, but Dad's control was needed in those important years of my life, like it or not. Dad held control with a loose grip. A wise man indeed!

Then once I got a few years older, I discovered much more about his wisdom. It always was more than a "stijfkop Dutchman" was willing to admit during those teenager years. Really Dad was a very wise man.

I recall a couple of experiences which reflect my questioning mind. One of the things I enjoyed, as a boy, was to visit some of my relatives during the summer. One special place for me was to go to Cedar Lake. Uncle Menno and Aunt Dorothy Musch lived there. He was working on a beautiful dairy farm in the country, seems to me the man's name for whom he worked was Cutler.

They rented a small house near the lake. Spiders were everywhere, so Aunt Dorothy wanted me to kill them. I got one penny for a huge yellow and black spider, while I had to kill all kinds of small ones for another penny. My weapon was a fly swatter.

But I spent my time also playing with the boys. A few years later they had me over again. They picked me up in their Model A Ford. I sat in the front, while Aunt Dorothy sat in the back with the boys. At that time they were living on the Doak Farm near Leroy. This farm had a silo. A creek ran through the farm near the house.

Uncle Menno went fishing with me in that creek. One day we caught a number of fish, about five nice ones. We put them in a washtub. They never got cleaned.

Aunt Dorothy was so crabby. It had been hot, so when she acted that way I thought she wasn't very nice to Uncle Menno. I still recall the baby being in the high chair near a wall. She waited for Uncle Menno to carry the baby and high chair to the table so we could eat. I couldn't understand why she didn't do it. So I asked her about it.

She said it was too hard for her. (I did notice she had a very large belly, which prevented her from carrying the baby and high chair.)

About that time, I thought I ought to tell her how I felt, so I did, "You could do it, you know, if you would not drink so much beer to get such a big belly!"

As a boy, I had no idea she was expecting a baby soon. Never had the slightest idea. In her extreme discomfort that hot summer, naturally she was crabby. But beer was not her problem.

During that week, with the tensions, I got very homesick. One evening I went back of the silo to cry. I cried my heart out. While I hoped to be alone, that didn't happen, for Raymond came by me to watch me cry. Soon he asked why I was crying. That bothered me, so I told Raymond to be still! He didn't leave. He never did go away, so he quietly watched me bawl.

Home felt a long ways away for the boy in Hoosierland.

Late one afternoon, with milking almost finished, Dad and I were in the cow barn together. I was singing a song, which I heard the bigger boys at school sing on the bus when coming home from a basketball game. Dad jumped on me for singing the song. I was stunned. Evidently, Dad felt the song had a questionable double-meaning. I thought it was only a funny little ditty, but it wasn't that for Dad. Dad gave me his interpretation, which I didn't accept at all.

So while we were separating the milk, we continued to talk. Dad was turning the cream separator. Dad was keeping the separator going the proper speed. The spigot would be open, allowing the milk to run out of the tank on top of the cream separator. Milk flowed through the cupped, thin, metal discs, allowing the separation to take place. Cream came out the top spout, running into a 5-gallon cream can. The skim came out the bottom one, splashing into a big bucket. was on top of the skim milk which had that bluish color. d's previous remarks got me to thinking. While we were usy with this chore, I decided to ask Dad about "the fe."

Dad could see out into the cow yard, as he stood beside the cream separator. He looked over my head through the open barn door. He spotted the cows and bull walking around in the cow yard. Evidently he had an illustration for me, so indirectly I got his answer, "You watch the old bull and cows, then you'll find out."

I had no idea why he decided to make his comment. To this day, I am puzzled by his answer. I asked him about real people. Perhaps Dad was too embarrassed to tell me, I don't know. I just thought he put me off. He certainly didn't give me a straight answer.

I left the barn that evening more confused than ever. But I didn't dare ask Dad any more questions. I kept still.

However, I do remember when I was a little older Dad talked more with me. I have memories of such talks while hoeing thistles.

One particular day Dad shared with me while the two of us were alone. We did not spray weeds in those days. We spent long hours chopping with our hoes in those thistle patches. We also worked on big patches of wild potatoes. It took a lot of hacking to get rid of those miserable wild potatoes and thistles. During those long hours we did take time to talk. Dad was more willing to talk, too. Slowly, I was gathering information about the facts of life.

Over time I was able to put things together. Naturally, I listened to older boys talk, sometimes a few younger ones. It taught me something about guys. Those who claimed to know "all about such things" were not near as knowledgeable as they tried to appear. Most of the time it was more boasting and bragging than knowing.

Generally, they passed on something they knew through stories, known, of course, as "dirty stories."

Now I know they did not have any concept from the point of view as a Christian. How much better to get the facts of life from parents or Christian teachers. Especially, getting the Biblical view about life. How wonderful it would have been to understand sex as a wonderful gift from our Creator.

277

Too much of it came from experimentation on the part of boys and girls. Sadly, they acted like they knew all about it, but it was mostly from a worldly point of view.

I know I can never go back in time. I do know it would have been easier for me to gain my understanding from the Bible alone. I wish some understanding person would have told me about the way God created men and women.

It took a long time before I found out most of those "facts" of my life. It was far more than learning "all about the birds and bees." As a boy my one desire was to know more about *me!*

David wrote about life, which I claim for myself, "For You created my inmost being; You did knit me together in my mother's womb. I will confess and praise You because I am fearfully and wonderfully made, the wonder of my birth! Wonderful are Your works, and that my inner self knows right well. My frame was not hidden from You, when I was being formed in secret and intricately and curiously wrought...Your eyes saw my unformed body, and in Your book all the days of my life were written, before ever they took shape, when as yet there was none of them. How precious and weighty also are Your thoughts to me, O God! How vast is the sum of them! If I could count them, they are more in number than the sand. When I awoke (could I count to the end) I would still be with You." (See Psalm 139.)

Life, and Death

"For me, to live is Christ—His life in me; and to die is gain—the gain of the glory of eternity." (Philippians 1:21)

There is the wonder of life! But there is also death.

When I was a small boy we visited with Uncle Dan and Aunt Grace Sipkema and their family. A few holidays were spent with them during those years. They had us over for Thanksgiving, but we did not eat turkey. Instead we had a big goose. Generally, Mom came home with some goose grease. Yuk! That was the stuff smeared on our necks at night, if we had sore throats. An old sock or piece of flannel was wrapped around our necks, after getting doctored with goose grease. How I hated that!

One summer night we went to the Sipkema's home for a visit. Their oldest child was not well. My cousin's name was Mildred, however we knew her as Tootsie. Toward the end she was bedridden.

That particular day Tootsie was very sick. Every now and then family members went into her room. I know I went in several times, while others were taking care of her. Aunt Grace was expecting, so it was hard for her. Dad and Uncle Dan were in and out a lot.

Before we left Mildred died. Dad helped by making a few preparations before the funeral director arrived. My Dad had been with the medics in World War I, so he knew what was expected and what had to be done.

After Tootsie died, I can remember we all sat quietly in the kitchen or the living room. At different times, I was in both rooms. I was nine years old. Mildred died on June 1, 1934.

A few days later we were back for her funeral. I still remember attending that funeral, which made me quietly reflect on death. After losing their daughter, who was 17, eighteen days after Mildred's death Aunt Grace gave birth to their youngest son. Danny was born on June 19, 1934. What a big change took place in their home. Death and life were experienced the same month. Our family returned for more visits that summer. Being nine, I had a lot of thoughts about life, and death.

As a little boy I liked to go to Uncle Case's home. I liked him. Then he died at the age of 45. He had brain cancer. That condition put him in a large hospital in Chicago. It seems the name might be the Billings Hospital. There he had brain surgery.

It seems I can still picture being in the hospital once. The surroundings of the room still linger in images I have in my mind. In a big steel bed I can see Uncle Case. It seemed so high. He told us about falling out of his bed one night, then having such a time getting back in bed again. After surgery he went blind. Uncle Case Walstra died afterwards in August of 1930. I was only five at the time. I can still remember seeing his body in the casket.

So many good things were said about the man. Uncle Case lived his life as a fine Christian. I liked my uncle, especially the way he would talk with me. His death made a deep impression on me.

Deaths of certain friends touched me. A big impact was made on me when the Marshall girl died. She will always be remembered as the girl sitting in the window at school during recess.

She got diphtheria, only to die a few days later.

Of course, we were unable to attend school for some time. I don't recall how long it was. Several days after her funeral we all had to go back to school for a mass immunization program.

I will always see that little girl sitting in the window. That picture has never left my memory.

Buddy Rowen's death was a big shock. He was killed riding a bike on Highway 53, going out of town.

We just got out of school for the summer when this happened.

Howard, or Buddy, as we knew him, was a grade ahead of me in school. I talked with him in basketball practice many times. We'd shoot baskets together, managing to get in line ahead or behind each other. He liked Marge Konovsky, who was in my class.

Marge got a new bike, so kids were taking turns riding it out of town. Howard had a turn, going north on the highway. A car behind him was waiting to pass. At the time a car honked, which made Howard think the driver wanted him to get over. So he swung over, riding into the opposite lane.

However, that car had not signaled, it was another person wanting to pass who had honked the horn. A college student hit Howard. The accident killed him.

I thought of Buddy many times that summer. I was going into the eighth grade, the grade Howard had just finished.

I missed Buddy.

Tyke Vander Zee would have been my choice. I thought of him as the All American Boy. While I did not get to know him so personally, I had several long talks with Tyke. The young man really impressed me. For a time he was working in the fields across the road from our farm. During his noon break he'd come over and talk. We'd sit in his car. I can't recall how we got started doing that, except one day Tyke stopped to talk.

Tyke was a handsome young man. He dated a very nice girl from Hebron. I had seen her at some basketball games we played with the Hebron School.

This young man was called Home by our Lord. When he died, I went to his home to view the body. Late that afternoon I had a long talk with Tyke's mother. I told her how I felt about her son. I know our Lord knows best, but his death was hard for me to understand. From what I knew, if any young person was prepared to die, I felt it was Tyke.

Cecil Meyers was another young man who died. Cecil died so tragically. His father had died earlier, so he was helping out his mother on their farm.

He and I ran around together a few times one summer. We'd drive to Hebron some nights, but many times we stayed in De Motte.

Cecil carried a gun on his tractor. The reason for having his gun along was to shoot a few unwanted pests in the field. The tragic mistake was in carrying the gun on the hood of the tractor while he was plowing. The barrel of the gun was pointed towards him. As he turned on the end of the field, the gun was jolted and discharged. As it went off, my friend was shot in his stomach, which took his life. I called at the funeral home. His death was very sad.

Milton Petersen was a fine Christian youth. As one of the young people from De Motte, I don't think any youth came any finer. Milt was planning on being a Minister of the Gospel of Jesus Christ. The family lived at first on the Potter Farm. The Petersen and Unzicker children rode on the same school bus with us.

One summer Milt worked on our farm picking pickles. That summer he and I had some good talks, while in the pickle patch. I knew he had committed his life to Christ to become a preacher. Milt was absolutely certain of his Call.

But, at that same time, I was still struggling, asking, wondering, "Is God calling me?" I did not have the answer.

One day in particular, I ventured to express what was in my heart, as I had some feelings about going into the Christian ministry. Yet I was not certain of my Call.

That stopped him. Milt stood up, turned to me, saying, "Don't you go until you are absolutely certain that God is calling you!" He was emphatic. The subject of "the Call" was discussed in depth that day in our pickle patch.

One year later Milt was at Winona Lake for a Youth For Christ Convention. It had just begun, only having a meeting or two. But it was break time. Young people could go swimming during the break. Milt decided to go for a swim in the lake.

Milt dove in...never to come up! That is, until they recovered his body from the water. Milt was called Home by his Heavenly Father!

Happening so suddenly, it was hard to believe. I even remember Bruce Todd, the funeral director, had commented he was hoping they made a mistake when they called him. As he drove to Winona Lake to pick up the body, he kept hoping it was all a mistake. But when he got there, one look, it was no mistake!

Standing next to his casket in the Todd Funeral Home, my thoughts returned to our talks. In quietness, my reflection drifted to our pickle patch, which was only a year before.

It was a sacred moment, the Holy Spirit was working, tugging at my mind and heart. The Spirit sent something through me. God presented this penetrating question: "Who will now go to preach the Gospel?"

I found an answer to that question, in a personal way. While I said nothing to any other person, I felt it all the way through college and seminary.

Finally, came a Sunday, when I was sent to preach in Milt's home church, the American Reformed Church of De Motte. There to my amazement, sitting to my left, in the front row, were his parents and other members of his family. A strange feeling came over me. As they looked up at me, were they thinking of Milt? I couldn't help but ponder what they had in their hearts, "If only Milt could preach the Gospel today!" That service I vowed to preach the Word in such a manner that my Lord and they, too, could approve.

As I greeted the congregation that Sunday, the last to leave the sanctuary was the Petersen family. I opened my heart, telling my personal feelings. I told them of my experience besides Milt's casket. I told how I wondered who would be called to fill his shoes. Ever since then, I confessed that I felt I was taking Milt's place.

Then it was his parents' turn, his father and mother told me how they felt—ever since they heard that I was going into the ministry, I was taking his place. More than that, his parents assured me that they had been praying for me all the way through my college and seminary training.

As God's children, we all stood there with some tears in our eyes. What assurance was given by the Holy Spirit!

God moves in some mysterious ways His wonders to perform! His people can only praise His Name. He is a kind, good, and gracious Father Whom we serve.

Some glorious day we'll understand it all.

One special day lives in my memory—December 7, 1941.

Sunday. In the morning we did the chores on the farm; Dad had gone to church for the morning service. In the afternoon, our turn came, so Mom took us to church and Sunday School.

We went to church at Dutch Corners, as we called our church. That Sunday we sat on the west side of the church, a little over half way to the front.

Pastor Schaap came into the pulpit. It seemed like a usual Sunday service, until his first announcement, the shocking news of the Japanese attack on Pearl Harbor! Our minister showed considerable emotion in his voice as he told us the war news. Before he was through, Pastor Schaap broke down. He cried.

It made me feel empty on the inside, then angry, and fearful. Oh, what horrible news! Our pastor prayed with us. We truly needed prayer. For his words touched all of us, for relatives, our family, the church family, for my cousin Bernie Tysen was stationed at Pearl Harbor.

Frankly, there is hardly anything else I remember of the day of infamy which lives on, the news left me numb.

At school, the following day, we gathered in the school assembly, all students from the 7th through the 12th grades. A large radio was on the desk in the front of the room. Our President spoke; we listened to his speech to Congress, and the nation. President Franklin Delano Roosevelt requested Congress to make a Declaration of War. They did.

In a matter of days, I recall young men coming to school to register for the draft. Some came to volunteer for military service, enlisting in one of the branches of armed services. During the breaks between classes and at noon we saw them coming all day in one steady stream. We were at war!

Our lives, but especially the lives of all young men and women, were changed from that day on. We were in World War II. One couldn't forget December 7, 1941. The battle cry in those days was heard again and again, "REMEMBER PEARL HARBOR!" Yet life had to go on for all of us!

Mom had some problems when she was expecting. Her legs gave her a lot of problems. Swollen in the summer heat, I would get a dishpan of water ready in the evening so she could soak her feet. Since it was hard to bend over, I'd wash her feet and legs before bed.

In between the birth of some of my younger sisters Mom had a large abdominal tumor. When the doctor did surgery to remove it, he claimed it to be as big as a football. Mom had this done in the Jasper County Hospital in Renssalear.

Generally, the family went to visit her. However, one night Paul and I were the ones who were to go to the hospital. We took the '37 Plymouth coupe that night.

Two girls went along to visit Mom. They were Frieda Cheever and Evelyn Osting. People made comments while we were in the hospital. One, we were rather young to come all that way to Renssalear. The other, we were pretty young to have those girls along with us.

The comments were both true. I have no further comment.

Grandpa Hoffman was in the Jasper County Hospital. Family members took turns being with him. Dad's turn came up, but he sent me to take care of "Daddy," his father. For some reason Dad couldn't make it, so I went in his place to help out.

It was in the summer of 1945. Grandpa Hoffman had fallen. In the fall he broke his hip. Grandpa was going outside to the toilet before going to bed one night. Instead of going down the steps, in the dark, he fell off the cement landing by their back door. It was a drop of at least a foot and a half. That fall resulted in his broken hip.

By this time Grandpa was 84 years old. His walk was unsteady anyway. He had a runaway with a team of horses years before. That runaway left Grandpa with injuries which bothered him the rest of his life.

The fall in the night had put Grandpa in the hospital. The news was a big schock to my Dad. I came back with the news, then went to the field to tell Dad. Dad's comment was prophetic, "Daddy will never make it." My father didn't look at me as he spoke, just stared off into space.

Grandpa never did make it out of the hospital. He died August 17, 1945. His birth took place on July 21, 1861. After 84 years his life on earth came to a close in Jasper County Indiana.

My little sister, Carolyn, had surgery when she was eight years old. She, too, was in the hospital in Renssalear. At the time she was in the third grade. She had appendicitis.

Turns were taken to stay with her while a patient in the hospital.

Since we did not have a telephone at home, I checked with the doctor while in town. Several times I stopped at the office personally to check on her condition.

One day he said she was running a fever, due to an infection. A change in her recovery caused me concern, frankly I was worried. At home, when alone, I would walk around praying for her. Even though her condition was never considered serious, I still wondered if she would recover. This caused a longer stay in the hospital. The family sent me to be with her for a day and through the night. Carolyn was in a room with an older woman. A very talkative person. Having that woman around did make time go faster.

At night I sat in a chair near Carolyn's bed. Most of the time we just held hands. Carolyn would fall asleep that way. Finally, I pulled my chair close enough to lay my head on the edge of the mattress. I did get a little sleep. However, any little noise in the hospital woke me up. Nevertheless, I did get some rest.

The woman in the room was very upset. She was upset with the nurses, she felt they should have placed a screen divider between the two beds at night. For our part, it really didn't bother us that much.

Once Carolyn's infection cleared up she was able to go home. I remember her school picture of that year. Whenever Mom and Dad were gone to see her I'd look at her picture, praying for her and asking God to heal her.

As a young person I felt my prayers were answered. Carolyn completely recovered from her surgery and infection. It was a good feeling to have her home again.

Left, Carolyn and Wilma on the southside of our home.

Youngest members of our family: Rita, Carolyn, Wilma, and Martin J.

Hunters

Dad had a gun. In fact he had a couple of guns, but I think his favorite was his 16 gauge shotgun. My father was always concerned about gun safety. For him that "unloaded" gun was very dangerous! He wanted guns unloaded in the field. Guns were never to be taken close to the house loaded.

Dad told of having his shotgun when he was still at home. On one occasion it was brought into their house. His oldest brother Ralph picked it up. Ralph next pointed it directly at the head of Grandma Hoffman. Then he called, "MA. . . "

My father rushed over, forced the barrel upwards towards the ceiling. Then he rebuked his brother for doing such a thing, saying, "You don't know if that's loaded!" Uncle Ralph sharply replied by insisting it was not loaded! Regardless of his brother's comment, Dad walked out of the house with the gun. Once outside Dad took the bullet out of the shotgun. It was loaded! And it had been aimed at Grandma's head. What a tragedy that could have been, except for the kind Providence of our Heavenly Father.

Dad went hunting when I was a boy. When I went along I would take our .22 rifle. Dad always used his 16 gauge shotgun. When I was very small Dad hunted rabbits. Generally, he came back with a number of rabbits, which he skinned by the clothesline. A few times he bagged some pheasants. Those times we ate pheasant or rabbit for dinner.

It tasted good, but I hated to find "shot" in the meat. Biting into "shot" hurt my teeth. Worse still was grinding the "shot" as I was chewing meat. While I enjoyed the meat, I didn't like to be surprised that way.

Later there was very little hunting for rabbits. Some kind of disease got into the wildlife rabbits, causing many families to be very cautious. If a hunter had an open wound, he could get infected while skinning the game. After that threat Dad didn't do much hunting anymore.

There was still enough other wildlife on the farm. It was inviting enough for others to hunt on our place.

Most hunters would ask for permission. A few did not. Some felt the farmer ought to permit them to hunt, those hunters did not pay too much attention to the rules. Others respected our instructions: No hunting around animals or where we were working.

Certain hunters came back year after year.

One who did was a barber from Hammond. That hunter liked to hunt squirrels. But before he went hunting, we needed haircuts. We'd sit on a heater chunk by the woodpile or on a chair. Naturally, being outdoors, he had to use a hand clippers. (During the Depression Dad cut our hair. Dad was pretty good, too.)

But, during squirrel hunting season, we had our own barber, right on the farm. Boys better hold still with a hand clippers. It could hurt like the dickens when one's hair got caught in hand clippers. It usually caught the hair in the neck. Those times it pulled out the hair before getting it clipped. Those times made me flinch or jerk away, making it even worse. It was best to sit still and take it. If the barber was in a hurry, then the clippers might dig into the neck. That made it smart.

Once the haircut was finished Mom's apron or the towel was unpinned. All the loose hair was brushed away, well, most were. Plenty of hair was still stuck to the collar of my shirt. Some managed to get down my neck. Oh, I hated that feeling. Even washing my neck did not always help. It generally took a change of clothes to get rid of those miserable, sticky hairs. As a kid I felt like I was wearing sackcloth.

Anyway, I had my ears "lowered" as we'd say in those days. All of the boys got haircuts. Sometimes Dad got one, too.

Once the barber finished he put away his tools and got his gun. Heading for the woods, he was going to hunt squirrels. We liked the man. Also, he hunted only where Dad gave permission.

There was a black man who came from Gary. He came out often to hunt. He wanted to hunt rabbits. The man had a big smile. His teeth had a number of gold fillings. Those sparkled when he smiled!

During the war he always had something for Mom, which was nice during food rationing. Some foods were rationed by points during World War II. Each purchase took points out of your ration book. His wife ran a grocery store. He came often with a five pound sack of sugar for Mom. No points. It was a gift. Then the man asked Dad for permission to hunt.

Other times he came with candy. But this man, too, would respect our rules about hunting.

However, others would not be that welcomed after a few times. While at first they did ask to hunt after a few times, they no longer asked. Instead they would tell you they were going hunting.

At first they did hunt where you requested they go. However, before too long, some of these men would go to the very place you asked them not to hunt.

Dad got into it with some of them. When they disobeyed, Dad ordered them to leave. And he meant—leave!

That was dangerous! After all, the hunters had the guns!

Some listened and left. Others were so arrogant, almost refusing to get off the farm even when they broke the rules. One group went right back of our barn, walking into the pig lot. It got very touchy that time. Dad was very angry with them. The hunters showed so much hostility. Openly quarrelsome too, it became a war of words. They finally left, but not before causing trouble.

Another time Dad was running the corn picker. I was unloading the corn at the crib. These black hunters were hunting in the very lands Dad was picking. Remember, we had always requested they hunt away from where we worked. But the rabbits were in those corn rows. Dad was chasing them out of the lands as he picked. Rabbits were running all over, so these hunters started to shoot whatever direction the rabbits were running. It was frightening! Our lives were in danger when they were so careless. Nor would they listen. Dad ordered them to leave. They refused, after seeing all the game in the field. I heard more shots. Dad kept yelling at them. I stopped, when I heard the last shots.

Dad yelled to me that I should call the sheriff. I continued towards the crib with my load. As I was leaving, I still could hear Dad and this one hunter arguing loudly in the cornfield.

I pulled into the yard, where I parked the tractor. Since we did not have a telephone, I had to drive nearly four miles to Uncle Ben Hoffman. I called the sheriff in Renssalear, which was about 25 miles away. He told me he'd get there as fast as possible.

Those hunters waited about as long as they dared, then left our farm. Right after they were gone, the sheriff drove on the yard. His car was steaming. Actually, he drove as hard as he could. But he was too late.

There was one thing. It helped. The one hunter was a policeman from Gary, Indiana. His badge was on his hunter's vest. That day, when he asked for permission to hunt, he threw open his hunting coat. It was done for my benefit. His badge was there for all to see! I looked at the number on his police badge.

I think I still recall that number—41. I mentioned that to the sheriff. While he couldn't do much to help us at the time, for that information he did thank me. Adding before he left, "That may be all we need." Given that information, he planned on reporting the hunter to the police department in Gary.

While the man had hunted year after year, as time went on, he became more bold. He was the type who told us what he wanted when he hunted on our land. But after that incident the policeman never came back. Remembering his badge number must have been enough to take care of him, and his kind.

One time a few had asked to hunt. Later a group joined them by walking into the field, without permission. They all lined up across the field, with a little space between hunters. They proceeded to march across the farm. They were making one big sweep to get all the game.

Dad was very upset. That was not hunting. They were ganging up to slaughter the wildlife. What unsportmanship!

Such people with a gun make it look bad for the true sportsman. Likely, we'll always have some poor sports like those characters.

The next story came from Neil, who had a turkey farm near Hebron. Hunters had asked Neil Morrow for permission. Year after year a certain man was permitted to hunt. The sad part was this very man betrayed a trust.

Once he "hunted" away from the buildings he would kill some turkeys. The birds were placed in a roadside ditch. After he returned from his "hunting" he left in his car. He drove off the turkey farm, down the road, where he could pick up the turkeys he killed.

However, this poor sportsman bragged a little too much. He got caught!

Some hunters did come for the sport of hunting on the farm. It is all right for them to return year after year.

The turkey-killer is the kind who ruin things for the good sportsman. They did more harm than they realize. It is hard to accept even the good ones after some ruined the good relationships you'd like to have with hunters.

We did have a colorful hunter who was welcomed for years on our farm. Bill Brown. He was a quail hunter. Bill enjoyed that sport immensely.

Brown was always dressed as a hunter, all in brown. He was a most careful hunter with his gun. However, in the end, a gun was his undoing.

One day Fred Wolff and Bill Brown met at the same woman's house. Both were there to see her. Green-eyed passion soon possessed both men, then raged between them.

Brown claimed that Wolff charged after him. Fred Wolff was a big man, a bricklayer. But Brown was big, too. Anyway, the way Bill told his story, he had to defend himself from Fred. That's when he grabbed a gun and shot Fred. Wolff was killed.

As the story goes, Brown then turned to the woman, threatening, "And you are next!" She dove through a window and fled into a field, where she hid.

Bill Brown took Wolff's car and left the scene of the crime. As he pulled into Leroy he spotted a police car, parked outside a small cafe.

He went inside, seated himself next to the officer. Then and there he confessed to the killing. Brown was immediately arrested and taken to jail. The man was held for his confessed crime.

Dad and Mom went to visit him in jail while he was waiting for his trial. At his trial he was found guilty and sentenced to prison for the murder.

I remember this whole sad and tragic experience in our community. I was touched emotionally by what happened. First, Bill Brown was well-liked by our family. He was always welcomed to hunt on our farm. Bill was a friend to our family.

A second way I was touched, Mrs. Wolff was one of my teachers. Her husband had been killed. I felt for her. The other woman involved was the mother of one of my friends.

It truly was a very sad tragedy in the lives of many close people of our community. It jolted many in our town when it happened. It jolted me, too.

One experience with hunters still remains a dark mystery. It was late in the afternoon, several hunters drove on our yard. One got out of the car to ask permission to hunt.

It appeared another hunter was getting out of the car when we heard a loud gunshot. The shot echoed around our yard.

Loud voices began speaking. Without asking to hunt, the man ran back to the car.

I was standing a short distance away from the open car door. They talked about getting hit in the knee. After quickly looking at it, they got the injured hunter back in the car. Both doors were slammed shut, then they roared off the yard.

What a mystery! What really happened? How serious was the injury? Where did they take the poor man for help? Who were they?

I remember looking around for blood, but never discovered any on the ground. Likely, if he was bleeding, it was in the car or on his clothes. Faintly, I recall his moans. But it all happened so fast, at the most, they were on our yard only a few minutes.

We thought someone might come back to tell us what happened, but nobody did. We looked in the papers and listened to the radio for any news about this mysterious incident. We saw and heard nothing. Some thought was given by our family that perhaps the sheriff might investigate the shooting. A doctor or hospital would have to report it, which would surely call for the law to look into the incident.

To this day we have no more answers or information than we did the evening those mysterious hunters stopped for a few minutes, then disappeared with their dark mystery.

Likely, we'll never find the key to unlock the secrets of that strange mystery.

Now I Can Drive the Car!

I had been driving the cars and trucks for years, yet I still looked forward to getting my permit. More important than a driver's permit, I wanted to get my license.

When I was old enough Dad and I took the green 1937 Plymouth to Renssalaer for my permit. We had to go to the Schlosser Creamery. First of all, we had to give the usual information. The fellow in charge said that he'd fill it out, while I read the eye chart.

I was requested to read the lowest line I could see on the chart. I hesitated, so he urged me to go ahead. I waited some more. By that time he was insisting that I go ahead and read it, assuring me he would fill out my application.

Embarrassed as I was, I had to ask him a very foolish question. After a few moments, I blurted out, "Where's the chart?" Slightly irritated, "The one on the wall!" he said. More confused than ever, I confessed, "I don't see any chart on the wall."

In disbelief he looked at me, laid down his paperwork, walked over to me—took my hand, then walked me towards the eye chart. Halfway there I exclaimed, "Oh, there it is, now I can see it."

Utterly disgusted and frustrated, he tore up my application, and threw it in the wastebasket. Turning to Dad, he said, "Don't come back here with him until he has glasses."

Finally, that was something Dad could now "see" for himself. Something he never accepted before. Teachers mentioned my need for years. I tried to tell him. Paul would bring home comments from my teachers. But Dad thought too many quacks were in the business of selling glasses. Those guys would put glasses on a kid, even if they didn't need them. That day Dad had his eyes opened, I certainly needed them.

As we drove out of Rensselaer Dad mentioned stopping in De Kock's Store in De Motte to talk to Rudy Zylstra. Rudy was the butcher in the store, who recently got new glasses. Dad felt we should ask him where he got them.

Dad stayed in the car. I was sent to the meat counter to ask Rudy. He told me, "From J. C. Schosser, in the Norris Building in Kankakee, Illinois. You go there, I think you'll like their glasses." I thanked him, then went back to our car.

But before we left town, we had two stops to make. We first got sweet rolls and doughnuts from the bakery. We also had to make a telephone call, which was done from the telephone office in town. Again Dad stayed in the car, while I called Dr. Schosser's office. I got an appointment for that afternoon. In fact they'd be ready for me when we got there. So we drove straight to Kankakee. Dad and I ate the whole bag of sweet rolls and doughnuts on the way over there.

I had my eye exam. We were then told that I was very nearsighted, also had astigmatism. They assured us they could make the corrections needed with glasses. I picked out my new frames. They would mail the glasses to me; they arrived in a few days.

Wow! That was a whole new world for me. I saw things I could never see before. Everything was so blurred and distorted before. No matter how I tried before that, I could not bring images into focus. I'd practically close my eyes trying to focus, but that never worked.

Uncle Ben Hoffman was by our place when my new glasses came. I walked out of the house wearing them. Naturally, I was very proud of them. But best of all, now I could see! It was just great, I thought.

However, something happened which opened my eyes to something else. I stood on top of the hill, with my new glasses on. I looked downhill by the toolshed where Dad and Uncle Ben were talking. Uncle Ben immediately called me "Four Eyes." Boy, did that ever hurt. I don't know what I expected, but I didn't think he'd do that to me. I quietly took the hurt.

Inside I knew how badly I needed those glasses. Really I had needed them for years.

That afternoon I went to the little forty to cultivate corn. For the first time I could distinctly see leaves on a tree—from a distance! Colors were brighter. Figures appeared unmistakably clear. It was a wonderful world I was seeing as a young man, actually for the first time in my life. I tried to tell Dad how wonderful it was to be able to see things so clearly. It was exciting. Dad's comment back was, "Willie, you don't know all the things you missed!" But I wouldn't miss them anymore.

Dad and I returned to Rensselaer to get my permit. That time I saw the chart—I spotted it when I walked through the door!

Several months later I took my driver's test. George Grevenstuk and I took it the same day. Others were there, even one girl who had moved from Kentucky. She stood out from all the others. The family came with an old Model A Ford. Her turn was just ahead of mine. The girl's parents were sitting in the back seat. The officer informed them that they would not be permitted in the car during the test. A lot of time was wasted in convincing them to get out. Once out, the examiner crawled in the front seat and the test was underway! A whole group of us were watching from the sidewalk.

She got the Model A started. With several jerky stops-and-starts she tried to back up. Eventually, she got it into the street. He pointed ahead—with one big jerk she took off. She was headed for the first stop-and-go light less than a block away. Pointing to take a right turn, she turned the corner. However, she barely missed the light, driving up and over the curb. It was cut very, very short! The old Ford jump in the air, then bounced back down again. Soon out of sight, only to reappear after circling the block. She pulled in her parking space, after bouncing off the curb—one more time. The examiner jumped out of the car, slammed the door. He made another jump—away from the car, as if his life was in danger. He left the poor girl sitting in her Model A Ford. Shaking his head in total disbelief, weakly he asked, "Who's next?"

I was. We got in my old green Plymouth for my test ride.

I did everything he requested. Once the test was over, he gestured for me to park on the side of the court house. The man praised me for my good job of driving. Even though I was slightly nervous, I was only glad to give him a good ride. I think the poor guy needed to relax a little after his life-endangering ride in the Model A Ford!

I got my license. I proudly announced, "Now I can drive the car!"

The first car Dad and Mom had was a Baby Overland, with side curtains. I remember riding in the front with Dad. One time he needed parts for his small Rumley threshing machine. It meant we had to travel to Laporte to pick them up. Mom was in the back seat with the baby when we made the trip.

That Overland was the car in which Dad would sing. As a kid I'd glance in his direction while he sung. All the time, Dad acted like he was not aware of my watching him. He saw me staring all the time. His voice got louder and louder. Never looking in my direction, Dad just continued to turn up his volume. I kept getting closer to him, almost looking directly into his face, Dad never cracked a smile. Instead, he'd sing even louder in the Overland.

While he never let on, Dad was having a lot of fun with me. It was fun.

After the Baby Overland our family got a Chevy, one with a green body and black fenders. That was a common color combination in those days. After that car Dad got a black Chevrolet, about a 1931 model.

The one I thought was the best as a boy was our 1934 Chevrolet. On the dash was a special emblem. It was the seal of the Chicago World's Fair. Actually, it was one of the cars used for demonstrations at the fair. People were given rides in a new car. After the fair, those cars went on sale, so Dad bought one. I enjoyed showing other kids that special car, always pointing to the dash emblem.

When I was twelve Dad went to Graves in Lowell to get a brand new car. They had to go to South Bend to pick a car up right off the assembly line. This one was our 1937 Studebaker, a light blue-grey color.

By the time Dad got back it was dark. He drove up our big hill, parking it near the house. That was very exciting, Dad

Late '20s Chevy, with green body, black top and fenders.

Our Chicago World's Fair Demonstrator Chevrolet.

Our 1937 Studebaker, with which we had many experiences.

299

came home with a new car! Dad sat behind the wheel, with his door open. I stuck my head inside to get a good look. Oh, it smelled so new. How many miles? I looked—exactly 72 miles. That was the miles from the factory in South Bend to our home place.

The trunk was so big, at least we thought so as kids. It was fun to crawl in it, holding the lid almost shut. But just to be sure, we used a corncob to hold it open. One time we rode from Uncle Ben's place to Rensselaer in the trunk. Paul, Howard and I were in the trunk. We took a corncob with a string tied to it, which we watched bounce around on the pavement. Aunt Edith was very upset about "those kids back in that trunk!" For us boys it was a barrel of fun to ride in our big trunk.

The '37 Studie, as we nicknamed it, had an overdrive. Paul and I drove that car all the time. I started when I was only twelve, but Paul was younger. Almost daily we drove to get the mail, our mailbox was almost two miles from home. One of us would drive down, while the other one would get to drive back home. We'd take turns.

One hot day we were sent for the mail, I drove. Lois rode in the front with me; Paul and Marty were in the trunk.

On the return trip we were to trade places. Paul was to be behind the wheel. However, before starting home, even by the mailbox, Marty was begging to drive the car. Realize he was only five at the time. Paul and Lois protested letting him drive, while I gave in, saying that he could drive. Of course, this left Paul to oversee this young driver! Lois and I went along for the ride, in the trunk.

Just before reaching the Carter place, it happened! Marty decided to made a sudden turn to the right—right into the ditch. Paul tried his best to correct it, but Marty had too good a grip. The car went nose-first into this ditch.

Of course Lois and I had no idea what happened. We were passengers traveling in the trunk. I threw the trunk lid open, we gazed into the sky. Then I exclaimed, "The Studie...in the ditch!" All of us scrambled out of the car. Standing on the road, we knew we were in trouble. Here we were, just over half a mile from the mailbox, but still almost a mile and half from home. I said that I'd run home.

Believe me, I had plenty of thoughts racing through my head while I ran home. I was hot, as I ran home. Mom had all the shades down, to keep the house cool, so she could not see me coming. Dad was taking a nap. Mom was caring for Wilma. I ran into the house, coming up to her with my beet-red face. Excitedly, I tried to tell what happened. I felt safe telling Mom, but how would I ever tell Dad. Dad heard me talking to Mom, so he got up, half-asleep, asking, "What happened?"

The truth? The Studebaker was in the ditch! So the first question from both of them, "Who was driving?"

Oh, boy, the truth had to come out, "Marty." What more could I say, it was the truth. But they must have had their doubts, both questioned me, "Marty?"

Dad turned to me, "Get the truck out; get a log chain." I did both, in a hurry. Dad crawled in with me, I drove off the yard and down the road.

When we arrived at the scene we had all kinds of spectators! Any suggestions? They predicted it was going to roll over! Frankly, they were right, it could have rolled. It wouldn't take much to tip over.

Dad took charge. He told me to back the truck up to the car. We hooked on the log chain. Dad then told some of the sightseers to hold down the driver's side, by standing on the running board. Dad got behind the wheel, then yelled at me to pull with the Dodge truck. Both vehicles spun in sand at first, then gripping the road, our Studie came out of the ditch back onto the road.

After unhooking the chain, I was told to go to the corner and turn the truck around. A few comments were also made to those people standing around. They were thanked for helping. (The car was not damaged at all.) Everybody got into the car, except me, I got back into the truck, which I drove home. Marty did *not* drive the Studie home!

Orders were given not to let him drive again. I guess he wasn't old enough yet! After all, he wasn't ready either, because he flunked the first time behind the wheel.

The Studebaker was one car Paul and I drove many times. Once we went with Dad to Grandpa and Grandma Hoffman. The weather was bitter cold. Dad wanted to check on his folks, did they have enough wood and coal? They were low on coal. Wood burned too quickly, but coal would last longer, so they had to have some coal to keep them warm through a frigid night. Dad told Paul and me to get a couple of sacks from the crib, then go up town for coal.

After finding the sacks, we tossed them in the car. The coal yard was by Konovsky's Lumber Yard in De Motte. All the car windows, except the windshield, were covered with frost. As boys we turned up the radio; the music was loud. North of Grandpa's house was the railroad, less than a quarter of a mile away. Slowly, I drove the car over the tracks, after crossing the tracks I turned left towards town. Immediately, a train flew by! I asked Paul, "Where did that train come from?"

We thought little more about it. Upon returning with a couple sacks of coal, Dad asked us if we didn't see the train. With the frosted-over windows, no. Dad said the whistle blew again and again. The engineer sounded his warning long and clear! With our loud music, we never heard it. From the kitchen window Dad had to watch us creep over the tracks, while the train was getting closer and closer every moment. Really, we just cleared the tracks when the train went whizzing through the crossing. Dad and our grandparents only could watch helplessly from the kitchen window.

God in His Providential care watched over two boys. Two Hoosier boys who were totally unaware how close a brush with death they were having. For some long agonizing moments Dad thought he would watch a tragedy happen before his very eyes. It must have seemed like "eternal" moments! But God was gracious to those boys who were only eleven and twelve. God indeed was merciful to a father and his sons.

Mrs. Swisher died suddenly on the night of October 20, 1937. She was 54. They had stopped at our house earlier that same evening, so this was shocking news to hear she died.

The family asked to use our car to make funeral arrangements. They had the funeral director from Rensselaer handle Liz's funeral. They had to contact other people, too. Dad said that they could go ahead and use our Studebaker.

Each time, upon returning, they first would tell how nice our car was, afterwards added it stunk. Over those few days, we wondered what they were talking about. We took it on a few short trips—nothing smelled. But upon the return of their next trip, they again complained about that terrible smell. That was a big mystery to us. We didn't smell anything.

A day or so later, I was told to get the mail. Wow! I got a whiff! The odor was very, very ripe!

Between the Hodge Ditch and Carters I pulled over to check it out. I lifted the hood. Something was overripe! Something died.

I spotted it, between the motor and the manifold, one well-roasted rat. Yuk! No wonder it stunk! It was about enough to gag me while I tried to get it out of there. Its hair and hide were burned and baked on the manifold. Finding a stick along the road, I rubbed the stuff off. After some circulation of air under the hood that repulsive smell drifted away.

The mysterious repulsive smell, which they endured every trip, was solved. However, I have no idea why nobody ever took the time to look under the hood. If they did, they could have gotten rid of the rat. They could have enjoyed the ride in a nice car, which didn't have to be a stinking ride.

One job I had, along with Paul, was to take our cream to the depot in De Motte. Our cream was shipped to Western Creamery in Chicago. It was shipped in 5-gallon cream cans. After unloading the cans on the platform, we went inside the depot to see Charlie Curtain, who made out the papers. A yellow card would be wired to each can.

If Dad had to go to town we'd go along with him to the depot. But if he was busy, then Paul and I took it to the station. After several trips, Charlie began to asked questions about how old we were. He let it be known that he thought we were very young to be driving a car. Once his comments included that we could get caught by the police. Upon getting home, we told Dad what he said.

After that, for a number of weeks, Dad said we'll ship it from the depot in Lowell. But it was much farther away. At times I was really worried about meeting a policeman when going to Lowell. Going to De Motte, we mainly could take back roads to town. I couldn't do that when we shipped out of Lowell, for we had more highway travel.

I got so frightened one time coming from Lowell. No, I didn't see a policeman. But the Studebaker began to shimmy. At a given-speed the front wheels would get this abnormal vibration. When Dad drove, he would just step on the gas, that would stop the shimmy.

I got too frightened to go faster, instead I almost came to a stop. I drove very slow after that happened to me.

One night, upon our returning home, we parked the Studie in the shed downhill. As we closed the door, we heard and smelled something. There was a dripping sound and the smell of gas. Getting a flashlight we took a look under the car. We discovered a sharp stick had punched a hole in the gas tank, on the edge of the steel strap which held the tank in place. Not a big hole. That night we found a cork in the house to plug the hole. Once we pulled out the stick, the cork was pushed into the hole. Years later, when we traded the car off, that cork was still in the gas tank. It never leaked again.

That never could be said for another gas tank. My little green 1937 Plymouth's tank leaked quite often. That car was always dragging bottom!

With another hole and the smell of gas, it was time to take it back to Cheever's Garage. Caleb would fix it one more time. But there came a time when he had fixed it enough, so he ordered a new tank. I brought it in to install the new gas tank. When I got there to take it home, I could not spot the "low-slung" tank under the trunk. Old Caleb smiled at me, then opened the trunk. There it was—in the middle of the trunk. Never again would we have to worry about a hole in the tank.

Dad hated it, mainly because there wasn't room for anything else in the trunk. After all, we needed the room. It was only a coupe, already the smallest kid had to lay in the back window. Dad told Caleb to put it under the car, where it belonged.

Dad's favorite name for the green Plymouth was "The Roller Skate." It seemed to skate all over the road. That car never wanted to go straight down the road, always sidetracking. The frame of the car must have been out of alignment, whatever caused that happened before we bought it.

One night I ran it low on water. Even after stopping at filling stations, I couldn't find any water. They were all closed.

I didn't want to run it that way, but some boys with me wanted me to drive it anyway. We were following a fellow who was on a date with one of the single teachers. Finally, I said that I had to go home. When I reached home it was boiling hot, with a burning smell under the hood. As I turned off the key it didn't want to quit running. Since it was so hot, I decided to leave it outside for the night. When I lifted up the hood, I could see the glow of the gaskets on the motor in the dark. I was sick, but I couldn't do anything until morning. I went to bed.

The next morning I was anxious to get it started. But it would not start, no matter how hard I tried. After that we hooked a chain on it, so we could pull it. We circled the little timothy field, again and again. Now and then it chugged a few times, then quit. I couldn't keep it running. I questioned myself: had I ruined the motor? Finally it took off. Once it started, it kept running. I was so relieved.

We did have one car of class. It was a luxury car, a 1927 Packard. It looked in excellent shape when we bought it in the 30s. It was in top condition. That Packard had a large trunk mounted on the back. The upholstery was the best quality. The big wheels had wooden spokes. One had to say it rode like a Pullman, pure comfort.

One day Dad and I were coming from Hebron, but the ride was not that smooth. At a certain speed it was so jerky, Dad made a crack about it. We both laughed, then he stepped on the gas. I watched the old speedometer roll around to 72! It was rolling along so smoothly you felt like you were sitting in a living room chair. Man, that was class.

It was fun to get some guys in the Packard for a ride. One Sunday morning we picked up Dick Evans and Hermie Belstra, just for a ride. Soon we ended up in Pondville, exploring the roads. Eventually, we got on some private property. It was time to get out of there, so we turned around. However, we discovered they locked the gate on us. We couldn't get out of there. Several times we drove up to the gate, each time some people came towards us. They were not going to permit us to go back that way. Our only way was to go to another, private property. We found a road, stepped on the gas and made the Packard roll along the backroads of Pondville. We escaped!

It got scary when this one guy picked up his gun. No more rides through Pondville on Sunday morning. We found other places to take rides with the old Packard.

Other cars we had were a 1931 Graham Paige, a 1935 Pontiac and 1937 Packard. That Pontiac was a neat car. Paul generally had it polished like a mirror. A black car with red wheels, and whitewalls, would catch anybody's attention.

It did. One night at school it caught somebody's eye. Paul just gave it a fresh polish job. With the keys in it, some guy stole it while we were in basketball practice.

I got out of practice first. We were to pick up Mom's groceries from the store, so Paul told me get the groceries while he showered. The keys are in it, he said. I looked for the car; I could not find it. So I asked him again where he parked it. It was supposed to be right by the door. I tried one more time, but I couldn't see it. Once again I told Paul I couldn't find it, by that time he was disgusted with me. Not having showered he ran outside in his practice clothes. As chilly as it was, he would show me. It was gone!

At first the best guess was that the cheerleaders took it for a joy-ride. It so happened a State Trooper was in town, so our coach suggested we give those girls a good scare. Paul rode around with the policeman looking for his car. They came back, unable to find it either.

Our friend, Malcolm Bozeman watched the car go out of town that night. He was standing in front of the American Reformed Church. According to him, the person in the car was having trouble keeping it running as he was leaving. However, once he got it running he floored it as he left town. He was speeding as he took the curve out of De Motte, heading south.

The State Trooper put out a bulletin on it.

Nothing was heard. Absolutely nothing. We felt we might as well accept it was stolen and gone for good.

That following spring, before school started in the morning, our school principal asked me if we had a car stolen. Somebody had called school saying the Pontiac was located in Lafayette, Indiana. Paul and a few classmates took our 1942 Buick down there to get his car back.

Something very interesting was found out when Paul got there. His car was discovered behind a school the very next morning after it was stolen. It was behind St. Mary's School in West Lafayette. It so happened an officer was going through the storage garage when he spotted Paul's black Pontiac. He was the one who informed us that it was found.

It lost a little of the luster of the polish job, being so dusty from the months of storage. One small dent was on the hood, which must have been caused by a 2x4, which was close by, when it fell on it. It was in that garage all the time. Only those miles from De Motte to the garage where added to the odometer. So the speculation was that the city police located the car, but were waiting for a reward to be offered. Further, in all likelihood some student was not getting a ride back to Purdue, so he took it. He was tempted to take the polished Pontiac, which caught his attention! After all, it even had the keys in it. Far too tempting. Paul had it looking too sharp to resist.

Years before this, my brother Paul and I had our eyes on another car. A Ford Model T. It was Grandpa Hoffman's coupe. A dandy little one, really nifty, in our eyes. We dreamed of getting that one for our very own. If only he'd sell it to us, wow! For, after all, when Grandpa got older, he parked his Model T. There it sat!

As boys we tried more than once to deal with Grandpa to buy it. Over and over we asked him, but Grandpa would not budge. No sale! Nothing doing! No!

Grandpa was not going to sell it to us. Why? We wanted to know, why? Well, he felt it would be too dangerous to let us have his Model T coupe.

Even to this day, I can almost hear Grandpa's answer, a refusal given in the form of a question: "Think I want you kids *kilt?*"

No matter how we pestered him, he gave the very same answer. His Ford coupe was put up on heater chunks of wood. It was in the far end of the corncrib shed. There to gather dust, while it went nowhere.

It made us sick. Every now and then we'd go look at it, what a waste! So useless looking. We just couldn't understand it. But Grandpa was not about to have some grandsons *kilt!*

However, we were to feel much worse later on. One night Uncle Ben had a fire on his farm. That fire burned down a number of buildings, including the shed with Grandpa's Model T. There is no way to express how I felt when I saw it. In the middle of the ruins of the fire was a burned-out shell of our favorite Ford Model T coupe. Now, that was a terrible waste! we thought. Depressed over it, we felt Grandpa made a big mistake. He should have sold it to us, then it would not have burned in that fire. But he didn't. And, why? Grandpa did not want us kids *kilt.*

Maybe it was best that way. Maybe the old Ford lives better in my dreams and memories this way, I don't know. But we never got to own his tin lizzie. Maybe it would have been an old flivver for us. (Those were some of the favorite names given to the old Model T.)

When Henry Ford first made the Model T a muffler could be replaced for a quarter. Right, a quarter of one dollar. In fact, a whole new fender cost only $2.50. The first ones Ford made were seven feet tall. One comment I also recall people said Henry Ford made, the Model T could be in any color people wanted, provided the buyer chose black!

Regardless, in my heart, I still lament not getting Grandpa's little black coupe.

Aunt Edith used Grandpa's car every now and then. Uncle Ben's family lived on the same yard, so they had use of his coupe at times.

Aunt Ed, as we knew her, came to our place, with all her kids in that little coupe. She parked it by our toolshed downhill. I think she came to help Mom wallpaper.

As kids, naturally, we played in the car during the day. After the papering was finished, Aunt Ed was anxious to go home. So she yelled, rounding up her kids to go home. Get in the car, she ordered. They all climbed in.

No key! She left it in the switch, generally everyone did the same thing. It was no longer there. No telling, likely one of the smaller kids lost it. It was gone!

Right away all the darn kids were blamed. All her kids were ordered out of the car. Searching everywhere did not turn up the key. Aunt Ed was one flustered woman. Finally, she was almost ready to pull out her hair. Instead she took out one of her large hairpins.

Aunt Ed stuck it into the key slot, jiggling and wiggling it. She moved it in every direction, then, believe it or not, it worked. Grandpa Hoffman's old Model T started. One more yell, all the kids piled back into the car. Stepping on the reverse pedal, the old Ford started to growl, then with a few jerks it was rolling out to the Old Grade, headed for home.

Everybody was smiling, kids were yelling good-byes, soon the last wave was seen. Only a little dust was floating in the air behind the Model T. Slowly the dust drifted over the fields. Soon they were out of sight.

I guess that's like Grandpa's old Model T Ford, it just drifted slowly out of sight...then...it's gone. But not from this Hoosier boy's heart, for he still sees it in the theater of his mind. While this causes tears to roll down my cheeks, for in some ways I'm sad, but I'm also happy for the memories playing on the stage of my mind and heart.

I'm glad Grandpa had his old Model T Ford coupe. Even though we could never buy it, Grandpa will never know how much he gave this boy from Hoosierland.

Who could forget our Model T Ford dump truck? It was one of the first things I learned to drive. Henry Ford came up with a car or truck which was easy to drive. Three pedals were on the floorboard of the old flivver. The first one was forward, rather slow. The middle one was the reverse. The third was the brake. Next to your left leg was a lever for "high speed" travel. When you got it rolling ahead you pushed the lever forward. Then a person was then moving, in those days.

Our dump truck actually had a small box on it, especially compared with other trucks. What made it special was the dump box. It was not a mechanical dump, we had to do the lifting to get it to dump.

Times were changing, as those trucks needed a transmission. Dad had one put in our truck. This worked by the pedals, but we also had a gearshift installed, with a first, second, third gears, plus reverse.

When you shifted into third gear it really went down the road. It made a grinding-singing sound. The strangest part was the reverse, with the lever ahead, the truck got going full speed backwards! Far too fast for steering it straight.

I know. One time Paul and I were sent to fix fence around the south pasture. Our job was to go around the whole fence replacing posts. We also had to patch the wire, if it had been broken in places. By mid-afternoon I was bored with the job. So the next time I had to move the truck ahead, I decided to go for a little ride. In my mischievous way I got into a peck of trouble. I wanted to find how fast I could make the old truck back up. I was backing all around the pasture. For some showing off, I started whipping the steering wheel back and forth. Suddenly Paul was flagging me down, "Stop! STOP!"

I had flipped the inner tube outside the tire. It was like a large balloon outside the rim and tire. Fortunately, it did not blow out. Quickly, I left the air out of the tube. After that I had to take the tire off the front wheel, which would allow me to put the tube back inside the tire. Once I got that done, I could use the hand pump to pump it up again. All this took a long time. Paul was pretty disgusted with me, for not too much fencing got done after that. My joy-ride was a big waste of time. Not only did the Ford truck go backwards, so did the job we were supposed to get done.

We still had a lot of fun driving that old truck. A lot of people thought Henry Ford made only a tin lizzie. But before we got to drive a Model T, most kids could purr like one of those Model T motors: "Bbbpt-n-bbbpt-n-bbbpt." Then to hear a horn honk would almost be enough to make you laugh. Those horns sounded like a hungry calf bawling. Maybe more like a sick calf! Anyway, those old Model T Fords gave many memories, and fun, but also frustrations.

Say what you like, there was nothing like a Model T.

One day Dad came home pulling an old Dodge truck. It was a 1927 model. Not very much to look at. Dusty. Spots painted everywhere, with bird droppings. Holes in the roof. Evidently, it had not been used for years. It needed a lot of work. Even the slats on the frame of the roof were just beginning to rot away. Dad sent to an auto supply place for a roll of

Our '27 Dodge truck, Paul seated on running board. I broke off my front tooth on the big black headlight on the other side.

311

covering. The underside of this covering was grayish in color, while the top was ribbed slick black. Dad replaced the roof with this new material. That took care of any further deterioration of the cab. (Left over materials were later used on my homemade wagon.)

Dad got the rest of the truck cleaned up. Once it was running again, we had a truck which we used for years.

I liked to drive it. As a kid I sat up high enough to be able to see where I was driving it.

This was the truck with a flare box mounted on the running board, just ahead of the driver's door. I stumbled over that flare box, while checking the oil. Unable to break my fall, I shattered one of my front teeth on the big black headlight. Whenever I look at that damaged tooth in a mirror, or my tongue feels it, I remember our 1927 Dodge truck.

With the passing of time, both the Model T and Dodge trucks had to go. Dad replaced them with a 1934 GMC truck. It had a wooden bed, around the outside were openings for the stakes. We had a red grain box and a blue stock rack for the GMC. Afterwards we built a gravel box, a little more than a foot high. That was a handy little box. It was good for grinding feed, hauling sand or gravel, or during planting time. I could reach over the side easily. I did not have to crawl or reach over the higher sides of the grain box. For other times we needed a grain box for harvest and the stock rack to haul cows or pigs.

However, we got the most use out of our blue rack during the Jasper County Fair. We hauled all of our exhibits and 4-H calves with it. Once there, we used it for our sleeping and eating quarters during fairtime. It was our make-shift mobile home for one week.

Sometimes Dad used the flatbed to haul hay. During the winter Dad hauled baled hay from the marsh to Sam Lev in Chicago.

We travelled many miles with our GMC, especially during World War II. It was very necessary on our farms.

After the war it was replaced with a new International truck, bought in 1946. That truck had a steel bed on it, which

Jerry Knip built in his shop. As we got closer to harvest time, Dad sent me to help Jerry get it finished. We made a small gravel box and grain box for it right away. Besides, we also added extensions to the sides so we could use it for hauling livestock. I spent hours putting in all those bolts and nuts on those boxes.

It was a big change to have a brand new truck, the 1946 International.

At first we had gas barrels on a high platform, near the big crib. It was located at the edge of the big hill. The posts had to be over seven feet tall, maybe more. On top of the platform were four 55-gallon drums. Our gas man had to walk up a slanting plank to fill those barrels. The fuel would be dumped into a large funnel, then drained into the drums. One had kerosene, while others were for gas. A long hose hung from the barrels, which was used to put the fuel in the tractors, cars, trucks, or a gas can.

One day somebody had parked a car on the big hill. This was east of the house. Marty was small at the time, nevertheless he adventured getting into the car. Soon it was rolling—downhill! Straight for the platform. He hit it! Barrels went flying and bouncing in every direction. None hit the car. Other than knocking down the whole works, not much damage was done. Once again, Marty was just too young to drive!

Uncle George Hoffman was our Standard Oil gas man when I was a small boy. I can remember when he came to bring gas to our farm. It was a balancing act to walk the plank to fill those barrels. Later Mel Struble got the route. Our Mobil gas man was Harry Mochler from Hebron. Dad bought from both of them.

Dad later bought an underground tank, a used one. Rich Grevenstuk brought it to our place. A used gas pump came with the tank, both were delivered at the same time.

The small slip scraper was used to dig the hole for this large 500-gallon underground storage tank. We buried it at the foot of the hill, north of the toolshed.

A small cement slab was poured, on which we mounted the pump. The globe on top of the pump was partly broken. At first we simply used it that way, but later we took it off. A small piece of tin covered the opening. Dad put a stone on top of the tin to hold it in place. With this pump we could put fuel directly into the tractors or vehicles. Later we purchased another tank, which was a 300-gallon overhead tank. After we got that one, the old tank was used for distillate for the tractor fuel. Gas was in the new overhead tank.

During the Depression people wanted to buy a little gas from time to time. Generally, they would want only a gallon or two. We didn't like to do that too often, but we did help them out in a pinch.

One day Kenny Swisher pulled on the yard with his old Model T jalopy, a stripped down version. Most of the body had been removed, so it was down to the frame. Kenny was sitting on the gas tank. A small wooden box bolted to the frame back of him.

He offered Paul and me a ride. Kenny wanted to go to town that morning. However, he needed some gas. As boys we were to ask Dad for some gas for him. Dad declined to give him any, too expensive, Dad claimed.

Kenny then asked for some free distillate, fuel oil. That fuel was cheaper. Dad said we could give him a couple of gallons. So we dumped it in his tank, mixing the two fuels. Immediately, his jalopy became a smoker.

Since the car was warmed up, we took off for town. It ran all right to De Motte, even if a cloud of smoke came out the exhaust pipe. Kenny kept his old Ford running in town. We parked north of Swart's IGA Store, where we picked up a few things before we left again for home.

As we headed back home we took the road next to the railroad tracks. At the dead end, east of town, we turned north, heading for the Old Grade in the marsh.

By that time his old jitney was having some trouble with the fuel oil in its system. Even so, as long as we ran it hot, we still were able to ramble right along. Still smoking. People would look at all the smoke, we laughed as they stared at us. It was polluting the whole countryside.

Dad with four horses in front of the grain drill, likely sowing winter wheat.

Once we got about two miles from home Kenny started doing some "hot shot" driving. He was hauling the steering wheel from one side to the other. Near Marion Carter's place he decided to drive into a little ditch, down one bank and up the other. It was fun—several times.

However, Kenny tried it once to often. He cramped the front wheels sharply, for a sudden turn, they locked in that position. The car shot sideways...and stopped! He killed the motor.

Trying over and over, he could not keep it running. Once the motor was cold his old Model T refused to drink that distillate.

I ended up walking all the way home. After telling what happened, the folks gave us a gallon of gas. We drained all the junk out of the tank, replacing it with a gallon of good gas. It started right away.

Our ten mile trip, to town and back, turned out to be a very long trip. Much longer than a few boys thought it would be.

Even an old Model T Ford could not be fooled about what it liked in its tank.

315

Horses

My favorite horse was old Benny. I should say that horse was everybody's favorite. There was only one Benny. There never was, or will be, another like that horse.

Two teams were Doc and Charlie, and then, Dick and Minnie. The day we got Dick and Minnie we had company. Uncle Dick and Aunt Minnie Peterson came to visit for the afternoon. When they got out of the car, they walked straight over to the barn. Dad was standing near the horse barn with his new team. One was a grey mare; the other the black gelding, next to her, was her teammate.

Aunt Minnie looked at them, then asked, "Nu, wat jou call dat?"

Dad looked at her, without batting an eye, popped up with, "Dick and Minnie!" From that moment on, that team of horses were called by those names.

My Dad would do things like that. One horse he bought from Tice Punter, that horse was called "Tice." It was one ornery horse, almost every runaway we had on the farm, Tice was involved.

Tice had a huge growth over the hoof on one leg. Afterwards, we found out how he got it, when he was younger. It happened during a runaway. He was hitched to a disk, which caused him to get cut up. After the injury, healing took place, but his hoof became deformed. It didn't seem to bother his work. Tice was a hard worker. Yet, for some reason, this ornery bugger would get spooked or feel his oats—and away he would lead another horse on a runaway.

Prince was a gentle horse. Not a big horse, but such a good worker. He could be worked by himself, or with another horse, as a team. Prince died of some kind of blockage. A vet worked to save him, but he died an agonizing death just east of the big crib. It was hard for me to see him die.

But one horse with life was Little Dick, a black horse. You would almost think he was related to Dick, of the Dick and Minnie team. But big Dick was a gelding; Little Dick was a stallion, full of life!

Later, when the big horse was struck by lightning, he began running around the farm with the old grey mare. Neither did any work at that time, so they lived a life of ease on lazy acres. Dad said they never had it so good!

When I was small I recall a severe electrical storm, which had so many close lightning strikes. Three animals died. The mother was standing near the fence, with her two-year-old and a baby colt by her side. After the storm they were found in one pile, each touching each other. One bolt killed the mother, along with both offsprings.

We went down the lane after the storm. I felt very sad to see those pretty horses dead. Her little colt was so cute, but there he laid dead in the pasture.

A few years later we lost another little colt. One morning a man stopped with a trailer out on the Old Grade road. There was a lot of stomping going on inside the trailer. Kingma had his stallion in the trailer. He walked that big horse on our yard. That stallion looked like a monster, he was really big. He took the stallion behind the corn crib. Dad got one of our mares out of the barn, taking her downhill. I wondered what was going to happen. Dad held the rope on the mare; Sam held the stallion by the bit. First the big horse bumped the mare, then bit her. She whinnied. Suddenly the stallion mounted the mare, to breed her. Dad and Sam talked for a little while, a price was mentioned if the mare had a baby.

Sam walked his stud over to the horse tank for a drink. Dad took off the halter, letting the mare run out into the pasture. Kingma went out the gate, across the yard to his trailer parked on the road. Once again the big monster stomped back into the trailer. It bounced around, when he was stamping down his big feet. A few strange sounds were made by the stallion as they pulled away and headed down the road to the north.

The mare did have a baby. However, it lived only a few days. I thought he was so cute, but he died at the bottom of the big hill. Again I felt sad, for it seemed we could not raise our own horses.

When I was a little boy, my Dad had a large number of horses on the farm. I remember Dad having five horses together pulling the gang plow. While it was only a two bottom plow, that many horses were needed to plow all day.

That was hard work for horses, causing them to sweat so much, making them very smelly on hot days. They were wet all over. The sweat made the leather harness smell, too. A harness would then be sticky, so I didn't like to touch it. I hated to get the slimy stuff on my hands and clothes. But all that came with working with horses in the summertime.

The first job Dad gave me with horses was to harrow. Four horses pulled our four section harrow. Dad put a board on the back of the harrow, where I could stand. Since the ground was rough, I didn't care to ride on it. So at first I walked from one end to the other, back and forth. However, after walking those long rounds for about an hour, I decided to ride on the harrow. Man, that first morning was so long. And I never walked so far as I did that day. I got so tired. My biggest problem was to get the horses to turn around on the ends of the field. Even though I was small, it was the first job Dad gave me with horses.

We had a two row horse cultivator, which took four horses to pull. Only a few times did I use it. Mine was a single row, to which one hitched only a team of horses. I covered many acres of corn with that single row. The seat hung low, where I sat. The cultivator had hand grips and feet stirrups, which were used to guide the cultivator closer or away from the row, but they helped me sink the cultivator shoes deeper into the soil also. Our single row was not hard on horses. Even so, every once in a while I would let them rest on the ends.

When they cultivated with four horses on the two row, Dad would switch horses at noon. A half a day was enough,

Cultivating corn with horses and one row cultivator. *Courtesy of Farm Progress Co., Carol Stream, IL.*

especially when the corn was getting taller. Then it was too hot for horses to work all day in tall corn.

The hottest work was when corn had to be laid-by. Corn was tall, and very little breeze was felt in the fields. It was extremely hot for horses walking between rows of tall corn.

One summer during the dry, dusty and hot Thirties, it was continually hot. In the east field, near the Cook Ditch, a horse went down. The animal overheated. The poor horse just dropped by the end rows. They unhitched the others and came home.

Some of us went back to the field to see what happened. Dad and the hired men tried to help, but it was too late. The horse died where it dropped. Later the men went back to dig the grave. The horse was buried right where it died in the corn field.

Dad gave orders to rest the horses. Even working

Unloading ear corn by the elevator into the crib. *Courtesy of Farm Progress Co., Carol Stream, IL.*

319

the horses only half a day, this still happened. Times were hard in the Depression, it was a big loss to have a horse die. Worse, everybody hated to see an animal suffer by being overheated. But it was hot for man and beast.

Those steel seats were hard! The only thing a guy could do was to use a folded burlap sack for a cushion, but that only added to the heat. A man's pants or overalls stuck to the seat, with all his sweat. The heat of the day just hung between the rows. It was hot!

It felt good to get off at the ends, while giving the horses a rest. At least one could walk around a little. It gave your blood a chance to circulate some. The ground was scorching from the sun beating down all day. Relief came only at the end of the day. Finally, one could quit and go home. Horses hung their heads down as they walked home. They were tired, and ready for water. But if it was extremely hot, one had to be careful, not giving them too much water all at once. They were unharnessed, then given something to eat and more water. Horses would seem to get a second-wind, especially if they were turned out to pasture in the evening.

Each spring there was one big job: hauling manure. During the winter manure piled up outside the cow barn. It got to be a big pile. A pile which was scattered over a large area of the hillside, south of the barn. Once the pile started to freeze, then a plan was used to dump more on top. Whenever we cleaned out the gutter we'd scoop it into a wheelbarrow. Getting a run at it, one would push it up the plank. But the trick was to keep it balanced, otherwise it would dump over. Oh, that happened, too often, right where you didn't want it to flop. A person had to wear boots to clean out the gutter, for it was one dirty job.

Once the gutter was clean lime was dusted from a loose-knit sack. It took care of some of the smell. Also it gave the barn a clean look. Fresh bedding was given to the cows at the same time.

Most of the time bedding was thrown on the manure in the horse stalls. After some time, the horse would be standing downhill, with his hind legs higher than his front ones. Eventually, you had to clean out the stall. Our calf pen would also have a build-up, as bedding was thrown over the manure. The same happened in the hog barn and chicken coop. But eventually, all the manure had to be hauled away.

Come spring those piles had to be cleaned up. Springtime meant it was time to fertilize the land. Pile after pile was pitched into the manure spreader. Load after load was spread in the fields.

We would hitch up a team to pull the spreader. Once alongside the pile, one had to start pitching manure. Every pile, pen, stall, or coop had an aroma all its own. Your nose gave the signal somebody was hauling manure. The air was filled with the smell around the buildings. It also could be detected on a guy's boots and clothing.

The cow manure pile had its own stench. Hog manure could smell awful. Wow! A calf pen could stink, too. It was ripe, we'd say. Still cleaning out the horse stalls gave a strong stink of a different kind. My eyes always burned when I pitched that manure. Eyes burned in the chicken coop, too. Those offensive odors were there no matter what animals or birds left their manure or droppings behind. Mix it with urine, then it was bound to smell—awful! Pee-uu! Wow!

After hauling away the manure piles and cleaning out the buildings, there was still more to haul away. This was found around the strawstacks. Cattle would eat around the stacks, but also lie down there overnight.

Maybe it was springtime, but this job had the foul "fragrance" which went with the job, a back-breaking one. It was hard to dig out the manure after it had been stomped for weeks or months. Sometimes it came out in layers, or a little would tear away with the tines of the fork. A person worked for each pitchfork thrown into the spreader.

It was a relief to get it loaded. Throwing the seat back, you could climb on the spreader and sit down. The team would pull the spreader out to the field.

I always hoped the wind was right, blowing the manure away from me. I did not want any of this "fertilizer" to fly all over my clothes. Those old beaters in the back would really whirl and cause the manure to fly!

The back of the spreader was a very dirty mess, filthy. One didn't want any of those parts to break on the spreader. There was enough pollution on all those moving parts to make it the most dreaded job of fixing any machinery.

My cousin Howard Hoffman had a terrible injury from their manure spreader. While he was climbing on the spreader he was severely injured. Once the load was off, then a person could stand inside the box. They were in the field, when he tried to crawl over the beater in the back. As they hit a bump, the drive chain dropped on the main gear—spinning the beaters. Two of the prongs raked into his forearm. Since it had been just unloaded, some manure was on the parts. Naturally, some of it got into his wounds. Providentially, those prongs missed the vital parts of his arm. While spared permanent damage to his arm, his injuries were very serious. It turned out to be a rough summer for Howard, as healing was slow. I visited him once, when he was in bed at home. During that time, a repulsive smell was coming from his wounds. Howard told me that it stunk so much he hardly could stand to keep his arm in bed with himself. Part of the night before, he put it outside the covers, so he didn't have to smell it so much.

The biggest job I had with horses lasted for weeks each summer. A hot job too, since we did this work in July and August. It was when we baled the slough hay on the land a mile north of our home place. I drove a team on the dump rake, my job for all those weeks.

During certain times of the year, our horses had plenty of free time. They had long periods to spend in the pasture or woods. Free time for them was a life of ease.

However, when the spring and fall work began, they had to give up the easy life. Then we had to round them up. If they were in the pasture, they tried to act like they were not paying any attention to my coming. They kept eating, all cropped the grass busily, until I was almost by them. Swinging their heads sideways, each kept ripping away. The horse would rip off the last mouthful, then up came his head. One of them would snort, lift his tail, like he was alerting the others. They'd all take off.

Sometimes they acted like they were heading for the barn. They could run like mad, looking back at times. They wanted to know where I was. One would start turning, to double-back. If possible, they'd run to the Hodge Ditch. It was a race to cut them off. If I failed, then I'd have to go all the way to the ditch and start over again.

Crossing to the other side, I would race, waving my arms and yelling,

Unloading loose hay into the haymow. *Courtesy of Farm Progress Co., Carol Stream, IL.*

"WHOA! WHOA!" Should I make it close enough to cut them off, even with only one to wheel around, then likely the others would go back, too.

Sometimes I won; others I lost. You only needed one of those ornery buggers to get all of them to run for it.

It was a good way to get you to reach wits' end. They made you mad enough to shoot them, if you had a gun. It could be so trying.

Once Dad got that aggravated with the horses. They ran and ran, as they had been in the open fields after the corn was picked. One kept leading all the others away from the barn. Eventually, Dad got his shotgun and his car. He drove after them until he caught them. Stopping the car, he jumped out with his gun. He yelled! (Wanting them to run, when they did, he'd give them some buckshot in their butts!)

Dad quickly raised his gun to shoot, giving them a start. But at the last moment one of his best horses wheeled around, facing Dad. Dad shot!

He reared, veered slightly—and got hit in the shoulder, near the heart. For a moment, he staggered. The rest of the horses ran off. Dad knew the moment he pulled the trigger, it was a terrible thing to do. But it was too late.

Dad did get the horse in the barn. All night long Dad kept after the animal. Dad did not permit the horse to lie down and die. And he didn't.

The horse recovered.

Usually, we thought we almost had it made, if we got them into the lot by the barn. Many times they'd come for a drink, then we'd slip around and shut the gate.

Even then we could have problems. Several of us would join together, to drive them into the barn. Certain days they did not want to be cornered. Only one would make the break. The animal would try to outsmart us. If one got such an idea in its head all the waving and shouting only caused the bugger to gallop right passed us. One better get out of the way!

Then we had to start all over again. Round them up, driving them together, hoping all would head for the barn door. One had to watch the trouble-maker very carefully, bluff him, or outmaneuver him. Sometimes it worked. Not always, then we had to repeat it over for another time.

If they had been out to pasture for some time, then it meant a lot of running and chasing. That's when we reached wits' end. It could be so aggravating. One day Dad was utterly disgusted with the whole bunch of horses. He wasn't alone, for we all had had it.

All our chasing, waving, shouting was worthless, it seemed. About then a person would pick up a stone, stick, or corn cob to throw at them. Enough to threaten them. At times it was enough to distract them, so they would go in the barn.

Dad discovered a rock not far from the water tank, which he picked up. They were making their move to run again. Dad hollered, then fired the rock. The leader was trying it again, so Dad aimed for that horse. Only the animal veered to one side. Old Doc, who had only one eye, stopped in his tracks, tragically, he turned his head. The rock hit Doc squarely in the good eye!

From his darkened world the poor animal reared up into the air. Shaking his head, he blindly staggered around in his dark world. Some blood and other fluids ran down his face. Finally, we tried to quiet him, he stood still. He looked the likes of a helpless creature. Dad continued to speak softly to Doc, grieving over the injury he caused his good horse. Dad was sick, but gently continued to clean the wound. Doc had a tear go down his cheek, but we all could have cried.

Doc was destined to live out the rest of his life in that dark world. Other horses seemed to sense it. Other horses became his eyes, as they led him around. From then on, he was always in touch with the other horses. Together, after such a tragic loss, they still had some old fashioned horse sense, Old Doc was with us for years.

Dad took care of his animals. Oh, at times he got angry enough, which he would regret later.

One day Dad got it himself. It happened when he stepped into the horse barn. Just as he was through the door, the horse in the first stall kicked. A vicious kick! A hoof caught Dad on the side of his knee. That put Dad down.

Once he got out of there, he had to half crawl back to the house. I still recall how painful it was for him. It caused him to hobble around for days. Later he favored it for some time, as he limped along.

Horses would get cut on a fence from time to time. Dad would take great care of such wounds. Many times horses got sore necks. Dad day after day would be seen doping with some kind of salve. It was watched closely until it completely healed.

For years we had horses. Our farms had a lot of them throughout those years, but one day we had none. I can't exactly remember when or how it happened. But one day the days for horses were over. Only the memories remained.

I'm the barefoot cowboy, without his spurs, on his faithful pony.

Ride 'Em, Cowboy!

I have to add another part of my boyhood in Hoosierland. There were all kinds of animals on the farm. As boys we would try to ride them. I tried riding a big pig. Sometimes a pig would let you stay on for a short ride. It would grunt, move a few feet, then stop. That was as far as I was going to ride. If the pig got frightened, with this kid on its back, then it would take a few galloping jumps—I thought it was high time to dismount. Time to jump off!

As a small kid I tried to sit on the back of our biggest dogs. Generally, the dog would cave-in, so there was no ride there.

Most of my memories have to do with ponies and Benny.

One year Grevenstuks boarded a pony on our farm. The oldest of us kids were still small at the time. There is a picture of me on the pony, downhill, near a trumpet vine. It was taken near the gas pump. Others are pictured on the same pony. I barely remember that Shetland pony.

Later we got Daisey, one I remember much better. Where she came from, I can't recall. She had a funny trot, which jiggled the daylights out of me. I never got her going fast enough to gallop. Her walk was slow enough; it took a long time to get any place. I could have jumped off and walked faster myself. If one of us wanted a slow, easy ride Daisey did all right.

Benny was my favorite. As kids we could do anything with him. For a short time I kept him in the cob shed. I cleaned out the north end so Benny would stay in there. But the door was too low, while Benny was too tall to go through the door. I dug a hole, so I could get Benny inside. Benny had to step down into the dip, as I led him in and out of the cob shed. He had to duck his head. His back would nearly scrape the top of the door frame and the edge of the roof. Nevertheless, I managed to get him in and out of there.

327

In my imagination that was my horse barn. This play did not last very long, Benny was soon back into the big horse barn. Anyway, for a little while, I had my own horse barn.

A gentle animal, so easy to handle. God gave him to be the best friend for us kids. We'd hitch him to the buggy, mudboat, wagon—anything. Best of all, we could ride Benny. When we did, he had plenty of plain horse sense to have all of us kids around.

One Sunday morning Paul and I wanted to take a ride. Never on Sunday! Mom's rule. Mom didn't think boys should be riding a horse on Sunday. For her, she had the feeling something bad would happen to us if we did. As boys could do, we kept on nagging Mom until she gave in.

So, in a way, she gave permission. However, we needed more than that, we needed help to saddle up Benny.

Dad was in church, as usual on Sunday morning, so he couldn't help. Mom would have to help us saddle up. Naturally, Mom kept protesting all the way to the barn. She drug her feet, every way she knew how. Once in the barn, she tried to say she didn't know how to put a saddle on a horse. Both of us boys assured her that we'd show her what had to be done.

Soon the saddle was tossed on Benny's back. Hanging over his sides was the belly band, which had to be fastened. Mom didn't think we got it tight enough. Good enough, we felt as boys. (It wasn't. Benny outsmarted us. He held his breath.)

With his bridle on, we backed him out of the stall, then led him outside. Paul sat in the saddle; I was sitting behind him. I wrapped my arms around Paul to hang on. Off the yard Benny trotted, with two boys going for a Sunday morning ride. Soon we were out on the Old Grade, heading north. Mom watched us from the top of the hill, as we got ready to go a little faster.

With encouragement Benny began to gallop. Just as we were passing the back driveway—it happened! The saddle slid sideways. First I fell off, landing on the dirt road. Paul rode the saddle around the side, then under the belly of Benny—hanging upside down.

Then he, too, dropped to the road. One hoof barely kicked us. Instantly, Benny stopped! Dead in his tracks, showing how much horse sense he had.

Sure we got hurt—a little. However, not as badly as we could have been, if we had another horse. Sure, we cried.

Mom saw it. She ran to the road, getting there as two boys were picking themselves up from the dirt road. Her first words, "See, I told you kids not to do this on Sunday, for I knew something was going to happen!"

With a few tears we walked Benny back to the barn. That was one time we did not "ride 'em!"

Paul never gave up very easily. He tried to ride any number of horses. One day he was seated on a horse in the middle of the cow yard. The horse just stood there. That horse wasn't going anywhere. Paul was unable to prod the plug to move on. So Paul asked me to give the horse a whack on the flank. I did. Once more I slapped him. Still he didn't move.

I looked around for a stick or something to hit the horse on the butt. I only spotted a corn cob. I picked it up, lifted the horse's tail, placed the cob under it. Instantly, the horse clamped his tail down. There was just enough irritation to make the horse move.

He did. Up and down! Up and down! The plug started to buck for all he was worth. Paul had to hang on or get bucked off.

Ride 'em, cowboy! Paul had to. But he did not like the stunt I pulled on him. While he was trying to hang on, I was getting a tongue-lashing for doing such a dirty trick.

I knew he was in a terrible predicament, a real pickle, yet I couldn't keep from laughing. It was really funny—for me.

After all those up and down bucks, eventually the cob did fall to the ground. The horse stopped bucking. Paul was able to get off safely. With that horse, after all, he wasn't going for a ride anyway.

Paul didn't give up easily. Paul and Red Evans bought a white or grey horse—hard to say just what color it was. A fancy saddle had been borrowed for this ride.

Paul led the horse into the field across the bridge. All saddled up, and ready to go, Mom was asked to hold the horse. Paul mounted his steed!

A spirited horse, indeed. No more than Mom got hold of his bridle, the horse reared, front legs pawed the air. Mom quickly backed away, almost fell backwards. She got out of the way of the crazy beast. Within a blink of an eye, Paul was unseated.

This did not turn out to be a bronc buster experience. No chance to ride 'em!

Instantly, the crazed animal took off across the field. Running towards the bank of the Cook Ditch, leaping into the middle of the old turtle hole. After swimming to the roadside bank, he climbed up to the Old Grade. In a crazy-frenzy he galloped off towards the Hodge. Kicking continually at the fancy saddle, as it became loose. It had enough damage. Also it cost enough to get repaired. Paul and Red got rid of that old plug in a hurry.

One other horse was also very spirited, Little Dick. He was the small black stallion. Sometimes I'd ride him to get the cows from the pasture near the Hodge.

He scared me, I admit it. At times I was afraid of that stallion. Yet I liked to take a chance and ride him. There was a long, level stretch in the pasture, east of the old barn. I'd race him all the way to the Hodge Ditch. Every ride I'd encourage him to go as fast as he could. The stallion would almost flatten his ears to his head—and go! I kept wondering what would happen if I ever fell off, yet that didn't stop me. I wanted him to go as fast as possible. I kept talking to him, urging him to go faster. It was like we had a game we played. While I'd repeat it, never did I feel comfortable about it.

Little Dick was an animal that could not be trusted. The reason, he was a stallion. This horse would rear up and strike down with his front feet. Such actions were scary.

One Sunday afternoon he did this, unexpectedly. I was getting ready to get the cows from the pasture. I had a bridle on him.

Company came on the yard, while I stood there holding him. He was a pretty horse. Violet came over to us, with the idea of petting him. Instantly, he was up, striking out with those pawing front feet. Yanking at his bridle, I pulled him away. Frightened, I asked her to leave the little timothy field immediately. My heart was pounding, but I don't know if Violet sensed the danger or not. I still think he might have trampled her if she were alone with him. I never did completely trust that stallion after that scary experience. It still disturbs me as to what might have happened.

With that, I'll leave you with the last "Ride 'em, Cowboy" story.

Cows

When I was a small boy we milked our cows by hand. It was much later when we got milking machines.

Cows stood in the barn in one long line of stanchions. A gutter was behind the cows. Manure and urine "perfumed" our barn. Worst time for that was when the cows were in the rye in the spring. Then their manure was so soft and runny. It seemed the smelly stuff splashed everywhere, including those of us in the barn. It stunk. Just as bad was the calf manure. The yellow stuff was a big mess if the calves had the scours.

As kids we had to watch where we walked. In the summertime we liked to go bare foot. One got pretty good at dodging the cowpies and horseballs in the pasture or cow yard. At times we didn't walk carefully enough. What a mess—to step in the middle of a soft cowpie. The awful stuff squeezed up between your toes. Yuk! And the best one could do was wipe his feet a little clean in the grass.

The safest thing was to wear shoes. Even then, I never wanted to get it smeared all over my shoes either. Best of all decisions was to wear boots or rubbers around the cows and calves.

In the winter evenings we had lanterns hanging in the barn. We did the chores by lantern light before we got our Delco system. Lanterns were not needed during the summer. Then it was light enough to get the chores done before dark.

During the summer we had the barn doors open. That way we had a little breeze blowing through the barn. Evenings were hot for us and the cows. Cows generally panted because they were so hot in the stanchions. Flies added to all our problems in the summer. Cows had their tails constantly switching, trying to chase away those miserable flies. Nothing was more repulsive than to have a well-urine-soaked tail smack you in the face. Some cows with one swing could wrap it around your face. Yuk! Man, I hated it when it happened.

In the winter time, the barn doors were kept closed. One comment we heard repeatedly as kids was, "Shut the door! Were you born in a barn?" No. Nevertheless, we still tried to keep the warmth in the barn by having the doors shut on cold days and nights.

At times I felt I'd like to give a cow a good whack. Some had the habit of pushing against you while milking. One could be a kicker. Every now and then a cow would step on your foot too. About that time you felt like taking the stool to give the critter a good whack.

But I felt sorry for cows when we dehorned them. Some had a mean-streak, using horns on other cows. Should that happen too often, Dad felt it was time to cut off those horns. A few cows had odd-shaped horns, those had to be removed with a hacksaw. That was easier than using a huge clippers. A cow could not get out the the stanchion, no matter how much they tried to move around. Dehorning always made the cows bellow. Bellowing at times from pain, but mostly from being so frightened while the critter was dehorned. Since it was such a bloody mess, I hated to watch it. Their bellowing went right through me. With the blood spurting out of the wound, I was bothered by that, too. Yet it never lasted long, even though at first I thought the poor animal might bled to death. It didn't. I was glad when the job was done.

Dad had names for all our cows. Only three names stick with me: Grandma, Dynamite and Plushbottom. Grandma had a small utter. Dad generally gave me the job of milking her. That old black cow was pretty gentle. Dynamite and Plushbottom both had huge utters. It was not easy to get a bucket under them when milking. Their utters hung so close to the floor. Plushbottom was the most endowed. Most of the time those two came in with dirty utters, especially when the lane and lot were muddy. After a good washing they were clean enough to milk.

One morning Dad had plans to ship a cow. He sold her. Generally Kaper, Grevenstuk or De Fries would haul them to the yards in Chicago.

This morning was different. Two black men came to pick up this cow. For some reason they could not get the truck close to the barn. Backing it up to the barn doors made it much easier to load into the chute. Then the animal could go directly from the barn, into the chute, and into the truck. But that day the truck was parked halfway down the hill. The chute was back of the truck. It was going to be difficult to get her to go up that chute.

Two long ropes were around her neck. Dad gave one rope to those two black men; Dad held the other rope. Strict orders were given to get a tight hold on the rope. Just to be sure of his grip, Dad wrapped the rope around his hand several times, not wanting it to slip away.

With the barn door open, they tugged on the cow to get her to come out. The cow went crazy, more like berserk! It took about two seconds for the black men to let go of their rope. Dad could never hold her by himself. Though he tried. The crazy cow took off down the hill, running wild.

With one big yank, Dad was flat on his belly. She was dragging Dad down the hill, then all over the cow yard. Dad was unable to get his hand loose from the wrap of the rope. His wrist was badly sprained. It was swollen when Dad got untangled and walked back to the barn.

Those two black men stood there with their eyes wide open. You would have thought they had just seen a ghost! Dad was angry. Why didn't they hang on to the rope? Dad bawled them out. They stood silent. Finally, they admitted their fears. They were frightened out of their wits once the cow went into her frenzy and took off.

They got back into their truck, leaving without the cow. Dad was more than disappointed, more like, totally disgusted over the whole thing. It was a big waste of time. And Dad got hurt. Those injuries were with Dad for a long time.

After the cows were milked we still had to separate the milk. A cream separator had a hand-operated crank. A few clothespins held the cloth used for our strainer. Once we got it turning fast enough we opened the spigot so the milk could flow through the separator discs. Cream went into a cream can; skim milk, bluish in color, ran into a five gallon pail.

Cream was sold to Western Creamery in Chicago. We shipped our cream by train. We fed the skim milk to the little calves or our pigs.

During the Depression some were glad to get skim milk for their table. Swishers came in the evening for their skim milk. They carried it in syrup buckets, generally a gallon size. Each pail was full when they left, plus all they could carry in their tummies. Each pail would be held under the spout. It would foam up, so it had to be blown away, in order to see how much the pail would hold yet. While getting close enough to blow, and get some milk out of the pail, they couldn't resist a slight tip of the pail. It worked each time. Foam would rise each time, but the milk went down. This was repeated until each tummy was filled first, then finally, the pail was filled to the brim.

Jokes were made about the foam. Eventually, the tummy showed a slight bulge, then the syrup pail was ready for the lid. Each time there was the joking and laughing as they got their milk. Their tummies tanked away more than the pails.

This was warm milk. By no means did it have the taste of a glass of cold milk from the refrigerator. Milk was still warm from the cows. But it was fresh. It was good to share it.

We, also, got our milk from the barn. Each evening we carried some fresh milk to the house in a bucket for our own family.

While we had a lot of work to be done in the cow barn, we also had fun.

Later we changed the whole barn. Plans for remodeling came from Purdue University. A pipeline was installed for our milking machines. The changes permitted us to milk more cows. At the same time we built a milkhouse.

A milk truck came everyday to pick up our milk. We shipped Grade B milk to Hammond. Jim Wiers was our milk hauler. Every now and then he'd ask if we wanted to ride along to the milk plant. If we were not too busy we'd take him up on his offer. I liked the ride. But better yet, it was the free chocolate milk we got to drink at the plant. That made it worth the ride. Chocolate milk was really a special treat for me.

We later built a stave wood silo. The company sent out a man to oversee the project. We erected a scaffold from a wooden framework. This was used to drive the staves into place. Basil Hall would be on a higher level than the rest of us. He used a 16-pound sledge to drive down the staves. Every now and then it looked like Basil would fall over backwards off the scaffold. He'd lift the sledge over his head, then pound down on a stave. Each one had to be driven into place.

I worked on handing the staves to the workers. On a Saturday Paul and Red Evans helped out. Walt Mak also worked with us. Paul and Red liked to jump on the scaffold to give me a scare. It did! Man, I was so glad they didn't work with us during the week.

Walt and I put on the roof, which was very scary being that high. What made it worse was the wind for a couple of days. It made the scaffold framework around the silo sway back and forth. It took a while, but we did get into the rhythm of the sway. Walt was tall, so he could reach to put on the top boards on the roof. Both of us were very glad to get the roof on the silo.

We added to our herd during this time of expansion.

All of this did not turn out the way we had hoped. Some cows we bought were diseased. Too late, we found that was the reason he sold out. Eventually, those diseased animals infected our whole herd.

All those problems caused the veterinarian to make many trips to our farm. In the end our barn seemed full of medication. We had it on the beams in the cow barn, enough, Dad felt, to start our own business. It was plain grief trying to keep ahead of our problems.

Some cows were sold at first. Later more went. But we started buying our own milk from Uncle Ben. Dad, in the end, sold the few we had left.

I think Dad felt relieved when those last cows were gone. For that matter, Dad never really enjoyed milking all the time he had been farming.

With all the problems we had, I was glad to quit milking, too.

Besides, we had enough other work on the farms to keep us very busy.

Pigs

When I was small we had pigs in the big barn. On one side was a row of stanchions for the cows; on the other side were the pigs. There was an aisle between the stanchions and the divider by the pigs. I could barely get over it. I could reach over it to dump skim milk into either a large wooden or steel troughs. There would be plenty of pushing and squealing at feeding time. Each pig tried to be a hog and get more than its share.

On the big hill east of the buildings, was another shed on the southern slope. It was a bank-shed, with a number of pens. It had been built into the side of the hill. The shed was made out of rough sawmill lumber, which never was painted.

Later two other small open-front sheds were built. One was in the large timothy field, while the other was located east of the barn and silo.

Most of the time we kept them in the barn when we got them ready for market. Dad's red Durocs were a pretty sight. I liked Durocs, for I thought they looked like a hog ought to look. This litter was ready for market.

But Dad noticed one was really sick. Before we knew it, the hog died. Afterwards, a couple others seemed somewhat sick. A vet came out, in order to check them out. He gave us terrible news: hog cholera!

We were not the only ones who had heard such news.

Earlier Evans lost hogs to the same disease. They had a big loss. It was thought pigeons flying from one farm to the other were spreading cholera.

Dad was told that he better sell immediately. But it was mentioned, Dad was not permitted to sell them himself. Some fellow came over, who had a permit to look at them. This man

338

made an offer for his Durocs. $400 for all those pigs! Here we had about 140 hogs ready to go.

Dad had no choice. Several trucks were on our farm within a couple of hours. All the pigs were loaded on a truck and trailer. That was the first time I saw a trailer behind a truck. One more truck was loaded besides those. Quickly, they left our farm.

We could only speculate what he did with them. Some commented that the fellow had to make out very good by selling most of them. Only a couple were getting sick when they were loaded. Almost every hog looked like a perfectly healthy pig. As a person thinks about it now, how many were seriously infected? What happened to all those which looked so healthy?

But a more serious question, how badly was the cholera spread by the trucks being on our farm? Were the tires and beds contaminated by the exposure? Did he bother to disinfect everything after getting rid of the loads?

A lot of questions still come to mind, as I reflect on this big loss. Believe me, for those times, it was an enormous loss for Dad. Dad had plans of getting a good price for that litter of red Durocs. Times were tough, any profit was desperately needed by the farmer and his family.

And to think, for all those beautiful animals he only got four hundred dollars!

As a kid I gave them ear corn and checked the feeders, cleaning out the junk under each lid. I also had to see they had enough water.

When I tried to get a pig back in, which happened to find a hole in the fence, as a kid, I thought a pig was the dumbest animal. They failed to see—every time—the same hole they got through! Ten times they would run right by it. And miss the hole in the fence every blasted time. Dumb!

As dumb as they were, I still have to admit something, I liked taking care of pigs much better than milking cows.

After the cholera scare, we eventually got back into the hog business again. We got away from the Durocs, having other breeds to replace them. Their build never caught my eye, for the Durocs were my favorite as a boy.

Row Crop Farming

The term used was broadcast, when seeds were cast in every direction when planting. That form goes back a long time, even to primitive farming, when they did it by hand.

We had a few hand-operated spreaders. We had to walk while using them. Mostly we used an endgate seeder, which was attached to the back of a box wagon, the endgate. I scooped seed into the seeder or drove the team for Dad.

That seeder was used for planting oats and barley. However, a hand spreader was used when planting timothy seed. Later Dad bought a small attachment for the endgate seeder to spread the variety of small seed. Our endgate seeder was chain-driven from the back wheel of the wagon.

Seed would be covered by a harrow or disc. Broadcast crops always had to battle the weeds. Weeds gave plenty of competition to such crops.

Many other crops were planted with our grain drill. Our first drill had a wooden box for the seed. Later we bought a new one with a metal box. With our drill we planted such seed as rye, wheat, buckwheat, soybeans, millet and Hungarian. Years later we started planting the soybeans with the corn planter.

Dad had a two-row Hayes corn planter. While planting corn Dad used the most steady team on the planter. If he planted from early morning to late afternoon, then he would change teams at noon.

Corn planting on our farm started on Dad's birthday, the tenth of May. Either then, or when the oak leaf was the size of a squirrel's ear.

My father could plant straight rows. Dad was able to get his fields to look like a checkerboard. He used a wirecheck when planting corn. Evenly spaced buttons on the wire

Dad is on the Fordson, holding Paul. I'm seated on the gang plow. Mom had just brought lunch to the field.

tripped the planter. That was the way corn rows were both up and down, and across the field, the same. When it was wire-checked cultivating could be done both ways. Our first culti-vation would be as the rows were planted. If the weeds got bad we would also cross-cultivate the field. When Dad had a good check, we had no trouble cultivating crosswise.

Row crop farming changed things on our farm. My father's comment, repeated often in explaining the change, was, "I never made much from farming until the row crop equipment came along." The biggest change came with the Farmall, a row crop tractor.

Plowing the fields was done with horses on the gang plow, or with the Fordson tractor. Five horses pulled the two-bottom plow. There were the lead horses, then the other three behind them. When the plow wasn't in the ground, the back wheel whipped back and forth, like an animal with a broken leg. But once you tripped it to plow it ran level and straight. As the farmer plowed, one horse walked in the furrow. The lines could hang slack, until he reached the other end. A plow con-tinued to turn over the soil until it was kicked out of the ground. Driving across the end the farmer had to grab the lines. He found the other furrow of the land he was plowing,

341

so he could plow back to the other end. It took a lot of rounds to plow a field. A strip was not very wide, so he had to keep plowing all day. Horses had to be rested on the end.

Out in a field our Fordson tractor would howl away. The tractor had wide wheels in front. When the front wheel was in the furrow it would hug the edge, so the farmer didn't have to drive it very much.

But getting a Fordson started was another headache. On a cold morning men would jack up the back wheel. It made it easier to start, but not every time. If it was really cold, then a fire would be built under it. The fire was under the oil pan, to warm it up. Oil that was stiff made it almost impossible to start, so if the oil was warmed up, the back wheel turning, eventually it started.

That is, as long as the tractor decided not to kick! Those old gray Fordsons could be "arm-breakers!" The farmer had to watch out it didn't kick while cranking it.

Cousin Neil Tysen got kicked by our old Fordson. It broke his arm, so his arm had to be in a sling that summer.

One summer we had some big problems with weeds. Dad borrowed a Fordson tractor which had a single front wheel. It had a cultivator mounted on it, to use in the corn fields. It was a big help, but we used it for only one summer.

Dad bought a F-20 Farmall with steel wheels. With such big lugs, it could do two things—kick up the mud and kick up the dust!

The next year we bought a second one, so we had two Farmalls. Both had steel wheels. While in the field one day, the International Harvester dealer from Lowell came over with his pickup. We were working near the Hobbs Ditch, on the east side of our farm. In the back of his pickup he had a set of new rubber tires and wheels. Dad wondered what he wanted. The dealer offered to put those rubber tires on one F-20, just for a few days. So we jacked up the tractor to change to the rubber tires. The steel wheels were dumped in the field. Now we had rubber tires on the front and back. What a big difference! As we used to say, a night and day difference!

It was fun having tires on our tractor. But several days later the dealer came back. Dad asked him what he wanted this time. He told Dad he had come to get his rubber tires back. He had sold them to another farmer. But they were on our tractor.

Dad refused to budge! Dad was going to keep them, so the dealer never got them back. We were so happy to have tires on our tractor. Those old steel wheels were stored in the old barn. They stayed there for years.

Farming made a big change when they put rubber tires on tractors. Both Paul and I were cultivating with those Farmalls, even while we were still in grade school.

When the corn was very small, not many rows were cultivated before dinner. Two boys hunched over the steering wheel were only creeping along the corn rows. It was slow going. The shields helped protect the young corn.

As the corn grew we got to drive faster. We had to be careful, for if we got off the row, we dug out the corn. Any stalk hit meant it never made it. Sometimes we'd try to transplant it. Never worked though, soon it wilted, and slowly died.

There was plenty of corn to cultivate. When we were boys we had about 225 acres on the home place. Each year we had some land a mile north, near the hay fields. Maybe we had

Our two F-20s in the big cornfield, where we were cultivating in 1945.

343

about 35 acres of corn at first, but later we broke more ground. Over half of our tillable land was planted to corn.

Soybeans planted each year amounted to over 110 acres. The beans had to be cultivated, too. All our row crops, we hoped, would be ready to lay-by around the 4th of July. Our one goal was to get it all done before we had our Sunday School picnic on the 4th. I remember one year I worked in the moonlight, just to be able to say we got done in time. I told other boys about it at the picnic.

Dad and I were both cultivating near the Hobbs Ditch when we had a surprise visitor. Our corn was rather small.

Suddenly we noticed an airplane. Several times he came close to the ground, then would circle again. We could see the pilot when he made another low pass. He waved at us. One more time he circled, then landed in the field with his Piper Cub plane.

The pilot was John Worland, a funeral director who was from Rensselaer. Mr. Worland had bought a farm nearby, but that day he landed in our field for a visit with us. As a boy, I was so fascinated with his plane. We got to look inside, so he told us all about his airplane. While he didn't have time that day, he did promise to give us a ride later. (I never did get the ride he promised. He sold his farm, so we didn't see him after that.)

The pilot turned the plane around, then the little Piper Cub took off in a cloud of dust. Especially, in those days, Mr. Worland's visit was one great big surprise. I told my friends all about him landing very near us in the corn field.

A few weeks later we could still see his plane's tire tracks in the field. Soon we cultivated them out, so his visit was only a memory.

Probably the most frightening experience happened to me while I was cultivating. It was some storm.

Storms! They could be rough. It was a big problem to get caught in one while being out in the field. Especially if a person didn't have protection from a building or shelter.

Dad had some stories he'd share with us. One he told was about a hired man getting caught in a hailstorm. It turned out to be a bad one, having large hail. The fellow had a team, which had to be let go. The animals had to seek their own shelter. In some way, I thought Dad mentioned the hired man was Bill Twa. In that hailstorm the only kind of protection Bill had was a large scoop shovel. A few stones had hit him. It was time to protect himself, so he grabbed the shovel. Bill put it over his head.

He soon discovered an awful racket from the stones pounding the shovel. Finally, he could not stand the noise, so he put it down. Getting hit with hailstones was even worse! So he ducked under the shovel again.

Afterward he told Dad about his terrible experience. Certainly he didn't know what was worse—all the noise from the hailstones banging on the scoop or suffering the pain of getting banged on the head and back. Bill must have discovered he was caught between a rock and a hard place!

Many times we wanted a good rain. A good thunderstorm was most welcome, most of the time. That is, only if a farmer could find shelter.

I remember a sudden thunderstorm. Man, this one came up fast. It caught me a long way from the house or barn. Tractors never traveled very fast. Our first Farmalls never had too much speed anyway.

It was easy enough to handle a heavy rain, by getting beside the back wheel to stay out of the driving rain. Sometimes I'd crawl under the tractor. Even doing that, I still got plenty wet.

Rough electrical storms meant big trouble. They frightened me so much. Lightning strikes were dangerous. More than that, they could be deadly. I saw animals killed when they were too close to a fence. Trees were no better. I saw large trees ripped apart by a direct hit!

I hated summer lightning. Once Dad and I were watching such a storm, while standing in the doorway of the horse barn. Wind was blowing some rain around, causing the door frame to get wet. Every now and then we were blinded by a flash, which was followed by hearing a sharp crack. Too close! Leaning against the wet frame, another close one hit. I felt a

345

jolt. Not a tingle, this charge went into my hand and down my arm. That was scary, I backed into the barn, away from the doorway.

Another storm hit, when we heard a few crashes. Frankly, at times, it was hard to tell how close they were. Some were too close for comfort. While this was going on, Paul and I were in the driveway of the big crib. We picked up our large log chain, taking it off the truck. Both of us were carrying it. As we were walking with it—crack! Bang!

One bright flash was seen. No doubt, that time it hit! At that very moment, Paul and I both felt the jolt. The charge in the air was picked up by that strike. We got rid of the chain in a hurry. It was close. Later we discovered it hit a big oak on top of the hill, next to the wood pile.

For a few seconds fear rushed through my whole being!

Yet the most terrifying happened while I was cultivating. I was trying to finish the field. While I saw the storm coming, I thought I might still beat it. So I pushed it, while out west it was looking worse each round. I watched two things: the sky and the rows.

But this storm moved faster than I expected. When it hit, it poured—buckets. A black sky in the west turned white with sheets of rain.

I was going to be soaked. I knew that, but in the middle of the downpour, a most vicious electrical storm erupted. Lightning that day struck absolute terror in my heart.

As a kid, I thought it best to stay on the tractor, which had rubber tires. Yet, to get home, I had to go down the narrow lane. Fences were on both sides. Certainly, I did not like those fences so close. Flash after flash crisscrossed the sky. For me the tractor seemed to be creeping down the lane toward home. It felt like a snail's pace.

Mom and some others of the family were watching me coming out of the field. With those lightning flashes they spotted the dark tractor.

Sharp strikes kept hitting, one after another. Finally, I was getting near the bridge, south of the little crib.

But just before reaching the bridge, another strike of lightning flashed, the thunder crashed. Very terrifying. Standing up on the tractor, I trembled. I was close enough to hear the charge in the air above the drenching downpour of rain. The lightning struck the huge cottonwood tree by the bridge. That strike ripped large chunks of bark and wood out of the side of the cottonwood.

I'll never forget those raindrops! Never! They were big. Each one. And they were colored. Purple. Violet. Lavender. It was the only time in my life that I saw such colored raindrops.

For a few moments I could barely see where I was going. Those looking from the kitchen saw it, too. It shocked Mom and the others. It happened at the very same time I was directly in line with the tree. For a brief time, they, too, were blinded by the flash. They had no idea what happened to me. All of them were relieved a few moments later, when I was seen crossing the bridge with the tractor.

Oh, I was so glad to be home!

I wonder if David was in such a storm, which helped to inspire Psalm 29, "The voice of the Lord is over the waters; the God of glory thunders, the Lord thunders over the mighty waters. The voice of the Lord is powerful; the voice of the Lord is majestic. The voice of the Lord breaks the cedars; the Lord breaks in pieces the cedars of Lebanon."

Adding also, "The voice of the Lord strikes with flashes of lightning."

I know what the Bible says is true, for I heard His voice that day as a boy!

I heard that voice in Hoosierland.

Husking Corn

Husking corn was a big job, especially when it had to be done by hand. One year Dad had 39 different huskers help him.

It was a race to get out in the cornfield each morning. That meant rising early! But before that, most men wanted a good breakfast. As they usually said, "Need something that will stick to your ribs." At our house it meant having plenty of Mom's buckwheat pancakes.

We raised our own buckwheat. I can remember taking buckwheat to the mill in Rensselaer, which was by the river. Our grain was left at the mill for about a week. Upon returning we were able to get our buckwheat pancake flour. It was in big sacks, about a hundred pounds each. All those sacks were stored in our front bedroom. Naturally, we had a few mice in our old house, so we patched the holes in the floor to keep out the mice. Two or three knotholes were covered with tin can lids. A flat lid was nailed over each hole.

Each morning Mom took some of the buckwheat flour for her pancake batter. Her griddle would be getting hot on the cookstove. Her griddle covered two plates on the stove. During corn husking time the smell of pancakes filled our house every morning. The aroma was also in our bedrooms and even on the porch.

Mom would put them on a big platter. This platter would be put in the warming closet to keep them warm. This was done while the men harnessed and hitched up their teams. They would have to feel their way around, as it would be still dark.

Once the men came in to eat, those pancakes didn't last very long. Those hungry huskers put away several platters each morning. Once a man had his fill, with a grin, he'd pat his belly. Likely he would add, "That ought to hold me until noon." Pushing his chair back, he was ready to husk corn.

With the early morning darkness around him, he'd check on a few things before leaving for the field. Did he have his cornhusking hook? Did he have his doubled-thumbed mittens? (After one thumb was gone he'd turn the pair over.)

Those mittens were soft. Besides them, he needed his picking sleeves. Maybe they were an old pair of socks or the legs from an old overalls. Mom kept such things in her rag bag. Sleeves protected his other clothing. He'd pull them in place and pin them.

It was time to go. With a breakfast sticking to his ribs, he had to hurry. Daylight was just beginning to break. The fastest husker wanted to get the lead. The last thing he wanted was a slow poke ahead of him. If that happened, then he wasted time when he had to pull out of the way, or getting held up until reaching the end. To avoid such a problem, he hurried to get the lead.

It was some sight to see the wagons leaving for the field. With those big bangboards, each wagon looked like it had a high sail on one side. It almost looked like boats sailing away in the faint light of the dawn on the horizon.

The bangboard could be spotted above the corn, long before you could see the Hoosier husker and his horses. Slowly, it would sail across the field. Once you got closer you heard the banging sound. It was similar to hearing gun shots. Bang! Bang! Bang! as the ears hit the board. A good husker had a rhythm as the corn continually banged into it. Each ear dropped onto the yellow pile in the wagon.

Horses were almost in step with the rhythm of the husker. Slowly, they pulled the wagon ahead. Horses walked in the downed or previously picked rows. Rows still standing, next to the wagon were the ones being picked.

A cornhusker had his hook strapped to his right hand, while he grabbed the ear with his left hand. His hook ripped open the ear's leaves, tearing away the husks. Just as quickly he grabbed the exposed ear, snapping it loose. Once it was snapped off, with a toss it sailed in the direction of the bangboard. Bang! Another ear slide down the yellow pile in the wagon. Slowly, the mound grew higher. Taking a step forward, as the wagon moved ahead, he was ready to husk the next ear. Grab, husk, snap, throw. Bang! Over and over this was repeated, hour after hour, until noon. By that time the golden yellow mound was higher than the wagon box.

For a little break, he crawled into the wagon, just to level off the load. At the same time, he took a good look to see where the other huskers were in the field.

Once he reached the end he turned into the next rows. Corn was soon flying again. It was plain hard work to husk a load of corn. More than once, he couldn't resist a peek, to see how his load was coming. Hopping upon the hub, he got a better look. A man's wrist could get sore, but he had to keep at it, if he was to make any money that day.

Finally, it was time to head for home. Time to level it off, so it could be measured. A yard stick was used alongside the wagon box. From those inches a husker could figure out how many bushels were in his wagon. Since he got paid by the bushel he kept a careful record. Each man had his little book, where he wrote it down. Fertilizer companies gave these little books out. Dad kept his in the pocket on the bib of his overalls.

At the end of the day, the men would compare how much each fellow picked that day. There was some real competition. It was a challenge to get the most bushels for the day. Maybe one had a couple of bad rows, a dead furrow or a poor stand. Naturally, the fellow having that happen to him would pick less.

I can remember them talking about husking one hundred bushels a day. Many huskers had that for a goal each day.

With our open pollinated corn production, that was a good day's work. Such seed was picked out from our own crib. Only the best ears were picked for seedcorn. I helped do that a few times. We took the best we could find. On our hand corn sheller was an attachment, which shelled off the kernels on both ends of the ear. Those were generally misshapened, so we culled out those kinds. The more uniformed kernels in the middle of the ear were put through the sheller.

After that a small grader, with a hand crank, was used. It graded the kernels into certain sizes. That helped us use the right planter plates when planting our corn. Open pollinated corn did not produce outstanding yields. So one hundred bushels a day was very good for a husker.

Naturally, that much was impossible if the wind blew down the corn. Such backbreaking work held a husker back. Should there be a lot of down corn, the farmer had to pay more per bushel to get it picked.

Dad's crop had blown down badly one year. It was a nightmare for our cornhuskers. That was the year Dad had so many different huskers. Some didn't last very long. At the end of the year, only three stuck with Dad. They were there with him when they finished in the spring. It was April before all our corn was in the crib. Thirty-nine different fellows were in our cornfields that year.

When the crib was full, then the last sack of buckwheat flour was empty. The guys ate all those pancakes, which stuck to their ribs! And Mom flipped all the cakes.

As a boy I remember the fellows talking about Vilis Jacks, who was from Jasper County. A champion cornhusker. Jacks first won the county contest that year, then went to the state.

Dad, Paul and I went to see the state cornhusking contest for the championship. We had to find our man from Jasper County. On the end of each bangboard was the husker's name and county. I found Jacks.

Dad, Paul and I were watching him. I kept following behind him, as he fired one ear after another against the bangboard. For me it was so fascinating watching him. He was our champion!

A little later I looked around for Dad and Paul, who were no longer around. They had moved on to watch some other huskers. I searched all around, but they just were not there anymore.

I ran to the next land, to look. They were not there either. So I ran to the next one. Nowhere to be found, I raced on and on.

I was panic-stricken. Fear possessed me. I ran and ran. From one land to the next, from one husker to the next. I could not find Dad.

I was lost!

I felt so frightened. Alone! People were everywhere, but I still felt alone. All alone.

I felt like crying. Halfway I did, mostly inside.

Soon all my racing around made me out of breath. My heart was beating so fast. Not just because I was running so hard. It was doing it because I was lost! And nobody found me yet.

Finally, I stopped running. I walked back to Vilis Jacks. A shot was fired, the contest had ended.

I followed his wagon. It went to an elevator where they would measure and weigh the corn Jacks had picked. I wanted to know how good he was. Even though I didn't know where Dad and Paul were, I had the feeling they would come to find out how Jacks finished. I was hoping they would come to the same place.

And they did.

Oh, that was a good sight, to see my Dad and my brother. I quickly asked if they had been looking for me. Dad said, "No, we didn't bother to look for you, for sooner or later, we'd find you."

That didn't make me feel very good. Well, even though they didn't even bother to look for me, I was happy to be found. That felt good! Very good!

And I was feeling very good for another reason, Jacks was the state champion that year. A man from our county was champion for the whole State of Indiana. Jacks was the Hoosier husker of the year. And I got to see him win.

I'll not forget that. Nor will I ever forget that I got lost! That was a terrible feeling, even when hundreds and hundreds of people were everywhere around me.

Since we were in school, as boys we did not do much husking. We were too small for a number of years. But we did help unload corn, in the evenings or on Saturday. We had an old wooden elevator at first. Horses were used to run the elevator. A gear box, which ran a tumble rod, would turn the elevator. The horses walked in a tight circle, continuously around and around. Once we got them started, they kept going until the load was all in the crib.

Later we bought a new metal elevator, which we ran with a tractor. Whenever we were around we were expected to help with unloading corn. Most of it would slide out of the wagon box, except some up front. If it couldn't be shaken loose one of us would climb inside the wagon and kick it loose.

However, one year, Dad wanted some help to open up a field. It was a Saturday, so he felt Paul and I could help out that day. We were given a team, wagon, each some mittens, and each a hook.

We were going to try our hand at being corn huskers. It was slow going. No steady rhythm of ears hitting the bangboard. Tearing off the husks didn't work like it did for the men. It was hard to snap off an ear, too. After a lot of struggling the ear would hit the bangboard with a little bang!

How tired our arms got, sore wrists. Hooking back the husks made them hurt, but so did the snapping and tossing the ear.

Paul was picking next to the wagon; I was a couple rows farther from the wagon. When two are husking together, one must stay ahead of the other one. One time, Paul and I were too close to each other. Paul got in line of my fire. After I picked an ear, I turned to throw it underhanded into the wagon. I caught Paul right on the cheek of his buttocks! Thump! Right on his rump!

Husking stopped for a few moments, except for Paul's dance. It seemed rather funny, for me. But then, I soon found out, it was not that funny. My brother didn't find it a bit funny. After he told me off, I found out that it was *not* funny!

Oh, well, what could you expect from such immature Hoosier huskers spending their first day in the cornfield?

That day we got some corn picked, but not that much. It was more like a small jag. At the time we were about ten and eleven. But I still have a few memories of being cornhuskers.

Dad had gone to the little forty to pick corn. Since it was Saturday morning, I had to grind feed. This ground feed was given to our cows and horses. The feed was kept in a bin in the barn.

The feed mill was in the big crib. I hauled the feed in our Dodge truck. If it was dry weather, I had no problems. However, if we had rain or it was springtime it was hard to get near the bin by the barn doors. Manure mixed with mud made it one sloppy mess. Sometimes you had to make several tries to get close enough to scoop into the bin.

I could not get close enough that day. It was a mess, so the truck got stuck. I wasn't close enough, nor could I back out. The truck was stuck in the middle of the slop hole.

I had to pull it out with horses. Then I could make another run for it. But to get it out, I needed help.

Dad just came home from husking corn. He pulled his team up to the gate by the big crib. His team just stood there, still hitched to the wagon. Dad crawled off the load, only to walk up the hill to the house. Since Mom had dinner ready, I figured he was ready to eat.

Others had gone to the house, too, including Paul. Before I went in, I wanted to get the truck pulled out. Paul refused to help me. Mom wanted everyone to sit down and eat, too. In the afternoon we were to go to Dutch Corners for Christmas practice.

I didn't feel like eating. At least not until I had the Dodge out of the mudhole. Since nobody was going to help I'd do it myself. First, I took Dad's team standing by the gate. After getting a log chain, I hitched the team to the back of the truck. Next, I had them pull ahead, to take the slack out of the chain. Quickly, I jumped into the truck and got it started. I shifted it in reverse. With my door open, I yelled at the horses, "Giddi-up!" While they pulled, the wheels on the truck spun. Soon we were moving backwards, dragging it out of the mudhole.

But then we had to stop! Again I yelled, "WHOA... WHOA!" Both horses stopped in their tracks. But the truck didn't stop that soon—it rolled, backing downhill. Our horses got bumped in their rumps. Again they took off!

This time, with a jerk! They were getting out of the way. Only this time they drug the truck a little sideways, into a stump. It tore into the mudflap and runningboard of the truck. Good grief! Now I was in big trouble.

Quickly, I unhitched the team, and put them in the barn.

Then I ran for the hill, east of the cow lot. I watched to see who would come out after eating dinner. I peeked from behind some bushes, where I was hiding. What would Dad say about the damage done to the Dodge truck?

So I kept out of sight. For at least a couple of hours I stayed hid in the woods. I noticed one thing, nobody went to Christmas practice that Saturday afternoon. Another thing, Dad never came out of the house.

Finally, I decided that I better come out of hiding. I ventured closer to the house. I spotted Mom, so I called to her. Quickly, I asked Mom, "Was Dad mad? Is he upset with me? What about my breaking things on the truck?"

To my total surprise, Mom answered, "Oh, he's sleeping. Dad's been sleeping since he came home with his load of corn. He doesn't even know about it."

Later I found out why it didn't bother Dad.

Some hunters had requested permission to hunt. Dad gave them permission. In their way, they thanked Dad by giving him a few drinks. Besides that, they told him the bottle was in the car, help yourself. Dad did.

That was so unusual for my Dad. However, when he got home, then he was ready for a good nap. Dad didn't eat either, just laid down and went sound asleep. That was the way he spent most of the afternoon.

Later he got up, so when he came out by the barn he found out what happened. I confessed how it all happened. He simply said that he knew I was trying to get the work done. With that said, he helped get the truck by the bin. We got the ground feed unloaded. We hammered out the tin mudguard, then went about the rest of our work. Nothing more was brought up about the whole thing.

Dad did explain to me that he had taken a few drinks from the bottle of the hunters. I can't recall anything like that ever happening again.

In 1937 we got our 22B mounted corn picker, a two row. It was mounted on our F-20 Farmall. It was one of the first pickers International Harvester made. What a big change for us. No longer did we unload only a few loads into the cribs. Instead picking fifteen, even eighteen, a day, was not unusual. The most I remember picking in one single day were the twenty-one loads. It was a long day, quite dark when I came up with the last load. However, since we did not have lights on our F-20, we could not stay very late in the field.

After getting out our corn we did some custom picking. I helped pick corn for Bill Peterson, Orin Bell, Uncle Ben Hoffman, and a few others.

Corn at that time was planted on the Gus Safstrom property, where there is a large housing development now. One year I picked in town, just back of the American Reformed Church in De Motte. Since those days, the town has seen tremendous growth.

One day I was picking corn behind the church and the Lageveen's property along the main highway.

I watched a boy in his back yard, as he'd walk up to his fence, then back off. A few movements were made, only to return again to the fence.

As I got closer, I noticed he was shooting a gun. He was aiming his gun directly down the rows I was picking. Immediately, I stopped the picker, then yelled at him! Jumping off, I ran away from the machine—getting out of the line of fire. Avoiding getting hit, I circled around in the boy's direction. He watched me, with his gun in hand. Angry and frightened I demanded what he thought he was doing! He told me he was shooting cans and bottles off the fence posts.

I wanted to know what kind of gun he was using. A .22 rifle, he told me. I had no idea if he were using long or short bullets. Generally, a warning is on the box of shells, informing

356

a person that they could travel up to one mile! I mentioned that to him. Did he know that? No, was his answer. Showing his ignorance about the danger, he commented that he thought they just went over the fence and fell to the ground.

Upset, I told him his father ought to have told him how dangerous a rifle could be. Warning him, in no uncertain terms, if he continued using that gun, while I was picking, I'd personally take it away from him. Out of fear, I added, I felt it was necessary that he learn more about guns and bullets. Before leaving I again made it plain to him, as long as I was working so close by, he was not to shoot his gun again.

After my lecture, he turned and went into his house. Much to my relief.

Then I recognized he was Art Lageveen, Jr., who had to be in the eighth grade at the time.

It turned out to be a very scary day for me. Here I thought it would be perfectly safe picking corn in town! Really, it was far from being safe, I could have gotten shot by a boy playing with his gun.

Shelling Corn

From those early days, corn was picked by hand, then ear corn was put in our big crib, and, later, in the little crib. When they were filled, sometimes we used the driveways of the cribs, too. When we ran out of room after that we put up round cribs.

When the corn was to be sold it was time to shell corn for the year.

From an old family picture, they were shelling corn when there was snow everywhere. The sheller was pulled by a large tractor. Corn was hauled in a wagon. But my first memories are about an old wooden sheller by the big crib. Names get mixed for me, when I begin to think about it, either Gibbs or Phipps. The man came from the east of our farm, near Bomb's Bridge. He had an unique sheller. His sheller was mounted on the chassis of a Pierce-Arrow. The cab had been cutoff back of the front seat. Then the chassis had been lengthened, so the wooden sheller could be mounted on it, a big red one.

A tall exhaust pipe was on the side of the cab.

However the front of the Pierce-Arrow had not been changed. It looked elegant, real class. What a motor, running so smoothly, like it was purring. This Pierce-Arrow totally fascinated me, especially the way the motor sounded.

Parked on the west side, the drags would be placed in the driveway of the crib. Each time we shelled, the bottom 1x4s were taken off the side, so corn could be raked into the drags. After it was in place Gibbs or Phipps would shift the drive shaft so it could run the sheller. That's when it would purr! The motor ran with such ease. Speeded up, the whole unit would get into a rhythm-bounce as the corn was shelled.

Corn just rolled out of the machine. We put some in wagons. Our Model T truck didn't hold many bushels. Since it didn't have duel-wheels, 75 bushels was a load for it. Uncle Fred Hoffman hauled most of the corn for us to the Konovsky's Grain Elevator in De Motte. At times the elevator furnished a truck. Since loads were not too big there was plenty of waiting for a truck to get back.

On the north side of the sheller was the huge cob pile. By the time we had the five thousand bushels shelled the pile was very high. Leaves were blown away from where we were working, depending on the direction of the wind.

Most of the time, it was routine, plain work. Generally, it became a "rat race" when the crib was almost empty. Until then the rats were in hiding, but eventually they had to make a run for it. Scoop shovels and corn rakes were used for weapons. A war was declared on those pests. Rats move very quickly, so we had to be faster to kill them. To hit your target required several strikes—keep banging away. Some naturally got away. By the time the crib was cleaned out, we also had cleaned out some of the rats. They were thrown in a pile. When we did the little crib they would run toward the ditch many times. Mom and the kids would help, each one using a hoe. They would hack away until they got their rat.

During the dry years, especially during the Depression years, I remember watching rats on the roof of the crib or lean-to shed. Mostly they came out during thunder storms. Those rats crept out cautiously to get water. As the shower continued, from the house we saw them crawl out for a drink. Some chewed holes in the shingles, while others gnawed on the boards to make an opening. One by one rats would crawl out. A few times Dad tried to shoot some of them with his rifle. After a few shots, they would run for cover. We never killed very many that way.

As a boy I always hated rats. To me they were "vies." Every time I had to pick up a dead rat, I began to spit. I never liked a rat.

Later Simon Belstra came to shell our corn. His John Deere sheller was mounted on a Ford truck. The Belstras also had a number of trucks to haul corn to the grain elevators. During those days we sometimes shipped to the Chicago markets.

Near the waterways were large elevators, which may be known as the Port. If the price was that much better we took the time to haul it all the way to Chicago. Some were very large grain companies.

Early boyhood days corn was shipped mostly by rail. I used to like to look inside the boxcars. They were on the siding by the elevators. If we hauled to De Motte we could watch them load the cars with corn, or some other grains. Elevators were always windy and dusty places. Since we knew most of the men working there, I felt free to look around. To me the railroads were so interesting.

Later the trucks were larger, then came semitrailers, when more corn was shipped that way.

If we could, as boys, we'd try to get rides to town or Chicago with the drivers.

Time to Make Hay

Years ago we put loose hay in our big barn. Hay was lifted from the rack with a hay fork. Our haymow had hay and straw stored in it.

The hay had to go through the big door high on the west end of the barn. One year Uncle Jake Walstra was there when the door had to be opened. Uncle Jake said he'd go up there to open the door. To unhook the door he had to climb the ladder on the inside. It had hooks on both sides. With a rope attached, the door was slowly lowered until it hung down, flat against the side of the barn.

After the fork came off the track, it was lowered to the load of hay. It was on the hayrack next to the barn. Uncle Jake pulled the fork back, reaching out for it, as it was swinging on the track. One of those prongs raked across the top of his head. I should add—his bald head. A point of the fork broke the skin, naturally the blood started to flow! Standing in the opening of the big door, bare to his waist, blood was running down his face and body. What a sight!

It looked very bad, but it looked far worse than his injuries really were. Because it was a head wound, it continued to bleed profusely. Naturally, it took time to get it stopped. The family made more of a fuss over it than Uncle Jake did. I must admit though, at first sight, one got the idea he could bleed to death! Uncle Jake joked to those who took it so seriously. Shortly we had him patched up, then we got started unloading the hay.

The fork was pushed and forced into the hay. At the bottom of those two prongs were small flaps, which would flip out to snag the hay. That way the fork held onto the hay, when it was lifted up into the mow.

361

A team of horses were on the east side of the barn. They were hitched to the large hay rope. When the signal was given they began to pull on the rope, which ran over a series of pulleys. When the team began to pull, slowly the forkful of hay was lifted off the hayrack. It went higher and higher, while a few little bunches of hay fell off. The fork went through the big door, then ran down the track to where it was to be dumped. At the right spot a trip rope was jerked. The fork let go and the hay fell in a pile.

The horses were backed up, which allowed the rope to pull back the fork. Once again more hay was lifted off the hayrack. After several large bunches were lifted off it was all unloaded. The whole load was soon in the haymow.

Putting up hay generally was hot work, and hard work. In a way, putting it in the mow was the easy part. Later it was so hard to dig hay from those bunches dropped in the barn. The hardest part was to get it out of that big tangled mess. It took a lot of tugging to pull loose a forkful for feeding. Sometimes I could discover a layer in the pile, which made it a little easier. Most of the time it was hard to dig out enough to feed the horses and cows. I always thought bean hay was the hardest stuff to dig out for feed.

After we got our old hay baler it was much easier to handle. Bales were in neat piles in the mow. One bale was removed at a time.

Generally, at haying time, it could be very hot! Early afternoon it would be so hot out in the field. However, if there were little or no breeze, then the hottest place would be in the haymow.

I felt drained during those days. One day, which I still remember, I felt strange feelings surging through my body. It was hot enough loading the hay in the hot sun, but that day the heat in the mow was stifling. About mid-afternoon, I honestly felt I would not live. I wondered how I could go on working. Those strange feelings went through my whole body.

After we finished the job my body cooled down. While I can't explain it, what happened to my body while working

362

through one of the hottest days I can ever recall, still lingers in my memory.

When we put up the slough hay a mile north it was different. Even though we spent part of July and most of August, we had some breeze. Even with a small breeze, the air was moving.

While we had woods all around us, we still were in the open. We moved from one area to another. Bale piles were scattered over the hay fields. Those stacked piles stayed there until Dad hauled them away. During the winter Dad hauled them to Chicago with our GMC truck. One day Dad let me go with him, when we took the hay to Sam Lev. Sam paid Dad $6.00 per ton for our slough hay. Just that much for all our work, including the hauling. Mr. Lev had an outlet for our hay. It was used to cover freshly poured cement. That hay protected it from a freeze, when the weather turned cold.

By the time Dad loaded the truck, drove to Sam Lev's Hay Market, unloaded and returned home, it turned out to be one long, long day.

During the winter, we'd wait for Dad before we ate supper. I know I'd go to the window in the front room on those nights. I'd look toward the highway, again and again. The sight I wanted to see was one of colored lights on the cab of our GMC truck. When I spotted them, it was a big relief. I'd tell others Dad was coming home! That news made us all feel better, especially if it happened to be a bitter cold day.

Some were extremely cold, so cold, in fact, we got very concerned about Dad's trip to Chicago. One night it got much later than usual. Chicago was 60 miles away, but it was much too late that night. Dad did not come home. We waited and waited. All of us were wondering what happened. Did Dad have trouble with the truck? Or, did Dad have an accident? We did not know. Since we had no telephone, we just had to wait.

So when Dad finally came home, our family was very glad to see him. Naturally, we all wanted to know what happened.

A back spring had broken on the truck. While Dad was crossing a railroad track, the wheel hit a large pot hole. Since it was so bitter cold, the spring broke! It snapped all the leaves in the heavy-duty back spring, under the load. The leaves continued to fall out, as Dad drove down the street. It happened near the hay market, which was the best part of Dad's misfortune. Yet Dad said he heard each piece fall out of the spring, then hit the pavement. Since Dad was so close to Lev's market, he kept going, even if he was just creeping down the street. The farther he drove, the more the load leaned, so he drove slower and slower.

Finally, he got there with his load. Most of the pieces were gone by then. After he got unloaded Dad had to find replacement parts and a place to get it fixed. Along with his troubles, this took a lot more time. Being a severely cold day, more problems were added. Dad told how the whole truck frosted-over when he pulled in the garage. That took more time to get it repaired.

Finally, after all that, it was fixed, but Dad still had the long trip back from Chicago. Dad didn't make much that day. At $6.00 a ton, with that repair bill, he didn't have much profit for all his work that day.

Just think, it took a crew of seven to bale the hay. A lot of machinery was needed, when our stationary baler did the baling. It took a lot of work to get all those bales into the piles. Then on a winter morning, Dad loaded it. After that, Dad had to haul it to Sam Lev, where he had to unload the hay. After all that, he had the long drive back home in our GMC truck. For all the time, work and investment, Dad got only $6.00 per ton.

When it was time to make hay the farmer had to do it. In those days, the margin of profit was very small.

Remember, many men in those days worked hard for the dollar. Dad did!

Threshing Time

We believed in neighborliness when it came to threshing time. Farmers could not do without their neighbors.

My first memories go back to when I was very small. The crew was on our farm to help Dad with his crop. It was dinner time, so the men were in the house eating. They washed up before the meal. Straw hats were in trees or on the ground. A number of them were tossed next to our shanty. I stayed outside, playing by myself. One hat fascinated me, so I picked it up. It had little red balls hanging from the brim. Each one was like a little red cherry hanging at the end of a red string. Likely it was really a Mexican hat, very colorful.

It wasn't long before I started picking the red cherries. One by one I pulled each one off, except three in the front. After the meal the hat's owner came out to discover what I had done. (His cherry crop had been harvested while he ate dinner!) Only three balls wiggled in front of his eyes. Then he commented about "the darn kid" who left only three of them on my hat.

The man was Howard Black, who was working for one of our neighbors. Later he teamed up with Reggie Cross, to become the Hoosier Sodbusters. They sang over WLS in Chicago. We'd listen to them over the radio, especially on Saturday Night Barn Dance over WLS.

When I was a little older, Dad and Mom took us to Chicago to see a live performance of the barn dance.

Dad spent a lot of time in the fields before it was time to thresh the grains. All the grain had to be cut. Dad did that with his McCormick-Deering binder. It had been stored in the little tool shed by the old barn. It had to be pulled out of the shed. Since it had such a wide apron, we had to pull it into the field first, in order to get through the gates. Once we got there we could screw down the bull wheel on the binder. Also the small wheel at the end of the apron had to be screwed down. Once we had those wheels down the dolly wheels could be removed. Those were the ones used to truck the binder into each field. Generally, they were placed in the fenceline, out of the way.

Our binder canvases were gotten out of storage. Those had to be stored in a safe place, rolled-up, away from the mice. One of the first things was to check each canvas. Were any slats broken? Did they need to be replaced? Rivets were checked. A short piece of railroad iron was out in the field, just in case a rivet had to be fastened.

Each canvas was put in place. The biggest one had to be placed on the apron of the binder. It was long. Two shorter ones carried the cut grain up to the knotter.

I thought it was fun to watch Dad sit on the binder seat, with rope lines. He had the old Fordson tractor in front of the binder. Lines went to the steering wheel, so Dad could turn the tractor by pulling on one of those lines. Another was attached to the clutch. Dad could actually run the tractor from his seat on the binder.

It was always neat to watch the sickle cut off the grain. The big reel gently pushed the cut grain backwards so it fell on the apron canvas. It moved along towards the knotter, where a bundle was made. Once it was pressed together, twine was wrapped around it. Just that quickly the knotter would tie the ends of the twine into a knot. All of this happened so fast. No more than the knot was tied, that bundle was kicked out. Right behind it another bundle was getting ready to be kicked out.

Bundles would fall into a carrier. When six bundles were in the carrier Dad would dump them. Bundles were dumped into a row. That made it much easier for shocking.

One of the most frustrating part of cutting grain had to be when the farmer had trouble in the field. Trouble with the knotter was the worst. Every now and then a loose bundle would be kicked out. However, maybe the next one would be tied. When that happened, it wasn't too bad. It was when the knotter got out of adjustment, all bundles came out loose. Dad had big problems when that happened. Dad would try to get it working again. Sometimes it took only an adjustment of the tension. Things could run smoothly for a long time. If everything failed, then a serviceman would have to be called from the dealer to fix it.

Dad had an aggravating job when we had so much rust in the wheat. That happened during the Drepression. Dad would come home covered a dusty cinnamom color. The red rust in the wheat was terrible that year. Added to that, it was such a hot summer. Also the binder would not always work, so my father had some very frustrating days in the field.

When I was a boy, we had large fields of shocks. Some of the grains we would thresh would be either rye, wheat, millet, oats, timothy, or buckwheat. For me it was a wonderful sight to see those shocks in the field. Bundles were set up in a small circle. Somewhat like a little tepee, with one bundle on top, called the cap. Grain would dry out this way, but it also kept out the moisture from a summer shower of rain.

For me it looked like so many golden huts across the landscape of our farm. All the huts, or little tepees, were in the stubble fields.

Most of the shocks were curing for several weeks or more. It depended on how soon the threshing ring got to your farm. Finally, the day would come. Other farmers came, with teams hitched to hayracks. Also the tractor and threshing machine pulled on the yard. Women were busy, too.

After all, dinner had to be served to that crew of hungry threshers. Some farmers brought one or two kids along. Kids had some work to do, but generally found some time to play each day. Any kid who came along felt it was a big treat. It was fun to watch the threshing, or playing with other kids, but best of all would be eating that dinner!

Dad had a small threshing machine when he was first farming. It was a little Rumley, a 28-inch. This one was used for a number of years. Later he bought one larger, which was an International Harvester. I helped with both machines. I knew where all the belts had to be stored at night. I knew exactly where they fit on the threshing machine. Besides, I knew how the machine was to be greased and oiled, and the blower adjusted. Naturally, the blower was adjusted as the straw stack got higher. Every now and then, only the rope to lift the hood on the blower pipe had to be changed.

It was important how the machine was set up. It had to be leveled. One had to check the direction of the wind that day. Nobody liked the straw, chaff and dust blowing on the threshers. Even with a slight wind change, things could get aggravating enough.

By the time I was twelve I could line up the tractor and the threshing machine. We put our biggest tractor on it so it could pull the machine. It was one long belt from the tractor pulley to the threshing machine.

The elevator from the grain hopper was put over the wagon or truck. The grain hopper had a counter on it, which counted the dumps. That way we knew how many bushels we threshed. We got paid by the number of bushels threshed on a farm.

With the blower cranked around to the straw pile, straw would be blown in a small semicircle. Most of farmers wanted the stack in his cow yard. A few farmers wanted it blown into their barns. What a dusty place the mow could be. It could be very bad if it was very dry. It was the farmer's job to keep the straw away from the blower. If he didn't pay attention, which happened it would plug the blower. Belts would fly off the machine. Everything came to a standstill. Straw was plugged all the way from the blower fan to the end of the blower pipe. All this had to be dug out. What a waste of time!

That did not happen when blowing it on a stack outside. I just cranked the blower higher, as the stack was built up. However, wet bundles could plug the machine, too. If there was too much moisture the machine speed slowed down. If that happened, then it plugged up things. The guy pitching bundles into the machine could be a big help at such a time. Either throw bundles into the feeder at a slower rate, give more space between bundles, or stop, so the speed on the machine could get going again.

Loads of bundles came from the field. These were loaded on bundle racks. Some of those racks had boards "V" shaped on the side. Bundles were pitched through the "V" opening. A team of horses pulled a bundle wagon. Pitchers were in the fields. The one on the rack had the bundles pitched up to him. If he did a neat job his load was stacked in layers. It would be easy to unload it in layers by the machine.

A threshing ring had to have enough wagons to keep the machine busy. Some would be loading in the field. A load or two would be waiting to unload. One load would be by the machine. The one who was going to unload would pull alongside the feeder. Standing on top of his load, he'd pitch it off, bundle by bundle, into the feeder. Heads first! The grain would go into the concave before the straw. That way the grain would get knocked out of the straw. As the cylinder whipped the grain through the concave, the grain was separated from the straw and chaff. Next, the straw went over the shakers, to finish the job of threshing.

When Dad had the small Rumley we threshed with a crew to the south. Some farmers in that ring were Borman, Slager, Hunter, and Madison, along with us.

One experience is remembered from threshing on the Gus Borman place. One of his boys, younger than I, wanted to lift me. We were by their barn. Walking up to me, he grabbed me around the waist. All of us were waiting, for the rig had to be moved. Their haymow couldn't hold more straw.

There we were, he had my legs lifted off the ground. I begged to be put down. When he let go, I got cut! His straps on his overalls were adjustable. One of those sharp points stuck through the material on his strap. A sharp point was protruding out from the strap. It sliced into the muscle on my upper arm. The white of my muscle showed. Only a slight amount of blood came from that cut. On my left arm, it left a cut about an inch long, above my elbow. The scar is still there. It is a reminder of those threshing days.

Most of those farmers did not have many acres to thresh. Small grain was threshed for personal use. Mostly those farmers were interested in getting the straw. All farms needed straw. However, with animals the farmers could use the grain on their own farms.

Shortly after that Dad got into another ring. He bought a larger threshing machine, which meant he could handle more custom work. Our International Harvester threshing machine had a larger capacity, when compared to the little Rumley.

Those in the new ring were across the Kankakee River, to the north. They all lived toward Hebron. Those farmers were Orin and Howard Bell, Jack Bell, Yankauskus, Buchanan, Dick (Blake) Morrow and Neil Morrow. Of course, this same crew came to help us thresh. Some of these had larger acreages of small grain. There was some rye, maybe a little barley, but mostly oats.

After the threshing went on for a few weeks, it got a little boring—for some. It was much harder to keep things going toward the end of the run. Pranks were pulled on some fellows. A few would go looking for eggs in the barn. In those days, a farmer would have a hen or two laying eggs in the horse mangers. Should a nest of eggs be found, then some poor guy got a trick played on him. Generally, it was some unsuspecting fellow who became the butt of the prank. Maybe he was busy talking with somebody else, near the barn or machine, even standing in the shade. While chatting with another guy, who had his attention, an egg would be slipped into his pocket. Slowly, it would drop to the bottom. But before the poor guy knew what was happening, the "bad egg" would slap his pocket! Pop!

Now in the bottom of his pocket was one scrambled mess—the yellow yolk, the white, broken shell, plus anything else in the man's pocket. One egg mixed with his pocket knife, coins, chew, handkerchief, and who knows what else! One big mess! Oh, yuk!

An ornery trick had been played on him. All those in on it, naturally, were laughing like mad. At first, the guy himself didn't know if he should laugh, or get mad. But he had to wonder what he could do with an egg in his overalls!

Sometimes a fellow's hat would be fired on top of a roof, or hid some unlikely place. A few times water got dumped on some tired thresher, who was relaxed and half asleep, ready for a short nap. Some prankster would get water from the horse tank and dash it on him! A rude awakening!

Those were ornery jokes played on each other, not too serious. Far worse, I felt, a few would start drinking on the job.

One day I was left in charge of the separator. Dad had gone home, so he told me to watch things. At the time, we were threshing by Dick Morrow.

This one fellow pulled his load of bundles up to the machine to unload. He was sitting on the bundles, as he pulled alongside the machine. After stopping his horses he stood up, or tried to stand up.

Soon he staggered around on top of the load. I closely watched him. At first I thought he was a little unsteady standing on those bundles. Maybe he lost his balance. Even so, I continued to keep an eye on him.

My concern was to have him fall into the feeder. That would have been a horrible tragedy. There were two sets of knives and prongs on the feeder of the threshing machine. These chopped away at each bundle pitched into the feeder. My worst vision was to see the man fall on his back into the feeder. He would have been hacked and knifed to pieces before I could begin to get the machine stopped!

That would have been one of the worst nightmares!

I stood by the tractor, with my eyes glued on him.

After a few more staggers, I went to his wagon. (Realize I was in my early teens, but still in charge.) I crawled up the side of his load, then I gave him one stern lecture. I told him to stay away from the feeder. I gave it to him with some harsh words. He became angry, trying to give it back to me. I told him to sober up! I did not want him to fall into our threshing machine.

My message got to him. Backing away from the feeder, he finally got his load off. Afterwards he came over to me, to ask who I was. I told him that my name was Bill Hoffman. He shot back, "You relation to Marty?" (Marty was the name he had for Dad.) His son, I told him. With sharpness, he replied back to me, "Well, you don't act like it. You are sure different than he is!" After that he told me how upset he was with me. But after that conversation, I was more certain than ever, he had been drinking—too much. Once again, I simply told him that I'd rather have him safe than falling to his death in that machine!

Regardless how he felt, it was evident he had had too much!

A footnote to that incident came later. It was when we were filling silo for Dick. The story is that this same man was sitting on the edge of a rack. They were going back to the field for another load. Once again, he had been drinking on the job. But this time, just sitting there, he fell. Flat on his face! On the cement highway! He looked a mess, I was later told.

That confirmed to me, as young as I was, I made the right decision when I sternly lectured him that day. I am certain he could just as well have fallen off the top of the load of bundles—right into the feeder. Just like he fell on his face on the highway. The thought of it just makes me shudder!

Such things were the exception. Most of the time those guys were hard workers. During the threshing season a lot of hard labor was accomplished. Some of those summer days were extremely hot.

All the fellows looked forward to dinner. Wherever we were threshing the woman of the house put up a real feed. Other women generally helped her get everything ready.

Before they came into the house, everyone had to wash up. Some dirt got washed off by the horse tank. Then after hanging his cap or hat in a tree, or throwing it in the grass or on the cellar door, he washed again. On a bench were some basins and pails of water, along with soap. After soaping himself—his arms, neck, and face, he rinsed it off with water. A towel would be used to dry himself, then hung back on a tree branch. Hair was combed by the mirror on the tree. All used the same comb. After everyone was all washed up, the whole crew marched into the house together. Generally, the most talkative one led the way to the table.

It smelled good. Some guys joked with the woman of the house. The tables were loaded. She had two kinds of meat, roast beef and chicken. Some women added one more, pork. Mashed potatoes and gravy were a must. If the sweet corn was ripe, plenty of hot, steaming fresh corn was on the platter. Fresh tomatoes, too, Pickles. Green beans, fresh ones. At times fresh fruit would be on the table. Oh, always plenty of seconds!

Before some had a chance to dig in, some fellow would be asking about dessert, "What kind of pie are we going to have?" That was always part of such a dinner. A big piece of fresh pie. Every woman could expect compliments for her meal. They were good cooks. But if she came out with a large slice of delicious pie—that made the meal! She would then get a nice word from most of the men. If she was in the corner of the kitchen, she'd be found, to be thanked by the threshers.

While the men wanted to get the threshing done for another year, which was important, those big dinners were almost as important. Farmers worked hard, then enjoyed eating.

Sometimes these guys would get to talking about dinner. A few could remember what we had been served at that place the year before. The best cooks were remembered. As a boy, I looked forward to dinner every day we threshed. Those days were my favorite days to pull up to the table.

After a big meal, most were not that eager to get back out there in the hot sun. It was tempting to find a shade tree, some did, saying they had to rest for a few minutes.

Generally, we headed for the threshing machine. We had to check things over. Maybe we could spot something which needed our attention. So we made good use of that time, before everything got going strong for the rest of the day.

I spent much time around the threshing machine, I liked it. It was one of the great times to be on the farm.

Oh, I must admit, if the wind switched, causing chaff and dust to blow the wrong way, that was awfully aggravating. A switch in the breeze in the afternoon could be so frustrating.

That happened one day while threshing timothy. That was the worst stuff. Oats and wheat were fairly clean grains to thresh. It was the best day when the breeze blew the chaff away from you.

Times have changed. No longer do farmers enjoy a threshing ring. Something was lost among neighbors when threshing time was no longer an annual experience on the farm.

It was so important, for there was that special bond of neighborliness. Once we lost that, we lost so much. Too much, I believe.

Even to this day, it is with fond memories I look back at that special time, threshing time. Time with great people, our neighbors, our friends.

Combines

Change comes slowly. Farmers can have a lot of doubts about anything new. That was true about combines. Threshing grain the old fashioned way worked! After all, we've always done it that way. Why change? Nobody needed to prove threshing. It worked—for years.

Skeptics had plenty of questions about combines. How could we combine grain in *one* operation? At our farm we joined those being somewhat skeptical about the whole business.

Since we had Farmalls, it was only natural that dealers wanted us to buy one from them. On the market was their new six-foot International Harvester combine. A new dealership was trying to get started in our area, so they were very interested in trying to influence us with their new combine. Allis-Chalmers came out with a five-foot machine. IHC had an auger behind the cutter-bar; Allis-Chalmers had a canvas. Both dealers wanted to sell Dad on their machine's merits.

Our 40 acres of wheat was not quite ready to harvest, yet the field had turned a golden color. Both dealers were eager to give us a demonstration of their equipment. They felt they could do the job, even though the wheat was not completely ripe enough to combine. Both came out to the farm the same afternoon. Others had heard about it, or had an interest, so they showed up in our wheat field.

Each machine would take a swath. First one, then the other. However, after each swath cut, farmers and dealers were busy looking and scratching in the wheat stubble. They checked the grain heads. Did the combine get all the wheat out? The International Harvester combine was first. Next it was the turn of the Allis-Chalmers. Once the swath was cut, more checking continued by the skeptics.

After repeated times, each taking a turn, critical checking took place by marking out a square foot. How many kernels of wheat could be found? Also, how many were left in the head?

Dad asked the IHC dealer to detach the straw spreader. When the same request was made of the other dealer, he protested. More kernels were found behind his machine, after the next count. The man wanted to put the belt back on again, so he could spread the straw. Dad felt that would be unfair, for any kernels going through the machine would be spread over a wide area. Dad was wise enough to know that wheat kernels would fly in all directions. In the end, the IHC combine left fewer kernels per square foot, plus it was doing a better job getting the grain out of the heads.

Both dealers tried to convince Dad that his machine would do the best job when the field was ripe.

When these test-runs were over, we had a winner.

The winner that day was the six-foot IHC combine.

The loser left, very upset. The supervisor for Allis Chalmers ran the equipment for the local dealer. He headed north, going to the dirt road on that side of our farm. But he got stuck. All that loose, sugar sand was too much. He buried the whole outfit when he tried to go up a hill. That's when all his frustration came out. Hot! Then all the extra work. On top of not making a sale. Thirsty. His attitude and language were bad. One neighbor said she was about ready to deny him a drink for the way he acted and talked. It was afterwards she mentioned this to me.

Dad bought the No. 60 combine. Dad was among one of the first to accept the change coming to the farm.

I learned how to run this equipment from the very beginning. I soon found out how rough it was to unplug a slug. Our wrench, which came with the machine, didn't last that long. We soon bent it out of shape when we used it to turn back the cylinder. To do that, it took a lot of hard straining to bend it out of shape. Eventually we had to get it welded, for we cracked it.

Later we welded a piece of pipe to the handle so we got more leverage. That about doubled the strength of the wrench. It made our job easier, sometimes. Too many green weeds meant grief. Green weeds were nothing but trouble. Too many weeds meant it was slugged again, and again. In the fall we hoped for a hard frost to take care of those weeds. Big lamb squatters generally gave the most grief. At times we walked through a patch of weeds to break the stems. The reel could not handle those big green ones. Most of the time they would be whipped into the machine, but should it hesitate for a moment, that meant trouble. Along with a pile of grain and the weeds, that would be too much fed into the combine at one time. It was bound to slug.

This International Harvester combine had an overhead bin. In order to unload, one had to back the machine next to the truck or wagon. If the bin was very full, then the chute wouldn't clear the box.

The first dumps generally caused problems. More than once, it wouldn't clear, so a chunk of wood was gouged out. If it barely cleared, once the bin was emptied, then you pulled away with no trouble. The bin raised; the truck lowered. Should there be a furrow in the field, then the back wheel of the truck was put in the furrow. Once several dumps were made, for the rest of the load the box was low enough to clear it easily.

But I remember the overhead bin for forgetting it. Especially, the corner of the chute. It was hard! And sharp! If I forgot to duck I would get a bump on my head. This generally happened when I was working under the bin. Most of the time I was in a hurry, while greasing or unslugging the combine. In my hurry I would jump off the frame, forgetting to duck or not ducking far enough. Those times I'd hit my head on that hard, sharp corner.

Then I ended up walking around the field—rubbing my head! After taking off my cap, carefully I'd search for the lump. I'd press it, just to check for blood. More than once I did cut my head. However, most of the time my cap protected my head enough from getting cut. Oh, it still hurt like the dickens! I'd mumble enough to myself. Also tell myself how

377

dumb I was to forget that bin was there. My hair would be all messed up, after I rubbed my head with my cap.

I swore that I'd remember it the next time. Sure enough, while in a hurry, I did forget. I'd repeat the same dumb mistake again. I must have a few scars in my hair, for I certainly collided enough with that chute.

Later Dad bought another used six-foot combine. I think it was a No. 61 model. Later he found one almost like the other two. That one was used for repair parts. That proved to be very handy, for during World War II it was difficult to find parts. Most of the time we were able to keep the two best machines running.

I ran it when we did some custom work for other farmers. I started doing custom work when I was twelve and thirteen years old. One of the first jobs was for Glenn Hunter east of De Motte. During those first years I could barely reach the crank to raise or lower the reel. I hung on the steering wheel with one hand, leaning as far back as I could, then I could reach to make the adjustment.

My favorite job was combining wheat. Wheat had a golden, slightly bronze glow over the field. With a slight breeze, the wheat heads would sway back and forth. I felt the field was praising God in harmony. What a picture, as the wheat heads would bow down, then lift their heads to praise our Heavenly Father. The wheat field was rendering a symphony to the Lord, telling the creation of the glorious splendor of the Lord's majesty and wonderful works. What a beautiful sight in the bright sunlight.

I liked to chew on new wheat. During the early harvest, a little more moisture remained in the grain, then it was more chewy. I'd take a whole handful of wheat to chew. After chewing it for a little while it would become like white gum. Some days I'd enjoy chewing it for hours.

When wheat and oats got ripe, it was enjoyable to combine those grains. I didn't mind soybeans, if they were not weedy. Most fields were clean, but in wet spots weed patches could be found. Sometimes those weeds would stay green too long. A few slugs soon took the joy out of the job.

Dust could be another problem. That happened when it became extremely dry. A cross-wind helped a person avoid most of the dust. However, some days there would be no breeze, then one could work in a cloud of dust. Worst still, when the wind came from the wrong direction, I'd sit constantly in dust. That would be aggravating.

The soybean harvest could give us big problems, if we had an extremely dry fall. Most of my suffering came from a wild potato patch. A small particle of that dust felt like you had a thorn or needle in your eye. Tears! It really hurt, believe me. It felt like a thorn was scratching over your eyeball. At first I tried to keep working, but not for long. It made me so miserable, something had to be done. Hopefully it could be flushed out with tears. Then gently rubbing it, hoping it would move to the corner of my eye. When it did not work another person would have to help. A corner of a big red or blue handkerchief would be used to wipe it out. At the same time one had to pull out or pull down on your eyelid. I knew immediately if it came out. Too often a person couldn't see anything. Your kind helper only saw a bloodshot eye, with a lot of tears. If it didn't come out, then both of you had to try again. Gently with the corner of the handkerchief another try would be made. Test it, a few blinks would be made, a shiver would shake your body, "Oh, it is still in there!"

More tears. Finally, one gentle pass through the watery tears got it. Instant relief. When it was gone, I was so grateful. Before expressing thanks again, each person had to tell how it was so painful. For such relief from misery, you thanked that person again.

Now you could again get back to the bean harvest.

Naturally more changes came. When I was on the farm we only had pull-type combines. Later farmers got their self propelled machines. That was a far greater change than the one we made in the late Thirties, after Depression Days.

Special People and Times

Fond memories flood my mind when I think about some early vacations. Special places like Turkey Run, Shades, Starved Rock, Bass Lake, and the Jasper-Pulaski Game Preserve all come to mind.

One of our earliest vacations seems very special to me. It was connected with a six-day bicycle race. I can still picture standing next to a fence, as we watched the riders go by. As kids we only watched for a short time. The race held our attention for a little while, then we'd run off to play.

I met a little girl there. Just the two of us would be the ones who ran off the play together. Her family were by some tents and cabins at the bottom of the hill; our family had a cabin almost all the way up the hill.

Bill and Paul, dressed in knickers, white shirts, and caps, ready for a picnic.

A vacation in 1930, in a cabin where we stayed. Mom is holding Lois, with Paul in front of her. This was the place I found "little girls"—love, or something!

How old was I? I have no idea. We had a 1928 Chevy, green with black fenders. One day Dad and I drove around looking for a grocery store, but we got lost. Seems Dad got directions mixed up, so after going the wrong way for several miles Dad decided to turn around. It made me anxious, so I sat on the edge of the seat. Dad talked to me while we rode around. Eventually, we found our cabin back. Once we got into the area of our cabin, I sat back, away from the dash, relieved we were no longer lost. Dad did talk to me all the time about our mix-up.

But the best part was my new-found friend. I didn't fall down the hill, but I did fall for her! She won my heart. During that vacation I made the amazing discovery of "little girls." I mean, really discovered them. It was the first time in my life I had such feelings. That new, strange feeling was a sensation I felt all the time we played. All the waking hours were spent together. It was such a happy time.

Finally came the time to go home. Our family was busy packing things to leave. Suddenly, I realized I was not going to see her again. My special friend wouldn't be there when I wanted to play with her. I told Mom and Dad I had to say good-bye to her. They let me go, so I ran with excitement down the hill for the last time. Her family saw me come back, so they let her talk to me again. Neither one wanted to say good-bye, for it made us feel so bad. We talked for a long time. I didn't want to go. We held hands for a last time, then I turned. I walked up the hill, with a heavy heart, and out of her life. It was harder to make it up that hill, for I was carrying my heavy heart.

I have never forgotten her. She has crossed my memory many, many times. That sensation of being with her was a special feeling I had never experienced before as a boy. She was the reason for making that time one of the most unforgettable vacations of my life as a boy.

Starved Rock in Illinois also triggers more memories. There were stories about Indians. Some were heard with fascination while vacationing there. Some, I'm sure, were just big stories, which grew even bigger by being retold.

I remember climbing up some of those big rocks. Mom was quite concerned when we went for walks. We'd reach the top of some large rocks, which was even more dangerous with us kids running around. If one of us went over the edge, it would have spelled tragedy. Mom generally wanted to hold tightly to our hands. She had a hold on the little ones, but Paul and I would rather run by ourselves. We scampered all over the flat tops of some rocks. One time Paul got way ahead of all of us. All of a sudden his steps changed—one big step! and a leap! He stopped. Then he turned around. Looking back at us, not making a move.

He just stood there, waiting for us. When we caught up with him we all saw it, too. A large crevice was there! Paul made it across by his leap. Two huge rocks had split apart, leaving this yawning opening. Everybody stared down into a very deep crevice!

But Paul was safe on the other side. Mom must have had nightmares about that one, for she often talked about it. However, Paul stretched his little legs long enough to clear the big crack between those rocks.

We did a lot of running and playing at Turkey Run and Shades in Indiana and Starved Rock in Illinois. They were exciting places of my early childhood.

Other outings were only a day-trip to Bass Lake. Some of the first pictures with Mom were taken at that lake. Mom is holding my hand as I walked in the water of the shoreline. Another early picture is one taken beside our Baby Overland car. Mom is holding me. I had a little white cap on. Our car had an Indiana license plate: 412-788 IND '25.

Later we spent some days at Bass Lake with relatives. Cousins would be there with us. Uncle Ben and Uncle George's families came at different times. Those would have been a day's picnic by the lake. Generally we'd also visit the State Fish Hatchery, while we were there.

When I became a little older we took a day to visit the Jasper-Pulaski Game Preserve. They had fish and wildlife there. They had some special animals which I liked to see. But the biggest attraction was the tall tower. It was a lookout tower, for spotting fires in the wooded areas of the preserve. Boys would accept the challenge to see how high they dared to climb up that tower. Some adults also tried to climb to the top. Most turned around before they got there. I never made it myself. I tried often, but every time I turned around before getting to the top landing.

One of our first trips was to visit young guys in camp. A truckload of people went that time, a whole group of fellows rode in the back of a truck. We drove behind them. The camp was for young men who worked there during the Depression. There young men were in what was called the CCC. They did a lot of reforestation in many areas of our country. This camp was the nearest one in Indiana.

Other fun days for us were Memorial Days. Our annual event was spent by having a picnic at Uncle Dick and Aunt Minnie Peterson's ranch. Uncle George Hoffman's family, along with Uncle Jake Walstra's, were there on Memorial Day.

Memorial Day at Uncle Dick and Aunt Minnie's place. Left, George's Bill, Howard, Paul, hired man Paul, Marty J. on pump handle, Kenny drinking.

A few other cousins also were invited. Ralph and Johnnie Walstra generally were there, too.

Most of the men and boys had to check on the 500 from time to time. We all wanted to know who won the Indianapolis 500! In those days most of us could name the drivers and winners of recent years.

Names we talked about were: Louis Meyer (2), Bill Cummings, Kelly Petillo, Wilbur Shaw (3), Floyd Roberts, Floyd Davis, and Mauri Rose (3). Depression Days winning speeds ranged from 96 to 117 miles per hour.

Besides listening to the race on a radio, we ate. This was always a big picnic, so we had plenty to eat.

About once or twice a year we visited with Uncle Ralph Hoffman's family. I liked to go there to visit with my cousin William, who was born in 1923, so he was a little older than I. William was comical, we had a lot of fun together. One day we gathered around the table, well before Aunt Minnie had the meal ready. The older people were talking, so we decided to entertain ourselves. William decided to put his tie up and over his face and head. Slowly it would slide, then drop and plop into his empty plate. As kids we giggled and giggled. Aunt Minnie told Uncle Ralph that he had to tell William to stop it. Something was said, but we continued to have good clean fun.

This bothered Aunt Minnie. It seemed to us that she was embarrassed that we were acting that way. This didn't bother our parents, so they didn't request that we behave any differently. With our egging him on, William put the tie up over his face and head one more time. We were all ready for the slide drop and plop.

Aunt Minnie demanded that Uncle Ralph put a stop to William's antics. Instantly, Uncle Ralph slapped William across the face.

Immediately the mood of our visit changed. William was embarrassed beyond measure, so he hung his head down during the meal. I ate my meal feeling very sorry for my cousin. None of us dared to have a good time at that Sunday dinner.

For several summers I later visited their vegetable farm in Blue Island. One visit stands out, the one when I was thirteen. That would be the summer of 1938.

Daily we got things ready for market. The load would be ready the night before, so we could leave very early the next morning.

We picked all kinds of vegetables, so it was a mixed load. So the day was spent picking tomatoes, green peppers, green beans, or melons. Besides we'd cut a lot of cabbage. These vegetables would be hauled out of the field and brought to the yard. Underneath their shade trees we'd pack them neatly into baskets.

This one day William took his 410 shotgun to the field. We were going to shoot some pesky crows. That morning we were working along the big canal. Several shots had been fired. All misses. Finally a black crow landed on a tree near the canal. William jokingly challenged me to shoot that crow. Chances were pretty good the bird would fly away, I attempted to get a little closer to him. Finally I was next to the bank, yet I wanted to get closer. I started up the steep bank, getting about as close as I could. William called out that I better shoot.

Halfway up the bank, I aimed. Fired! The gun kicked back. William laughed. Afterwards he told me why he thought it was so funny. After I fired the shot he figured I was going to fall backwards down the bank. Oh, I missed the crow!

Late afternoon we loaded all the stuff on Uncle Ralph's Diamond T truck. That was some truck, at least I thought it was as a boy. For the size rack he had on it seemed too small for all the power the truck had.

Since I wanted to go to market, I had to get to bed early. Early to bed for the alarm was going to ring early! Around 1:30 a.m. Uncle Ralph's alarm would go off. Shortly after that he and I would be in the Diamond T. It was chilly, after crawling out of bed in the middle of the night. I'd sit humped up from the night's chill. We were headed for the Randolph Street Market.

Once there, Uncle Ralph would pull it into a row of trucks. Many truck farmers lined the middle of the street at the market. Certain baskets were set on the tailgate. A few more were put under the back of the truck, right on the street.

While it was still dark, people started stirring on the street. Voices in the dark shadows could be heard. As the dawn was breaking more buyers made their way down the back of the trucks. Every now and then one would stop to look over a few baskets, ask a few questions. Maybe ask the price. With a wave of the hand, the once prospective buyer walked away.

But, if he liked what he saw, he got serious about the price. Maybe he'd make an offer. Uncle Ralph would repeat his price. Maybe the fellow suggested a new amount. That began the haggle over the price. As they went back and forth, their bargaining voices would get louder. Sometimes I got a little frightened. Man, to me, it sounded like they were mad at each other. I didn't care for that to be going on in the shadows.

Finally, a price would be agreed upon. Then came the question, "How many do you want? How many?" Maybe five baskets. Ten. One took all we had left on the load. Anyway we got rid of the whole load very early. We were back on the road from the Randolph Street Market before daylight was very bright. The family could hardly believe we got back so soon that morning.

We did a lot of work on Uncle Ralph's truck farm, but I thought it was fun, so different from our farming.

I know they took me to some baseball games. Finally, came the day for me to go home. When my family came, Mom was not along. Then I got the exciting news that I had a new baby sister. She was born while I was on vacation. Carolyn Ruth was born July 31, 1938.

As a boy, it would have been great to stay longer, but I was rather anxious to get back home. I wanted to go home to see the new baby in our family.

When I was small the marathon was the craze.

It was the latest fad. Dad and Mom would go to see such an event. Some people were dancing, while others would be walking. Chicago had one that went on for 119 days in 1930, which was when I was five.

Couples would dance until they were staggering near exhaustion. Eyes half shut, arms hung over a partner's shoulders, then drag their aching feet over the floor. It was sheer agony to try to win one of those. Times were rough, so this was one way to get some money.

It was the latest craze. Dad and Mom went to one in Gary. Chod Swisher, one of Pete's sons, was in that contest.

Short rest-recesses were given to the contestants. Yet it was so hard, some people did die of heart failure.

While our folks went to see one of those events, we had a hired man take care of us kids. John Systsma was working for Dad. It was still early evening, before Dad and Mom got back home. John, Paul and I were eating supper.

Afterwards John decided to give us a little home entertainment. And how! It frightened the daylights out of Paul and me.

John could roll his eyes back in his head, so far back we only saw the whites of his eyes. Scary enough in itself, as he pulled that stunt several times. We didn't know where his eyes were! But he still had a climax to his act. He let out a groan—

twisted and turned, then rolled sideways off the kitchen chair. There he laid, still as death on the floor.

Naturally, to us kids, we thought he was dead!

With a dead man in the house, it was high time to get away from the corpse. Fast! Now!

I ran west, into the living room, hiding behind an open door. I used the crack between the door and the frame to get a peek. I wanted to keep an eye on the dead. Would the dead move? No, our dead hired man didn't move a muscle.

Paul ran to the east, out the door—outside. It was a much safer place to be. But Paul ran into Dad, who had come home, so he told on John.

John remained dead still. Motionless, well, at least, until Dad walked into the kitchen. Dad was soon standing over John. Dad spoke! And one dead hired man was instantly standing on his feet! It was time for John to be shocked. Wow! John caught it from Dad. Dad told him he was not given a job to scare kids. He was to care for them.

The show was over. Then it was John's turn to have his heart beat fast! Likely he didn't forget how he was bawled out for his evening entertainment.

Later on our folks told us a little about the walk-a-thon in Gary. I got the idea we had a more lively show in our kitchen.

When we were kids we looked forward to the big event of the summer—the 4th of July picnic. It was our Sunday School picnic, one which the First Reformed Church and the American Reformed Church celebrated together. The earliest one I can remember was north of Dutch Corners, in a picnic grove. Later we went to one about two and a half miles south of our farm. Finally, it was held in the Kingma grove, just north of De Motte.

There were the food and pop stands. Before noon we had a speaker; afterwards we ate our picnic dinner.

Most of us kids were anxious to get the games started. One year I won the foot race for those of my age. I got a pocket knife for the prize. Another time I got some money for winning.

The two churches would have a softball game. But the most exciting event was the tug-of-war between the men. Always the biggest man got to be the anchor at the end of the rope.

I still remember one very hot 4th. Neither team could get the advantage. Nothing was moving. The two church teams seemed to be dead-even.

It was a killer. They tugged and tugged.

Finally the First Reformed Church team won. Afterwards Bill De Young was having problems. Bill felt funny after it was over. It was no wonder, for they had gone at it so hard. Some comments were made about some men could have gotten heart attacks. Most of the exhausted men found the shade, trying to recover after their war. It was a war, for neither side wanted to give up. Men dug-in and held their ground! Eventually the American Reformed Church moved and gave up.

I hated to go home from the picnic. Each 4th finally came to an end. We had to go home, for our cows were waiting to be milked.

Funny thing, if those old cows got out, breaking through the fence, likely it would be the 4th of July. Often it happened that way, whenever we were going away for the day. We wondered if those old cows didn't want us to go away.

Sometimes we would go somewhere to see fireworks at night. That meant we had to hurry to get our chores done.

Labor Day was another special time for us. That day we would generally go to Lowell. Their American Legion Post sponsored that celebration each year.

They had a midway, with sideshows and rides. One year they had a "wild" man in a show. He had been found in a swamp, so mosquito infested he was almost eaten alive. Also, we were told by the barker, the only thing this wild creature would eat was raw hamburger. Every now and then they tossed him a raw chunk, which he'd grab and devour instantly. Some of the most weird sounds came from him, as he stuck out his tongue and would spit.

Our wild man would suck in his breath, "AAEEEEEHHH... PHITTTHHHH..." His first sound was made while sucking in his breath, following it with his tongue sticking out, and spitting. As boys, we soon got this down so we could imitate him for weeks after Labor Day.

His hair was tied in a ponytail, coming together on the top of his head. His face was all painted up. A big stake was driven in the ground, to which he was chained. Naturally, that prevented the wild man from getting away.

One mother commented, as they fed him some raw meat, "Oh, my kids eat raw hamburger, whenever they can get away with it." Frankly, she was not impressed by this raw meat eater.

For the longest time, we'd talk about this wild man. Once it was mentioned, immediately we'd each give our version of his weird vocabulary, "AAEEEEEHHH...PHITTTHHHH..."

Another year we had a long-remembered experience at Lowell. Again there were strange sounds, which came from the Ferris Wheel. As it would go up, a very strange scream would rise above the midway. However, when the wheel came down, then a different kind of scream could be heard. It was repeated over and over, as the wheel went round and round. Heads turned. Eyes from all over the grounds were focused on that Ferris Wheel. Screams going up! Then screams coming down! Up...down...up...down...

It was coming from one seat of the wheel. There sat Lois, my sister, and Evelyn Hoffman, my cousin. Evelyn was doing all the screaming.

Before the ride was over, everybody on the grounds had heard and saw what was going on. It was no secret who took a ride on the Ferris Wheel that night. It was a ride to be remembered for years!

When we were small we liked to go to town on Wednesday and Saturday nights. Families did their shopping for groceries and any other thing they needed. It was a time to visit and socialize, taking a break from the hard work on the farms. If the barber was not too busy, then some got a haircut. Most kids looked forward to getting an ice cream cone, if they had a nickel to spend.

During the summer we had a bandstand for our school band. Some nights they gave a short concert. Once it got dark they showed free movies. This took place in a vacant lot across from most of the stores on main street. That is where we heard the band and saw the movies.

Dad told me about my first haircut. My folks felt it was time for that first haircut. So Dad took me to the local barber on a Saturday night. I think Dad mentioned his name was Sam Cross. Naturally, I was not too happy with this first adventure in the barber's chair. I fussed. I jerked around. The ordeal was rough on me, but also on Dad and Sam. Then came the moment for the wrong move. I made one; Sam made one. My ear got clipped!

I let them know about it! I must have wanted to let the whole town know about it. I bawled my head off. The longer I yelled, the worse it got. Finally some women in town heard my cries, so they came to see what was going on. There they stood looking through the big window of the shop. That poor little kid! Things were getting a little tense, as time went on. More and more women crowded around the window outside Sam's shop. It was getting to Sam, so he turned to Dad, "Maybe I ought to lock the door, before they come in here." Under his breath he mentioned that they may be lynched before the night was over.

Eventually, I had that first haircut, plus an ear clip. Dad ventured into the angry crowd of women. Everybody settled down and went about their own Saturday night chores.

Dad would tell the story, adding that I almost caused a riot in town that night. Say, maybe that is why Dad bought a hand clippers to cut my hair at home. If I wanted to kick up a fuss, Dad had a much better chance of getting out alive. Besides, if I wanted to holler my head off, then I could go right ahead. Neighbors didn't live that close by.

I could have tested that one out, I suppose. One would be to test how good my lungs were, then the other for testing the hearing of our neighbors. Really I did not have to do either one, for my Dad was a fairly good barber.

At least he never clipped my ear. But he could sure pull the short hair in my neck! That was very easily done with a hand clippers. Oh, boy, that could hurt. As a kid I knew it was not done on purpose, mostly it was the fault of that old hand clippers.

By the time I was a teen-ager I headed for town to get a haircut for 25¢ at the barber shop.

More Special People and Times

Interesting people came to town in the summertime. It was really a special time when the traveling medicine man came to our town. Generally, he had some kind of "cure-all" to sell.

Often it was an Indian, with headdress and all. Each one had his sales pitch. He'd talk on and on of his wonders for sale. Most people figured it was nothing more than snake oil. However they all stood around to listen.

As the show got started, many would gather closer to the show. What he needed was his first sale. Somebody in the crowd in town had to be his first sale. Once he got some person to let loose of the first dollar or 50¢, then other people decided they would buy, too.

Dad was one to purchase some kind of medicinal oil. He bought the kind to relieve pain. A vial was supposed to have curative powers. The little glass vial was about the size of a fountain pen, with a small cork in the end. Dad either paid 50¢ or 75¢ for each little bottle.

Dad used this on his shoulder. This injury gave him a lot of problems. It was injured when he hit a stump with the tractor in the hog lot, just east of the big barn.

It happened in big weeds. Those weeds were pretty high, that was the reason Dad never saw the stump. The pulley on the tractor was in the exact spot to hit the stump.

It stopped his tractor all right—dead in its tracks. That sudden stop threw Dad into the steering wheel with his shoulder. Dad got hurt. Later the doctor felt he had cracked a bone, which left him with continual pain from the injury. So whenever it was giving him pain he'd get out this little vial of Indian oil to rub on his shoulder. Only a little was put on the tip of his finger, then rubbed in. It was strong stuff. Stunk! If you got close enough your eyes would burn.

For years Dad used what he bought from the old Indian who came to town. When Dad felt the pain, out came the concoction from the medicine man.

A few years later, towards fall, the medicine man was back in town. He was in the bandstand for the evening. Wires were strung from corner to corner of the stand. They supported the lights. He was busy giving his pitch to any takers. A few older boys thought of giving him a hard time, at least some little prank was in order. One young guy got tomatoes from his mother's refrigerator. While driving slowly down main street, they were going to fire tomatoes from the car. A couple hit the wires strung around the bandstand. Direct hits! Splitting and splashing tomatoes around the stand. The visiting medicine man had some sharp words for those guys. One local merchant felt sorry for the poor man.

Only trouble, after getting home that same evening, she made a discovery. Her tomatoes were gone!

One week, when I was older, we went with Uncle Jake Walstra and family to the Hammond Civic Center. The main feature for the evening was professional wrestling.

That started it all. Several times cousin Lawrence went with us. After a while a number of young fellows got together to go on our own to the Civic Center. It wasn't long before we went almost every week. For that summer we were hooked on wrestling.

At first I thought it was *real!* I totally failed to see those wrestlers were only acting, playing a part of the character they wanted us to see.

One night I remembered "The Blimp" being on the card. This big blimp was from Boston. 840 pounds! His belly hung to his knees. Shortly, before coming to Hammond for an evening appearance, he had gotten married. We were told his wife was about a hundred pounds!

The night we saw him he was on the card to get in the ring with a local boy, who was in the Navy. The sailor was on leave. Nothing big about him, well under two hundred. But he was to be matched with this Blimp, who was dressed in sweats. They put on a show. This sailor could not even get close to The Blimp, who pawed away at the little sailor.

The crowd cheered when the sailor jumped on the back of The Blimp. From that position he hammered at the temple area of his head. The crowd loved it. Just as suddenly the big guy bent forward and flipped the sailor to the mat. One leap, he pinned the sailor. Who could tell—he totally covered him with his winning move. Naturally, the crowd was furious for doing that to their underdog favorite.

Once we caught on, that this was entertainment, we soon lost interest. A couple more times we went back. Then it was over. That ended it, for we never again returned to the Hammond Civic Center.

However, it didn't mean we completely lost interest in wrestle-mania. No, that didn't stop. It only put more of a personal interest in it, fellows around De Motte wanted to wrestle. That took some time before we got over that.

One who really got caught up in the wrestle-mania was my cousin Bill, of Uncle George. Along about this time people had trouble with two cousins, both called Bill Hoffman. Who are you talking about? To keep it straight, Bill of George or Bill of Mart? So before long, Bill of George was known as Wild Bill; Bill of Mart was known as Tame Bill.

One Sunday morning I drove over to Kniman, where Wild Bill lived. Uncle George and Aunt Jennie were in church. In those days we attended the two o'clock afternoon service. Sunday School was after church.

Generally the folks were in the morning service, while the kids were at home. We talked on the lawn for a little while. Soon we got into a wrestling match, Wild Bill vs. Tame Bill. At first it was more messing around. After a few moves, things changed. Our struggle got more intense.

Good holds were made. How do you break out? Both of us put plenty of push into our moves. Naturally, we were rutting up their lawn. Chunks got pushed out of place. Then more chunks of sod were plowed up. Before too long, a whole section of their lawn was a sight.

That horrible sight was what Aunt Jennie spotted walking into their yard. And she was upset! Two young wrestlers soon found that out. She let us know about it, then and there!

Her sharp words were enough to dampen the wrestling mania around their place. But the struggle went on, in a new arena. Next time it was at Tame Bill's place. A few weeks later Wild Bill came over on Sunday morning. To talk, we went into my bedroom. Dinner was not ready, we had plenty of time to wait for Mom to get it ready. We spent our time sitting on the edge of the bed talking.

Wild Bill started again. Our wrestling mania match was taking place on top of my Hollywood bed. Twisting and turning, both struggling with each other. A sharp crack was soon heard, then a bang! Two legs were snapped off my bed. Good grief! One side was eight inches higher than the legless side!

All the noise brought inspectors on the run. The rest of my family came to inspect the damage. Well, we were told we did it, that's the way you'll have to sleep in it. Only one trouble with that consequence, Wild Bill would not have to sleep in my bed. I had to sleep in that lopsided thing!

I tried it for one night. No good at all, the whole night I was prone to roll downhill. Gravity pulled on me all night long. Getting a few boards, I slipped them under the low side, which made it slightly more level. During the week I spent my time attaching the legs back on the frame. It never was as solid after that wrestling match.

Never again did we use it for a ring or match.

Between church and Sunday School fellows gathered by the old outhouse behind church. Each week we went there, before Sunday School got started.

One Sunday Wild Bill began popping me in the muscles of my upper arms. His knuckle made it hurt. It was painful, with each punch. I told him to stop. In front of the other guys, he punched away. I was plenty mad, but couldn't do too much about it. Finally the bell rang, so it was over, for then. I was glad to head for Sunday School, for I had enough.

When I got home, my arms were so sore. I felt it all the time doing the chores that evening. While in the cow barn I told Dad what Bill had done. Soon Dad heard enough of my complaining, so he just said, "Don't tell me about it. Take care of it yourself." Not exactly what I wanted to hear. Still I thought about it.

A few weeks later, some of us were uptown. It was before Christian Endeavor, our young peoples' meeting on Sunday evening. I got out of my car to talk to another couple. We were in front of De Kock's Store, on main street. While they sat in his car, I talked with them through an open window.

Who pulls up in his car—Wild Bill. Some other fellow was with him. They joined us, as we talked for a short time. Bill grabbed me, getting a hold. Great, when we had on our Sunday clothes. We soon were into a wrestling match. Something I did not like at all. I thought of what Dad said. This old stuff was getting to me, in a hurry.

I reached back, wrapped one arm around his neck, then I reached back to grab his one leg. I lifted it off the ground. While off balance, Bill struggled to break my hold.

Since he was off balance—I just dropped him. Just like that he found himself lying on the street in front of the store. Only trouble for him, it was where he landed. Some car on Saturday night had left some oil spots there. That dirty oil is what Bill got on the back of his white Sunday shirt.

It messed up a nice shirt. He complained.

I felt I had not started it. So I walked away. Each of us got into his car, heading for Dutch Corners to go to C.E.

Bill had to go home with his oil stained shirt. And face his mother. Aunt Jennie was not happy again, about our wrestling-mania. So the next time Bill came uptown he had on clean work clothes. That's when he told us he couldn't wear good clothes again, if we were going to wrestle.

Shortly after that he wrestled at softball games. I wanted no part of it. He turned to other guys, so they got into it. After getting a little older, this wrestle-mania ended. Fine with me.

With my small size, I simply was no match for those fellows with bigger builds. Any of them who wanted to continue that wrestle-mania, go to it, that's all right with me. Just leave me out of it!

I was not going to wrestle The Blimp! Nor anyone of them!

One form of home entertainment was with our old piano. It was one of those old player pianos. I remember the day we went to get it. We took the old Dodge truck. It came from a place near Uncle Jake and Aunt Ann Walstra, around Oak Lawn, Illinois.

That old piano was heavy! Once we got home, the truck was backed up to the front door of our house. It was placed along the west all of the front room. There's where it stayed.

The weight of the piano pressed down on the floor next to the wall, causing the floor to dip down.

In the corner of the room was a big box of rolls. Some rolls showed a lot of wear and tear. Through the years before we got the player piano those old rolls had a lot of hard use. A few were in pretty rugged shape. Some had the hook missing, so one had to hook it carefully to the roller. Every now and then a roll would have a large section missing, which gave extra music as it rolled over the player part.

It was a lot of fun to get a roll out, then pump for all you were worth. This meant sitting on the edge of the bench, gripping under the keyboard so you could push down hard while pumping. That made for some loud music.

One of my favorite numbers was the "Stars and Stripes Forever" roll. I'd play it, then roll it back—and play it again. If I had one that I enjoyed I'd play it over and over. On some rolls they printed the words which went with the music. Some songs I liked to play and sing along at the same time. That was fun, too.

Mom and Dad did buy some new rolls, so we played them over and over, too. Hours were spent at the old player piano in our home.

One day a piano tuner took out the player part. That ended our fun with that old piano. Then one day the old piano was gone. In my memories I'd like to sit down on the bench again, pump away, listening to "Stars and Stripes Forever."

I had a small ivory colored radio. I listened to it by the hours in my room. The Hit Parade on Saturday night was my favorite when I was a teenager.

Yes, Dad did tell me to turn it down. I liked to have the volume turned up, especially while listening to some big band.

Two voices were heard, week after week, those of Kate Smith and Frank Sinatra. Kate would sing, a great favorite of millions, "God Bless America." Since we were in a war, that was our prayer. Nobody had that special sound as did Kate Smith. Young and old alike appreciated hearing her sing.

But during those years one was called "The Voice"—Sinatra. Bobbysoxers would swoon when he sang. Oh, those girls screamed!

It became well-known that wherever he appeared there would be screaming-meemie kids, as some thought of them. Even some girls would skip school to hear him sing.

So often when Sinatra sang some girls squealed, others swooned, then all bedlam would break loose. They said that an epidemic of "Sinatreitis" swept like measles among the nation's teenagers. Different ways were used to explain all that swooning or fainting among the young girls at his performances. We heard it explained as mass hypnotism, frustrated love, his personality, even mammary hyperesthesia. One of my classmates in high school, Dale Schwanke, would tell us that it was a special response only girls could have. Dale felt Frank Sinatra would hit notes only girls could hear which stimulated them sexually so they passed out!

Anyway Frank was a hit. Some of his first hit records were "Fools Rush In," "White Christmas" and "Night And Day." Sinatra appeared on *Your Hit Parade* each week. That was a spot he held from 1943 until 1949, when he was dropped.

Stranger than fiction, bobbysoxers even dug up his footprints in the snow to preserve them in the refrigerator. During World War II he was the hit! His income leaped to the million dollars a year high! Next to unbelievable in those days.

As a teenager, I would go into my bedroom to listen on my little radio. I'd listen to which songs were among the top hits for the week. My favorites were "Don't Sit Under The Apple Tree," "Peg O' My Heart," "God Bless America," "White Christmas," also, "Oh, Johnny!"

It was fun watching which songs would stay at the top for the most weeks in a row. My bedroom at the end of the house, off the kitchen and bathroom, was where I'd be found on Saturday night. With my door closed, so nobody would disturb me. It had to stay closed, unless I got excited about a favorite hit, then I'd try to get someone to come and listen to it with me. However, most of the time I wanted to be alone. If I had to keep the sound down, then I'd put my ear next to my radio.

Whenever I was in my bedroom, generally my little ivory colored radio would be turned on.

I never did much fishing. Oh, we saw a lot of people fishing. A favorite spot for fishermen was by the Hodge Ditch bridge. They parked by the bridge. Some fished from the bridge; others stood on the bank to fish.

One afternoon we decided to go fishing in the Hodge. Other people were fishing along the south bank. I decided to fish from the bridge. I leaned on the bridge structure, holding my pole.

It wasn't long before I had a bite. As I began to pull up on my pole a fish came out of the water, many were surprised by the size of my catch. I kept trying to work him through the bridge's framework, which wasn't going good at all. Finally a man on the bank told me to swing it over to him, so he could help me. He told me that he'd take the fish off the hook for me. Working my way closer to him, eventually I swung the line over to him, so he could grab the line and the fish.

My heart was jumping as much as the fish. I was excited. My heart was beating with an open-throttle.

Finally the man had it, as he talked, saying he'd get the hook out of the fish for me. He worked at it, and he got the job done.

But just as the hook came out, my big fish wiggled! Instantly that slippery fish leaped into the air—jumped right out of his grasp. Splash! My first fish-catch was back in the Hodge Ditch. I was crushed. With sadness, I had to admit, "That was the big one that got away!" With one sickening splash I lost all my desire to fish.

I only can remember one other time I fished. One night I went along with Tootsie and Dena. Dena mentioned that Paul went along, too. I can't remember that part. But I do remember what happened to me. We had been catching bullheads that night. Our catches were put in a gunny sack, which was lying on the north bank.

As the evening drug on, I got tired. Instead of standing, I decided I was going to sit on the bank. I put out my hand, behind me, to help me sit down. Only I failed to realize the sack was behind me.

Not for long!

One of the old bullhead spurs speared me—in the palm of my hand. Oh, it killed me! Agonizing pain shot through my hand and arm. It was so painful!

Once again, all the joy of fishing was quickly gone. I didn't care to fish any more that night.

Dena commented that she and I left for home after that. The two of us left in the car. Tootsie and Paul had to walk home afterwards. I can't recall very much of that, but I still remember the bullhead spearing me! I got the point, which I've never forgotten.

In the Spring of 1937, a huge rush of water caused flood damage in many places, but the greatest in the Ohio River Valley. Waters from the Wabash and Ohio Rivers resulted in grave problems for a city at the bend of the Ohio River in southern Indiana. Part of the problems began in January of that year. Evansville, Indiana, was hit hard by those flood waters. We heard about it in school. Children were asked to help those children who lost so much by that flood. Good used clothing and toys were shared with children in the flood stricken area. Our family gave to that cause. My sister Lois gave one of her dolls.

As kids we put our names and address in the pockets of the clothes. Lois had hers inside the doll's dress. We hoped to hear from some children who received these things. After months had passed, a letter came to Lois. It was from Jane Lenore Harris of Evansville. Since Lois was small, I wrote a letter for her. Jane told us she lost her father, who had died when they were small children. Charles was her older brother, while Randy was her youngest brother. Her mother had been a widow for years.

Jane and I became pen-pals, writing off and on for a number of years. Once after a long time between letters, I wrote one more letter, which was answered by her mother. Jane had gotten married.

That ended our correspondence. However, I must add one more experience related to this family. January 21, 1970, I had a funeral in Evansville for Thomas E. White. I drove down there from Fulton, Illinois, to conduct the services. Mrs. White, the widow, came along, as I drove her car. She stayed with her family. I was given a room in a hotel for the several days I was there.

All of a sudden, it hit me, could I possibly locate the Harris family? Going through the telephone book, I did discover a Charles Harris listed. I called the number. It turned out to be Jane's oldest brother, so his wife answered my call. Naturally I had to give her details of the background. She informed me that Jane was living out East, in one of the southern states. Her husband was a doctor. The youngest brother was a school teacher. Their mother had remarried, but was still living in Evansville.

She promised to make contacts with the family. I got a call back, asking if I could visit with them that evening. I told them that I could, after the visitation at the funeral home and a brief family service.

When I completed that brief service, I looked up, seeing two people waiting for me. Charles and his mother were there, so we met personally for the first time in our lives. I went with them to Randy's home, where we had a delicious meal.

We told many stories that night, which we shared in our hours of visiting. I saw pictures of Jane and her family. Late that night they brought me back to my hotel.

Near the hotel was a large cement wall, which was built after their big flood. It was a flood wall to protect the city of Evansville should another big flood threaten them. That wall was a reminder of how our pen-pal friendship started between Jane and me.

The following day I had the funeral for Thomas E. White, then his widow and I drove back to Fulton. It was such a bitter cold night as we returned home late at night and late in the month of January.

However, that trip had added a warm experience of having a personal visit with Jane's family in Evansville, Indiana. Now tucked away in my memories is that experience with other Hoosiers in Hoosierland.

Fair Time

I guess I would have to say it all started with the Jasper County Corn Show. At that show I won my first trophy and first ribbons. A little later I got involved in 4-H and the Jasper County Fair.

When I was in 7th grade my agriculture teacher was John Borman. As my teacher he encouraged me to get a ten ear corn sample for the show that fall. This teacher spent several evenings in the corn field picking out the best ears with me. That was in 1937. I won a champion and first place ribbons. The trophy I received was for my champion yellow corn display. Each year they had a banquet in Rensselaer, which we attended and I received my trophy.

The next year I also had corn in the show. Once again I got champion and first place in my class. At the banquet I picked up my second trophy.

In 1938, I had a picture taken with my ten ear corn display, along with my two trophies and ribbons. I made the case which held the ten ears. In the picture is a little white bench, which I also made. I marked the winning years in the picture. Notice I outlined the years with ears of corn: 1937 and 38.

That picture was taken on the southside of our big hill.

About the same time interest was show by our Ag teachers to start a 4-H club in De Motte, or Keener Township.

When we organized the 4-H club I was present. We were in the basement of our old school house. All kinds of names were suggested. Our final choice was the name we used for years: Challengers.

My brother Paul and I wanted dairy calves for our 4-H project. Our calves were purchased from a dairy just north of Rensselaer. The dairyman's name was Walters, who had pure-bred Holsteins. From his herd Paul got a calf nearly all white;

my calf was black and white. We showed these animals in competition for several years. I had membership in the 4-H club for at least five years. At least I have a 5-year pin, which was awarded to me.

Two people who influenced me in the competition at the Jasper County Fair were Ely and Walters. For one, Mr. Ely, the Ag teacher, helped us with entries and getting set up for our stay for the week. The other, Francis Walters, from whom we purchased our calves, but who also pushed us to get our animals in the open class competition. At first, I didn't want much to do with the open class, but with his help we finally did sign up for it. After all, we had purebred Holsteins. (Very natural for Dutchmen, who had relatives who also had Holstein-Friesian dairy cattle. Besides these cattle originally were developed in Friesland.)

That year I had exhibits in the dairy and poultry departments. This was only the beginning, for it wasn't long that I got involved in the horticultural and agricultural departments.

Fair time was fun time!

But we had a lot to learn, especially that first year. We had to thank Mr. Ely for his special attention.

Across the road from the county fairgrounds was the Jasper County Home. Known to most of us as the "Poor Farm." Elderly people lived there, who would show up at the fairgrounds when all the new activity started at fair time. One person we immediately met was an old Indian named "Kiki."

Kiki spent a lot of time hanging around where we had our tents and trucks parked. Also he was in the dairy barn. Mr. Ely noticed Kiki was there too much! Plus the man was too fascinated with young boys. Soon he brought pictures, which he had drawn and colored. At times he asked the boys to sit on his lap. That's when Mr. Ely kept his alert eye on us. He was extremely uncomfortable about Kiki's continual attention given to boys.

Once Mr. Ely had us alone, he warned us about Kiki. First he simply tried to tell us not to spend so much time around the man. However, the truth was—Kiki was around us!

Realizing we were not going to get his message it was time to give a plain warning. His plain order was: "Don't spend time with that man. Stay away from him!"

Typical of kids, I for one, had to ask, "Why?" His warning seemed to make us even more curious. So I just asked, "Why do you say that about Kiki? He's a nice man." Not wanting to get into it any more than that, he simply put it this way, "Well, someday you will understand. For now, just stay away from him!"

From that moment on—we did! If we spotted Kiki coming, we were gone! We slipped out of sight. If he was coming our way we took off the other way. If we saw him coming down the fair's midway we'd quickly duck between the tents of the sideshows or behind some ride. There we'd hide until it was safe for us—Kiki was out of sight. As we watched old Kiki looking around, you could tell he was out searching for us. However, a very wise teacher had given us a word of warning. As I've looked back through the years, I am so thankful Mr. Ely did. Some boys with country innocence could have been deeply troubled before it was all over. Now, more than ever, I do understand, for Kiki had far too much interest in us young boys. Far, far too much interest! So I still appreciate his fair warning at fair time, which was for the best interest of some very innocent boys from the farm in Hoosierland!

It was work to get ready for the fair. We had to work with our calves during the summer. We had to get ready for the show ring. Paul and I would lead those animals around by a halter. Besides that we had to get them to stand the correct way for the judge to look over our calves in the ring.

No matter how nice things went at home, sometimes it was a different story at fair time. More people were around, so one could end up with an ornery critter on his hands. That was very embarrassing when the animal caused this to happen in front of the judge. What a place to showoff! When it did happen, there would go any chance for a showmanship award!

But there were a lot of things to do before we got our calves in the ring. We had to get prepared to stay all week on the fairgrounds. The animals and all their feed had to be taken by truck to Rensselaer. Also we needed to get our food and clothes ready for the week.

Some 4-H members would drive back and forth each day. Others stayed in the barns with their animals. The first year we stayed in a tent. Red Evans had a small tent. Paul and I lived in one half, while Red had the other side for himself. As brothers, Paul and I, slept together; Red slept by himself. Others stayed in their trucks, which had to be cleaned up before you could live in them. After all, the animals had made things a little dirty on the trip to the fairgrounds. All the straw had to be swept or forked out, then the manure washed away. The tents and trucks were next to the fence around the race track.

It was fun to be at the fair the whole week. A rather comical thing happened one night in Red's tent. Kenny Swisher decided to be at the fair, with the carnival capturing his interest. So he hung around the midway most of the time. However, late at night, he needed a place to sleep. In the middle of the night he decided to stick his head inside our tent. Once he got his head inside, he crawled all the way inside. He was going to sleep with us. Naturally he crawled on Red's side. It was some time before Red discovered Kenny was sleeping with him. Soon there was some growling going on between them. Once he was awake enough he chased Kenny from his side of the tent. Red and Kenny exchanged some harsh remarks before it was over. Kenny had to move. So did Paul and I! We moved over, so Kenny could crawl in with us. Three of us then shared the other half of the tent. Red could roll over, for he had plenty of room again. The three of us didn't roll too much. If we did, we had to do it together, as it was crowded on our side. We made it through the night. And we made it through the week in our little tent.

The following year we put the stock rack on our GMC truck. Above the rack we put a 2x4 through the center. Stretched over the top and sides was one of the large canvases we had from the farm. Up front we had planks across the rack. On those planks we put an old bed spring and mattress. That was our sleeping quarters—bedroom for the week!

In the back we had our kitchen. Borrowed from little Grandma Hoffman was her two-burner kerosene stove. We cooked on it, mainly warming up pork and beans, and sweet corn.

Harry Mockler, our Mobil gas man, got us some groceries. His wife had a grocery store in Hebron. Before the fair he brought out our purchases on his delivery: thirteen cans of pork and beans, a few cans of sweet corn, cream style, and corn flakes. Generally, we took a loaf of bread from home.

Milk we got from dairymen who had cows at the fair. They had to milk every morning and evening, so we got fresh milk from them. Warm! It meant we had milk to drink and for our bowl of cereal. We could heat up our pork and beans on Grandma's stove. The menu was the same every day! Water to wash dishes could be heated on her stove, too. This way we were set up for camping at the fairgrounds for the week. In the years to come, the routine was about the same.

Each year at the fair we'd get to see friends we'd seen the year before. Some 4-H members were back year after year, so it was good to be with them. Some were only seen at fair time.

One such man was born in De Motte, but each year he visited at the time of the Jasper County Fair. This man was United States Congressman Charles Abraham Halleck. Likely, this was a very good way to keep in touch with the people of his district. His children always showed up, too. They were Charles W. and Patricia, who were twins. They would come down to the dairy barn to talk to us kids. Both of them were not afraid to spend a lot of time around us. At times they visited us where we were camping out. Coming out of Washington, D.C., they seemed to be very friendly with us. They were nice friends, having a lot of fun being there with those of us in 4-H. All of us enjoyed each other's company.

As time went on, I got more involved in 4-H. I had the privilege of being chosen to attend the 4-H Convention in Indianapolis. Four attended, representing Jasper county. The only other person I remember now was Mary Felder, the Buick dealer's daughter. I think the other boy was from Remington.

Each county got to send four young people. In all, we came from 92 counties in Hoosierland. Our convention was held at Butler University in Indianapolis. Bud Schultz, our county agent, brought us there. We stayed in the dormitories on campus.

Each evening of the week we had a special religious service. One of the adult leaders or a young person would be asked to lead us in the service. I served on one of the committees to prepare for such an evening service in the big university chapel.

We got to the meeting one day, only to be told by our chairman we had no speaker for the evening. So we were without a person to deliver a message. Up until then, everything just fell in place. This was a shock to our committee. Over and over we talked about not having a speaker. It seemed no person had a solution, not even a suggestion.

Finally, I suggested a solution, I'd do it. I offered to give the message for that evening in the chapel. Immediately they accepted my offer.

That was the easiest part for the committee. But it was also the easiest part for me, saying I'd do it. What message was I going to give? Didn't I realize that? Yes, I did. I also realized it was only a few hours before the start of our chapel service. I left the meeting immediately, I hurried back to my room. First I got out my Bible, then prayed, and searched through Scripture passages. Coming back to me were some sermons I heard my minister preach at the First Reformed Church. So I jotted down notes of all the thoughts which came to me. Illustrations started coming back, I added them to my notes. From those notes, I began to get a theme together, then an outline, finally I had enough notes to prepare my message. After writing it, I rehearsed my message over and over in my dorm room. It still made me feel rather anxious. But I wouldn't have to wait too much longer, for chapel was held following our evening meal.

As we gathered in the chapel, I sat with others on the platform. From there I could see it was packed, every pew on the main floor was filled, as was the balcony. Between five and six hundred faces were looking back at me. And this was going to be my first public speaking experience! Suddenly all kinds of questions raced through my mind. I stumped myself with a big question: "What am I doing here?"

I began to compare myself with former speakers. Some were very capable speakers. They gave very good messages.

After all the preliminaries, which seemed quite long, suddenly they were finished—it was my turn!

I read several passages from my Bible, then gave my message. I delivered it pretty much the same way I put it together, in the short time I had. The delivery went well. Once I got started, it seemed to flow satisfactorily. All the young people were quiet and attentive as they listened.

The next day, when some of us went into the canteen for refreshments I got a big surprise. One of the students on campus, who was serving us, recognized me. Looking at me, she said, "You were the guy who gave the message last night in the chapel, didn't you?" I nodded I was. She further responded, "I thought so. It was very good." I thanked her.

My fellow-delegates from Jasper county talked to me about my message on the way home, after the convention. All of them were surprised by my contribution and the speech. Mary Felder thought it was good enough to hear again. She thought all the 4-H clubs in the county ought to hear it.

That never happened. It was war time, which limited travel for most of us. Anyway, none of us were looking for unnecessary travel, so nothing more happened regarding her suggestion.

Once we got back to Rensselaer, we separated. However, I had a problem. I did not have a way to get home. Besides, we did not have a telephone. Well, I could walk, which I decided to do—hitchhike. My first hike took me to the end of the city. Every now and then I'd stop, to try my thumb. No hitches—no rides. People kept driving right on by. So I was back to walking.

Eventually two young fellows came to a hurried stop. They were headed as far as Aix. Not that far, but far better than nothing. They had a little box on the back of their old truck. I tossed my suitcase back there. Three of us sat in the cab, I was stuck in the middle. We were on our way. Soon they were asking me questions, which I tried to answer. It kept the conversation going.

As we came to the little spot in the road, Aix, they turned off Highway 53. Once stopped, I got out. I stepped up to the side of the little box on the back. Just as I was reaching for my suitcase—they took off. Wheels spinning! They churned up the road. My reach came up empty handed!

My heart sank! I stood there—helpless. Mouth open. Flashing through my mind was this thought—that's what you get for riding with strangers! Forget it; it's gone!

Just as quickly, I heard tires skidding on the gravel road. They had stopped. Spun their wheels again—backing up to me. "Sorry," they apologized, "Never even thought of your stuff in the back." Grateful to them, I thanked them one more time.

Suitcase in hand, I began my walk again. My goal was to get to Uncle George Hoffman's by Kniman. I finally walked into their yard. They took me home after chores that evening.

While going to the fair was fun, we did go to put our calves in the ring and to show our exhibits. My brother Paul and I competed against each other. Results that first year were very interesting, which we discovered when we got into competition. Results of the judging in the 4-H: Paul got first place; I got second place. Later, the same afternoon, in the open class we were against each other. However, in the open class, we had to compete against farmers who came to show their dairy cattle at the fair. Results of the open class judging were reversed: I got first; Paul got the second. That happened with the same judge.

As boys we later asked him how that could be, complete switch in the results on the same afternoon. He tried to explain it to us, then in the end, he admitted he was surprised over his own judging. Maybe the animals were very close in being alike, therefore it could have gone either way. In fact, it did.

During my first year in 4-H, I got to know my way around a little. With some pushing, I got into some of the open class exhibits. I won two ribbons in 4-H with my dairy calf and with chickens. In all that year, I took twelve places with my exhibits. My prize money amounted to $14.25. I came home with more money than I had when I went to the fair. (Many kids blew a lot of money, but I disciplined myself, so that every year I won far more money than I ever spent.)

I got acquainted with two people at the fair. Superintendent George Wood of the County Fair Horticultural and Agricultural Departments. Another man, Harry Q. Holt, was Superintendent of the Martin County Schools, who had been a judge at the fair for over twenty years. They were extremely helpful, with their many suggestions.

But once I got started, Fuzzy Johnson from Johnson's Seed Store in Hebron did so much for me. He helped with the initial cleaning of the grains. Del, one of his men, worked with us too. They spared nothing, being so willing to help me get ready with my displays.

We'd change screens in his big fanning mill. It meant doing this for a small amount of grain. This took time and a lot of work. At his place we got the first cleaning of all these grains: wheat, rye, soybean, buckwheat, timothy, Hungarian, millet, oats, etc. Each grain came from our farms. Each exhibit was half a peck. After that cleaning at the seedstore, it still had to be hand-cleaned, which meant I had to sort through the half peck kernel by kernel. Fuzzy Johnson also gave me display sacks which I used for my exhibits at the fair.

Five-inch grain sheaf displays were made up for millet, Hungarian, timothy, wheat, rye, soybean, buckwheat, sudan grass, clover, etc.

Other entires were: longest stalk of corn, greatest number of pods on soybean plant, best inoculation of soybean plant, red radishes, pickles, etc.

My entries generally were three of the same kind. Many times, therefore, since I had the best exhibits, I would take first, second, and third places in each class.

As time went along, I gained better ways to display my exhibits. Later I also became an assistant to George Wood in the Horticultural and Agricultural Departments at the county fair.

A trophy was given to the township who scored the most points. Carpenter township had been the winner for years. They won twice. Permanent possession went to the first township winning it three years in a row. One of the first years I pushed for Keener township, we just missed it, for it was close that year. We had 154 points, while the winner had 156. Two others were close, with 150 and 148 points.

The next year, I was determined, we were going out to win the trophy. We did.

One year we scored 366 points to win. My total points that year added up to 286. The year we gained the permanent possession of the J. C. Spindler Company trophy Keener township scored 568 points. Of those, I scored 320 points, more than the next highest township, which had 256.

Harry Q. Holt, the judge, felt the quality of exhibits was excellent. The keen competition brought out the best in all of us. Once we got into the competition to win the trophy, we had some of the best displays ever at the Jasper County Fair.

Clippings from newspapers had such bylines: Bill Hoffman Is Multiple Winner At The County Fair, Mr. Hoffman Stages A One-Man Show, and Keener Wins County Fair Silver Cup.

For all the work I had many ribbons to show for it. While it was tedious work to get a grain sample ready, a sheaf took plenty of work, too. Since we did not raise some of these crops yearly, I still planted plots in our large garden. In such plots I had the following: Hungarian, millet, sudan grass (sometimes), buckwheat, etc. Others I got out of the fields. Before fair time I would make each sheaf, placing each stalk of grain in it individually. I'd time it so each sheaf would be ready for prime showing at fair time.

Included in my collection of ribbons are some I won at the Northwestern Indiana Broiler and Egg Show, which was also held in Rensselaer.

At last count I had the following in my collection: 2-champion, 91-first, 92-second, 59-third, 2-fourth, 2-fifth, and a sixth. Grand total: 249 ribbons.

413

Later, one of my younger sisters wanted my collection entered in the De Motte Hobby Show. I held back at first, thinking there would be one big temptation with such a collection, then end up losing some of them. Anyway, when she asked one more time, I entered them in the show. Now I have one more blue ribbon, first award, from the De Motte Hobby Show.

The Bible speaks of another prize: "But one thing I do: forgetting what is behind and straining toward what is ahead, I press on toward the goal to win the prize for which God has called me Heavenward in Christ Jesus." (It would do us all so much good just to read again Philippians 3.)

How easy it is to parade one's contributions, performances, achievements, conquests, victories, winnings, and successes. Memories helps us to recapture a few of the glory days of the past.

But then we must remember that even the best trophies in the case tarnish quickly. Really the glory of yesterday soon disappears.

Because our memories have some experiences and happenings in life which one can't forget so easily, it doesn't take much to uncover some failures which still haunt and hurt. One can't seem to forget the wasted days, the wasted tears. It is hard to forget it! But one must do it, says the Bible, otherwise those things have a downward drag on life, our souls!

We have an upward call, which is a must for a Christian. Paul felt that Jesus Christ reached out and grasped him. Paul could never forget what happened on that Damascus Road, when Christ seized and took possession of him. After that the press was on to win the prize for which God called him Heavenward. From that moment on, Jesus Christ is the Author and Finisher of our faith. We are to win the supreme and heavenly prize—all by the grace of God.

Even the best has to be counted as a loss, Paul reminds us.

The best of life's gains are to be given to Jesus. I am reminded of something that goes like this, after being congratulated, "When I receive a bouquet of applause, I take a quick sniff and hand it up to the Lord for His glory." What a reminder, quickly give them to Jesus.

May we be challenged to strain forward to glorify God and enjoy Him forever!

A New Year

It was January 1, 1947. A new year! At the time I was 21.

The weather was rather rough, as we entered the new year. After all, what could be expected, wasn't it the first day of January? Cold! I was so glad to get the chores done that evening. I cleaned up and wanted to warm up and take it easy that evening. Listen to the radio, and read a little, both sounded good to me.

Headlights were noticed, as a car drove on our yard. Couldn't imagine who it could be. Marty went to the door.

I was totally surprised! Marty came back to the living room, after answering the door. My brother informed me some fellow wanted to see me. Me? Well, who is it? I put these questions to him, as I began to get up to see for myself. He tried to answer my questions, "You know, that fellow, the one you said was getting married today."

Neal Knip? My mind wondered...sure he was getting married today. As I went to the door, I was puzzled, why would he come here? He must have made a mistake!

I got to the door—sure enough, there stood Neal Knip! The groom stood before me!

Alberdena Dykhuizen in 1947, in her beautiful yellow dress and gold belt.

416

I congratulated him, first of all. But for the life of me, I could not begin to imagine why he was there at our door on his wedding day! Why? Especially on the first evening of his married life—why?

Neal didn't keep me guessing. He told me Alberdena had stood up for Thelma at their wedding that day. (I had gathered that much, as they were friends.) She was in the car with them, he said. They wanted me to go along for their wedding dinner at Tieble's on Highways 30 and 41.

The boy in Hoosierland in 1947.

(Well, so much for my relaxing evening at home.) I agreed to go along. But, I'm not ready to go away, so I told him I'd have to get ready, as soon as I could.

Fine. Neal went back to the car to wait, with Thelma, his bride, and Alberdena.

I hurried. Soon I was seated in the back seat of their car. All ready to go!

But, not so fast, as we soon found out. We were going nowhere! Neal's car refused to start. Both of us got out, lifted the hood, trying to find out the trouble—in our Sunday suits. Man, was it ever cold!

Neal was sure it was the fuel pump. It had to be shot!

Everybody was getting cold by this time, either by just sitting in a cold car or standing in the snow and looking under the hood. Both Thelma and Alberdena went into the house. Mom opened the oven door, so they could warm up their cold feet.

Neal and I went into De Motte to get some parts. We took Dad's Buick. But it was New Year's Day, what place would be

417

open? We finally found the needed parts at Neal Sekema's Garage. He found a fuel pump among his parts. Then, back to the farm, where Neal put on the new pump—in the cold! In his wedding suit!

Now, would it run? Everything seemed to be fixed. Let's try it. It started!

All of us crawled in once again. This time was more promising, we were on our way to Tiebel's for that wedding dinner.

That evening we shared with Neal and Thelma on their wedding day.

Naturally I took Alberdena home.

To keep warm, I cut wood north of the chicken house. Then on the hill, in the woods, I cut down a lot of oak trees. Once they were fallen, I took them to a sawmill near Hebron. We had a house to build. A house to keep warm.

We had another wedding. That summer. Ours!

Alberdena and I got married June 26, 1947. Our Wedding Day!

So more than one thing was in the plans for that New Year. It is amazing how God invades our plans in life. In His kind Providence, He had plans for another couple which we didn't realize the first day of the New Year 1947.

Oh, I took Alberdena home again. But this time it was ours. The one we built in the woods that same year.

That's just the beginning of another chapter in the life of a boy in Hoosierland.

Pastor William Hoffman
903 Berg Blvd SE
Stewartville MN 55976-1483

The Hoffman Farms in Hoosierland.